Settler Society in the English Leeward Islands, 1670–1776

Settler Society in the English Leeward Islands, 1670–1776, is the first study of the history of the federated colony of the Leeward Islands – Antigua, Montserrat, Nevis, and St. Kitts – that covers all four islands in the period from their independence from Barbados in 1670 to the outbreak of the American Revolution, which reshaped the Caribbean as well as the mainland American colonies. Natalie A. Zacek emphasizes the extent to which the planters of these islands attempted to establish recognizably English societies in tropical islands based on plantation agriculture and African slavery. By examining conflicts relating to ethnicity and religion, controversies regarding sex and social order, and a series of virulent battles over the limits of local and imperial authority, she depicts these West Indian colonists as skilled improvisers who adapted themselves to an unfamiliar environment and who were as committed as other American colonists to the norms and values of English society, politics, and culture.

Natalie A. Zacek is a lecturer in history and American studies at the University of Manchester. Her papers have been published in journals such as *Slavery and Abolition, Journal of Peasant Studies, History Compass*, and *Wadabagei: A Journal of the Caribbean and Its Diaspora*, as well as in several edited volumes. She is a founder of the H-Atlantic listserv and has served as its book review editor for its first decade.

Settler Society in the English Leeward Islands, 1670–1776

NATALIE A. ZACEK

University of Manchester

CAMBRIDGE
UNIVERSITY PRESS

CAMBRIDGE
UNIVERSITY PRESS

32 Avenue of the Americas, New York NY 10013-2473, USA

Cambridge University Press is part of the University of Cambridge.

It furthers the University's mission by disseminating knowledge in the pursuit of education, learning and research at the highest international levels of excellence.

www.cambridge.org
Information on this title: www.cambridge.org/9781107518346

First published 2010
First paperback edition 2015

A catalogue record for this publication is available from the British Library

Library of Congress Cataloguing in Publication data
Zacek, Natalie.
Settler Society in the English Leeward Islands, 1670–1776 / Natalie A. Zacek.
p.   cm.
Includes bibliographical references and index.
ISBN 978-0-521-19044-2 (hardback)
1. Leeward Islands (West Indies)–Social conditions–17th century.   2. Leeward Islands (West Indies)–Social conditions–18th century.   3. Great Britain–Colonies–Leeward Islands (West Indies)–History–17th century.   4. Great Britain–Colonies–Leeward Islands (West Indies)–History–18th century.   I. Title.
F2131.Z33 2010   972.97–dc22
2010022341

ISBN 978-0-521-19044-2 Hardback
ISBN 978-1-107-51834-6 Paperback

Contents

Tables

Acknowledgments

Like so many academic monographs, this book has been a long time in its gestation, and in common with so many authors, I have amassed a host of debts of gratitude along the way. This book began as a doctoral dissertation at Johns Hopkins University, which was the ideal place for a novice graduate student to begin work in the fields of Caribbean and Atlantic history. There, the wise mentorship of Jack Greene, Sidney Mintz, Michel-Rolph Trouillot, and Michael Johnson, and later of Philip Morgan, was of immeasurable benefit, as were the comradeship and inspiration of the "Greene Team" of Jack's many Ph.D. students, particularly my fellow 1992 entrants James Baird, Nuran Cinlar, Carla Gerona, and April Hatfield. I was lucky enough to number among my friends at Hopkins Bill MacLehose, Lara Kriegel, Christine Johnson, Elaine Parsons, Phil Vogt, Ernst Pijning, Jeri McIntosh Cobb, Max Edelson, and Julia Holderness, all of whom helped to keep me (relatively) sane and happy over the long term in Baltimore, as did longer-distance friends such as Al Goyburu, Lina de Montigny, Bret Empie, Eric Trachtenberg, Joe Morgan, Andre O'Neil, Sharon Tulchinsky, Carol Sharma, and Maura Gallagher.

In the material world, the research that produced this book was initially supported by a graduate fellowship from the History Department at Johns Hopkins, supplemented by funding from the John Carter Brown Library, the Huntington Library, and the Folger Institute. A visiting position at St. Louis University came along just in time to fund me to the completion of the dissertation, and just as the final product was submitted to the Eisenhower Library at Johns Hopkins I was lucky enough to be hired by the University of Manchester. There, I benefited enormously not only from the university's financial support, including a well-timed research leave that allowed me to complete my revisions to the manuscript, but from the friendship and intellectual support of many colleagues, particularly Julie Gottlieb, Glyn Redworth, Norris Nash, Brian Ward, David Brown, Elizabeth Toon, and the members of our World Histories works-in-progress reading group: Laurence Brown, Paulo Drinot, Till Geiger, Anindita Ghosh, Steven Pierce, Bidisha Ray, and Yangwen Zheng.

My thanks also go to the many librarians and archivists who have been so helpful to me in a wide-ranging and long-drawn-out program of research. I am especially grateful to the library staff at my two "home" institutions, the Milton S. Eisenhower Library at Johns Hopkins and the John Rylands University Library at the University of Manchester, as well as to those at the British Library, the National Archives of Great Britain, Lambeth Palace Library, the University of London's Senate House Library, the Institute of Historical Research, the Institute of Commonwealth Studies, Oxford's Bodleian Library, the Scottish Record Office, the National Library of Scotland, the Archives of Antigua, the Archives of St. Kitts, the Nevis Historical and Conservation Society, the John Carter Brown Library, the Huntington Library, and the Boston Public Library.

Some material from Chapter 3 appeared in Caroline Williams, ed., *Bridging the Early Modern Atlantic World* (Ashgate, 2009); from Chapter 4 in Merril D. Smith, ed., *Sex and Sexuality in Early America* (New York University Press, 1998); and from Chapter 5 in Robert Olwell and Alan Tully, eds., *Cultures and Identities in Colonial British America* (Johns Hopkins University Press, 2005). I thank these presses for allowing the inclusion of this material.

Working with Cambridge University Press has been a pleasure. Early on, Frank Smith expressed enthusiasm for this project, and closer to the finish line it was expertly aided by the efforts of Eric Crahan and Jason Przybylski. Three anonymous outside readers offered thoughtful and substantive comments, which resulted in a greatly improved final product – but all responsibility for remaining errors lies entirely with me.

Several friends went the extra mile, and more, helping me revise my dissertation into book form. Michal Rozbicki not only shared a series of enjoyable Tex-Mex lunches with me in St. Louis, but offered much-needed encouragement at a crucial juncture. Patience Schell more than lived up to her name as she plowed through a rather unpromising early version of the monograph, and her insightful comments were of great help. Norris Nash did the same yeoman service and even volunteered for a second go-around, truly earning his title as the Smartest Chap in the School. Christine Johnson provided months' worth of much-needed encouragement at a crucial juncture, and I can't imagine having been able to complete my revisions without her help. Nicholas Canny gave wise counsel about an earlier version of Chapter 2, and my fellow British Caribbeanists Trevor Burnard, Kenneth Morgan, Simon Smith, Mary Turner, James Walvin, Betty Wood, and Nuala Zahedieh all cheer-led along the way. But much of the credit undoubtedly belongs to Jack Greene, who believed in this project and its author in even the least promising circumstances, and who has provided me and his many, many other students with a model of intellectual rigor, creativity, and generosity of spirit to which we all aspire. Jack, I truly could not have done it without you.

Familial debts are of the longest standing and the greatest depth. My grandmother, Sophye Bernstein Cohen, taught me so much about how to live a good life and to have a lot of fun along the way. My mother, Judith Cohen Zacek, is sui generis, and it is to her that I dedicate this book.

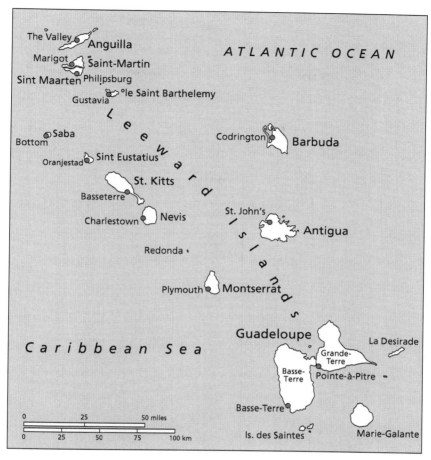

The Valley
Anguilla
Marigot
Saint-Martin
Sint Maarten Philipsburg
Gustavia °Ie Saint Barthelemy

ATLANTIC OCEAN

Leeward Islands

Bottom
Saba
Oranjestad Sint Eustatius

Codrington
Barbuda

St. Kitts
Basseterre
Charlestown Nevis

St. John's
Antigua

Redonda

Plymouth Montserrat

Caribbean Sea

Guadeloupe
La Desirade
Grande-Terre
Basse-Terre Pointe-à-Pitre
Basse-Terre

Is. des Saintes

Marie-Galante

0   25   50 miles
0   25   50   75   100 km

Map 1. Leeward Islands

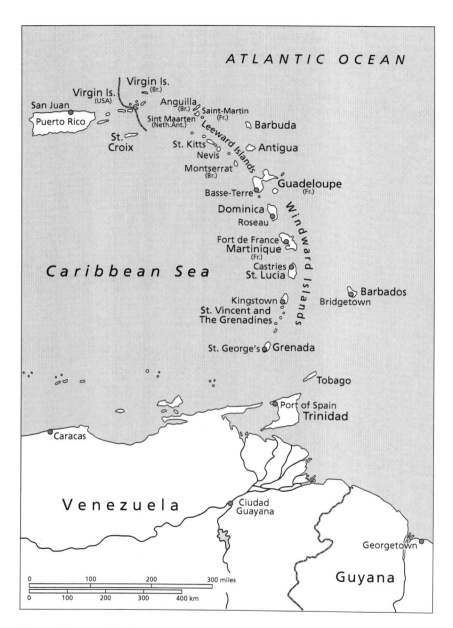

Map 2. Eastern Carribean

Settler Society in the English Leeward Islands, 1670–1776

Introduction

In the summer of 1753, fashionable Londoners were intrigued to read, in the August issue of the popular *London Magazine*, a vivid account of a murder trial that had taken place the previous winter in St. Kitts, one of the four islands that, along with Antigua, Montserrat, and Nevis, made up the federated British West Indian colony of the Leeward Islands. The magazine's editors explained that they had chosen to devote front-page space to these distant proceedings because the story "has of late been a subject of conversation, and contains some very extraordinary circumstances." Specifically, "the proof [of the defendant's guilt] was founded entirely upon presumption, without any one witness of the fact, which is a dangerous sort of proof, but more necessary to be admitted in the West-Indies than here at home, because negroes are not admitted as witnesses."[1] In other words, the defendant, a young attorney named John Barbot, had been found guilty of murder and executed for this crime largely on the basis of testimony of several black slaves, who under both English and colonial law were not legal persons and whose testimony had to be presented in court as hearsay evidence from the lips of white men. A careful reading of the *London Magazine* article and the transcript of the trial, which appeared in London in pamphlet form that same summer, makes it clear that, although both the victim, Matthew Mills, and his alleged murderer were white, they were very different sorts of men in the eyes of their fellow white Kittitians.[2] Mills was a third-generation islander, the owner

---

[1] "Tryal of John Barbot," *London Magazine*, August 1753, 1.

[2] The pamphlet, whose publication was presumably financed by friends of Barbot, was entitled *The Tryal of John Barbot, Attorney at Law, for the Murder of Mathew Mills,*

of a large plantation there as well as of a sugar-importing firm in London, and was known within his island community as a gentleman of unimpeachable honor and integrity. By contrast, Barbot was a man of faintly exotic Huguenot descent, a Londoner recently arrived in the islands, and a lawyer who owned neither slaves nor land, who had quickly made himself deeply unpopular throughout St. Kitts because, rather than accepting his relatively low social status in comparison with men such as Mills, he was a "most provoking" individual who constantly demanded that the local planters "treat him as a gentleman," despite the fact that neither his character nor his socioeconomic status entitled him to demand such a degree of respect.[3] When Barbot killed Mills, apparently over a trivial exchange of insults, the community was apparently so pleased to be rid of such a troublesome man as the former that it accepted the prosecution's deployment of hearsay evidence that had originated from the ranks of the enslaved, undermining a fundamental tenet of white legal and cultural dominance, in order to ensure that Barbot would be convicted and executed.

The story of John Barbot, an obscure man who came to brief public notice only through his inimical relationship with a West Indian planter of considerably higher social and economic status, may appear initially to be nothing more than a diverting footnote within the larger history of Anglo-American jurisprudence. But the Barbot trial can claim a broader importance to scholars interested in the histories of the West Indies and the Atlantic world, as the event itself and the reception it elicited in the metropole challenge long-held understandings of the nature of the societies that arose in the English settlements of the Caribbean. A close reading of the eighty-page trial transcript affords the reader a strong sense of the large degree of social diversity that characterized the populations of St. Kitts and its near neighbor, Nevis, in the middle decades of the eighteenth century. The dramatis personae who appear in this account include not only the expected figures of planters and slaves, but also physicians and merchants, managers and attorneys, mariners and tavern keepers, free colored laundresses and wealthy white dowagers, constables and slave boatmen, men and women, white, black, and racially mixed, enslaved and free, English and foreign, immigrants and creoles, all of

Esq.; to which is added, The Prisoner's Narrative of the Cause of the Difference between Mr. Mills and Himself, and of the several Steps that led from thence, to the Commission of the Fact for which he suffered (London: John Whiston and Benjamin White, 1753).
[3] "Tryal," 1.

whom, however they may have been advantaged or disadvantaged by virtue of their race, gender, or socioeconomic status, contributed to the formation of an English settler society in two small tropical islands that had by then become some of Britain's most profitable colonies.[4] Moreover, the document's "thick description" of Kittitian and Nevisian life belies the persistent historiographic conception of Britain's West Indian colonies as being as socially and culturally impoverished as they were commercially successful. The picture that emerges from these pages is of a small but vital community, one whose white inhabitants displayed a strong sense of identification with the mother country, an emotional as well as a financial investment in the island's continued peace and prosperity, and a commitment to upholding both metropolitan and local law and ideals of polite public and private behavior. The magazine and pamphlet offer a recognizable colonial echo of eighteenth-century Britain's self-image as a "polite and commercial" nation and of communities that had undergone a mimetic process in many ways comparable to what had been experienced in such North American mainland colonies as those of the mid-Atlantic and Chesapeake regions, rather than a strange new world that lay "beyond the line" and that was characterized by "a hectic mode of life that had no counterpart at home or elsewhere in the English experience."[5]

Contemporary commentators and modern historians alike have repeatedly depicted these colonies as social failures, as places in which fortunes were soon won and sooner lost, where indentured servants and, later, African slaves labored under worse conditions and their masters lived in greater luxury than in Britain's other plantation colonies in North America, and where skewed sex ratios, an unpredictable tropical environment, and the constant threat of foreign attack and slave rebellion forestalled the emergence of many of the institutions that are seen as having exerted a calming and civilizing force elsewhere in Britain's American empire. This lurid picture arose initially from popular but frequently inaccurate, and in some cases entirely fictitious, depictions in

---

[4] According to Margaret Rouse-Jones, St. Kitts was, for its size, the most profitable of Britain's American colonies in the half-century between the Treaty of Utrecht (1713) and the Treaty of Paris (1763); see Rouse-Jones, "St. Kitts, 1713–1763: A Study of the Development of a Plantation Colony" (Ph.D. diss., Johns Hopkins, 1977).

[5] Paul Langford, *A Polite and Commercial People: England, 1727–1783* (Oxford: Oxford University Press, 1989); Richard S. Dunn, *Sugar and Slaves: The Rise of the Planter Class in the English West Indies, 1624–1713* (Chapel Hill: University of North Carolina Press, 1972), 45.

popular narratives such as Edward Ward's *Trip to Jamaica* (1700) and William Pittis's *Life of Bavia, or, The Jamaica Lady* (1720), which gave the Anglo-American reading public what it wanted, a vision of the West Indian islands as tropical hells where, in the words of Thomas Hodges, "it is grown a Proverb with the English Merchants, that tho a Man goes over never so honest to the Plantations, yet the very Air there does change him in a short time."[6] Over the course of the eighteenth century, as many of the wealthiest West Indian planters left their estates in the hands of managers and attorneys and relocated temporarily or permanently to Britain to enjoy the luxuries and to influence the commercial policies of the metropole, they appeared on the metropolitan social scene as "the most conspicuous rich men of their time."[7] Whether in London's Portman Square, on estates in the English countryside, or at Bath and other fashionable watering places, West Indian planters "formed a social circle of their own and were bound together by intermarriages, common interests, and firm and lasting friendships," a circle from which the majority of Britons, even those of the greatest wealth and highest social status, felt themselves alienated.[8] Even George III professed himself surprised by the "Extravagance and Luxury ... and a certain Species of Vanity" that he considered characteristic of the West Indian planters and was wary of the political and economic power wielded by the West India Lobby.[9]

If contemporary observers were often moved to dismiss West Indian colonists' repeated assertions that they were "but Englishmen transplanted" rather than examples of supposedly inevitable creole degeneracy, modern historians have frequently succumbed to the temptation to accept at face value the critiques of English West Indian colonial society posed by scandal-mongering pamphleteers, by metropolitan commentators appalled by and perhaps envious of what they considered the shameless excesses of wealthy absentees, and particularly by the many impassioned denunciations of plantation society produced by antislavery activists in the late eighteenth and early nineteenth centuries. Although most current scholars of the West Indies would most likely dismiss as hyperbole Gordon Lewis's assertion that "the Caribbean plantocracy constituted the most crudely philistine of all dominant classes in the history

---

[6] Hodges, *Plantation Justice* (London: A. Baldwin, 1701), 10.

[7] Richard Pares, *Merchants and Planters* (Cambridge: Cambridge University Press, 1960), 38.

[8] Philip C. Yorke, ed., *The Diary of John Baker* (London: Hutchinson & Co. Ltd., 1931), 49.

[9] Robert Robertson, *A Detection of the State and Situation of the Present Sugar Planters of Barbadoes and the Leeward Islands* (London: J. Wilford, 1732), 3.

of Western slavery," and that "the general Caribbean society formed during the four centuries after the Discovery was marked throughout by a spirit of cultural philistinism probably unmatched in the history of European colonialism," scholarly opinion has for the most part echoed Richard Dunn's contention that "ever since the eighteenth century the sugar planters have *deservedly* received a bad press."[10] In his recent monograph on seventeenth-century Barbados, Larry Gragg astutely summarizes the prevailing historiographic view of English settlers in the West Indies as "grasping capitalists intent on getting rich quickly by exploiting their slaves and servants, but also as ill-mannered and immoral ... as men who made fortunes, turned over their plantations to an abusive overseer, and returned to England; or as degenerates who sank into a hopeless moral torpor."[11] The largely unquestioned image of West Indian colonists either losing their Englishness under the negative influences of a tropical climate and a lack of necessary checks on their behavior, or clinging too tenaciously to an English identity and thus failing to develop a recognizable version of the creole nationalism that eventually resulted in the mainland colonies in a rebellion against imperial authority, has continued to influence even the most recent historiography of colonial British America. To T. A. Milford, the Leewards in the revolutionary era were notable for their "grotesque character of life," and in his award-winning biography of Alexander Hamilton, Ron Chernow quickly dismisses mid-eighteenth-century Nevis as "a tropical hellhole of dissipated whites."[12] Alternatively, Andrew O'Shaughnessy's otherwise exemplary study of the American Revolution in the Caribbean attributes the West Indian colonies' continued loyalty to Britain to "the strength of the social and cultural ties with Britain [which] restrained the development of a nationalistic creole consciousness among whites." In his view, "These British sojourners ... bequeathed shamefully little toward developing an infrastructure in the islands" and their ethos was "materialistic, individualistic, competitive, [and] exploitative."[13]

---

[10] Lewis, *Main Currents in Caribbean Thought: The Historical Evolution of Caribbean Society in Its Ideological Aspects, 1492–1900* (Baltimore: Johns Hopkins University Press, 1983), 109; Dunn, *Sugar and Slaves*, 335, emphasis mine.

[11] Gragg, *Englishmen Transplanted: The English Colonization of Barbados, 1627–1660* (Oxford: Oxford University Press, 2003), 8.

[12] Milford, *The Gardiners of Massachusetts: Provincial Ambition and the British-American Career* (Durham: University of New Hampshire Press, 2005), 89; Chernow, *Alexander Hamilton* (New York: Penguin, 2004), 8.

[13] O'Shaughnessy, *An Empire Divided: The American Revolution and the British Caribbean* (Philadelphia: University of Pennsylvania Press, 2000), 4, 5, 7.

Some recent scholarly work has, however, begun to explore English West Indian society in a more nuanced way. In his survey of the history and historiography of colonial British America, Steven Sarson has made the welcome claim that "there was a common pattern of historical development throughout the [English] West Indies, and it matched that of most of the mainland colonies," and recent work by Trevor Burnard, Sarah Pearsall, and B. W. Higman has delved deeply into manuscript sources to present a vision of eighteenth-century Jamaica that calls into question long-established stereotypes of the island's planters as profligate philistines and debauchees.[14] Yet given their commercial and strategic preeminence in the eighteenth-century British Empire, we still know very little about the West Indian colonies, in comparison not only with Massachusetts or Virginia, but with less exhaustively studied Anglo-American colonies such as North Carolina and Georgia. Without a doubt, the study of these islands presents scholars with particular challenges. The base of documentary evidence, particularly for the seventeenth and early eighteenth centuries, is far narrower than that which has survived for the majority of the North American settlements; warfare, natural disasters, and the effects of a tropical climate have damaged or destroyed many records. The ongoing imperial rivalries between Britain, France, Spain, and the Netherlands meant that some of the islands passed repeatedly back and forth between empires, complicating their histories and rendering them problematic objects of study within a dominant historiographic paradigm that remains centered on the study of the nation-state. Moreover, the islands' physical separation and distance from British North America, as well as their non-participation in the American Revolution, has placed these settlements in an awkward position in relation to teleological narratives of American history. Taken together, these factors have rendered these islands historiographically marginal, too Anglo-American to be part of a circum-Caribbean story focused on the syncretic "black Atlantic" cultures developed by slaves and free people of color in the French and Spanish colonies, and too Caribbean to figure significantly in the story of the formation of the United States.

---

[14] Sarson, *British America, 1600–1800: Creating Colonies, Imagining an Empire* (London: Hodder Arnold, 2005), 117; Burnard, *Mastery, Tyranny, and Desire: Thomas Thistlewood and His Slaves in the Anglo-Jamaican World* (Chapel Hill: University of North Carolina Press, 2004); Pearsall, "'The late flagrant instance of depravity in my Family': The Story of an Anglo-Jamaican Cuckold," *William and Mary Quarterly* s3: 60 (2003), 549–82; Higman, *Plantation Jamaica, 1750–1850: Capital and Control in a Colonial Economy* (Kingston: University of the West Indies Press, 2005).

These problems are particularly characteristic of the study of the Leeward Islands. By virtue of their small size and population, as well as their distance from the Greater Antilles and the North and South American mainlands, the islands can seem to constitute a margin of a margin, existing historically and historiographically in the shadow not only of Barbados, with its self-image as the "civilised island," but of Jamaica, the source of the greatest sugar fortunes in the era of slavery and the site of the most powerful political and cultural struggles for black liberation and enfranchisement in the nineteenth and twentieth centuries. In 1702, the Leewards' governor, Christopher Codrington, observed that "ye Sugar Ilands dont much love One An'Other," and indeed, all that bound the four Leewards together in 1670, when the Board of Trade removed them from Barbadian jurisdiction and reconstituted them as a separate, federated colony, was their relative geographic proximity to one another and their long-standing resentment of what they considered to be Barbados's unwillingness to protect them from foreign attack or to aid them in the development of their sugar industries.[15] Initially, Antigua, Montserrat, Nevis, and St. Kitts were rivals at least as much as they were partners. By 1682, the Leeward planters had recognized that their patterns of social and economic development diverged sharply from one another and that, although the four islands might share a governor general and commander in chief, each island required its own governing council and assembly.[16] The Leewards' proximity to the French stronghold at Martinique left them vulnerable to invasion in the seemingly endless rounds of Anglo-French hostilities that raged between 1660 and 1713, and the prevailing paths of the trade winds made communication and trade with Britain more difficult than with any of England's other West Indian colonies. The term "Leeward Islands" itself epitomizes their apparent marginality, as "leeward" is a term that holds meaning only in relation to some other, more central location.

But despite the Leewards' small size and population, and the challenges their settlers faced from French attack and from the natural disasters – floods, earthquakes, and hurricanes – that occurred more

---

[15] Codrington to William Blathwayt, March 15, 1702, Blathwayt Papers 351, Henry E. Huntington Library, San Marino, CA.

[16] The laws of each of the Leeward Islands were not binding in the other islands, unless the individual laws received the specific approval of the General Assembly of the Leewards; see Wavell Smith, *Two Letters to Mr. Wood, on the Coin and Currency in the Leeward Islands, &c.* (London: J. Millan, 1740), 11.

frequently and wreaked greater devastation there than almost anywhere else in the Caribbean, they are not marginal to the histories either
of the West Indies or of the Anglo-American world. From the records
that have survived the ravages of fire and water, time and neglect, it
is possible to learn a good deal about the day-to-day lives of the men
and women, white and black, free and enslaved, who lived in these
islands and who in many instances considered them home. We can see
these people struggling, individually and communally, to find solutions
to the same problems that vexed the populations of New England or
the Chesapeake. As Trevor Burnard has observed, "However oddly
constructed West Indian society might appear in England, it took little
time for the English coming to the islands to be caught up in a system
that seemed internally logical and perfectly natural."[17] The same comment might be applied to modern scholars as to contemporary visitors: Antigua or St. Kitts might initially appear exotic and chaotic when
compared with Plymouth, Providence, or Philadelphia, but sustained
inquiry into the island colonies' patterns of social development encourages the observer to see these patterns as logical responses to the particular circumstances that confronted emigrants and creoles in this part of
colonial British America.

The principal challenges that Leeward colonists faced over the period
from their political separation from Barbados in 1670 to the outbreak of
the American Revolution, the event that would recast the Anglo-Atlantic
world in terms highly unfavorable to the continued economic prosperity
of the British colonies in the West Indies, were those that challenged all
colonial Anglo-American societies:

developing and maintaining an identifiably English society in territories with large Scots and Irish elements within their populations;
benefiting from the commercial acumen and trade networks of
Huguenots, Jews, and Quakers while promoting the Church of
England's spiritual monopoly and material welfare;
regulating sexual and marital relationships in a way that accommodated the unbalanced sex and race ratios, yet established formal
and informal institutions to manage difficulties that might result
from interracial or nonmarital sexual relationships;

---

[17] Burnard, "Thomas Thistlewood Becomes a Creole," in Bruce Clayton and John A.
Salmond, eds., *Varieties of Southern History: New Essays on a Region and Its People*
(Westport, CT: Greenwood Press, 1996), 100.

developing ideologies and practices through which island residents
   could develop and express their political allegiance both to their
   colonies and to British imperial authority; and
creating what they considered to be recognizably English societies on
   small and isolated tropical islands whose most numerous inhabitants by far were African-descended slaves.
It is on these concerns that this book centers its analysis.

At its outset, this study delineates what Fernand Braudel called "the
limits of the possible," by exploring the significant challenges settlers
faced in their attempts to establish political, social, and religious institutions in the Leewards. The islands were subject to frequent natural
disasters, menaced by foreign invasion, threatened by an ever-increasing
imbalance between the white and black populations and thus by a constant and frequently justified anxiety about the individual or communal revolt of slaves, and unsettled by the challenges inherent in the
relationship between local and imperial authority. By understanding
the difficulties under which Leeward residents lived and labored, individually and communally, we can better comprehend the development
of both their mentalities and their societies in the period with which
this study deals.

The monograph then addresses the significant elements in the white
population of the Leewards that were other than English by birth and/or
expressed confessional allegiance to a faith other than that of the Church
of England. Island societies that were as small as those of the Leewards,
with respect to both geography and population, and that faced so many
internal and external challenges, could not afford to discourage such people from settling among them, nor could they either disperse them within
a larger English population or concentrate them in a distant hinterland.
The "deficiency laws" that were reissued regularly over the course of the
period under study show that both colonial and imperial authorities were
determined, and even desperate, to increase not only the absolute number of white residents, but the percentage of whites in the total population. At the same time, however, they expressed considerable concern
over the presence of potentially "dangerous tenants," and the legislative
records of the islands, as well as the occasional censuses that Leeward
governors commissioned and sent on to the Board of Trade in London,
display ongoing anxieties about the extent to which these at least initially
suspect groups could be trusted to work for the peace and prosperity of
the islands.

Sizable populations of Irish and Scots were present in the Leewards throughout the seventeenth and eighteenth centuries. Popular opinion, supported by some historians and anthropologists, has long conceived of Montserrat as "Ireland's only colony" and as "the Emerald Isle of the Caribbean," simultaneously emphasizing the importance of the island's Irish settlers and claiming that the majority of them were political prisoners transported by Cromwellian and later by Stuart authorities as rebels against English authority, and that these indentured servants made common cause with African slaves, creating a syncretic "Black Irish" culture that, they assert, characterizes Montserrat to this day. But this picture is both limited in scope – all four of the Leewards had Irish populations, although Montserrat's was the largest both in raw number and as a percentage of the total white population – and historically rather inaccurate. Many Leeward Irish were indeed indentured servants or former servants who led materially impoverished lives in Montserrat's isolated St. Patrick's Parish, but their masters too were often Irish, many of whom were members of the "Fourteen Tribes" of Galway, powerful and prosperous merchant families who dispatched younger sons and cousins to the West Indies to take advantage of new commercial opportunities as planters and merchants. Descendants of these Frenches and Lynches, Skerretts and Trants, among others, established planting and mercantile dynasties that persisted in some cases up to the era of Emancipation. Some maintained private or, on occasion, public adherence to the Church of Rome, which would have prevented them from acquiring political power in Britain and throughout its North American colonies, yet at least some of these Irish Montserratians entered the ranks of local officeholders, in which positions they worked to consolidate the political, social, and economic dominance of the islands' great planters, rather than attempting to ameliorate the harsh conditions in which their poor Irish Catholic neighbors lived.

Surviving census data show that the Leewards, like other Anglo-American colonies, were home to few Scots prior to the beginning of the eighteenth century. But there, as elsewhere in the British Empire, the Act of Union (1707) unleashed a great wave of Scots emigration to the colonies, a wave that included many men of little fortune but good education, who thus were well positioned to gain a measure of success as the managers, attorneys, and bookkeepers who played a crucial role in the commercially maturing plantation societies of the West Indies. By examining these white subpopulations at both the communal and the individual level, utilizing census data to discern the general patterns of experience, and drawing on surviving archives of individual families, such as the Irish Blakes and the Scots Tullidephs, it is possible to explore at a microlevel the strategies by which particular Irish and Scots settlers succeeded in attaining positions of wealth and status in the Leewards.

The religious life of the Leewards was in many ways as heterodox as the ethnic makeup of its white population. Throughout the seventeenth and eighteenth centuries, despite the attempts of spiritual and temporal authorities in the metropole to encourage Leeward settlers' material support of and participation in the affairs of the Church of England, the Church struggled to furnish itself with adequate churches and sufficient clergy, and even when both were available it was not always easy to interest island whites in religious matters. Although Charles Leslie, writing in the 1730s, dismissed West Indian planters as being "more fond of a pack of cards than of the Bible," the impression gained from legislative records and from the memoranda that island clergymen sent to the Society for the Propagation of the Gospel is that islanders were at worst indifferent, not hostile, to the Established Church, and that local officials and clerics were frequently able to mobilize a critical mass of planters in support of building or repairing churches and filling vacant ministerial positions.[18] But it is equally important to explore the role of religious minorities, specifically Quakers, Huguenots, and Jews, in the social, political, and economic life of the Leewards in order to understand how, and why, the first two groups were far more successful than the latter in assimilating themselves within the islands' white communities.

In studying the social development of the Leewards, it is crucial to understand the ways in which sexual behavior shaped and was shaped by life in these plantation-centered slave societies. As Foucault stated, sexuality is an "especially dense transfer point for relations of power," and in slave-based societies power was the most important difference between whites and blacks, the free and the unfree.[19] The centrality of slavery to the society, politics, economy, and culture of the Leewards meant that sexual behavior was a contentious issue not only in relation to concepts of individual and communal morality, but also with respect to questions of ownership, inheritance, and legal personhood; as Hilary Beckles has noted, "The entire ideological fabric of the slave-based civilization was

[18] Leslie, *A New and Exact History of Jamaica* (Edinburgh: R. Fleming, 1740), 37.
[19] Foucault, *The History of Sexuality: An Introduction*, trans. Robert Hurley (New York: Pantheon Books, 1978), 103.

conceived in terms of sex, gender and race."[20] Under such circumstances, the perceived sexual license of the colonies was not necessarily greater, and may in some circumstances have been significantly less, than that experienced within the metropole. I address these issues first through an analysis of the laws that political and religious authorities in the Leewards enacted in their attempts to regulate the sexual activity of white and black residents alike. I then discuss a series of instances in which Leeward settlers flouted local norms of sexual behavior, and the communal response these scandals evoked.

It is similarly essential to fully understand the ideology and practice of political life in the Leewards, especially the various attempts, led primarily by members of the four islands' Houses of Assembly, to adjust the balance of imperial power in favor of the colonies. Through such analysis, we can see the formation of a core of political ideology and behavior among white Leeward settlers through which they articulated a strong sense of British identity and "their overwhelming desire to be judged according to British values."[21] Because of the highly idiosyncratic structures of political authority in the islands and the extent to which, in island colonies boasting very small white populations, the line between interpersonal and political conflict was frequently blurred, it is highly instructive to examine a variety of situations in which islanders resorted to verbal, physical, and even murderous attacks against individuals who, they believed, were attempting to undermine what they considered to be their natural rights as Englishmen.

Finally, we return our attention to the Barbot trial. By reading the event in light of the interpersonal relations it dramatized, the goal of this concluding section is to explore the murder of Matthew Mills and the trial and execution of John Barbot as incidents that show the rich texture of eighteenth-century Leeward society and to offer final thoughts on the historical evaluation of Leeward society.

Writing a generation apart from one another, Edward Kamau Brathwaite and Trevor Burnard have attempted to alter the conventional historiographic wisdom on the subject of colonial West Indian society. In an essay first published in 1970, Brathwaite contradicted the prevalent picture of the planter as slothful and dissipated, unwilling or unable to

---

[20] Beckles, "White Women and Slavery in the Caribbean," *History Workshop Journal* 36 (1993), 69.

[21] Trevor Burnard, "Ethnicity in Colonial American Historiography: A New Organising Principle," *Australasian Journal of American Studies* 10 (1992), 10.

exert himself in the service of his community in the manner that would in England have been expected of a man of his rank. In Brathwaite's understanding,

> within the white section of society there was a great deal of building – churches, forts, public buildings, plantation houses – much of it of lasting architectural interest; there was an active Press and there was at least as much theatre as there is today. In the field of literature itself, a great deal of energy was given over to treatises on horticulture, fevers and diseases, sugar and sugar manufacture, estate management, sermons, and descriptive and historical works.[22]

In his recent monograph based on the diaries of the eighteenth-century Jamaican overseer Thomas Thistlewood, Burnard argued that these private writings

> help us to see that whites did manage to create a viable society in the Caribbean that was characterized by more than just untrammelled individualism, self-centeredness, and lack of concern for the commonweal.... [Thistlewood] was part of a society with rules and reason, founded on the recognition of whiteness as the defining condition for social privileges.[23]

Both Brathwaite and Burnard were writing specifically about Jamaica, and their works have played a valuable role in inspiring other scholars to question long-held assumptions about that island and the English colonial society that developed there in the era of sugar and slavery. However, their work is also of importance in encouraging scholars to engage in new interpretations of the histories of other West Indian islands, particularly those that, like the Leewards, were literally and figuratively situated within and between two vital systems, that of Britain and its American colonies and that of the Caribbean basin. Shaped by the same elements as Saint-Domingue and Cuba, Curaçao and Puerto Rico, yet simultaneously developing within the imperial parameters that created New England, New York, and Virginia, facing the same challenges as Barbados and Jamaica, often augmented by additional difficulties relating to size, location, and topography, the Leewards appeared to their seventeenth- and eighteenth-century European visitors to be both alluring and alarming, splendid and squalid. Travelers' narratives recount their authors' surprise, positive and negative, at the patterns of creolization they observed

---

[22] Brathwaite, "Creative Literature of the British West Indies During the Period of Slavery, *Savacou* 1 (1970), 46–7.
[23] Burnard, *Mastery*, 250.

in architecture, diet, dress, and behavior, and at the ubiquity of slaves and free people of color. But however exotic these colonies may have seemed to outside observers, their white inhabitants were determined to make their polities as recognizably English as might be possible on small, tropical islands whose economy rested almost entirely on slave-based plantation agriculture. Moreover, from their public and private writings we can see that, on the whole, these white islanders were confident that they had been notably successful in achieving this goal. In the chapters that follow, we will learn more about the challenges Leeward whites faced in creating and sustaining an identifiably English society in the West Indies and, I hope, will gain a deeper understanding of the ways in which they met these challenges and achieved, on their terms if not always on ours, social success.

I

The Challenges of English Settlement in the Leewards

INTRODUCTION

In recent years, historians of colonial America have become accustomed to including the larger British, as well as the French, Spanish, and Dutch, colonies in the West Indies on their mental maps of the Atlantic world. The Leeward Islands, however, have for the most part remained literally on the margins of that world, with many scholars still uncertain about their precise location or about which individual islands made up the Leeward colony. The very term "Leeward Islands" is a purely relational one, which owes its origin to the need of London-based administrators to distinguish between Barbados, the first of England's colonies to commit to large-scale sugar production and African slavery, and the more northerly and easterly islands, which until 1670 were essentially Barbados's colonies. In 1995, the historical geographer David Lowenthal dubbed these islands the "wayward Leewards" and described them in the following terms:

Marginality is the key to [the] distinction between the Leewards and the rest of Plantation-America, especially the rest of the Caribbean.... Leeward Islanders have more in common with small islanders elsewhere from the Pacific and the Indian Ocean to the Mediterranean and the North Sea, than with the rest of plantation America, even the Caribbean.[1]

[1] Lowenthal, "The Wayward Leewards," in Karen Fog Olwig, ed., *Small Islands, Large Questions: Society, Culture, and Resistance in the Post-Emancipation Caribbean* (London: Frank Cass, 1995), 183–4.

Lowenthal's statement echoes that made more than half a century earlier by the imperial historian Ruth Bourne, who described the Leewards as "the hottest, the most disease-ridden, the most subject to earthquake, and the most open to Maroon and enemy attacks of all England's possessions ... the most undesirable place imaginable to live in." But although she described the Leewards as "on the whole sparsely settled and poor," Bourne admitted that "they produced a considerable amount of sugar," an accomplishment that places them squarely within the boundaries of "Plantation-America."[2] This chapter will examine the four Leeward Islands, individually and together, in terms of their topography and demography, so that we can better understand the factors that drew settlers to these colonies and allowed them to flourish economically under often challenging conditions. It will also discuss the circumstances under which the Leewards became their own colony, as well as the extent of their socioeconomic development at the moment of independence, giving a sense of the challenges this colony faced and, to a large extent, overcame in the century that followed.

TOPOGRAPHY

In geographic terms, none of the four Leewards was ideally suited to the large-scale cultivation of sugar. Antigua, named by Columbus for the great Seville church of Santa Maria de la Antigua, is the largest of the four at approximately 108 square miles; it is also the flattest, and thus the only one in which planters could turn the majority of the land over to sugar production. At least as important, it possessed three excellent natural harbors: at English Harbour to the south, which by 1725 had become the British navy's principal base in the eastern Caribbean, at St. John's in the west, and at Parham to the north, although the latter two were surrounded by rocks and shoals that rendered navigation challenging. Antigua's soil was considered to be "very fertile and productive ... retentive of moisture, and respond[ing] readily to tillage and manures," although it was only "to be wrought with a good deal of labour," and the island's place in the path of the trade winds simultaneously provided power for mills to grind the newly harvested sugarcane and made it difficult for the French at Guadeloupe and Martinique to launch naval attacks against the island. The almost complete lack of streams, rivers,

---

[2] Bourne, *Queen Anne's Navy in the West Indies* (New Haven: Yale University Press, 1939), 51, 32.

or other sources of fresh water rendered the island extremely vulnerable to drought, yet after a slow start, Antigua had by the early decades of the eighteenth century become not only a major sugar producer, but an important British naval station and the administrative center of the Leeward colony.[3]

Montserrat, Nevis, and St. Kitts share a mountainous topography and a history of volcanic activity, but their respective productive capacities varied greatly throughout the period under study. Montserrat, named by Columbus for its alleged resemblance to a mountain outside Barcelona, although having an area of just fewer than 40 square miles, boasts a wide variety of microclimates and -environments, including woodlands, wetlands, drylands, and forests. On the island's leeward side, the gentle slopes and plentiful sources of water allowed sugar, cotton, and indigo to flourish, while in the southern parish of St. Patrick's the soil was rocky and subject to erosion, and the area suffered from drought even when the rest of the island was well watered. Montserrat's economic development was significantly undercut by its lack of harbors, which made it necessary for ships to anchor offshore and employ lighters or other small craft to load or unload goods. The island was fortunate in that its Soufriere Hills volcano remained dormant for half a millennium, but its size could support only a small white or black population, and problems of soil fertility and hydration destined it to remain economically and politically marginal within the Leewards. Nonetheless, an anonymous contributor to the eighteenth-century volume *American Husbandry* claimed that it was the healthiest and most pleasant part of the West Indies and that its valleys "yield[ed] all the West Indian productions in perfection."[4]

---

[3] Vere Langford Oliver, *The History of the Island of Antigua* (London: Mitchell and Hughes, 1894), vol. 1, v; Mr. Morris, "The Colony of the Leeward Islands," *Proceedings of the Royal Colonial Institute* 22 (1890), 245; Robert V. Wells, *The Population of the British Colonies in America before 1776: A Survey of Census Data* (Princeton, NJ: Princeton University Press, 1975), 210; Michael Craton, *Testing the Chains: Resistance to Slavery in the British West Indies* (Ithaca, NY: Cornell University Press, 1982), 115; Governor Hart to Council of Trade and Plantations, July 11, 1722, in W. Noel Sainsbury et al., eds., *Calendar of State Papers: Colonial Series* [hereafter C.S.P. Col.], 1721–1722 (London: HMSO, 1934), 109.

[4] Lydia M. Pulsipher, *Seventeenth-Century Montserrat: An Environmental Impact Statement* (Norwich: Geo Books, 1986), 6; Pulsipher, "Galways Plantation, Montserrat," in Herman J. Viola and Carolyn Margolis, eds., *Seeds of Change: A Quincentennial Commemoration* (Washington, DC: Smithsonian Institution Press, 1991),140; Pulsipher and Conrad M. Goodwin, "A Sugar-Boiling House at Galways: An Irish Sugar Plantation in Montserrat, West Indies," *Post-Medieval Archaeology* 16 (1982), 25; Howard A. Fergus, *Montserrat: History of a Caribbean Colony* (London: Macmillan, 1994), 4, 7; Harry J. Carman, ed., *American Husbandry* (New York: Columbia University Press, 1939), 448.

Nevis, like Montserrat, was a small island, consisting of just 36 square miles, and even more mountainous than the latter, with similarly stony soil and variable rainfall; Columbus called it "Nieves" (snows), because the clouds that often surrounded its highest peak made the mountain look as if it were capped with snow. Early planters claimed that its hot springs were "as successful against Distempers as ours in Somersetshire [Bath], or those of Bourbon in France," and by the 1770s the springs had begun to draw tourists to the lavish Bath Hotel outside the capital, Charlestown. Still, as the planter William Hacke wrote in 1684, "The fresh water on this island is not very good; it is so hot that you can scarce keep your hand in it; the Inhabitants save raine water & keep it in Cisterns made of stone for theire necessary occasions." Although Nevis flourished in the seventeenth century – Charlestown served as the administrative center of the Leewards for the federated colony's first twenty-five years after it gained its independence from Barbados in 1670, and throughout the century the soil remained "very productive, and yields great quantities of sugar" – by the middle of the eighteenth century the island's physical and social fabric had been shredded by a series of human and natural disasters. Moreover, the thin, clayey soil became increasingly worn out, leading to a dramatic decline in the annual production of sugar in the decades leading up to the outbreak of the American Revolution.[5]

In sharp contrast, St. Kitts, just 2 miles away across the strait, was widely regarded as the producer of the highest-quality sugar in the West Indies. With an area of 76 square miles, it was significantly larger than Nevis or Montserrat, but still considerably smaller than Antigua, let alone Barbados (166 square miles) or Jamaica (4,400), and its interior was so mountainous that a third of the land was unfit for any type of cultivation, resulting in the island's plantations being strung out along a coastal road, a far from ideal pattern of settlement in the face of foreign attack or slave rebellion. But a commentator in *American Husbandry* described its volcanic soil as "a light hazel mould on brick earth, of a surprising fertility ... the best for producing sugar," a sentiment echoed by the Jamaican planter and historian Bryan Edwards, who described it as "more especially suited to the production of sugar than any other in the West Indies." Edwards claimed that "canes, planted in particular

[5] Herman Moll, *Atlas geographus: or, a compleat system of geography, ancient and modern* (London: John Nicholson, 1717), vol. 5, 518; Governor Hart to Council of Trade and Plantations, July 11, 1722, *C.S.P. Col., 1721–1722*, 109; Vincent K. Hubbard, *Swords, Ships, and Sugar: A History of Nevis to 1900* (Placentia, CA: Premiere Editions, 1991), 5; Joyce Grenfell, *Nevis, Queen of the Caribees* (London: Macmillan, 1994), 25.

spots, have been known to yield 8000 lbs. of Muscovado sugar from a single acre" and that the island's average annual produce in the late eighteenth century was 16,000 hogsheads of sugar, "a prodigious return, not equalled I imagine by any other sugar country in any part of the globe." On the eve of the American Revolution, the quality and quantity of sugar produced on St. Kitts had enabled the island to surpass Jamaica and Barbados and to become the richest colony in the British Empire.[6]

NATURAL DISASTERS

In addition to the very limited amount of arable land available throughout the four islands, Leeward planters had to cope with the constant threat of several types of natural disaster. Although the volcanoes of Nevis, St. Kitts, and Montserrat remained dormant throughout the seventeenth and eighteenth centuries, the Leewards were particularly vulnerable to hurricanes; simultaneously, however, they were prone to excesses of dry weather, which might inflict considerable damage on the health of canes, slaves, and planters alike, and bring with them the threat of unquenchable fires. The Nevis clergyman Robert Robertson gave voice to planters' anxieties about these disasters, asking, "Does not a Hurricane, or Dry-weather Year, set a Planter farther back than a seasonable Year can advance him? ... Is not the Planter undone when a Mortality seizes the Negroes, if he has not the wherewithal to renew his Stock?" In a pamphlet aimed at giving Whitehall administrators a sense of the "state and situation of the present sugar planters of the Leeward Islands," Robertson enumerated "some Contingencies to which the Leward Islands are especially subject, such as Hurricanes, Accidental Fires, and Dry Weather, any one of which will make a vast Diminution" in the islands' production of sugar.[7] Robertson's subsequent pamphlet was concerned entirely with the effects of the hurricane that struck the Leewards at the end of June 1733. Although Robertson described the damage to Nevis as "but small," he reported that "Trees in several Places are torn up by the Roots; many

---

[6] Carman, ed., *American Husbandry*, 445; Craton, *Testing the Chains*, 33; Edwards, *The History, Civil and Commercial, of the British Colonies in the West Indies* (London: John Stockdale, 1801), vol. 1, 430. By comparison, the far larger island of Jamaica in 1773 produced 77,000 hogsheads of sugar, and in 1784 Barbados made 57,500 (Richard B. Sheridan, "The Wealth of Jamaica in the Eighteenth Century," *Economic History Review* 18 [1965], 303; Eric Williams, *From Columbus to Castro: The History of the Caribbean* [New York: Vintage Books, 1984], 124).

[7] Robertson, *A Detection of the State and Situation of the Present Sugar Planters of Barbadoes and the Leeward Islands* (London: J. Wilford, 1732), 25, 48.

of the Negro-Huts, Mayors-Houses, and slighter Sugar Works, are beat down," a degree of devastation which promised that Nevis would indeed experience a "vast Diminution" in its productive capacity. Robertson asserted that "the Loss of Sugar alone in the Shipping of Nevis and St. Christopher's, with what lay expos'd to the Weather on the several Bays, is computed at about Two Thousand Hogsheads; and, which must prove of far worse Consequence in this and next Year's Crop, the young Canes are almost everywhere stript and twisted, or blown out of the Ground, and the old ones laid flat upon it."[8] Yet Nevis and St. Kitts had gotten off lightly in comparison with Montserrat, where, Robertson claimed, two dozen houses in Plymouth, the island's capital, had been destroyed, as had "many more in the Country, with most of the Boiling-houses, and the Sugar in them, which was considerable." Montserrat's inhabitants had fared as poorly as its buildings; Colonel William Liddell, a leading planter, "was so bruised with the Fall of his House, that he died," and "many of the Whites, and more of the Blacks are hurted, and some killed by the falling down of their Houses; and in short, they are in so miserable a Condition all over that Island, that if I had credit enough to presume so far, I wou'd recommend their Case to the publick Favour and Compassion."[9]

As destructive as this hurricane was, it was neither the last nor the worst the Leewards would face in the later seventeenth and eighteenth centuries. In the 1670s, one report to the proprietors of Carolina suggested that they might recruit white settlers from Antigua, as the planters there "would willingly come off and transplant themselves farther from the terrible Hurry Caines that doth everie yeare distroye their Houses and Crops." Another asserted that many planters were "removing from Antigo weary of Hericanes," perhaps referring to the 1667 storm that had torn through the Leewards and "reduced most of these miserable people to their first principles."[10] Had this blast failed to convince Antiguans to try their luck in the apparently calmer climate of the North American mainland, that which struck in August of 1681 might have delivered an extra dose of persuasion, as "it was not the Ships only that felt the fury, of this storm, but the whole Island suffered by it; for the Houses were blown

---

[8] Robertson, *A Short Account of the Hurricane, that pass'd thro' the English Leeward Caribbee Islands, on Saturday the 30th of June 1733* (London: Privately printed, 1733), 10, 12.

[9] Ibid., 12.

[10] Matthew Mulcahy, *Hurricanes and Society in the British Greater Caribbean, 1624–1783* (Baltimore: Johns Hopkins University Press, 2006), 19, 28.

down, the Trees tore up by the Roots, or had their Heads and Limbs sadly shattered, neither was there any Leaves, Herbs or green Thing left in the Island, but all look'd like Winter, Insomuch that a ship coming thither, that used that Trade, could scarce believe it to be the same Island." To add insult to injury, another storm ripped through the island just two weeks later, also devastating St. Kitts.[11] In 1707, at a time when the Leewards were already destabilized by the effects of ongoing Anglo-French warfare, a hurricane "almost entirely destroy'd their Sugar-Works, threw down their Houses, tore up their Trees and Plants by the Roots, and left them in a most miserable Condition," particularly in Antigua and Nevis. In the wake of this tempest, Leeward governor Daniel Parke informed the Board of Trade that "I have lost almost all I have ... I have been building a House at St. Kitts, which is now blown down, and the ffload has caryed away all the timber into the sea."[12] In June 1733, thirty of Montserrat's thirty-six sugar mills were blown down in what the French marine engineer Jacques Bellin described as a hurricane so terrible that it destroyed three-quarters of the structures on the island, while on Antigua the damage, exclusive of shipping, was estimated at £50,000.[13] Just four years later, Montserrat's surviving or rebuilt windmills were leveled by another hurricane, and many of the island's slaves and livestock, along with those of St. Kitts, were swept into the sea, while the cane crop was destroyed. The Antiguan planter Walter Tullideph wrote at this time to his brother in Scotland that "at Montserrat the rains were so violent that it had like to have carried away all of Town into ye Sea, part of the fort with two or three white people was carried away and at [the planter] Mr Tuite's seventeen of his negroes ... were carried away by the floods and lost nay he writes himself that 150 Acres of Cane land is carried away & now no more but a heap of Rocks & stones, his two mills blown down &c."[14] In 1751, Montserrat and St. Kitts were struck again, resulting in losses

[11] William Dampier, *Voyages and Descriptions* (London: James Knapton, 1700), vol. 2, 70; Philip P. Boucher, *France and the American Tropics to 1700: Tropics of Discontent?* (Baltimore: Johns Hopkins University Press, 2008), 281.

[12] John Oldmixon, *The British Empire in America* (London: John Nicholson, 1708), vol. 2, 218; Mulcahy, *Hurricanes and Society*, 91.

[13] Mulcahy, *Hurricanes and Society*, 72; Bellin, *Description géographique des Isles Antilles possédées par les Anglois* (Paris: Didot, 1758), 126; *The American Gazetteer* (London: A. Millar, 1762), vol. 2, unpaginated. All translations are mine unless stated otherwise.

[14] Thomas Southey, *Chronological History of the West Indies* (London: Longman, 1827), vol. 1, 264; Walter Tullideph to David Tullideph, October 3, 1737, Letter-Book of Walter Tullideph, Ogilvy of Inverquharity Papers, GD205/53/8, Scottish Record Office, Edinburgh. My thanks to Baron Ogilvy of Inverquharity for allowing me to quote from these letters.

estimated at more than £100,000 sterling and the destruction of many "Houses, Mills, and Works," as well as all of the harvested and processed sugar stored in the islands' mills and warehouses.[15] But the worst was yet to come; in August 1772, the Leewards were devastated by the most powerful hurricane of the century, in response to which Sir Ralph Payne, the islands' governor, wrote that the "Misery and Distress from the Fury of the Storm, [was] unknown I believe before, to any Part of the human Creation," that it was "scarcely, if at all, inferior in Horror, to the dreadful Catastrophe of Lisbon," and that it "baffles all the Powers of Description and can only be conceiv'd by those, who were the unfortunate Victims of it." Another observer painted a vivid picture not only of the hurricane's destructiveness, but of the way in which it turned the islands into sites of phantasmagoric terror, as "the crash of falling buildings," "the rattling of timbers," and "the tumbling of stone walls" mingled with "the shrieks of those who were left destitute of shelter," as "some houses were ... whirled into the street, others not a vestige of them left behind," and as "a war of wind and rain" tore St. Kitts's new courthouse from its foundations and ripped the roof off of Basseterre's principal church, reducing the island's symbols of temporal and spiritual power to rubble.[16] The Leewards' sole newspaper, the *St. Christopher Caribbean and Leeward Gazette*, expressed itself in less florid terms, but noted that "the dreadful effects of the hurricane ... will be so long felt by the unfortunate inhabitants of this country, that they must make the deepest impression upon every sensible mind."[17]

As terrifying and destructive as hurricanes were, however, they were far from being the sole disaster Leeward colonists had to fear; a lack of rainfall could be as destructive to people and plants as a surfeit thereof. Antigua, whose agricultural productivity was always limited by the island's paucity of sources of fresh water, was especially vulnerable to drought, despite its inhabitants' efforts to conserve rainwater in cisterns or in clay-lined ponds.[18] Shortly after the arrival in December 1721 of Governor

---

[15] Mulcahy, *Hurricanes and Society*, 2.

[16] Ibid., 22, 24; *An Account of the Late Dreadful Hurricane, which happened on the 31st August, 1772, also the Damage done on that Day in the Islands of St. Christopher and Nevis* (Basseterre, St, Kitts: Thomas Howe, 1772), 4, 5. The "dreadful Catastrophe of Lisbon" refers to the earthquake of 1755, which devastated that city.

[17] Mulcahy, *Hurricanes and Society*, 141.

[18] In a 1721 act for "the Preservation of the Body Ponds, and making them Publick Ponds," Antiguan residents were reminded that "in the Times of extreme Drought, when other Ponds and fresh Waters have been dried up, the aforesaid Ponds, called *The Body Ponds*, have afforded fresh and wholsom Waters, and have been the Support of the Inhabitants,

William Hart, the island finally came to the end of a four-year drought, and welcome rains heralded a rapid return to prosperity, even in the face of a series of minor hurricanes in the autumn of 1723.[19] Yet in May 1726, Hart wrote to London that the island was again "in a most deplorable Condition from the Dry weather, which has Continued for Eight Months past," in the course of which the planters had "not only lost their Crop for this Year and the next, But they have been oblig'd to bring all their Water from Guadaloupe and Mountserrat, which was Sold at fifteen shillings a Hogshead which has occasioned the loss of many of the Cattle and Negroes." Hart's anxieties appear to have been swiftly relieved, as he recorded three days later that he had ordered a "Thanksgiving" for rain, much as he had decreed a fast for lack of rainfall the previous March, but Antigua continued over the following decades to suffer from drought. In March 1731, the fashionable London periodical *Gentlemen's Magazine* published an Antiguan correspondent's plaint that "there is a great Want of Rain ... if the Rain don't fall, there will be no Crop next year. The young Canes are much burnt. The Crops are very short at Nevis and Mountserrat. The Ponds are almost dry, and Water so scarce that a Pail of Cistern-Water is sold for 3s." In June 1736, Leeward's governor, William Mathew, ordered a "Fast ... for the blast and dry weather," and June 1741 saw a "Fast appointed for want of rain."[20]

Although the risk of fire was, of course, greater during periods of drought, this danger was omnipresent in towns in which residents and structures were tightly packed, most buildings were made of wood, and winds were often heavy. On August 17, 1769, St. John's, Antigua, suffered a fire, supposedly caused by an unattended coal pot, which consumed two-thirds of the capital's buildings, including 260 houses, and the damage was estimated at £400,000 local currency. The Scots traveler Janet Schaw, who visited at the end of 1774, pronounced the town to be "very neat and pretty" but noted that "it still bears the marks of ... the dreadful fire." In 1776, a "disastrous fire" devastated Basseterre, St. Kitts, the damage from which was partly recompensed by an appeal, backed by George III, through which metropolitan Britons, probably including

---

the Slaves and Cattle," and were asked to refrain from cutting down the trees and shrubs surrounding them, as this would leave the waters "exposed to the Heat and Exhalation of the Sun, [and] the Waters [would be] not only rendred much worse, but are in great danger of being dried up" (*Acts of Assembly, Passed in the Charibbee Leeward Islands, from 1690, to 1730* [London: John Baskett, 1734], 181; italics in original).

[19] A. P. Newton, "Introduction," *C.S.P. Col., 1724–1725* (London: HMSO, 1936), liv.

[20] Oliver, *History of Antigua*, vol. 1, xcvi, xcviii, ci, cxxxi.

many expatriate West Indians, donated thousands of pounds for the town's rebuilding.[21]

Most devastating to the social and economic life of the Leewards were the earthquakes to which all of the islands were vulnerable, due to their geologic location near the juncture between the Caribbean and North American tectonic plates. In the century between 1670 and 1776, the islands experienced no fewer than nine major earthquakes, as well as numberless milder shocks. The Reverend William Smith, who served as rector of the parish of St. John's, Nevis, in the 1730s, claimed that, during his five years on the island, he had experienced at least a dozen of the latter, and in the aftermath of a particularly "violent Shock" he was convinced that "all that part of Charles Town will one time or other sink down into the Sea (by the Shock of a more violent one) as Port Royal in Jamaica did."[22] Smith might have felt still more pessimistic had he experienced the earthquake that struck the Leewards in April 1690. Each of the islands suffered significant damage, particularly at St. John's and the French settlement at Basseterre (where an estimated 12 million tons of sugar were destroyed), but the tremor was strongest at Nevis; there, landslides occurred on Nevis Peak, "all the Houses in Charles Town that were built of Brick or Stone, dropt of a sudden down from the Top to the Bottom in perfect Ruines," and an observer decreed that "it was a dreadful thing to see Men, Women, and Children flying up and down from Place to Place in Fear and Consternation," while "the Earth in many places ... broke open and swallow'd some Thousands of great Trees, that were never more seen," and "the Surface of the tottering Earth ... open'd, and from the yawning Clefts, vomited up a sort of hot, bituminous Water, whole Tuns full at a time, no less offensive to the Smell, than dreadful to the Sight."[23]

---

[21] Sir Probyn Inniss, *Basseterre: The Story of a West Indian Town* (Basseterre, St. Kitts: Privately printed, 1985), 27; Schaw, *The Journal of a Lady of Quality*, ed. Charles M. and Evangeline Walker Andrews (New Haven: Yale University Press, 1923), 87; Matthew Mulcahy, "Weathering the Storms: Hurricanes and Plantation Agriculture in the British Greater Caribbean," Program in Early American Economy and Society, Library Company of Philadelphia, http://www.librarycompany.org/Economics/PDF/Files/C2002-Mulcahy. pdf, 29. See also Bonham C. Richardson, *Igniting the Caribbean's Past: Fire in British West Indian History* (Chapel Hill: University of North Carolina, 2004).

[22] Mulcahy, *Hurricanes and Society*, 125; Smith, *A Natural History of Nevis, and the rest of the English Leeward Charibee Islands in America* (Cambridge: J. Bentham, 1745), 65. In 1692, Port Royal experienced a severe earthquake that killed an estimated two thousand people and virtually obliterated the town.

[23] G. R. Robson, "An Earthquake Catalogue for the Eastern Caribbean," *Bulletin of the Seismological Society of America* 54 (1964), 789; *An Account of the Late Dreadful*

For Nevis, this earthquake was just one in a series of disasters that devastated its population and productive capacity and doomed it to marginal status among the Leewards. In 1689, yellow fever had struck, apparently killing half of the island's residents, leaving few to face the prospect of rebuilding after the ravages of the 1690 quake. Smaller shocks hit in 1692 and 1696, and in 1706 a French invasion left the island virtually in ruins, the majority of its buildings, including the courthouse and churches, destroyed, the cane fields laid waste, and the coppers and other machinery used in the refining of sugar plundered; the remaining English settlers were then struck by the 1707 hurricane. Although the island to some extent recovered from these depredations, it never regained the position it had held in the late seventeenth century as the most prosperous and best governed of the Leewards. In 1734, Governor Mathew asserted that it had "quite lost its Trade, & is a desert to what it was Thirty Years ago," and in 1770 the Abbé Raynal, in his renowned *Histoire philosophique et politique des établissements et du commerce des Européens dans les deux Indes*, claimed that "since this series of disasters, it has recovered a little. It contains six hundred free men and five thousand slaves, the taxes upon whom do not exceed £1875, and who send to England three or four millions weight of raw sugar."[24]

How, then, did Leeward colonists cope with the physical and psychological effects of life in the shadow of disaster? Why did they choose to remain in islands so prone to floods and fires, droughts and earthquakes? As Matthew Mulcahy has observed, such disasters "did not simply halt colonists' social and economic improvements," but "violently and dramatically knocked them backward, reversing the trajectory of development."[25] Yet evidence suggests that the settlers developed a variety of methods by which to cope with emotional and environmental trauma alike. At any moment in the late seventeenth and eighteenth centuries, the islands' population would include people who, if they had not personally lived through a disaster, had heard their elders' accounts thereof and had drawn from them strategies for limiting or repairing their ravages. By

Earth-Quake in the Island of Mevis, St. Christophers, &c. which happen'd in the Beginning of April, of this present Year 1690 (London: A. Smith, 1690), 1; Moll, *Atlas geographus*, 517; Boucher, *France and the American Tropics*, 226.

[24] Brian Dyde, *Out of the Crowded Vagueness: A History of the Islands of St. Kitts, Nevis & Anguilla* (Oxford: Macmillan, 2005), 85; Hubbard, *Swords, Ships, and Sugar*, 35, 41–2; Raynal, *A Philosophical and Political History of the Settlements and Trade of the Europeans in the East and West Indies*, trans. J. O. Justamond (London: A. Strahan and T. Cadell, 1788), vol. 6, 304.
[25] Mulcahy, *Hurricanes and Society*, 126, 73.

the end of the seventeenth century, Leeward settlers had learned, supposedly from the Carib Indians of Dominica and St. Vincent, how to predict hurricanes, preparing for their onslaught when "the Skies are very turbulent, the Sun redder than usual, and the Hills clear of Clouds or Fogs," and when "in the Hollows of the Earth or Wells there's a great Noise, the Stars at Night look very big ... the N.W. Sky very black, and the Sea smells stronger than usual."[26] They had realized that hurricanes and earthquakes tore stone and brick buildings to pieces, but that "those that were built of Wood were no less violently shaken, but stood however, which shew'd that the Rivetings of wooden Structures are far stronger, and not so easily disjointed as the Co-agmentations of Cement and Mortar."[27] In 1701, the Assembly of St. Kitts expressed its concern that the destruction of "deeds and grants by accidents of fire or water or wind" left property holders "exposed to every wicked man's molestation," and an act of 1712, citing "the frequent Accidents of Hurricanes and Fires" that left many people without "their Writings, Deeds, Conveyances, and other Evidences whatsoever of the Lands and Tenements of which themselves and their Ancestors have been so many Years quietly and equitably possessed," ordered that "every Proprietor of Land within this Island shall be adjudged legally instated and reinvested in such Estate ... as he, his Ancestors, or they whose Estate he hath legally had at the Time of this Island being surrendered to the French" in 1689.[28]

Over time, islanders learned to rely on themselves, by building with wood against earthquakes and hurricanes and conserving every drop of rainwater in the face of drought, but they also became increasingly aware of the assistance they might gain, from the metropole and other colonies alike, by virtue of their membership in the British Empire. After the hurricane of 1772, Ralph Payne wrote to his fellow royal governors in Barbados, Virginia, and Pennsylvania, requesting that they send the Leewards fish, cornmeal, and other foodstuffs to "avert the Threatening Prospect of Famine," and the notoriously independent-minded and assertive Assembly of Antigua proposed that small boats be stationed in the Caribbean sea-lanes in order to meet any vessels carrying food supplies from North America to Britain and divert them to the Leewards, although

[26] Moll, *Atlas geographus*, 520.
[27] *Account of the Late Dreadful Earth-Quake*, 1.
[28] "An Act for Settling the Estates and Titles of the Inhabitants of this Island to their Possessions within the Same," *Laws of the Island of St. Christopher, from the Year 1711, to the Year 1791* (St. Kitts: Edward Luther Low, 1791), 10.

the plan was in the end rejected by the island's Council.[29] Fortunately, "great Numbers of Planters, Merchants, and others, in the British West India Islands" came forward to offer "the most liberal and benevolent Assistance to their poor Neighbours in the Day of Distress," fulfilling the prediction of the *Virginia Gazette* that "there will be a charitable attention paid to it, even in a distant clime, the metropolis of our empire; particularly all those who have had and have been benefited by the existence of so fruitful a spot."[30] In a similar vein, in the wake of the Antigua fire of 1769, British merchants active in the West Indian trade donated £500 sterling from their general fund for relief of the sufferers.[31] In 1776, as his North American subjects moved to sever the bonds of empire, George III created a charitable fund for the rebuilding of Basseterre after it was devastated by fire, a "performance of imperial theater" that emphasized the paternalist nature of British colonial rule and the sovereign's concern and compassion for those subjects who remained loyal to the mother country.[32]

As Leeward colonists looked to the metropole and to their fellow British American colonists for physical relief from the suffering caused by natural disasters, they, like their contemporaries in Britain and North America, also turned to Providence. In times of drought, governors ordered days of public fasts in the hope that a communal display of piety and repentance would bring an end to the presumably divinely ordained lack of rainfall. When rain finally came, it would be marked by a communal thanksgiving for God's mercy; a similar gathering took place if an approaching hurricane suddenly veered away from the islands, as happened in Antigua in 1683.[33] Both the French marine engineer Jacques Bellin and the Scots writer Tobias Smollett, who visited the West Indies in his capacity as a ship's surgeon, were struck by what they saw as a curious practice at Nevis. According to Smollett, "The Nevisians are said to have three public annual fasts, to implore the Divine Protection against hurricanes; and if none happen in July, August, or September, they have

---

[29] Mulcahy, *Hurricanes and Society*, 106.

[30] *Virginia Gazette* (Purdie and Dixon), November 5, 1772, 3; October 29, 1772 (Rind), 1.

[31] *Virginia Gazette* (Rind), March 3, 1770, 2.

[32] Alan Taylor employs this phrase in reference to the king's efforts to relieve famine in Quebec and the Canadian maritime provinces in 1789; see Taylor, "'The Hungry Year': 1789 on the Northern Border of Revolutionary America," in Alessa Johns, ed., *Dreadful Visitations: Confronting Natural Catastrophe in the Age of Enlightenment* (New York: Routledge, 1999), 171.

[33] Mulcahy, *Hurricanes and Society*, 38.

a public thanksgiving in October"; in Bellin's account, these fast days were also employed as attempts to forestall earthquakes.[34] In the wake of a calamity such as the St. Kitts hurricane of 1772, the governor might decree a day of "Fasting and Humiliation" to signify the inhabitants' acceptance of the disaster as an expression of God's will and their gratitude that the ravages had not been still greater.[35] But as traumatic as floods and droughts, earthquakes and conflagrations were to Leeward colonists, as frequently as they occurred, and as devastating as they were to the islands' social and political and particularly their economic life, they nonetheless failed to discourage the majority of colonists from attempting to rebuild their destroyed homes, businesses, and estates or to convince new migrants to look elsewhere when trying their luck in the West Indies. However "weary of Hericanes" the islanders might become, the threat of natural disaster was just one of the challenges they faced in the attempt to build families and fortunes in the Leewards, and for the most part they were no more unnerved by the prospect of flood and fire than they were by that of foreign attack or slave rebellion.

SLAVE REBELLION

For the most part, the Leewards were "creole islands" that lacked settled indigenous communities at the onset of European settlement.[36] Of the four islands, only St. Kitts was by the early seventeenth century home to a Carib Indian population, and the majority of these native people were exterminated by a joint Anglo-French expedition within the first year of European settlement, while the survivors fled to the Carib stronghold at Dominica.[37] For the following half-century, Dominican Caribs, sometimes led by a man known to Europeans as "Indian" Warner, allegedly the son of Thomas Warner, the first English governor of St. Kitts, and a Carib woman, launched occasional raids against the Leewards. In 1672, for example, Sir William Stapleton, the first governor of the independent Leeward colony, reported to the Council of Trade and Plantations that the Caribs had "lately broken the peace made with [Barbadian governor] Lord Willoughby, having killed and left for dead two more of his

---

[34] Smollett, *The Present State of All Nations* (London: R. Baldwin, 1769), vol. 8, 487; Bellin, *Description géographique*, 121.

[35] *Virginia Gazette* (Purdie and Dixon), November 5, 1772, 3.

[36] The phrase is taken from Megan Vaughan, *Creating the Creole Island: Slavery in Eighteenth-Century Mauritius* (Durham, NC: Duke University Press, 2005).

[37] V. S. Naipaul, *The Loss of El Dorado* (London: André Deutsch, 1969), 117.

Majesty's subjects in Antigua, where thirty of them are in the woods; has secured two periagoes [canoes] and twenty-eight Indians who came to Montserrat to commit the like outrages." In a "remonstrance" of 1676, Antiguan settlers claimed that, two years earlier, Caribs had landed on the island, "killed severall Christians and carried away sixteen negroes, and one Christian child, whom they afterwards cruelly murdered."[38] But these raids appear to have halted after "Indian" Warner's death in 1674, after which time the principal source of anxiety among Leeward settlers, with reference to rebellious populations, stemmed from the rapid increase in the enslaved population, both in absolute terms and in comparison with the population of white settlers. In 1678, only Nevis had more black inhabitants than it did white, but by 1707 the whites on all four islands were outnumbered by the blacks by a factor of 2, a tendency that grew still more pronounced over the course of the eighteenth century. By 1756, the percentage of blacks in the population ranged from 86.1 in Nevis to 90.2 in Antigua.[39] The ever-increasing ratio of blacks to whites, although both a cause and a symptom of the Leewards' rising prosperity, was a source of concern to the planters, who came to view themselves as an embattled minority constantly at the mercy of a potentially hostile majority. Moreover, the geography and topography of settlement in the Leewards created their own problems of security. Settlers in the plantation colonies of North America understood that, should their bondspeople rise against them, they at least possessed the option of flight to the interior, but residents of the tiny Leeward islands had nowhere to run. Under such circumstances, the planters' perpetual sense of vulnerability to their "numerous and disaffected herd of African slaves" and the absence of sufficient "low and middling men of a free condition" necessary for "the security, as well of the solid wealth of every nation," encouraged them to see conspiracies everywhere and to punish these alleged plots with great severity.[40]

White residents of, and visitors to, the Leewards had since the late seventeenth century noted that the islands' slaves were prone to running away and to "committing depredations" against the plantations. In 1686, the Antigua Council authorized a Captain Carden "to pursue & capture

---

[38] Stapleton to Council, May 27, 1672, in *C.S.P. Col., 1669–1674* (London: HMSO, 1889), 364; Peter Hulme and Neil L. Whitehead, eds., *Wild Majesty: Encounters with Caribs from Columbus to the Present Day* (Oxford: Clarendon Press, 1992), 91, 97.

[39] Wells, *Population*, 212.

[40] William Burke, *An Account of the European Settlements in America* (London: R. and J. Dodsley, 1759), vol. 2, 114.

or kill 40 or 50 runaway slaves in the Mountains," referring to the steep and heavily forested Shekerley Hills in the southwest of Antigua, and when the physician and naturalist Hans Sloane visited Nevis in the late 1680s, he noted that "the Ground is cleared almost to the top of the Hill [Nevis Peak], where yet remains some Wood, and where are Runaway Negroes that harbour themselves in it."[41] In 1723, the Assembly of Antigua passed an act for the "better government" of the "great numbers of slaves" who had taken advantage of the apparent "lenity of the laws & fled to the mountains, whence they issued in armed bands to damage the plantations." The ringleaders were attainted of felony, and the Assembly announced that it would pay a reward of £3 to any white man who killed a runaway and £6 should he take one alive. Moreover, although slaves would continue to be granted their customary three days' holiday at Christmas, during that time the island would be placed under martial law, "on account of the usual riotous behaviour of the blacks."[42] In September 1724, a planter informed the Nevis Assembly that there were "Severall Negroes in this Island Run Away who Dayly Commit Thefts and Robberys" and that "Incouragement [should be] given to the Publick to such Persons who shall take and apprehend the said Negroes," a suggestion that encouraged the island's chief justice, John Dasent, to order that the considerable sum of two pistoles be given to anyone who apprehended one of these maroons.[43]

As already noted, the Leeward Assemblies rewarded white residents more generously for taking runaways alive than for killing them upon their apprehension. This divergence might initially seem surprising; if runaways were so destructive and disruptive to the peace and prosperity of the islands, would not killing them on sight provide an immediate solution to the problem? But Leeward whites, like those elsewhere in the slave-based plantation societies of the Americas, were keen to strike fear into slaves' hearts through the use of exemplary punishments, such as public executions, often by burning. Bringing runaways back in chains, placing them in jail, trying them in court, and then publicly executing them created a scripted drama of crime and punishment that aimed to teach the condemned man or woman's fellow slaves that resistance was

---

[41] Oliver, *History of Antigua*, vol. 1, lxvi; Sloane, *A Voyage to the Islands Madera, Barbadoes, Nieves, S. Christophers and Jamaica* (London, B. M., 1707), vol. 1, 42.

[42] Oliver, *History of Antigua*, vol. 1, xcv, cii.

[43] Mr. Parris to Nevis Assembly, September 10, 1724, C.O. 186/1: Minutes of Assembly, Nevis, National Archives of the United Kingdom, Kew, London.

futile and would almost certainly end in a painful death.[44] One of the many paradoxes inherent in Atlantic slavery was the idea that slaves were not merely persons possessed, like Russian serfs or medieval European peasants, of fewer legal rights than their social superiors, but were actually chattel – living property. Thus, when slaves ran away from their masters, they were not only depriving their owner of his labor value, but were actually stealing his property; runaways were "slaves who stole themselves."[45] And because a slave, particularly one young and strong enough to feel confident that he or she might be able to evade surveillance and survive in the harsh, wild hills of Nevis or Antigua, was a highly valuable piece of property, such "stealing" was a felony, not an act of petty theft, and had to be punished accordingly.

Because of the spotty record-keeping in the Leewards, it is difficult to acquire reliable statistics about the extent of slave resistance. But according to the legislative records of St. Kitts, between February 1740 and June 1746, thirty-eight slaves were executed for felony. They included one woman and a number of men whose African names, such as Cudjoe, Quashie, and Cadenda, may have indicated that they had been born free and had been enslaved and brought to the West Indies as children or youths.[46] From the amounts of sugar awarded to the owners of these executed St. Kitts slaves as compensation for the loss of their laborers, we can infer that the majority of the runaways were exactly the sorts of strong younger people who would be most likely to take their chances as fugitives and whose absence would not merely display their defiance of their masters, but would represent a significant loss to the latter's productive endeavors. Of the thirty-five executed slaves whose values were given, all but two were appraised at 3,000 or more pounds of sugar, and fifteen at 4,500 or more.[47] In Nevis, owners of executed slaves were reimbursed with cash rather than sugar; in the early 1730s, the average allowance per slave was £30, and twenty years later it had risen to a little

---

[44] On the relationship between slavery, law, and punishment in the eighteenth-century Caribbean, see Diana Paton, *No Bond but the Law: Punishment, Race, and Gender in Jamaican State Formation, 1780–1870* (Durham, NC: Duke University Press, 2004), and Vincent Brown, "Spiritual Terror and Sacred Authority in Jamaican Slave Society," *Slavery and Abolition*, 24 (2003), 24–53.

[45] Peter Wood, *Black Majority: Negroes in South Carolina from 1670 through the Stono Rebellion* (New York: Norton, 1974), 239.

[46] On the conventions of naming of slaves, see Trevor Burnard, "Slave Naming Patterns: Onomastics and the Taxonomy of Race in Eighteenth-Century Jamaica," *Journal of Interdisciplinary History* 31 (2001), 325–46.

[47] Entries taken from throughout C.O. 241/5: Minutes of Council and Assembly, St. Kitts.

more than £70.[48] In the former period, the average price of a West Indian slave was approximately £25, and in the latter £40, so clearly these slaves were of average to high value to their owners.[49]

Even more worrisome than runaways were those slaves who took violent actions against their masters. The Nevis records depict slaves rebelling against white authority in a variety of ways. In 1734, a slave named Limerick, the property of James Emra, "Committed a Barbarous Murder on the Body of John Wattis," a white man. Emra's neighbor, John Brodbelt, received ten pistoles for recovering Limerick, but the slave "Laid Violent hands on himself" and cheated the executioner. In the following year, John Huggins was reimbursed by the Assembly for £30 in relation to the execution of his unnamed "Negroe Woman," who had allegedly poisoned a white woman, and in 1738 George Webbe was granted £70 for a male slave who was executed for having burned down the house of another white woman, Elizabeth Neal.[50] William Smith, a Cambridge graduate who spent most of the 1730s as the rector of St. John's parish, Nevis, recorded in his *Natural History of Nevis* that "a Parishioner of mine, baptized a Black Woman, and had her well instructed in our Religion here in England, but she had not long been arrived at Nevis, before she poisoned four White Persons, and was executed for so doing."[51] In St. Kitts just before Christmas 1753, a female slave named Baby was executed for having murdered her owner, Thomas Barnaby, and in the summer of 1760, Elizabeth Morgan's slave François "Barbarously Murdered a White Man and a Negro Slave and Wounded another White man." The Assembly reported grimly that François "has not been brought to Justice for his said Crimes ... [and] still continues upon this Island," and offered the sizable reward of £150 to anyone who might apprehend him.[52]

The legislative records of the Leeward Islands do not present a full picture of the varied ways in which slaves continued to resist bondage, as they deal only with specific breaches of island laws. The surviving plantation records, however, offer a more nuanced sense of the patterns

---

[48] Entries taken from throughout C.O. 186/1–3: Minutes of Assembly, Nevis.

[49] David Eltis, Frank Lewis, and David Richardson, "Slave Prices, the African Slave Trade, and Productivity in Eighteenth-Century South Carolina: A Reassessment," *Journal of Economic History* 66 (2006), 1057.

[50] Petitions of Catherine Emra, May 23, 1734, John Brodbelt, May 27, 1734, and John Huggins, June 21, 1735, C.O. 186/1; petition of George Webbe, March 24, 1738, C.O. 186/3.

[51] Smith, *Natural History*, 230.

[52] Assembly meeting minutes of December 7, 1753, C.O. 186/3; Assembly message to Council, July 29, 1760, C.O. 241/8.

of life and labor on the estates that generated so much wealth for masters and such misery for slaves. For example, the letters that circulated between the absentee Nevis planter William Stapleton, grandson of his namesake the governor, and his several managers and overseers in the 1720s and 1730s provide additional insights into the lives of the enslaved. In the summer of 1731 Joseph Herbert, the estate manager, informed Sir William that two newly purchased slaves, William and Daniel, had hanged themselves. Some months later Charles Pym, a neighbor who had purchased that particular consignment of slaves for Stapleton, claimed that "the two negroes hanging themselves surprised me when I heard it," as "when I bought I thought them the finest parcel that I had ever seen and everybody that saw them said the same." Pym went on to attribute the suicides to the captives' African ethnicity, asserting that "such accidents frequently happen from negroes of that country and notwithstanding every planter is fond of buying them," because these Coromantines, from the Gold Coast, were supposedly able to survive "vast Heats" and "scarcity of Provisions," conditions they were likely to encounter on West Indian sugar plantations.[53] Keith Mason has argued that Daniel and William, men who had been born free on the African coast, might have shared a belief common among the various ethnic cultures of West Africa, that when they died their souls would fly back to their homeland. Lacking any further information about these men, however, we cannot know their precise motivations for killing themselves, but whether or not they believed that death would bring them home, they no doubt would have appreciated any means of escaping the daily hardship and misery into which they had suddenly been thrust.[54]

The Stapleton plantation records also provide evidence of the many less dramatic ways in which slaves rebelled against overseers, masters, and the entire system of plantation slavery. Although slaves themselves were, in legal terms, chattel, they frequently undercut the claims of their owners and other planters to the sanctity of property by stealing or destroying their goods. In May 1723, overseer Timothy Tyrrel informed Stapleton that "the still house by the camp is burnt down and suppos'd to be burnt on purpose, by Wells's negroes," referring to the slaves of a neighboring

[53] Herbert to Stapleton, July 21, 1731, and Pym to Stapleton, December 3, 1731, in Edwin F. Gay, "Letters from a Sugar Plantation in Nevis, 1723–1732," *Journal of Economic and Business History* 1 (1928), 168, 169.
[54] Mason, "The World an Absentee Planter and His Slaves Made: Sir William Stapleton and His Nevis Sugar Estate, 1722–1740," *Bulletin of the John Rylands Library* 75 (1993), 129, 123.

planter.[55] Another Stapleton slave, Pompey, "was cut to pieces stealing corn" from a nearby estate, and Marcellus stole a piece of pork from a neighboring plantation. These actions may seem rather trivial, but for slaves to leave their quarters, enter the grounds of another estate, and make off with even small amounts of a white man's property actually represented a considerable risk.[56] That slaves were willing to risk severe punishment or even death for such small gains adds another dimension to the more overt forms of resistance represented by those who ran away or who killed themselves or others.

A further form of resistance that the Stapleton correspondence illuminates is so-called *petit marronage*, the process by which some slaves ran away from plantations not in the hope of permanently escaping bondage, but simply seeking a respite from unremitting work or a temporary escape from a particularly onerous task, a time of poor rations, an anticipated punishment, or a quarrel with a fellow slave. As Keith Mason has noted, "Fleeing the plantation ... required a great deal of courage, initiative and planning ... it meant cutting oneself off from family, kin and friends," the relationships with whom were a slave's greatest source of happiness and represented a haven from the harshness of daily labor.[57] The surviving Stapleton plantation accounts from 1725 to 1736 list twenty-six slaves who had run away, amounting to one in eight of the estate's laborers. All but one were returned to the plantation, either because they chose to return to reunite with loved ones or could not find subsistence in the hills, or because they were captured and, as they had not been long absent nor committed any crime against the person or property of a white man or woman, were brought back to their owner rather than executed. But their absence, however long it persisted, resulted in the plantation's being understaffed and its productive capacity undercut. A number of these runaways, unusually, were women, who were valued as a source of reproductive as well as productive labor, or came from the ranks of more experienced laborers, whose absence was particularly damaging.[58]

From these examples, we can gain a deeper understanding of the zero-sum game that slaves and masters played, of the "mutual mistrust at the heart of the slave regime."[59] Clearly, it was with the slaveholders that the

---

[55] Tyrrel to Stapleton, May 30, 1723, in Gay, "Letters," 154.
[56] Joseph Herbert to Stapleton, August 25, 1731, in Gay, "Letters," 158; Mason, "World," 127.
[57] Mason, "World," 129.
[58] Ibid., 128.
[59] Ibid., 130.

advantage lay: they made the rules under which their bondspeople lived and died, and enforced those rules with the power both of law and of brute force. Theirs were the whips and the guns, the horses and the ships, and all of the authority of state, church, and capital. It was they who enforced draconian punishments for any show of resistance, who decreed that "if [a slave] strikes a White Man, the Law condemns him to loose the Hand that he strikes with; and if he should happen to draw Blood, he must die for it," while at the same time holding that "[i]f a White Man kills a Black one, he is not tried for his Life," but merely was expected to make financial restitution to his victim's owner. Yet these rules can be seen as stemming not from Leeward slave owners' sense of power and confidence, but from their striking vulnerability. As the Nevis clergyman William Smith addressed his readers, "You will say, that these Proceedings are very despotick; But if you consider, that we have near Ten Blacks to one White Person, you must own them to be absolutely necessary."[60] Under such circumstances, planters' overriding sense of themselves was that of people who were embattled rather than privileged.

As much as white islanders tried to convince themselves that their slaves were either slow-witted or childlike, and that slavery was an at least relatively benign system of labor, no one who had spent any time in these plantation societies could maintain these beliefs in the face of so much evidence to the contrary, where anxious gossip circulated tales of slaves who stole whites' property, burned their houses and sugar works, or undercut both their agricultural success and their facade of absolute control by removing their labor, temporarily or permanently, through desertion or suicide. Even a slave who over many years had proved himself so skilled and so apparently trustworthy that he was placed in a position of authority over his fellow slaves and rewarded with better conditions of life might, at any moment, decide to strike for freedom. Such was the case of Frank, who by 1729 had become both the Stapleton plantation's driver and its distiller of rum. Intimations that Frank might be other than entirely loyal to his masters came in the course of the investigation of an alleged slave conspiracy in the summer of 1725, when Mary Combs, the wife of a Charlestown tailor, claimed that she had heard Soco, another slave, tell Mrs. Symonds that "Frank (Meaning a Negro Man formerly belonging to the Lady Stapleton Deceasd) is to be our Captain."[61] Unwilling to

[60] Smith, *Natural History*, 234.
[61] Deposition of Mary Combs, C.O. 186/1.

believe that Frank had indeed been connected with the plot, let alone its leader, the overseer Joseph Herbert and other whites testified to Frank's excellent character and unimpeachable loyalty and secured his release from prison, then sent him on to England because they believed reports that several white islanders, convinced that Frank was indeed guilty, had promised to administer their own justice by killing him. Herbert and his friends continued to lobby the Leeward governor for an official pardon for Frank, which was granted in 1729, two years after Frank's return to Nevis. Yet within two years, overseer David Stalker reported to Stapleton that "Frank is run away," and Herbert added that the "great rogue" was likely bound for England. Although Frank was apparently spotted in St. Kitts and then in Jamaica, he was never recaptured.

If a man such as Frank, who was tied to the Stapleton plantation not only by a position of relative authority and respect, but by a wife and perhaps children, and who had so impressed his white supervisors with his apparent loyalty that they had discounted evidence that he was at the heart of a dangerous plot, could rebel, then could white islanders feel confident about the trustworthiness of any slave or of their own ability to understand the people who literally surrounded and so greatly outnumbered them? Equally alarming would have been the incident, recounted by Reverend Smith, in which a female slave who had been baptized and had allegedly embraced the Christian religion in England had, soon after her arrival on Nevis, poisoned four white people. We can speculate that this unnamed woman might have been angered by the fact that her religious conversion had not altered her enslaved status, or perhaps that she had opted to adopt Christianity as a strategy to gain the trust of white people, and thus allow her to infiltrate their lives and homes and bring about their deaths. But whatever the case, it is easy to imagine that the fact that the poisoner was a person who appeared to have accepted white values to a far greater degree than the average slave would have aroused shock and horror among the Nevisian public. Moreover, it most likely would have become one of the many stories of slave resistance that circulated by gossip and hearsay throughout the islands and across the decades as a constant reminder of the apparently inherent rebelliousness and untrustworthiness of the bondspeople who every year increased their number in relation to the white population of the Leewards.[62]

---

[62] Smith, *Natural History*, 230.

If the rebellious actions of individual slaves were a source of considerable alarm to Leeward planters, instances in which large groups of slaves, sometimes augmented by free people of color, conspired against white dominance were the cause of far greater terror. In 1725, as Nevis's planters agonized over the threat that the dry weather posed to their sugar crops, their slaves' already difficult lives became still harsher, as they labored beneath the blazing sun and struggled to survive on ever-decreasing amounts of food and water. By September, at least some of them appear to have reached their breaking point, apparently conspiring to "cut off all the whites, and take the island for themselves."[63] Upon being informed of this turn of events, Governor William Hart left his base at Antigua, the capital of the Leewards, and made his way to Nevis, where, after he had jailed ten of the alleged conspirators and sentenced two others to be burned to death, he pronounced the "Negroes" to be "sufficiently terrified" that they no longer constituted a threat to the island's security.[64]

Of course, the rebels' plans were never put into action, and, indeed, it is difficult to discern whether a plot had actually existed. As Brian Dyde has noted, "The main evidence came from a slave informing his owner of overhearing talk among his fellows of a rising, and of their appointment of leaders." From this accusation, the tangled trail of hearsay led to a white woman named Sarah Lytton, who, on September 29, 1725, claimed that she had heard a man named Samuel Bayley "Say that he heard his brother John Bayley Say that a Negro Man named Tom Cleverly belonging to Collonel Jorey knew as much or more of the matter meaning the Riseing of the Negroes, than the Negroes that were already Brought in upon that Account." It then moved on to the aforementioned Mary Combs, who made a deposition that she had overheard a slave named Soco, the man who had incriminated Stapleton's slave Frank, inform his owner, Mrs. Symonds, that when passing one evening by the hut inhabited by the slaves Johnny and Sambo, he had heard these men respond in the affirmative to an unknown guest's asking if "all you Negroes [are] agoing to Rise upon the White Men."[65] But none of those slaves imprisoned or executed confessed to the existence of a plot, let alone their own involvement

[63] Mason, "World," 129.

[64] Hart to Board of Trade, January 1726, C.O. 152/15: Board of Trade: Original Correspondence, Leeward Islands, 1725–7.

[65] Dyde, *Out of the Crowded Vagueness*, 104; Deposition of Sarah Lytton, September 29, 1725, and deposition of Mary Combs, same date, C.O. 186/1.

in it, and it is impossible to discern whether this conspiracy had actually been organized and might have succeeded had a single slave not chosen to tell his master about it, or whether it was simply an instance of slaves' wishful thinking or of planters' deepest anxieties, a question that has been raised in relation to a number of alleged slave conspiracies in the slave societies of the Americas. It is entirely possible that the Nevis plot of 1725 existed only in the paranoid mind-set of slaveholders or in their bondspeople's dreams of revenge and liberty.

Similar questions arise in relation to the Antigua slave conspiracy of 1736, an incident analyzed exhaustively and provocatively by David Barry Gaspar.[66] In January 1737, Leeward governor William Mathew sent the Council of Trade and Plantations a box of public papers that, he claimed, included convincing evidence of "a most dangerous conspiracy of the negroes to destroy all the white inhabitants of this island." The conspirators had apparently planned to take a leaf from Guy Fawkes's book and, under the direction of a slave carpenter called Tomboy, fill with gunpowder the seats that the latter was building for use at "a great ball to be held on 11 October last, at which all the people of note in the island would be present." After blowing up the building, several groups, each consisting of three or four hundred slaves, would seize the town of St. John's and put all of the surviving whites to the sword, then would take control of the island's fortifications and the ships in its harbors.[67] Although the conspiracy, if indeed it had ever existed, never came to fruition – the ball was postponed, and in the meantime the persistence of rumors circulating among black and white Antiguans alike led Mathew to begin his inquiries – the rumor itself horrified the white community, not least because a number of the alleged conspirators were slaves and freemen of color who up to that moment had impressed their owners and fellow islanders with their good characters. The carpenter Tomboy had been born on the island, and was so respected and trusted by his master, Thomas Hanson, that the latter allowed him "to take negro apprentices and make all the profits he could." Secundi and Jacko, named in Mathew's report as "the most active incendiaries," were also creoles, converts to the Catholic faith whose "employments were crafts, overseeing, and house-service," and the freedman Benjamin Johnson was a devout Christian

---

[66] See Gaspar, *Bondmen and Rebels: A Study of Master–Slave Relations in Antigua* (Baltimore: Johns Hopkins University Press, 1985).

[67] Mathew to Council, January 17, 1737, *C.S.P. Col.*, *1737* (London: HMSO, 1963), 10, 12.

who, witnesses claimed, had been seen "every Sunday for twelve months past go[ing] to or returning from church."[68] Like Stapleton's Frank and the unnamed Christian female slave, these men had appeared through their behavior over many years to merit the trust of whites, and therefore had gained a greater degree of freedom than was usually vouchsafed to individuals of their color and status. If men such as Tomboy and Jacko were secret rebels, who among the slaves and freedmen could be trusted, and if the answer was, as many Antiguans came to believe, none, then how best might fewer than 4,000 whites, many of whom were women and children, defend themselves against nearly 25,000 slaves?[69]

Governor Mathew himself claimed that "the particular inducement to the slaves to set this plot on foot ... was the inequality of the numbers of white and black" and expressed his desire that "gentlemen should reside on their estates; that men of the best figure and fortune should not put slights on the commissions of peace and militia; that slaves should not become craftsmen, overseers or tradesmen; that more of our menial servants should be white; and that no fiddlers for gain, except white, should be suffered."[70] Not surprisingly, it was far easier for Mathew to convince the Antiguan House of Assembly to pass increasingly draconian legislation limiting the economic and social lives of slaves and free people of color than it was for him to increase the number of white indentured servants or to persuade planters to remain at all times on the island and to take up responsibilities as constables, magistrates, and militia officers. Although some Antiguan planters echoed Mathew's concerns, including Samuel Martin, who wrote in his *Essay upon Plantership* that "intestine wars [are] not possible to be suppressed by a few" and that "a numerous body of brave white men" was needed to prevent further slave rebellions, more prevalent was the sentiment expressed in the 1737 petition of the island's leading citizens, which saw the island's best hope for security lying with an increased presence therein of royal troops, a frequent request from eighteenth-century West Indian planters.[71] Lacking a white

[68] Ibid., 11; Mathew to Alured Popple, May 11, 1737, in ibid., 147.

[69] These statistics are taken from "Abstract of the Commissions and Instructions formerly and at this time given to the Governors of His Majesty's Plantations in America," 1740, Add. Mss. 30372, British Library, London. According to this document, in 1734 Antigua was occupied by 3,772 whites and 24,400 slaves; the small free black population was aggregated with that of the enslaved.

[70] Mathew to Council, January 17, 1737, 20.

[71] Martin, *An Essay upon Plantership* (London: A. Millar, 1765), x, xi; petition of John Yeamans and others to George II, February 21, 1737, in *C.S.P. Col., 1737,* 50. See also

population sufficiently numerous or motivated to act in their islands' defense, and usually unable to attract the desired military support from the metropole, Leeward residents, like those of other British American colonies and other colonial Caribbean societies, "lived on their nerves," in Richard Pares's phrase, telling and retelling stories of slaves' individual and communal perfidy and excusing their brutal punishments of suspected rebels through pronouncements regarding the supposedly savage nature of black people and the fragility of white control over them.[72] As Governor Hart wrote, several years before the discovery of the supposed conspiracy at Nevis, although a St. Kitts act against runaway slaves, provoked by the fact that "St Christophers has a ridge of very high and inaccessible mountains that runs east and west through the Island, which has encouraged great numbers of the negroes to run away and resort thereto; and these mountains according no sustenance, they descend in the night to get provisions which they secretly steal or rob by open violence from the neighbouring Plantation," "may seem to contain several severities to those that are not acquainted with the sullen and barbarous tempers of the negroes," such drastic punishments were wholly necessary under the exigencies of life in flourishing plantation colonies.[73]

Yet these punishments clearly failed to prevent slaves from running away or from committing individual acts of resistance, and they similarly seemed unable to protect whites from gnawing anxieties regarding the existence of slave conspiracies, not only in 1725 on Nevis and in 1736 on Antigua, but throughout the Leewards in the decades before the American Revolution.[74] Throughout the eighteenth century, as the increasing prosperity of the Leewards became both the cause and the

---

Andrew Jackson O'Shaughnessy, *An Empire Divided: The American Revolution and the British Caribbean* (Philadelphia: University of Pennsylvania Press, 2000), 34, 38, 43.

[72] Pares, *A West-India Fortune* (London: Longmans, Green, 1950), 25.

[73] Hart to Council of Trade and Plantations, June 21, 1722, in *C.S.P. Col., 1722–1723* (London: HMSO, 1934), 92, 97–8. The provisions of this "Act for the better Government of Negroes, and other Slaves" included the practice by which runaways and those slaves who assisted them were to be punished "for the first Offence [to] be publickly whipt upon the bare Back with any Number of Stripes, not exceeding fifty," with a second offense carrying a penalty of one hundred lashes (*Acts of Assembly, Passed in the Island of St. Christopher; from 1711, to 1739, inclusive* [London: John Baskett, 1739], 69, 71.

[74] Montserrat's authorities claimed in 1768 to have uncovered a "dreadful conspiracy" scheduled to erupt as the island's elite was occupied with the annual St. Patrick's Day festivities. The following year saw slaves troubling Antiguan planters with their "nocturnal Perambulations," supposedly aiming at the seizure of St John's, and in 1770 St. Kitts's slaves apparently devised "a grand plan ... to cut off every white man in the island" and crown the slave Archy king. See O'Shaughnessy, *An Empire Divided*, 38–9.

result of the enormous expansion of its slave population, planters would almost certainly have agreed with Thomas Jefferson's famous dictum that the price of freedom – their freedom to become some of the "most conspicuous rich men" of their time – was eternal vigilance. Even Samuel Martin, celebrated not only in the West Indies but in England and the North American colonies as a notably humane planter, an agricultural innovator, and a devout Christian, and who was described by Janet Schaw, a visitor to his Green Castle estate on Antigua, as "a kind and beneficent Master," preferred freedmen to slaves as his personal attendants, as "it is a maxim of his that no slave can render that acceptable Service he wishes from those immediately about himself; and for that reason has made them free." Schaw claimed that "the alacrity with which they serve him, and the love they bear him, shew he is not wrong," but her attempt to rationalize Martin's unusual arrangements rang hollow; if the slaves truly "appear[ed] the subjects of a good prince" and "cheerfully perform[ed] the labor imposed on them by a kind and beneficent Master," why did this master believe that "those immediately about himself" could not "render acceptable Service"?[75] It is possible that Martin was unable to dismiss from memory his father's murder at the hands of his own slaves, as well as the apparent involvement in the 1736 conspiracy of several of his own bondsmen, and thus that, despite his ongoing attempts to reframe the master–slave relationship as one of Christian paternalism, he could never feel entirely confident that this paternalism evoked a corresponding filial affection in the hearts of his bondspeople. Nor, it seems, could his fellow planters.

THE FRENCH THREAT AND LEEWARD INDEPENDENCE

As much as Leeward colonists feared the effects of natural disasters and slave rebellion, they had, up to the Peace of Utrecht in 1713, equal reason to be anxious about the prospect of raids by foreign powers. As one early eighteenth-century pamphleteer commented, "The Leeward Islands are in the greatest Danger, in case of a War with France, of being invaded, which the English Planters are most sensible of, and is what the wisest of them apprehend every Day."[76] The islands lay literally in harm's way, as they were situated downwind from Martinique and

---

[75] Pares, *Fortune*, 108; Schaw, *Journal*, 104–5.
[76] Nathaniel Uring, *A Relation of the late Intended Settlement of the Islands of St. Lucia and St. Vincent, in America* (London: J. Peele, 1725), 119.

Guadeloupe, the bases of French marine power in the eastern Caribbean, and if warfare broke out in Europe between England and France, as it did in 1666–7, in "King William's War" of 1689–97, and again in the War of the Spanish Succession, also known as "Queen Anne's War," between 1702 and 1713, the French settlers were quick to arm themselves and plunder the plantations of their English neighbors. Barbados, which lay upwind from the French islands, escaped such raids, but the Leewards, particularly St. Kitts and Nevis, were attacked repeatedly. In 1670, Leeward planters and merchants requested that the Council of Trade and Plantations assist them by encouraging the English planters of Surinam, which had recently been captured by the Dutch, to resettle in St. Kitts in order to help the latter colony recover from the effects of a French raid in 1667. According to the petition, "There were at least ten thousand planters and inhabitants of St. Christopher's before the French invasion, now reduced to about one-third … their number being so small cannot be safe from French rapine."[77] In 1698, a French expedition landed at Nevis and, after a pitched battle against the English settlers, burned many of the island's houses and sugar works and carried off three to four thousand slaves.[78]

Anglo-French relations were particularly tense in relation to St. Kitts, which from the beginning of European settlement occupied the uncomfortable position of a colony shared by the feuding powers. The colony's origin myth, or at least that deployed by its European inhabitants, held that the first French and English settlers had arrived on the island on the very same day in 1625. Lacking "any awareness of their [joint] arrivals," this situation "would cause between them a terrible dispute, and a process which could not end otherwise, because the Island would be divided between the two nations, and hunting, fishing, the volcano, the salt ponds, and the meres would be held jointly."[79] The resulting pattern of division, in which the English occupied the center of the island while the French controlled both of its ends, would probably have proved

---

[77] "Reasons why the planters and merchants of the Leeward Isles desire the planters of Surinam to be directed to St. Christopher's," October 10, 1670, in *C.S.P. Col., 1669–1674*.

[78] Oldmixon, *British Empire*, vol. 2, 217.

[79] "… les François arrivèrent a bout au même moment que les Anglais faisoient décente a l'autre, sans avoir aucune connaissance de leurs arrivées, ce qui causa entre eux une dispute terrible, et un procez qui ne put être termine autrement, sinon, que l'Isle seroit partagée entre les deux nations également, que la chasse, la pêche, la soufrière, les salines et les étangs seroient en commun" (G[autier]. D[u]. T[ronchoy]., *Journal de la campagne des isles de l'Amérique* (Troyes: Jacques LeFebvre, 1709], 35).

less than satisfactory even in a time of peace. But Anglo-French relations throughout the late seventeenth and early eighteenth centuries were notably bellicose, and when war broke out it not only embroiled the lands and seas of Europe, but flared up thousands of miles away in the West Indies, where the two nations' colonies engaged in hostilities as their metropoles' proxies. According to Richard Pares, this accident of geography made it inevitable that the island would "be lost or ruined again and again," an observation borne out by the anguish resonating throughout the settlers' repeated appeals to Parliament deploring the loss of their estates, slaves, and fortunes. The dangers of such an unsatisfactory arrangement were articulated by both English and French commentators; George Gardyner wrote that "the French and English are intermixed so together, that with much difficulty could either hinder a secret designe though there is constant guards upon each others Borders," while the Abbé Raynal stated that "this arrangement mixed too many persons together, who could not be agreeable to each other, and jealousy soon divided those whom a temporary interest had united. This fatal passion created daily quarrels, skirmishes, and devastations … in 1666 their subjects in St. Christopher's fought with a degree of obstinacy that was not to be found elsewhere."[80]

It was the ravages of French attack that facilitated the removal of the Leewards from Barbadian jurisdiction and their re-formation as an independent, federated colony. In the face of this devastation, the Leeward colonists insisted that they had done their utmost to resist the French invaders but that their valiant attempts had been undermined by the failure of their "mother island" to protect the interests of her "children." In a series of petitions from "divers merchants, inhabitants, and planters," the subscribers insisted that Barbados, under the leadership of William, Lord Willoughby, was nearly as culpable as the French themselves for the terrible state in which the Leewards found themselves. One petition claimed that Willoughby had retained for Barbadian use weapons and ammunition that Charles II had procured for the defense of Nevis and that "St. Christopher's after the French had taken it might have been regained if assistance had appeared within a reasonable time" from Barbados.[81] Another expressed the signatories' anxiety upon hearing the names of the

---

[80] Gardyner, *A Description of the New World, or American Islands and Continent: and by what people these regions are now inhabited, and what places there are desolate and without inhabitants* (London: Robert Leyburn, 1651), 73; Raynal, *Philosophical History*, 305–6; Richard Pares, *War and Trade in the West Indies, 1739–1763* (Oxford: Clarendon Press, 1936), 232.

[81] Petition, September 22, 1670, in C.S.P. Col., 1669–1674, 97.

commissioners, mostly leading Barbadian planters, whom the monarch had appointed to deal with the resettlement of St. Kitts, believing that these were men from whom they could "expect no kindness, some of them having been heard to say it were no matter if the Leeward Islands were sunk, for they hinder the trade of Barbadoes." According to the petitioners, Barbados's failure to come to their assistance was rooted in jealousy, because the Leewards were producing a better quality of sugar and indigo, to the degree that "their trade is so much to the disadvantage of Barbadoes, that the inhabitants thereof rather wish that said Islands were displanted than that they should contribute to their safety and prosperity, as may appear by their delay in re-establishing St. Christopher's." So that the Leewards might reach their commercial potential, they requested that "a Governor of said Islands be constituted under his Majesty, and not subordinate to the Governor of Barbadoes," a change that would allow the Leewards "not only to defend themselves, but to help even Barbadoes itself."[82] Stung by what apparently struck him as the Leeward planters' ingratitude, Willoughby vigorously defended his actions, informing the Council of Trade and Plantations that he considered the petitioners' claims entirely specious. Not only were they themselves to blame for the French seizure of St. Kitts, which he insisted was "lost by their own precipitancy and rashness in not attending the orders from Barbadoes, and had they attempted nothing against the French until the arrival of the fleet, the French had inevitably lost their own instead of the English," but he was convinced that the separation of the Leewards from Barbados would "put every island upon its particular guard" and thus "enfeeble the strength of the whole," and therefore "the matter of this petition will be found a design of very inconsiderable persons for their own private advantage." Willoughby was still more outspoken in a letter to Christopher Codrington, his deputy governor, who, as a leading planter in both Antigua and Barbados, had a foot in each camp; he insisted that the Leewards were "acting the part of him that saws off the bough on which he sits" and, in classic sour-grapes fashion, that he was overjoyed to be "quitted of the troublesome and hazardous part of his Government, from which he could never aim to reap any pleasure, profit, or advantage."[83]

[82] Ibid.
[83] Willoughby to Council, October 29, 1670, and to Codrington, November 7, 1670, in *C.S.P. Col., 1669–1674*, 120, 127.

The combination of the Leeward petitioners' desire for independence and Willoughby's lack of interest in the retention of Barbadian authority over them evidently proved convincing to the council. In a report to the king, the Board of Trade emphasized the desolate condition of St. Kitts in the wake of the French raids, as a result of which not only were the English plantations devastated, but the French with whom they continued to share the island had "much increased their people and their forces, trade, and plantations." Although the councillors presented no criticism of Barbados's alleged unwillingness to send forces to the aid of the English Kittitians, they noted that seven hundred miles separated the two islands, and that the wind patterns and water currents between the two were highly unpredictable, so that a squadron from Barbados might arrive at St. Kitts within a week or could spend as long as two months in transit, so "on a sudden attack, any of the islands may be lost before relief could come from Barbadoes, or indeed notice be given of danger."[84] By the end of 1670, they had issued a formal recommendation that the Leewards be separated from Barbadian jurisdiction and re-created as their own federated colony, to be ruled by a royal governor accountable to the council; the price of their independence, and of the increased administrative costs thereof, would be a duty of 4.5 percent on their exportable commodities.

Having accepted the recommendations of the Lords of Trade, Charles II commissioned Sir Charles Wheler, an army veteran and a prominent royalist, as the first captain-general and governor-in-chief of the new colony of the Leeward Islands. The appointment proved short-lived; by the beginning of 1672, Wheler had alienated his constituents and had been replaced by Stapleton, whose determined pursuit of personal wealth and prestige did not prevent him from fulfilling the responsibilities of his office.[85] During his tenure as chief executive, Stapleton oversaw the islands' recovery from the depredations of the preceding decade's warfare and the beginning of their slow but steady emergence as prosperous and dynamic producers of sugar. His administration created a formal legal

[84] Council of Foreign Plantations' report to Charles II, in *C.S.P. Col., 1669–1674*, 97–8.
[85] Richard S. Dunn, *Sugar and Slaves: The Rise of the Planter Class in the English West Indies, 1624–1713* (Chapel Hill: University of North Carolina Press, 1973), 124–5; C. S. S. Higham, *The Development of the Leeward Islands under the Restoration, 1660–1688* (Cambridge: Cambridge University Press, 1921), 76. Some accounts give his surname as "Wheeler." Wheler reappears in 1684 as naval commodore in the English colony of Newfoundland; see Peter E. Pope, *Fish into Wine: The Newfoundland Plantation in the Seventeenth Century* (Chapel Hill: University of North Carolina Press, 2004), 104.

structure aimed at providing solutions for many of the Leewards' most pressing problems, including questions of land tenure, credit and currency exchange, and legislative responsibility.[86]

THE STAPLETON CENSUS OF 1678

A census of the four principal Leeward Islands, which Stapleton dispatched to London in June 1678, provides a clear window through which one can discern the social, political, and economic processes at work in the Leewards at the beginning of their independence and their move toward exclusive focus on sugar production, the latter of which would transform them from small, vulnerable, and underdeveloped colonial outposts to highly prosperous, and thus greatly valued, imperial possessions.[87] The structure of the Stapleton census is quite straightforward. It is an allegedly complete list of "all the men, Woemen, & Children whites & blacks in the Severall Divisions in the Island[s]" and consists of an aggregation of the separate returns from the islands of Antigua, Montserrat, Nevis, and St. Kitts.[88] Its manifest purpose is similarly clear; it is a report from a Crown official in the colonies to his supporters and supervisors at home and was most likely compiled from data collected by a number of his subordinates. Both Stapleton's administrative skills and the improvements his term of office saw in the governance of the islands are embodied in this census. Yet the document also shows that, after fifty years of continuous English settlement, the four islands remained socially and economically underdeveloped, in comparison both with Barbados and with the Spanish and French settlements in the West Indies.

Although Stapleton submitted the census to the Lords of Trade as a single document, and the version held by the National Archives appears to have been compiled by a single copyist, significant differences exist between the structures of the census returns of the several islands. Of the four sets of returns, Antigua's contains the greatest amount of detailed information; it lists the name of every head of household in each of the

---

[86] Dunn, *Sugar and Slaves*, 125; Donald Harman Akenson, *If the Irish Ran the World: Montserrat, 1670–1730* (Montreal: McGill-Queen's University Press, 1997), 92–3.

[87] The Stapleton census is held by the National Archives in C.O. 1/42/193–243 and has been printed in its entirety by Oliver in his *History of Antigua*, vol. 1, lviii–lxi, and his *Caribbeana: Being Miscellaneous Papers Relating to the History, Genealogy, Topography, and Antiquities of the British West Indies* (London: Mitchell, Hughes and Clarke, 1910), vol. 2, 68–77, 347; vol. 3, 27–35, 70–81.

[88] Antigua census returns, in Oliver, *History of Antigua*, vol. 1, lviii.

island's divisions. The overwhelming majority of those who appear in these Antiguan returns are men, but there was a small female presence among the householders. After each name one finds enumerated the members of his or her household, listed not by name, but by categories of race, gender, and age. The returns from Montserrat, on the other hand, read more like a muster roll than a roster of a colonial population. Here, too, the subheadings bear the names of the island's divisions, but with a few exceptions, these were not administrative units or Anglican parishes, but military zones: "Major Gallwaye's Division," "Captn. Richard Basse his Division," and so on. As in the returns from Antigua, those of Montserrat list householders by individual name but differ by excluding women at the individual level. For example, the return from "Capt. Nicholas Mead his Division" enumerates each white man residing therein, often in pairs that probably indicate militia partners (e.g., "George Syms & James Stanley"; "John Finny & Peter Make"), but only at the foot of the column does it give the respective numbers of "Woemen Whites," "Children Whites," and "Negros old & young." Because women did not serve in the island's militia, the Montserrat returns do not list any by personal name in this section of the census, although it is highly unlikely that there was not a single female-headed household on the island. A similar approach was taken in the St. Kitts returns, with the distinction that these enumerate white men not only by name, but by ethnicity: "English, Irish & French," with a few Dutch and "Welch" men also appearing among them.

Nevis's returns provide in many ways the richest data; they are the only ones that list by name both white female heads of households and the wives of white male householders and that break down the number of children by both race and gender. Unfortunately for the historian, this form of tabulation does not appear throughout the Nevis returns, but only in their first section, "A List of Randoll [Randolph] Russell's Company or Division." The remaining sections of the Nevis returns, however, hold their own interest; although most of them list only their divisions' white male householders, some annotate the names with such descriptors as "old," "blind," "poor," "decripped" (crippled), and "Quaker."[89]

These raw numbers in and of themselves show the considerable variations that had developed within the populations of the islands (Table 1.1). In 1678, Nevis, though the smallest of the Leewards in geographic terms,

---

[89] The returns classed Quakers with the elderly and infirm because their pacifist principles, like others' age or physical or mental disabilities, prevented them from serving in the defense of their islands.

TABLE 1.1. *Population of the Leeward Islands, 1678*

	Nevis	St. Kitts	Montserrat	Antigua
White men	1,534	695	1,149	1,236
White women	828	540	691	544
White children	1,159	663	943	528
TOTAL WHITES	3,521	1,898	2,783	2,308
Black men	1,422	550	400	805
Black women	1,321	500	300	868
Black children	1,106	386	292	499
TOTAL BLACKS	3,849	1,436	992	2,172
TOTAL	7,370	3,334	3,775	4,480

Note: This and all subsequent tables are based on my own calculations from the 1678 census.

was by far the most populous with respect to both its white and its black populations. Antigua, the largest island, with a white population of 2,308 and a black one of 2,172, was a distant second. Montserrat had more whites than Antigua, but its black population was considerably smaller both in absolute terms and in proportion to its white population, giving the island the most lopsided racial makeup found among the Leewards. St. Kitts had a substantially smaller white population than Montserrat but a much larger black one, making these two settlements similar in terms of the size of their total population but quite different when those populations were subdivided by race.

These statistics impart a clear message about the respective degrees of social development that had taken place in each of the four islands. They emphasize the fact that St. Kitts, though the earliest English settlement in the Leewards and England's first successful West Indian colony, had suffered the loss of a considerable percentage of its white population; fewer than 700 white men resided there in 1678.[90] This depopulation stemmed in part from the effects of the 1666–7 war, in the course of which the French Kittitian colonists overran the English half of the island, evicted

[90] Throughout the 1640s and 1650s, St. Kitts had been the most heavily populated of the Leewards, perhaps even overpopulated, despite the fact that Kittitian tobacco was at that time of insufficient quality to be a profitable staple. Governor Thomas Warner claimed in 1642 that the English sector of St. Kitts was home to 1,600 fighting men, although this seems to have been something of an exaggeration (Dunn, *Sugar and Slaves*, 121; Gordon C. Merrill, *The Historical Geography of St. Kitts and Nevis, The West Indies* [Mexico City: Instituto Panamericano de Geografía e Historia, 1958] 35, 59).

its planters, looted or destroyed nearly everything of value, and refused to cede control of English lands until 1671. In 1677, Christopher Jeaffreson, formerly one of St. Kitts's most successful planters, wrote despondently to a friend in London that "the sad workes of the last unhappy difference, in the yeare [sixteen] sixty-six ... [are] not halfe worne out, nor is the island a quarter as well peopled as it then was."[91] Most of those opting to leave were small planters who were financially unable to make the transition from tobacco to sugar and who believed that they would find more opportunity elsewhere in the West Indies or in English North America.[92]

The population of Nevis, by contrast, was on the rise at the time the census was taken, despite the ongoing effects of the 1666-7 war and the fact that the island had suffered the effects of no fewer than twelve hurricanes in the years between 1642 and 1669.[93] These dramatic increases in both the white and black populations of the island resulted primarily from the fact that Nevis was the first of the Leewards to experiment with sugar planting on a large scale and therefore required a sizable labor force, black and white, to work its newly created plantations.[94] By 1678, approximately twenty-five years after the beginning of large-scale sugar cultivation, Nevis's plantation economy required a large laboring class, whether enslaved, indentured, or free. However, the island had not yet reached the point at which planters were sufficiently wealthy to live as absentees or at which landless whites faced such poor prospects that they fled the island in search of opportunities elsewhere. Finally, Antigua and Montserrat did not attract large settler populations until after 1660, possibly because the former not only was notoriously arid, but was staunchly royalist in its political sympathies, while the latter was heavily populated by Irish Catholics, thus making both islands likely targets for Cromwell's Puritan crusade against Cavaliers and "papists" in the Western Design, the Protector's attack on Spain's colonies in the West Indies.[95]

Specific examples from the 1678 census give an idea of the precarious nature of English settlement in the Leewards. St. Kitts was unique in

---

[91] Jeaffreson to George Gamiell, May 12, 1677, in John Cordy Jeaffreson, ed., *A Young Squire of the Seventeenth Century, From the Papers (A.D. 1676–1686) of Christopher Jeaffreson* (London: Hurst and Blackett, 1878), vol. 1, 215.

[92] Dunn, *Sugar and Slaves*, 129.

[93] Hubbard, *Swords, Ships, and Sugar*, 10.

[94] By 1655, Nevis annually produced almost forty thousand pounds of sugar (Dunn, *Sugar and Slaves*, 122–3).

[95] "An Act Prohibiting Trade with the Barbada's, Virginia, Bermuda's and Antego," in Oliver, *Caribbeana*, vol. 2, 171–3.

choosing to list its inhabitants by a unit other than that of the division, the latter referring to an area that lay under the jurisdiction of a military officer and that was responsible for raising a militia in its defense. But this did not reflect a lack of military organization within the colony. Although four of St. Kitts's administrative units, those of St. John Capisterre, St. Anne Sandy Point, Trinity Palmetto Point, and Christ Church Nichola Town, are referred to as parishes, the other three localities, St. Thomas Middle Island, Cayon, and Half-Way Tree, are classed as divisions. Hence, the St. Kitts returns, like those of the other islands, read more like a muster roll than a modern census. The most striking element of the St. Kitts returns is the fact that they list no individual women by name. Each parish or division enumerated only the names of its "able men bearing Armes"; each militiaman was listed by his first and last names, with the divisional commander, generally a lieutenant, a major, or a captain, being first among them.[96] Women, children, and "Negroes, great and smale," appeared only at the bottom of each list as categories and aggregate numbers, never mentioned by individual name or even by their relationship to the "able men"; the only "Inhabitants" listed by individual name were white men. The sense imparted by these returns is that St. Kitts in the 1670s existed less as a plantation colony than as a sort of armed camp.

This idea is supported by the fact that, again alone among the census returns of the Leeward colonies, St. Kitts's returns listed the nationality of individual militiamen (Table 1.2). Indeed, national origin was the sole descriptor of these men. The returns variously coded these Kittitian men as "E" (English), "I" (Irish), "F" (French), or "D" (Dutch). However, as Vere Langford Oliver noted in his gloss on the Kittitian returns, this coding does not seem to have been particularly accurate. For instance, the return from the Half-Way Tree Division lists all of its male residents as English, even though some bear such stereotypically Irish names as Teige O'Neale, Dermond Calahane, and Thurlogh Rayley.[97] This obvious disparity raises questions about how nationality might have been defined and attributed in St. Kitts. Was the Half-Way Tree return simply the work of an individual who might have been unable or unwilling to make such distinctions regarding others' nationalities? Were O'Neale and the rest typed English, and therefore unthreatening, because of certain personal

---

[96] These officers were generally drawn from the ranks of the island's most prosperous planters; those listed include members of the Crisp, Crooke, Phipps, Jeaffreson, and Willett families. For the aristocratic character of the Leeward militias, see Pares, *War and Trade*, 234.

[97] Oliver, *Caribbeana*, vol. 1, 73

TABLE 1.2. *St. Kitts White Population, by Division, 1678*

Division	White Men	English	Irish	French	Other
St. John Cap.	61	40 (65.6%)	10 (16.4%)	11 (18.0%)	
Sandy Pt.	158	85 (59.8%)	54 (34.2%)	19 (12.0%)	
Cayon	81		21 (25.9%)[a]	54 (66.6%)	6[b] (7.5%)
Half- Way Tree	70	70 (100%)	0	0	0
St. Thomas Mid. Island	121	51 (42.1%)	58 (47.9%)	6 (5.0%) 1S, 1W, 6D[c]	
Trin. Palm. Pt.	117	71 (60.7%)	35 (29.9%)	7 (6.0%) 4 Dutch (3.4%)	
Nichola Town	87	43 (49.5%)	19 (21.8%) 25 (28.7%)	0	
TOTAL	695	381 (54.8%)	176 (25.3%)	122 (17.6%)	18 (2.3%)

[a] These men are aggregated as "English Irish & Welch."
[b] "The Father Hermitts White men" (noncombatant clergy).
[c] Scots (S), Welsh (W), and Dutch (D).

characteristics they may have possessed: That is, were they island-born rather than natives of Ireland? Were they Protestants by birth or conversion? Were they married to English women? Or had they perhaps proved their loyalty and trustworthiness to such an extent that they had been reconstructed in the public eye as honorary Englishmen? We can only speculate about the explanation, but each of the six other St. Kitts divisions or parishes contained their complement of residents listed as non-English, although each area was under the command of an English officer. In St. Thomas Middle Island, 47.9 percent of the white men were Irish, and even St. John Capisterre, which had the lowest percentage of Irish residents of all the divisions, was 16.4 percent Irish. In some cases the returns broke down the numbers of women and children by nationality, and the list for Cayon Division distinguished among slaves owned by the English and those possessed by French colonists, presumably Huguenots. Cayon not only bordered on French territory, but was home to many colonists described in the census as French; of eighty-one white men, only twenty-one (25.9 percent) were "English Irish & Welch," while fifty-four (66.6 percent) were French and six (7.5 percent) were clergymen whom the enumerator placed in a separate category due to their noncombatant status. In St. Kitts as a whole, only slightly more than half of the white male population (54 percent) was described as English, while 25 percent were Irish, 18 percent were French, and 2 percent were "others," mostly Dutch.

These features of the St. Kitts census returns emphasize concerns about nationality and security, which reflect the island's recent difficulties. The war of 1666–7 had had severe and long-lasting repercussions for the Kittitians. In the course of their raids on the English half of St. Kitts, the French had destroyed many of its plantations, evicted its residents and seized their slaves, and then refused to return the lands to their owners until 1671. These developments no doubt encouraged the formation of a mind-set among English Kittitians that stressed security and military preparedness over all other societal concerns. Added to this anxiety was an awareness that, much as Nevis's servants had assisted Spanish invaders in 1629, a number of the island's Irish Catholic indentured servants had apparently aided the French attackers. Finally, although they had regained their estates, English Kittitian planters suffered the frustration of having to continue to share the island with the French, who appeared to never miss an opportunity to launch an occasional raid or other provocation against their English neighbors. Considering this recent history of dispossession and destruction, it is not surprising that the 1678 census depicted Kittitian residents' primary concern as physical security, with the militia serving as the defining unit of social organization and with the nationality of each white male resident carefully noted, to the exclusion of all other personal data. Although the island had the longest history as an English Leeward colony and boasted of its status as the "Mother of the Leewards," Stapleton's census depicted St. Kitts as having been scarred by its recent experiences and struggling with the legacy of national hatred.

Although the muster-like structure of the St. Kitts returns keeps them from offering as much detail as the documents from the other islands, a thorough examination of the data yields some valuable information about the island's pattern of socioeconomic development. As Table 1.1 reveals, the island's seven parishes and divisions contained a total of 3,334 people, 1,898 (56.9 percent) of whom were white and 1,436 (43.1 percent) of whom were black. Whites still outnumbered blacks by a ratio of about 3:2, and only three divisions had populations that were more than 50 percent black. The island's northern or windward coast, consisting of the division of Cayon and the parishes of St. John Capisterre and Christ Church, Nichola Town, were the most densely populated by slaves. Out of Capisterre's 400 people, 237 (59.2 percent) were black. Nichola Town's situation was similar; 269 of its 432 people (62.3 percent) were black. Cayon was somewhat more racially balanced: its 457 people included 224 whites (49 percent) and 233 blacks (51 percent). At the opposite end of the spectrum, 471 of the 652 residents of Sandy Point (72.2 percent) were white, as was true of 422 of the 580 residents of St. Thomas Middle Island (72.8 percent). The populations of Trinity Palmetto Point and Half-Way Tree were, respectively, 56.3 and 55.3 percent white. Because by the 1670s nearly all blacks on the island were slaves, these figures suggest a pattern of slaveholding and, in all probability, sugar production that was considerably more developed on the northern coast in St. John Capisterre, Cayon, and Nichola Town than it was elsewhere on St. Kitts.

The general picture one forms of St. Kitts is of a colony that by the late 1670s had undergone the social and economic processes associated with the development of a semi-monocultural regime of sugar production. These processes included the accumulation of vast acreage and a large number of slaves by a small group of wealthy and well-connected planters, most of whom had established their estates in the exceptionally fertile agricultural lands located in the island's northern coastal region. Had the Crown undertaken a census before the 1666–7 war, it would probably have depicted a settlement that was following closely in the footsteps of Barbados in terms of its economic, political, and cultural development. But the highly destructive nature of the conflict with the French and the Dutch had devastated St. Kitts, and in Stapleton's census the island seemed to be not a fount of prosperity, but rather a settlement that was essentially still in the process of recovery and lacked the resources of labor and capital that would have allowed it to retain its antebellum preeminence among the Leewards. It would be nearly a century before the island would return to its former glory.

The fact that six out of the ten divisions of Montserrat list slaves only in raw numbers, rather than by owner, complicates the task of interpreting patterns of slaveholding on this island, but to a lesser degree than do the returns from St. Kitts. On the whole, Montserrat contained far fewer slaves than did St. Kitts, in both absolute and relative terms (Table 1.3). The former's 992 blacks (26 percent of the island's population) contrasted sharply with its 2,783 whites, while the latter's ratio of 1,436 blacks (43.1 percent) to 1,898 whites came much closer to racial parity. Blacks outnumbered whites on Montserrat only in St. Peter's Parish, where 211 slaves were owned by 144 whites living in thirty-nine households. Blacks were in the minority in all other divisions, with their percentages ranging

TABLE 1.3. *Montserrat Census Returns, by Division, 1678*

Division[a]	White Men	White Women	White Children	Blacks	Total
Lt. Col. Cormack	147 (34.7%)	87 (20.6%)	149 (35.2%)	40 (9.5%)	423
Maj. Galway	128 (33.1%)	67 (17.3%)	118 (30.5%)	74 (19.1%)	387
Capt. Basse	120 (27.8%)	179 (41.5%)	98 (22.7%)	34 (26.0%)	431
Capt. Mead	117 (33.2%)	60 (17.1%)	93 (26.4%)	82 (23.3%)	352
Capt. Cove	102 (27.3%)	59 (15.8%)	117 (31.3%)	96 (25.6%)	374
Capt. Booth	149 (39.1%)	53 (13.9%)	84 (22.1%)	95 (24.9%)	381
Cove/Palm Pt.	107 (36.1%)	73 (24.7%)	69 (23.3%)	47 (15.9%)	396
St. Peter's	73 (20.6%)	29 (8.2%)	42 (11.8%)	211 (59.4%)	355
Northward	108 (31.7%)	24 (7.0%)	52 (15.2%)	157 (46.1%)	341
Devereaux	98 (22.5%)	60 (13.8%)	121 (27.8%)	156 (35.9%)	435
TOTAL	1,149 (30.4%)	691 (18.3%)	943 (25.0%)	992 (26.3%)	3,775

[a] The divisions of Montserrat are those of Lieutenant Colonel Cormack, Major Galway, Captain Richard Basse, Captain Nicholas Mead, Captain Peter Cove, Captain Andrew Booth, the Cove and Palmetto Point, St. Peter's Parish, the Northward Division, and Captain John Devereaux.

TABLE 1.4. *Slaveholding Households, Montserrat, by Division, 1678*

Division	Total Households	Households with Slaves	% of Households with Slaves
Cove/Palmetto	68	22	32.3
Northward	75	7	9.3
Devereaux	73	9	12.3

from a high of 46.1 percent to a low of 9.5 percent of the locality's total population. The returns from the Cove and Palmetto Point, Northward, and Devereaux's divisions, the only ones that break down slaveholding by individual owner, show that relatively few households within each division held any slaves at all. Of the sixty-eight households in the Cove and Palmetto Point, twenty-two (32.3 percent) possessed one or more slaves. Slaveholding was much more highly concentrated in the other two divisions; only seven (9.3 percent) of Northward's seventy-five and nine (12.3 percent) of Devereaux's seventy-three households contained slaves.

When one ascertains the number of slaves per household, the degree to which slaveholding was concentrated becomes still more striking (Table 1.4). Of the 157 slaves in the Northward Division, 64, or 40.7 percent of the total, were the property of a Lieutenant John Daines, who appears to have been a widower with four children; another 30 (19.1 percent) were owned by Thomas Canes. Fifty-one, or 32.7 percent, of the 156 slaves in Devereaux's Division belonged to the family of Captain Anthony Hodge. Another 38 (24.4 percent) were the property of Galway-born John Blake, and a further 24 (15.4 percent) belonged to a Mrs. Cane, who may have been the wife or another female relative of the aforementioned Thomas Canes.[98] The remaining slaves within these divisions belonged in smaller numbers to a few other planters, but in each instance they were too few to mark their masters as landowners of considerable wealth or substance.

The impression one receives from examining the Montserrat returns is that this society was in a state of flux, but of a different sort from that which St. Kitts was undergoing. The destructive warfare of the preceding decade had greatly affected the island, although the long-term results

---

[98] As discussed in the following chapter, the Blakes were early and prominent settlers on Montserrat. John Blake, the first of the family to settle on the island, was the son of a former mayor of the city of Galway, Ireland (Fergus, *Montserrat*, 57).

were less dire than those experienced in St. Kitts. But Montserrat had never attained the power, prestige, or prosperity that the older settlement had possessed; if St. Kitts's founder, Sir Thomas Warner, had left behind a long-standing reputation for practicality and probity, Montserrat's first governor, Anthony Briskett, and his immediate successors were better known for rapacity and, in the case of Briskett's successor, his son-in-law Roger Osborne, for lawlessness and even murder.[99] The quality of Montserrat's leadership improved significantly under the able rule of Stapleton, but in 1678 the island still lagged far behind the rest of the Leewards in terms of its agricultural productivity, wealth, and societal organization. In any case, the census shows that Montserrat, though less damaged by the events of 1666–7 than St. Kitts, lagged far behind the latter in terms of its economic development; the comparatively low ratio of blacks to whites and the concentration of those slaves among a few planters shows that Montserrat had not yet made the transition from indentured servitude to slave labor, and therefore that its society consisted more of small farmers than it did of substantial planters. Like St. Kitts, it remained a society whose primary goal, as the returns indicate, was security and military preparedness. Unlike St. Kitts, though, Montserrat, as we shall see in the following chapter, was not a "ruined and destroyed Mother island," but rather a settlement that was still at an embryonic stage of socioeconomic development.[100]

The Nevisian and Antiguan portions of the census show that these islands not only produced census materials that included a considerably thicker description of their respective populations, but also appear to have progressed much further in the processes of social articulation and class formation than had either St. Kitts or Montserrat. The Nevis returns listed each male householder's wife by name and included a number of examples of female-headed (thus non-militiaman) households. Although historians have frequently described colonial British America as having no place in its society for unmarried women, these women seem to have been able to provide a least a minimal livelihood for themselves and their dependents. Out of Nevis's 29 female-headed households, the returns classified only 5 (17.2 percent) as poor, while they designated 104 of the 305 male-headed households (34.1 percent) as impoverished. Of these

[99] In 1654, Osborne was accused of having murdered his brother-in-law, the prosperous Anglo-Dutch planter Samuel Waad, and seizing his property; see Chapter 2.

[100] Jeaffreson, *Young Squire*, vol. 1, 183.

29 female-led households, 18 (62.1 percent) included one or more slaves, while the percentage (166 of 305, or 54.4 percent) of male-headed households containing slaves was slightly lower. Of course, this does not necessarily indicate that more women than men could afford to buy slaves. Many of these women were widows and had almost certainly inherited at least some of their slaves from their late husbands. However, these statistics suggest that neither spinsters nor widows were automatically destined to spend their lives in poverty.

Whereas the St. Kitts and Montserrat census returns indicated that military preparedness against internal or external attack was the overwhelming priority, those of Nevis focused more on issues of rank and property. By 1678, this island was the most prosperous of the Leeward colonies, its early and comparatively smooth transition from tobacco to sugar as its staple crop having yielded considerable profits for its nascent planter class.[101] That Nevis had a higher economic profile is clear from the fact that it served not only as the seat of government of the Leewards but also as the Royal African Company's slave-trading entrepôt in the islands.[102] But this economic success did not create the sort of rising tide of prosperity that lifts all boats; instead, Nevis's comparative wealth had imposed a higher degree of socioeconomic stratification and class-related tension on its society. The island's wealthiest planter, Colonel Randolph Russell, owned 150 slaves; although few in the colony could aspire to such wealth, several other Nevisians, including Michael Smith, Thomas Cole, and Captain John Smith, each held 70 or 80 slaves, as well as complements of white indentured servants. But these men were anomalies; they numbered among the six landowners who possessed 60 or more slaves, whereas more than 150 settlers owned none at all, and dozens of others held only a few.[103] In only one of Nevis's thirteen divisions did more than half of the households include slaves; in four of these divisions, one-third or fewer of the households did so (Table 1.5). Social concentration was

[101] As early as 1655, Nevis planters owed 39,064 pounds of sugar to Dutch traders, whereas St. Kitts owed 2,444, Montserrat 1,741, and Antigua none (Dunn, *Sugar and Slaves*, 122–3).

[102] Merrill, *Historical Geography*, 56; George I. Mendes, "The Historical Notes of the Early Years of the Island of Montserrat," *Leeward Islands Review and Caribbean Digest* 1 (1937), 16. See also K. G. Davies, *The Royal African Company* (New York: Longmans, Green, 1957).

[103] Throughout the seventeenth century, a Nevisian who owned 50 slaves was considered a "big planter"; see Pares, *Fortune*, 24. In Barbados, though, by the 1650s only a man with approximately 150 slaves could claim to be a planter of substance (Dunn, *Sugar and Slaves*, 69).

TABLE 1.5. *Slaveholding in Nevis, by Division, 1678*

Division	White Households	No. Owning Slaves	% Owning Slaves
Col. Russell	111	28	25.2
Lt. Col. Morton	91	27	29.7
Maj. Lanhather	49	29	59.2
Capt. Hughes	94	24	25.5
Capt. Burt[a]	n/a	n/a	n/a
Capt. Bridgewater	87	31	35.6
Capt. Howard	53	22	41.5
Capt. Earle	90	31	34.4
Capt. Smith	66	20	30.3
Capt. Haymon	74	36	48.6
Capt. Butler	76	32	42.1
Capt. Choppin	48	21	43.8
Capt. Nethway	35	12	34.3
TOTAL	874	313	35.8

[a] The returns for Burt's division list only white men by name, and list slaves only by number, rather than by owners.

already extreme; a few planters owned most of the slaves, and many residents not only lacked slaves but were described as impoverished.

The number of residents the returns described as poor is a particularly striking illustration of the high degree of socioeconomic stratification that marked Nevis at this time (Table 1.6).[104] In some divisions, only a few individuals bore the appellation of "impoverished," but in Lieutenant Colonel Morton's division, no fewer than forty-three (47.3 percent) of the ninety-one households merited the term, and they were recorded separately at the end of the divisional return, under the heading of "Poor men having Wives & Children." Similarly, John Hughes's division listed fifty-one households, followed by another list of forty-three households of "Poor people belonging to the aforesaid Comp[any]." Poverty was a major attribute in the description of an individual or a household, and the poor were carefully demarcated from the rest of the population in the census returns. The lack of data for five of Nevis's thirteen divisions, especially the largest, Russell's, prevents one from ascertaining the full

[104] In the Barbados census of 1680, those residents who were listed as being "pore" or "very pore" were non-slaveholders who owned on average between three and five acres of land (Richard S. Dunn, "The Barbados Census of 1680," *William and Mary Quarterly* s3:26 [1969], 16).

TABLE 1.6. *Poverty in Nevis, by Division, 1678*

Division	White Households	Poor Households	% Poor and White
Russell	111	n/a	n/a
Morton	91	43	47.3
Lanhather	49	8	16.3
Hughes	94	43	45.7
Burt	94	n/a	n/a
Bridgewater	87	n/a	n/a
Howard	53	n/a	n/a
Earle	90	3	3.3
Smith	66	2	3.0
Haymon	74	1	1.4
Butler	76	n/a	n/a
Choppin	48	11	22.9
Nethway	35	2	5.7

dimensions of poverty on the island, but in the other eight divisions the average complement of poor residents was 18.2 percent of the total white population.

The census gave the occupations of a few of these impoverished Nevisians – John Davies was a "musitian," John Oliver a sawyer, and Edward Billingsley a doctor – but we know little or nothing about the occupations or economic circumstances of the majority of the island's poor residents. Nevis had begun its turn toward sugar monoculture a generation earlier, in the 1650s, and many of its numerous poor inhabitants may have been indentured servants who had served their time and, because they lacked sufficient capital to acquire land, slaves, and other implements of sugar production, were forced to eke out a living on the physical and economic margins of the island, drawing on their own labor and that of their wives and their children.[105]

If rank or economic status was an important marker of difference among Nevisians, nationality manifested itself as a lesser concern than it had been in, for example, St. Kitts. Although the Nevis returns concluded with a numerical breakdown of the white population into its English, Irish, and Scottish components, one senses that the enumerators made comparatively little effort to accurately identify residents in terms of their nationality. For example, the returns from Captain Burr's division specifically

[105] Dunn, *Sugar and Slaves*, 122.

marked some of its residents as Scots, Irish, Dutch, or "Jewes" but clearly overlooked many others; such Irish names as Matthew Gohagan, Brian O'Brian, and James Casey, and such Scots as Alexander Thomson and Richard Richardson, are not identified as such. Nevis's administrators, it seems, were far more concerned with the threat posed by a disaffected white lower class than that of a non-English or, in the case of the Jews and Catholics, non-Protestant element in the island; certainly the number of the former was far larger than the latter.[106] Moreover, the poor were, if not a menace, at least a problem, as they might require various forms of relief, the cost of which the planters were anxious to minimize.

The census returns leave the reader with the impression that, of all the Leeward Islands, Nevis was the best rich man's country and the worst place in which to be poor.[107] The island's total population of 7,370 (3,521 whites and 3,849 blacks) was by far the largest in the Leewards, despite the fact that Nevis was, in terms of its geographic size and arable land, considerably smaller than Antigua and St. Kitts and only slightly larger than Montserrat. The island had already become overcrowded and was likely to become still more so, as its white population included a higher percentage of children than that of any other island except Montserrat. The economics of sugar production favored the wealthy, who could afford both to engross large tracts of land and to acquire the slaves necessary for successful sugar cultivation. Although the six planters who owned sixty or more slaves each held only 17 percent of Nevis's entire slave population, the rest of the slaves were scattered so widely throughout the population that few other planters were anything other than small producers, those who remained trapped in a cycle in which a dearth of slaves meant that their estate could not produce enough sugar to reap substantial profits, which in turn forestalled the possibility of acquiring additional slaves. For the ambitious small planter, Nevis did not offer much hope for future prosperity, especially in comparison with Antigua, a much likelier venue in which a settler might "hew a fortune out of the wild woods."[108]

---

[106] As will be discussed in Chapter 3, Nevisian policies and attitudes toward Jews were sufficiently open-minded that a Sephardic Jewish community flourished on the island during the first half of the eighteenth century; see Malcolm H. Stern, "A Successful Caribbean Restoration: The Nevis Story," *American Jewish Historical Quarterly* 61 (1971), 22–3, and "Jews of Nevis" (unattributed typescript, Nevis Historical and Conservation Society, Charlestown, Nevis).

[107] For the idea of "the best poor man's country," see James T. Lemon, *The Best Poor Man's Country: A Geographical Study of Early Southeastern Pennsylvania* (Baltimore: Johns Hopkins University Press, 1972), xiii, 229.

[108] Quoted in Dunn, *Sugar and Slaves*, 130.

The returns from Antigua are similar in structure to those of Nevis, in that they list the island's households by the names of their respective heads, followed by the number of white and black men, women, and children resident therein. Antigua had endured pillage by the French during the preceding decade's conflict, but these depredations seem to have had a rather different effect there than they had had on St. Kitts. For the latter, the events of 1666 were disasters that had undermined the foundations of an affluent and prosperous society, but for the former, the destruction appears to have acted as a force for renewal. Antigua saw many new arrivals in the late 1660s, many of them refugees from the political changes brought about by the Restoration; the island had been strongly committed to the royalist cause during the Civil War, and the newly enthroned Charles II was happy to reward its loyalty by encouraging its settlement and economic expansion and by aiding its commercial integration into the empire. Although in 1678 it still lagged far behind Nevis in terms of sugar production, the census returns show that quite a number of Antiguan residents had managed to accumulate many slaves and large tracts of land.[109] The family of Colonel Philip Warner, son of St. Kitts's founder, Sir Thomas Warner, possessed more than a hundred slaves, while Lieutenant Colonel Rowland Williams, scion of another early settler family, owned seventy-four, as well as a number of white indentured servants. Planters who had arrived on the island during the Interregnum had also attained both wealth and influence, as represented by Samuel Winthrop, a cousin of John Winthrop of New England, and the Dutchman Bastian Baijer, both of whom owned a large number of slaves and served as the military commanders of their respective divisions. Such recent arrivals from the chaos of Surinam, newly fallen to Dutch forces, as Willoughby Byam (owner of thirty-three slaves in the division of Old North Sound) and Henry Meyer (who held thirty-six slaves and resided in St. John's, the island's capital) quickly attained membership in the island's elite.

Despite these examples, which imply that slaveholding was highly concentrated on Antigua, as it was on Nevis, the impression one receives from these returns is that the former's social and economic structure remained fluid and open, in contrast to those of war-ravaged St. Kitts, underdeveloped Montserrat, and increasingly stratified and overpopulated Nevis.

---

[109] According to David Barry Gaspar, "In 1672 there were only about 570 slaves in Antigua owned by a few individuals among the 600–800 English settlers, most of whom were 'very mean and lived much scattered'"; see Gaspar, "'To Bring Their Offending Slaves to Justice': Compensation and Slave Resistance in Antigua, 1669–1763," *Caribbean Quarterly* 30 (1984), 45.

TABLE 1.7. *Slave Ownership in Antigua, by Division, 1678*

Division	Total h'holds	Slaves	No. /% of Households with Slaves	Average no. of Slaves/ Household
Falmouth	53	284	23/43.4	12.3
Nonsuch South	79	83	23/29.1	3.6
Nonsuch North	55	92	27/49.0	3.4
Belfast	51	70	15/29.4	4.7
Old North Sound	35	372	26/74.3	14.3
New North Sound	56	260	24/42.9	10.8
Popeshead	61	178	40/65.6	4.4
Dickinson's Bay	54	233	31/57.4	7.5
St. John's	66	277	23/34.8	12.0
Carlisle Bay	42	323	27/64.3	12.0
TOTAL	552	2,172	259/46.9	8.4

As the examples of Baijer, Winthrop, and Byam illustrate, opportunities for social and economic success were sufficient to allow at least some newcomers to set themselves up as successful planters and gain elective or appointive office within a few years of arriving on the island. Slaveholding was more equitably spread among the residents of Antigua than it was elsewhere in the Leewards; in four of the island's ten divisions, more than half of the households appear to have contained one or more slaves (Table 1.7). Slaveholding was somewhat more concentrated in the southern portion of the island, which was probably at least in part the result of the fact that this region had been the site of Antigua's first English settlement and had had the longest time in which to develop a slaveholding planter elite, but even in Falmouth on the south coast, more than 40 percent of the households held slaves.

Furthermore, Antigua's population included far more of the "middling sort" of planters than did that of Nevis, the only other island in which we can determine the presence or absence of slaves at the level of the individual household. Many Antiguan residents owned between ten and twenty-five slaves, a number not sufficiently large to grant them a place among the local elite, but one that differentiated them from the struggling small farmers.

Antigua's status as the frontier of opportunity stemmed primarily from its comparatively low population density. Despite its relative size, being

TABLE 1.8. *Children in White Population, by Island, 1678*

Island	Total Whites	White Children	Children as % of White Population
Nevis	3,521	1,159	32.9
St. Kitts	1,897	663	34.9
Montserrat	2,682	943	35.2
Antigua	2,308	528	22.9
TOTAL	10,408	3,293	31.6

nearly twice as large as St. Kitts, the second biggest of the Leewards, its white population in 1678 numbered only 2,308 individuals, far fewer than were resident in either Nevis or Montserrat, and a scant few hundred more than lived on war-ravaged St. Kitts. Nor was Antigua in any danger of overcrowding through natural increase; only 22.9 percent of its whites were children (528 out of 2,308), a considerably lower figure than in any of the other Leewards (Table 1.8). As Antigua had of the Leewards the lowest percentage of women (31 percent) in its white population, overpopulation was unlikely to become a problem in the immediate future.

That there were more opportunities for individual advancement in Antigua than elsewhere in the Leewards is implied by the fact that the nationalities and religious affiliations of its residents were not manifestly a concern of the census takers. The Antigua returns concluded, as did those of the other islands, with a breakdown of the populations of English, Irish, and Scots on the island, but they did not identify any individuals in terms of their ethnic background or confessional allegiance, though many residents were clearly of Irish, Scots, or Dutch descent, and a few appear to have been Jews. Furthermore, these returns, unlike those of Nevis, do not mark any individual as impoverished, a fact that does not necessarily imply that no white Antiguans *were* poor, but rather that poverty was not sufficiently severe or prevalent to be a subject of great public concern. In 1678, Antigua was probably the site of the greatest social and economic opportunity among the Leewards: it appears to have been the island that boasted the fewest restrictions based on an individual's rank, nationality, or religion. Underpopulated as it certainly was, particularly in comparison with Nevis, it was probably the most receptive, socially and economically, to new arrivals. As such, it attracted many migrants, allowing it by the beginning of the eighteenth century to outstrip the other Leewards in

terms of population, productivity, and wealth, symbolized by its officially
supplanting Nevis as the colony's seat of government in 1708.[110]

CONCLUSION

The picture of the Leewards offered by the 1678 census is of four islands
whose social and economic development had been significantly retarded
by warfare and natural disaster; particularly in comparison with Barbados,
they were impoverished, marginal places that seemed as unlikely to cooperate with one another as they had been to cooperate with the latter.
As the seventeenth century drew toward its end, the Leewards remained
small, crude, frontier societies that seemed unpromising to potential settlers and investors alike. But over the course of the hundred years that
separated the Leewards' independence from Barbados and the outbreak
of the American Revolution, the islands, slowly at first, and then with
increasing speed, developed their sugar industries, invested in the purchase of African slaves, livestock, and machinery – in Samuel Martin's
phrase, the "nerves" of a plantation – and by the mid-eighteenth century
had produced a small but influential elite class that attracted both the
envy and the awe of metropolitan observers.[111] As will be explored in the
following chapters, stories abound of individual effort: of Azariah Pinney,
deported from the West Country as a "Monmouth Man" but surviving
transportation to build on Nevis and in Bristol the great "West-India
fortune" described by Richard Pares; of Samuel Martin, whose grandfather fled Dutch-conquered Surinam determined to "hew a fortune out
of the wild woods" in Antigua and founded a dynasty of colonial planters and imperial administrators that would span three centuries; of the
Scot Walter Tullideph, who arrived in Antigua penniless but parlayed his
modest business skills into a vast fortune and married his daughters into
the British aristocracy; of cadet members of the great Irish mercantile
families known as the "Fourteen Tribes of Galway," whose endeavors in
Montserrat and St. Kitts greatly enriched both themselves and their kin
in Ireland, enabling them to escape some of the miseries associated with
the Cromwellian and Williamite conquests; and of Jewish, Quaker, and
Huguenot settlers who rose to positions of wealth and respect despite
their initially suspect confessional allegiances. Although, in Pares's words,

[110] F. G. Spurdle, *Early West Indian Government* (Christchurch, New Zealand: Whitcomb and Tombs, 1963), 48.
[111] Martin, *Essay upon Plantership*, 15.

life in the Leewards was that of "a small and close-grained society, surrounded by men of another colour, liable to sudden ruin from hurricanes, fires or French invasions," in which planters "concentrated on getting rich quick in a trying climate and a strange landscape," and, according to Edmund Burke, "the expences of a plantation in the West-Indies are very great, and the profits at the first view precarious … neither is the life of the planter, a life of idleness and luxury; at all times he must keep a watchful eye upon his overseers," nonetheless the existence of a planter could be a highly rewarding one.[112] As Burke himself wrote, "Notwithstanding all this, there are no parts of the world, in which great estates are made in so short a time … the produce of a few good seasons will provide against the ill effects of the worst; as the planter is sure of a speedy and profitable market for his produce, which has a readier sale than perhaps any commodity in the world."[113]

These stories of individual prosperity did not occur within a social vacuum. In order that individual planters might acquire wealth and influence, and that the Leewards might become lucrative British colonies, it was crucial that these island communities learn how to deal with the numerous challenges they faced, not only the threats of natural disaster and slave rebellion, but the less obviously menacing but nonetheless destabilizing issues presented by a white population that was, for most of the period under study, significantly unbalanced in gender terms and that was notable for its national and religious diversity. In addition, the Leewards had to learn, individually and together, to create a workable form of representative government through which the islands could benefit from their position within the expanding British Empire while upholding their commitment to self-government and regulating the expression of interpersonal tensions within small, competitive, and inescapably intimate settler communities. In the following chapters, I will explore the varied ways in which Leeward colonists learned to live and flourish in an initially difficult tropical environment and through which they negotiated for themselves a sense of being at once English and West Indian.

---

[112] Pares, *Fortune*, 25; Burke, *Account*, vol. 2, 99.
[113] Burke, *Account*, vol. 2, 100.

2

Irish, Scots, and English

INTRODUCTION

A notable element of the 1678 census is the extent to which the putatively English settlements in the Leeward Islands were populated by people of Irish and, to a lesser degree, Scots birth or descent, and whereas the latter were aggregated within the section of the population described as "English," the former were counted separately in the returns for all four islands. In the century that followed, people of Irish birth or heritage continued to constitute a large segment of each island's white population, while the number of Scots increased dramatically after the Act of Union in 1707 and continued to rise throughout the eighteenth century.

Of course, the Leewards were not unique among the settlements that constituted late-seventeenth- and eighteenth-century colonial British America in including a substantial number of people of other than English nationality in their white populations. We might think, for example, of the many Dutch-descended settlers in New York, the numerous Germans in Pennsylvania, and the sizable Huguenot contingent in coastal South Carolina. However, the ethnic diversity of the Leewards merits extended analysis for several reasons. First, as this chapter demonstrates, it was a source of frequent comment, and at various times significant public concern, in the period under study. Second, and contributing to the first cause, the Scots and Irish populations of these four islands' were notably high even in comparison with the populations of the North American settlements just mentioned, to the extent that at various points Antigua and Montserrat, Nevis and St. Kitts had a minority of Englishmen and -women within their white populations. Finally, in these islands, the white population was throughout this period extremely small, both in absolute number and in relation to the enslaved; not only did these small communities "live on their nerves" regarding slave rebellion and the other concerns described in the preceding chapter, but they had reason for further anxiety about the Irish and Scots elements among them in a century in which Jacobitism was a recurrent threat. Yet, as we shall see, for the most part these miniature societies succeeded in integrating at least initially alien and even suspect ethnic minorities, and can even be said to have done as much as the far more intensively studied mid-Atlantic colonies in offering a model of successful ethnic coexistence and integration in the first British Empire.

This ethnic diversity within the white population has been a major source of scholarly interest in the histories of the Leeward settlements. Historical study of Montserrat, for example, has focused almost exclusively on the presence of a significant number of people of Irish descent in its white population throughout the era of sugar and slavery, and much of this scholarship has promulgated the idea that the island's white society was starkly divided into an oppressed Irish majority and an oppressive English minority. Even today, Montserrat is known as "the Emerald Isle of the Caribbean," a sobriquet whose use the island's government has encouraged by selecting the shamrock as the island's symbol, the emblem on its flag, and its official passport validation stamp. Admittedly, few historians have taken seriously the anthropologist John Messenger's hyperbolic assertion that contemporary Montserrat is replete with Irish cultural remnants, which he described as persisting over the centuries in traditions ranging from the culinary (a local delicacy known as goat-water stew, supposedly identical to a typical Connemara dish) to the linguistic (an allegedly broguelike inflection in the local accent) to the cultural (the use of a hand drum similar to the Irish bodhran in island music).[1] Yet the quasi-official propagation of the idea of Irish heritage, combined with a multitude of Irish-derived surnames and place names throughout the island, has encouraged many scholars to conclude that

---

[1] See Messenger's "The Influence of the Irish in Montserrat," *Caribbean Quarterly* 13 (1967), 3–26; "The 'Black Irish' of Montserrat," *Eire-Ireland* 2 (1967), 24–40; and "Montserrat: The Most Distinctively Irish Settlement in the New World," *Ethnicity* 2 (1975), 281–303. His ideas have been promoted by the anthropologist Jay D. Dobbin, who is skeptical of some of the former's findings but maintains that many of Montserrat's musical and folkloric traditions are of Irish origin; see Dobbin, *The Jombee Dance of Montserrat: A Study of Trance Ritual in the West Indies* (Columbus: Ohio State University Press, 1986).

Montserrat's historical importance stems almost entirely from its position as "Ireland's Only Colony."[2] Colonial government records and voyagers' accounts show that many seventeenth- and eighteenth-century visitors to Montserrat, including travelers, government officials, and clergymen, were struck by the fact that the island's white population was heavily Irish.[3] However, one ought not conflate this long-standing conception of Montserrat as a peculiarly Irish place in the first British Empire with an interpretation of the island's history that emphasizes its apparent marginality in comparison with the other Leewards and that assigns the responsibility for Montserrat's alleged socioeconomic failure to the presence of either a ruthless and bigoted English plantocracy or a shiftless and turbulent Irish underclass.

Historians' interpretations of the earliest migration of Irish indentured servants to Montserrat epitomize the problems that can result from indiscriminate deployment of oversimplified ethnic and national categories. Hilary Beckles, among other scholars, has asserted that Irish indentured servants experienced "the most intense day-to-day discrimination and humiliation" in the English West Indies and that their condition "was nearer slavery than freedom."[4] His implication is that these servants suffered persecution and prejudice at the hands of an English Protestant plantocracy that despised and feared them because of their nationality, their religion, and their inferior socioeconomic position. But while Beckles's observations may ring true in relation to the situation that developed in Barbados in the early and middle decades of the seventeenth century, at which time planters and magistrates had yet to draw definite boundaries between the statuses of slaves and servants, and when Cromwellian efforts

---

[2] Contemporary Irish place names in Montserrat include Kinsale, St. Patrick's, Farrell's Mountain, Broderick's, Sweeney's Well, Cork Hill, and Galway; see T. Savage English, *Ireland's Only Colony: Records of Montserrat, 1632 to the End of the Nineteenth Century* (London: West India Committee, 1930). Ryan, Daly, Meade, Tuite, and Farrell are among the most common surnames in Montserrat.

[3] For example, "Monserat is seated by Irish" (George Gardyner, *A Description of the New World, or American Islands and Continent: and by what people these regions are now inhabited, and what places there are desolate and without inhabitants* [London: Robert Leyburn, 1651], 75); "This Isle is most Inhabited by the Irish, who have here a Church for Divine Worship (Richard Blome, *A Description of the Island of Jamaica, With the Other Isles and Territories in America, to which the English are Related* [London: T. Milbourn, 1672], 114).

[4] Beckles, "A 'riotous and unruly lot': Irish Indentured Servants and Freemen in the English West Indies, 1644–1713," *William and Mary Quarterly* s3:47 (1990), 511; see also Beckles, *White Servitude and Black Slavery in Barbados, 1627–1715* (Knoxville: University of Tennessee Press, 1989).

to subdue Ireland encouraged English colonists to conceive of the Irish as dangerous rebels, they are not as useful for understanding the experience of Irish settlers in the Leewards. In Montserrat, the majority of these Irish servants were not vagrants or convicts that metropolitan authorities had inflicted on a resistant colony, but were instead individuals who had been recruited to emigrate by a number of the island's most prominent residents, many of whom were themselves of Irish birth or descent and who had drawn on their familial and commercial connections at home to populate the island with a white laboring class. As early in the course of white settlement as the 1630s, Anthony Briskett, an Irishman of Italian ancestry who served as Montserrat's first governor, succeeded in recruiting a substantial number of Irishmen from the vicinity of Wexford, his birthplace, to emigrate to Montserrat. Some of these recruits arrived as bondservants, others as free laborers.[5]

Montserratian planters were frequently unable, due either to a shortage of capital or to a lack of easy access to the entrepôts of the Royal African Company, to acquire a sufficient number of slaves to accommodate the labor requirements of their estates. Blocked in their preferred venues of labor accumulation, these planters often took advantage of a preexisting network of friends and family members at home to acquire the additional workforce necessary to expand the cultivation of sugar, indigo, and tobacco. Montserratian planting and trading families such as the Blakes, the Frenches, the Kirwans, and the Lynches all descended from the "Fourteen Tribes," an intermarried clique of wealthy and influential Galway-based merchant families of both "native Irish" and "old English" stock.[6] As members of such an elite, they quite likely looked down on the newly arrived servants, who in many cases were illiterate, Gaelic-speaking agricultural laborers recruited from the "Tribal" families' Irish estates, but an aloofness based on a perceived difference in rank is something quite different from what Beckles and other scholars have posited as a quasi-racialized and ever-widening divide between an

[5] Recruitment of indentured servants from one's home area in Britain was common among Leeward planters. The Tudways of Antigua, for example, drew on their contacts in their native Somerset to acquire servants for their plantations; see David Watts, *The West Indies: Patterns of Development, Culture, and Environmental Change since 1492* (Cambridge: Cambridge University Press, 1987), 362, and David Galenson, "Servants Bound for Antigua, 1752–56," *Genealogists' Magazine* 19 (1978), 277.

[6] Jane H. Ohlmeyer, "A Laboratory for Empire? Early Modern Ireland and English Imperialism," in Kevin Kenny, ed., *Ireland and the British Empire* (Oxford: Oxford University Press, 2004), 55; Donald Harman Akenson, *If the Irish Ran the World: Montserrat, 1630–1730* (Montreal: McGill-Queen's University Press, 1997), 68.

English Protestant plantocracy and an underclass of downtrodden and disenfranchised Irish Catholic laborers. As Donald Akenson has perceptively noted, "The idea of the Irish-as-slave, or as proto-slaves, or as black men in white skins ... [has] conjoin[ed] with a stream in Irish historical writing that presents Irish settlers ... as being passive emigrants," whereas in actuality "the overwhelming majority of Irish indentured servants who went to Montserrat did so by personal choice, with information in hand."[7]

The historiography of the Scottish presence in the West Indies has focused less than that of the Irish on a conception of them as a marginalized and oppressed group within an English-dominated white society. The "new British history" of the past three decades has encouraged historians to view the Act of Union between Scotland and England (1707) less as an English conquest of a defeated enemy than as a negotiated settlement between the commercial interests of North and South Britain.[8] More recently, historians such as Alan Karras and Douglas Hamilton have meticulously documented the experiences of individual Scots migrants to colonial British America in an attempt to understand both the challenges and the benefits that Scots heritage conferred on those who tried to make their way in the overseas settlements of the newly created "Great Britain."[9] Still, much of the scholarship on Scots in colonial British America has continued to center on their alleged exclusion from the more elevated social and political circles, and has perhaps taken too seriously comments such as that made in 1775 by William McLeod, a Glaswegian immigrant to Virginia, that "a man's being a Scotchman is sufficient to condemn him upon the slightest information, they being looked upon as the greatest enemys to America."[10]

Of course, categories of ethnicity and nationality, like those relating to race and gender, are not fixed terms of analysis, and they ought not to be automatically associated with ideas of poverty, disenfranchisement, or other forms of oppression, even if such linkages in many instances accurately represent the experience of particular national groups within the

---

[7] Akenson, *If the Irish Ran the World*, 49.

[8] The "new British history" is generally viewed as having originated as a response to J. G. A. Pocock's 1974 essay, "British History: A Plea for a New Subject." See "*AHR* Forum: The New British History in Atlantic Perspective," *American Historical Review* 104 (1999), 426–500.

[9] Karras, *Sojourners in the Sun: Scottish Migrants in Jamaica and the Chesapeake, 1740–1800* (Ithaca, NY: Cornell University Press, 1992); Hamilton, *Scotland, the Caribbean and the Atlantic World, 1750–1820* (Manchester: Manchester University Press, 2005).

[10] Quoted in Karras, *Sojourners*, 93.

metropole. What it meant to be "Irish" or "Scots" was subject to dramatic fluctuations over the seventeenth and eighteenth centuries. Rather than utilize "Irishness" or "Scottishness" as received categories of analysis, it is necessary to de- and reconstruct the ethnic history of the Leewards in order to gain a more nuanced understanding of the ways in which national and confessional identities intersected with other factors in the development of white society in the English West Indies, and more specifically in the Leeward Islands. "Irishness" developed in the Leewards as a term that people frequently used to demean others, while "Scottishness," despite certain negative associations, was an attribute people were willing to claim for themselves and value in others. Moreover, "Scottishness" as a label was far less likely to persist over generations; new arrivals might be so identified for some years, but within a generation they were generally considered to be, if not English, then recognizably British, whereas people of Irish descent might be described as "Irish" after their families had been established in the islands for a century. That this chapter discusses Irish migrants in greater depth than it does Scots is largely the result of the fact that Irishness was a far more significant element in writings by and about the residents of the Leewards, even in the eighteenth century, when new arrivals were far more likely to be Scots than Irish.

MONTSERRAT: "IRELAND'S ONLY COLONY"?

In actuality, the tensions that often arose between the upper and lower ranks of Montserrat's white society, rather than representing an ingrained hostility between an English "us" and a Irish "them," reflected the principal fault line running through the island's history in its heyday of plantation-based agriculture, that separating landed and landless, rich and poor. To the extent that ethnic prejudice existed in Montserrat, it centered far less on national origin than it did on religion, with Roman Catholics there, as elsewhere in Britain and its colonies, experiencing various civic disabilities. But as we shall see, at least some Montserratians of Irish descent were willing to conduct their public lives in a way that allowed them to accommodate their Catholic faith with at least outward compliance with Anglican practice; moreover, in some circumstances "the solidarity of the rich overcame the divisiveness of the righteous," allowing even relatively overt Catholics, if propertied, to attain positions of prestige and power.[11]

---

[11] Akenson, *If the Irish Ran the World*, 130.

As Howard Fergus has noted, Montserrat "was unique among the Caribbean English colonies in having freedom of religion as a dominant motive for its establishment."[12] In 1634, Father Andrew White, a Catholic priest en route from England to Maryland with Leonard Calvert's expedition, disembarked briefly at Montserrat, where he encountered "a noble plantation of Irish Catholique, whom the Virginians would not suffer to live among them because of their religion."[13] These Catholics had probably emigrated to Montserrat at the behest of its governor, Anthony Briskett, who owned property and had business associates in Virginia, and who was in search of white settlers for the newly planted island colony. But although Briskett played an important part in the Hibernicization of the population of Montserrat, he did not initiate this process. Rather, Sir Thomas Warner, the founding father of the Leewards, apprehensive that the English settlement he had established at St. Kitts in 1625 had, in the space of less than a decade, become both significantly overpopulated and confessionally divided, encouraged the Kittitian Irish Catholics to found their own settlement on the then-unpopulated island of Montserrat.[14] In the words of the eighteenth-century West Indian historian Bryan Edwards:

[T]heir separation appears indeed to have been partly occasioned by local attachments and religious dissensions, which rendered their situation in St. Christopher's uneasy, being chiefly natives of Ireland, of the Romish persuasion. The same causes, however, operated to the augmentation of their numbers, for so many persons of the same country and religion adventured thither soon after the first settlement, as to create a white population which it has ever since possessed.[15]

---

[12] Fergus, *Montserrat: History of a Caribbean Colony* (London: Macmillan, 1994), 17.

[13] "Habet Montserrate incolas Hyberos pulsos ab Anglis Virginia ab fidei catholicae professionem." See White, "Relatio Itineris in Marilandiam," in Clayton Colman Hall, ed., *Narratives of Early Maryland, 1633–1684* (New York: Scribner's, 1910), 101. All translations are mine unless otherwise indicated.

[14] Sir Henry Colt, who visited Montserrat in 1631 en route to Barbados, found it to have "noe inhabitants," but saw "ye footstepps … of some naked [i.e., barefoot] men," most likely Caribs on a hunting expedition from the nearby island of Dominica. See "The Voyage of Sir Henrye Colt Knight to the Ilands of the Antilleas," in V. T. Harlow, ed., *Colonising Expeditions to the West Indies and Guiana, 1623–1677* (London: Hakluyt Society, 1925), 83. In 1645, Guillaume Coppier asserted that Montserrat was the home of "Sauvages," but offered no evidence in support of this claim; see Coppier, *Histoire et voyage des Indes occidentales* (Lyon: Jean Huguetan, 1645), 28. Warner also encouraged St. Kitts's Irish settlers to consider emigration to Catholic Spain or its colonies; see Add. Mss. 36325, f. 16, British Library, London.

[15] Edwards, *The History, Civil and Commercial, of the British Colonies in the West Indies* (London: John Stockdale, 1801), vol. 1, 496.

Warner may have suggested such a strategy in response to his experiences in Guiana in the preceding decade. Throughout the 1610s and 1620s, several small English and Irish settlements had coexisted in relative amity along the Amazon River; indeed, one of Guiana's principal attractions to the Irish Catholic merchant families who subsidized these ventures was that the region constituted an unsettled frontier in which Irish people could settle and seek to turn a profit without encountering much English interference.[16] By creating a situation in which the Irish and the English were not obligated to live in close proximity or to compete with one another for scant opportunities in relation to commerce and land acquisition, Warner hoped to stave off the kinds of internal dissensions that might make the fledgling colony of St. Kitts still more vulnerable to European and Amerindian attack, and to limit opportunities for Irish Catholics to ally with their French or Spanish coreligionists throughout the Caribbean against the English settlers.

Throughout the 1630s, the families who made up Galway's Fourteen Tribes fastened on Montserrat, and to a lesser extent St. Kitts, and the economic opportunities the Leewards presented.[17] In the absence of a specifically Irish colonial project, families such as the Lynches, Kirwans, and Frenches, mindful of the economically fruitful if short-lived Irish settlements that had previously flourished along the Amazon, sponsored a series of migrations composed both of their younger sons and impecunious cousins and of laborers or cottagers living on their estates, the former to purchase and manage tobacco plantations and the latter to provide these plantations' indentured labor force.[18] Thinly populated and highly vulnerable to French and Spanish attack, Montserrat was grateful to receive a steady stream of planters and laborers from any source, and the island's initial commitment to freedom of religion meant

---

[16] Joyce Lorimer, *English and Irish Settlement on the River Amazon, 1550–1646* (London: Hakluyt Society, 1989), 43–6, 124.

[17] The Fourteen Tribes were the families of Athy, Blake, Bodkin, Browne, Darcy, Deane, Fonte, French, Joyce, Kirwan, Lynch, Martin, Morris, and Skerrett (Martin J. Blake, *Blake Family Records, 1300 to 1600* [London: Elliot Stock, 1902], iii). Of these fourteen families, at least nine (Athy, Blake, Bodkin, Browne, Darcy, French, Kirwan, Lynch, and Skerrett) sent one or more kinsmen to Montserrat in the seventeenth or eighteenth century. See Louis M. Cullen, "Galway Merchants in the Outside World, 1650–1800," in Diarmuid O'Cearbhaill, ed., *Galway Town and Gown, 1484–1984* (Dublin: Gill and Macmillan, 1984), 69–70, 87, and Kerby A. Miller, *Emigrants and Exiles: Ireland and the Irish Exodus to North America* (New York: Oxford University Press, 1985), 141.

[18] L. M. Cullen, "The Irish Diaspora of the Seventeenth and Eighteenth Centuries," in Nicholas Canny, ed., *Europeans on the Move: Studies on European Migration, 1500–1800* (Oxford: Clarendon Press, 1994), 126.

that Catholicism was not at this time a major obstacle to the acquisition of property and office, as it was in most other settlements throughout colonial British America. The amalgamation of the Galway settlers with those Irish whom Governor Briskett had previously brought to the colony ensured that, by the beginning of the 1640s, Montserrat had become "virtually an Irish colony."[19] By the end of that decade, commercial ties between Montserrat and Ireland were well established and potentially lucrative, as evident from an account of the "shippe Pellican of St. Mallo," which landed at Plymouth, the capital and principal port of Montserrat, in 1649, where it took on a cargo of "Tobacco, Sugar, Indigo and other Merchandizes" to the value of "the summe of ten thousand pounds sterl: or thereabouts (such Commodities then bearing a very great rate in Ireland)." Governor Briskett's request that Captain Hop, the master of another vessel trading with the island, send to him such implements as "three great Copper furnesses of two or three hogsheads each," "two Capp Ladles," and "two skim[m]ers" confirms that by the end of the 1640s Montserratians had begun to cultivate sugar, in addition to tobacco and indigo, and that the island was entering a period of relative prosperity and productivity, both for its residents and, presumably, for their sponsors in Ireland.[20]

Before 1650, metropolitan authorities had generally viewed Montserrat as an isolated and insignificant island that was "of so little consideration, especially to our Nation, that it would seem tedious to mention [it]."[21] If a place of so little value were to be swamped with Irish Catholics, England was unlikely to suffer any dire consequences. Indeed, Montserrat's attractiveness to Roman Catholics seeking the free exercise of their religion would do the fledgling Anglo-Atlantic empire a considerable service by concentrating these generally undesired colonists in a single place and by allowing the neighboring islands to rid themselves of these unwanted Catholic settlers. However, the currents of increased hostility toward both the Irish and the Church of Rome in the course of the Civil War and the Interregnum, in conjunction with the poorly organized but nonetheless alarming attempts of several of the English West

---

[19] John Oldmixon, *The British Empire in America* (London: John Nicholson, 1708), vol. 2, 189.

[20] "A note of such things as I would have brought me to Montseratt," Add. Ms. 34486, f. 89, British Library, London. Furnaces, ladles, and skimmers were used in the processes of boiling sugarcanes and extracting juice from them.

[21] *America: or An exact Description of the West-Indies* (London: Richard Hodgkinson, 1655), 470.

Indian colonies during this period to shrug off the proprietary yoke of the earl of Carlisle, transformed Montserrat in metropolitan eyes from an essentially unthreatening minor colonial possession to a potential hotbed of popery and anti-Cromwellian sentiment.[22] Furthermore, the fact that Montserrat had begun, albeit in a limited fashion, to produce sugar raised its perceived value among the English Caribbees; perhaps the island was not a barren rock after all, but a potentially flourishing sugar colony, in the mode of Barbados.

If Montserrat were to develop into a profitable sugar-producing colony, its inhabitants' Catholicism would require both surveillance and control. Between 1646 and 1668, local laws barred Catholic priests from residing on the island, or even visiting it to celebrate Mass or to dispense any of the other sacraments.[23] In 1650, Father Jean Destriche, a Jesuit priest who resided in the French section of St. Kitts, had to disguise himself as a merchant in order to obtain permission to land at Montserrat. Although Catholics constituted by far the majority of the island's population, priests were legally prohibited from celebrating Mass in public, and Destriche had to resort to officiating at a series of impromptu meetings in the woods. In St. Kitts itself, divided as it was between French and English jurisdiction, numerous Irish Catholic indentured servants, whom the English administration refused permission to erect a chapel and employ a priest of their own, often slipped across the border to the French sector, where they could receive the sacraments from Father Destriche and the other Jesuits from the college at Basseterre.[24]

Faced with the proximity of the Cromwellian expeditionary force of the Western Design, to which he was obligated to supply both provisions and recruits, the Montserratian governor, Roger Osborne, formerly of Ballycrenan, County Cork, was, despite his vast landholdings and his marital connection to the founding Briskett family, either unable or unwilling to protect his Catholic constituents from being "treated cruelly and miserably in temporal, and much more in spiritual

[22] F. G. Spurdle, *Early West Indian Government* (Christchurch, New Zealand: Whitcombe and Tombs, 1963), ch. 1.

[23] Fergus, *Montserrat*, 20.

[24] "Apres avoir pourveu aux plus urgentes necessitez des Irlandois de S. Christophle, il passa en l'Isle de Monserrat ... Le Pere, qui scavoit qu'ils ne souffriroient pas un Pretre dans leur Isle, se deguisa en Marchand, y alla sous pretexte de vouloir acheter du bois.... On choisit un lieu dans les bois, ou le Pere se rendoit tou les jours, pour y dire la Messe, et y conferer les Sacremens" (Pierre Pelleprat, *Relation des Missions des PP et de la Compagnie de Iesus Dans les Isles, et dans la terre ferme de l'Amérique meridionale* [Paris: Cramoisy, 1655], 19, 39–40).

things."[25] As the home of a population that was predominantly Irish and Catholic, Montserrat began to experience internal as well as external pressures in the era of the Protectorate.

The earliest example of a local dispute involving national and religious hostilities dates from May 1654, when Osborne ordered the execution of Montserrat's wealthiest planter, and his own brother-in-law, an Englishman of Dutch ancestry named Samuel Waad, after the island's general court had found the latter guilty of attempted mutiny, a charge focusing on an insulting letter that Waad had sent to Osborne. Despite the fact that Waad had lent Osborne the value of twenty thousand pounds of sugar and tobacco, Osborne apparently envied Waad his considerable wealth and resented the fact that Waad "lived in better estate" than he.[26] By dispatching Waad, Osborne at one stroke canceled a crushing personal debt, eliminated a hated rival, and laid his claim to guardianship of the estate of Waad's late wife, who was both Osborne's sister and the widow of the late Governor Briskett. This estate also included the patrimony of Elizabeth Osborne Briskett Waad's son, Anthony Briskett II, and represented the accumulated fortunes of the Briskett and Waad families, including "70 heads of cattle, 500 sheep, 2 horses, 2 colts, many pigs, 30 christian servants and 50 slaves."[27] Osborne's execution of his brother-in-law may also have been motivated by a desire to assert his authority as the head of the Osborne family on Montserrat by ridding himself of a troublesome relative by marriage whose wealth and authority, as husband of a governor's widow, threatened Osborne's prestige and what he viewed as his right to control the destinies and resources of his sister and her son.[28]

---

[25] Jesuit Father John Grace, quoted in Richard Bagwell, *Ireland under the Stuarts and during the Interregnum* (London: Longmans, Green, 1909), vol. 2, 345. Osborne provided payment in sugar for the purchase of eight sheep and an allotment of "Cassader bread sent for the use of the fleet and Army in this expedition"; see Rawlinson Mss. A.40, Thurloe's Papers, vol. 11, 427, Duke Humfrey's Library, Bodleian Library, University of Oxford.

[26] T. C. Barnard has described elite seventeenth- and eighteenth-century Irishmen and –women as constantly "scheming and spending" due to their consistent "preoccupation with making the right impression"; see Barnard, *Making the Grand Figure: Lives and Possessions in Ireland, 1641–1770* (New Haven: Yale University Press, 2004), xxi.

[27] Fergus, "Montserrat 'Colony of Ireland': The Myth and the Reality," *Studies* 70 (1981), 329.

[28] On the transfer of status in colonial British America from a man to his widow and her subsequent husbands, see Darrett B. Rutman and Anita H. Rutman, *A Place in Time: Middlesex County, Virginia, 1650–1750* (New York: Norton, 1984), ch. 5.

Nothing in the records of the Waad–Osborne imbroglio implies that national or confessional allegiance, rather than personal rivalry, had brought about the original rupture between the two men, but when Waad's family and friends demanded redress of their grievances against the governor, their denunciations of Osborne were inflected by a tone of strident hostility toward the Irish and Catholics in general, as well as toward Osborne as an individual. A "true Remonstrance" against Osborne's "Illegall Proceedings," which the Waads paid to have published in London later in 1654, maintained that the governor was a "late acquitted fellon," referred to him as an "Irish Murderer," and took pains to point out that under Osborne's leadership the Montserrat militia consisted of "a strong guard of Irish ... in Armes," officered by such island residents as "Nathaniell Read who married an Irish woman, Wm: Bentley a papist, [and] one Dabram an Irishman."[29] Samuel Waad, Sr., the executed planter's outraged father, took depositions from his two surviving sons, the merchants Henry and Richard Waad, and their indentured servant, Henry Wheeler, all of whom insisted that Osborne's criminality and his unfitness to hold office manifested themselves in his despicable treatment of Samuel, Jr., and stemmed from his identity as an Irish Catholic. Their depositions recounted incident after incident in which Osborne had supposedly behaved according to the seventeenth century's most negative stereotype of the Irishman. These infractions allegedly stemmed from Osborne's alcoholism (a witness "hath seen the said Go[verno]r. drunke & through drinke in danger of breaking his Horse"; "the said Gor. was ordinarily drunke & in his drunkennes would beat men whom he mett in ye high way"), his tolerance of the presence of a Catholic priest and the public performance of Catholic rituals (one of the deponents asserted that he had "heard a woman had a wooden Cross caryed before her Corps going to buryall"), and the fact that Osborne had blatantly defied parliamentary dictates by "maintaine[ing] a Trade with the Dutch ... by boats & shallops passing betwixt the Island & Stasha [the Dutch island of St. Eustatius]."[30] To further blacken Osborne's reputation, the Waads eagerly raised questions relating to his confessional adherence, his ethnic

---

[29] *A brief and true Remonstrance of the Illegall Proceedings of Roger Osburn (an Irish man born) Governor of Mount:Serrat one of the Caribba Islands, with his Irish Complices against Samuel Waad the younger, of Topsham in the County of Devon, Gent. And of his Barbarous and Inhuman Murthering of the said Waad in the said Island upon the First Day of May: 1654* (London: n.p., 1654), broadside. Note the ways in which the broadside's title emphasizes the protagonists' national identities.

[30] *Remonstrance.*

background, and his defiance of Cromwell's imperial policies; they con-
flated Irishness and Roman Catholicism with gubernatorial misbehavior and general malevolence, perhaps not surprising at a time in which
Cromwellian policies had brought Anglo-Irish relations to their nadir.

In the end, Osborne succeeded in retaining both his office and his freedom; the Waads petitioned Daniel Searle, governor of Barbados and the
Leewards, to take action against him, but Searle was distracted by problems within his own administration and he essentially ignored the Waad
controversy until the furor had died down, thus allowing Osborne to
hold onto his position. It might seem surprising that an Irish Catholic
accused of murdering a wealthy and well-connected Protestant planter
might escape censure, but Osborne was wily enough to gain the support
of both royalist and parliamentary interests in Montserrat. Although he
may well have countenanced the presence of a priest and the observance
of some elements of Roman Catholic ritual on the island, he technically
upheld the law, which at this time prohibited only the public celebration
of Mass and the erection of Catholic chapels. He also lavishly entertained
Cromwell's agents and made a great show of his willingness to provide
them with men and provisions for the Western Design, the parliamentary plan to seize Spain's Caribbean colonies, including the great prize
of Jamaica. Moreover, Osborne's aggressive promotion of trade between
Montserrat and the neighboring Dutch islands might have been unlawful, but it was also probably lucrative to settlers on both islands. Dutch
financing and expertise, the results of their endeavors in northeastern
Brazil, had laid the foundations of Montserrat's nascent sugar industry,
and this inter-island commerce brought substantial profits to local planters of all stripes, Catholic and Protestant, Irish and English. Osborne's
treatment of Waad certainly gained him a number of enemies, but his
skill in playing competing interests against one another and his success in
establishing Montserrat's trade with St. Eustatius and other Dutch-held
islands protected him from paying a high price for his actions.[31]

The position of the Irish in Montserrat underwent a series of changes
after the Restoration, as political and religious forces at work within the
metropole inflected the emerging rhythm of the island's socioeconomic
development. By the time that Charles II came to the throne, Montserrat
had been producing sugar for several decades, yet the industry remained
in its infancy. As was discussed in the preceding chapter, the majority
of the island's planters were small farmers, of whom less than a quarter

---

[31] Fergus, *Montserrat*, 41, 52.

owned even a single slave, which makes it clear that most Montserratians were not yet involved in sugar growing. The desire of these planters to expand Montserrat's sugar cultivation, coupled with their lack both of capital and of easy access to the Royal African Company's slave ships, made the importation of white indentured servants a logical economic choice, and long-established Montserratian connections with Ireland ensured that the majority of these recruits would be Hibernian. Although these servants provided a labor force that Montserratian planters desperately needed, their continued importation contributed to social tensions. The increasing degree of socioeconomic stratification, essentially an inevitable by-product of the slow but steady turn toward sugar monoculture, meant that, once their terms of indenture had come to an end, these men and women, lacking capital and other resources, had scant opportunity to acquire land of their own and set themselves up as independent producers in Montserrat. Their former employers were legally obligated to provide them with plots of land, but in general the planters, whether of English or Irish heritage, turned this obligation to their advantage; they effectively segregated the island by class and nationality by giving the former servants miniscule plots in St. Patrick's Parish, "a dry, inhospitable landscape that constituted just ten percent of the island territory" but that was home to more than 40 percent of Montserrat's population. Because former servants tended to be impoverished and un- or underemployed, both colonial and metropolitan observers soon came to see former servants in general, and Irish Catholic servants in particular, less as a sturdy yeomanry that might serve to defend the islands from foreign attack or slave revolt than as a turbulent proletariat with little if any stake in the maintenance of the status quo. Such people, many settlers feared, were as likely to disrupt local administration as they were to support it.[32]

By the end of the 1660s, European wars and the turn toward sugar monoculture had given rise to a situation in which Irish Montserratian planters found themselves facing a harsh choice: Either they could ally themselves with their fellow countrymen and coreligionists, regardless of the highly divergent nature of their socioeconomic interests, or they

[32] An anonymous poem of the 1730s, entitled "On the Occasion of the News of Andrew Buckler's being drown'd with his Cargo of Irish Servants, bound for New-England," encapsulates colonial British America's general feelings toward Irish servants: "Poor Buckler, with his Crew of Transports, drown'd / How sad the News, how doleful is the Sound! / Yet, had they all been safely set on Shore / Alas! New-England might have mourn'd much more." See Samuel Keimer, ed., *Caribbeana* (Millwood, NY: Kraus Reprint Co., 1968), vol. 2, 165.

could reject these ties of nationality and faith in order to retain their privileged position, which included the rights "to bear Arms, serve upon Juries, and do their Country's service in all other respects the same with the Protestants," although not to hold civil or military office, within an increasingly polarized settler community.[33] Although allegiance to Catholicism in and of itself became a lesser cause of persecution after the Stuart restoration than it had been in the era of the Civil War and the Protectorate, a number of other factors overdetermined the emergence of Irish servants as the particular *bête noire* of Montserratian society.

In 1666, England went to war against France and the Netherlands, a conflict that rapidly spilled over into the combatants' West Indian possessions. Not only did the islands lie "beyond the line" of European treaty obligations, but their status as valued and profitable colonies made them a tempting target for enemy raids.[34] Later that year, a French squadron commanded by Admiral de la Barre landed at Sugar Bay, near Plymouth, the capital of Montserrat; in conjunction with a force of Carib Indians from the nearby French colony of Dominica, it attacked and soon captured the Gardens redoubt, or "deodand," in the island's southeastern corner, forcing the surrender of the island's militia.[35] This defeat came as a crushing blow to Montserrat's planters, and their realization that a number of disaffected Montserratian indentured servants, nearly all of whom were Irish Catholics, had abetted the French in their attack made this loss still more galling. Some observers claimed that no fewer than five hundred servants had taken an oath pledging their allegiance to the devoutly Catholic Louis XIV.[36] In January 1668, several dozen

---

[33] William Smith, *A Natural History of Nevis, and the Rest of the English Leeward Charibee Islands in America* (Cambridge: J. Bentham, 1745), 306.

[34] The Treaty of Vervains (1598) between Spain and France set a precedent whereby, despite whatever peace existed in Europe, all territories west of the Azores and south of the Tropic of Cancer were excluded from the truce, and thus were "beyond the line" of treaty obligations; see Akenson, *If the Irish Ran the World*, 13.

[35] Marion M. Wheeler, *Montserrat, West Indies: A Chronological History* (Montserrat: Montserrat National Trust, 1988), 15; David Buisseret, "The Elusive Deodand: A Study of the Fortified Refuges of the Lesser Antilles," *Journal of Caribbean History* 6 (1976), 43–80. The term "deodand" derives from the French *dos d'ane* (back of an ass), which was the name of a refuge in the hills of Guadeloupe to which the settlers withdrew in case of an attack. "Deodand" soon became a generic term for such a redoubt or fortress in the islands.

[36] Thomas Southey, *Chronological History of the West Indies* (London: Longman, 1827), vol. 2, 74. The clergyman Patrick Barclay claimed that "de la Barre made himself master of [Montserrat] by the treachery of the natives. Having made above three hundred Irish prisoners, he left the Irish there with their families, having oblig'd them to swear

enraged and dispossessed planters drew up a petition to William, Lord Willoughby of Parham, captain general of Barbados and the Leewards, in which they bemoaned the

> most barbarous & unhumane manner [in which they had] been Robbed Plundred Stripped & allmost utterly Consumed of all that wee had in ye world by a P[ar]ty of Rebellious & wicked people of the Irish nation o[u]r neighbors & Inhabitants in such sort, as it is allmost Impossible either for man or penn to utter or describe ... they makeing advantages & pryvate bennifitt to themselves of part of what wee had with soe much care & industry (even to the very hazzard of o[u]r Lives) saved from o[u]r Ennymyes.[37]

The signatures affixed to this document are of at least as much interest as the virulently anti-Irish rhetoric. Of the twenty-seven Montserratian residents who signed the remonstrance, nearly half bore surnames that marked them as being of Irish birth or descent. Planters with such obviously Irish names as Dermot Sullivan, John Lynch, John Carmick, and Daniel Dawley were apparently quite willing to endorse a petition that described the Irish specifically as being a "Rebellious & wicked people." These signatories were men of significant property and standing in Montserrat. They had suffered the destruction of the fortunes that they had "with soe much care & industry ... saved from o[u]r. Ennymyes" and were angered both by the destruction of what remained of their estates through the depredations of the Irish servants and by a fear that they, by virtue of the nationality and, in some cases, religion they shared with these traitors, would suffer another loss, that of their prestige and of the concomitant privileges and opportunities they enjoyed in local society. If they were to salvage anything from this wreckage, these Irish planters needed to act quickly and decisively to differentiate themselves as clearly as possible from traitors and marauders and other "wicked people of the Irish nation."[38] The task that lay before them was to determine who

---

obedience to the conqueror." See Barclay, *The Universal Traveller: or, A Complete Account of the Most Remarkable Voyages and Travels of the Eminent Men of our Own and Other Nations to the Present Time* (Dublin: R. Reilly, 1735), 293.

[37] "The Remonstrance, Declaration & humble Peticon of his Ma[jes]ties. most Loyall subjects & yo[u]r. Excellencyes most obedient & obligged humble servants the Inhabitants of the Island of Mountseratt," C.O. 1/22/17, reprinted in Aubrey Gwynn, "Documents Relating to the Irish in the West Indies," *Analecta Hibernica* 4 (1932), 259.

[38] Ibid., 259. John Carmick's career is indicative of the socioeconomic background of the signatories. He had resided on the island from the earliest days of white settlement, had served as a colonel in the local militia, and as early as 1654 was recorded as owning a warehouse in which his neighbors stored their tobacco while they waited for Dutch

in Montserrat possessed the cultural authority to assign the meaning of Irishness. Would such a responsibility belong to a threatened and hostile English planter community, or could a certain element within the Irish population of the island exert this authority? If the latter situation prevailed, the old Galway elite and their allies would succeed in distancing themselves from a threatening rabble, rather than being lumped with them by unsympathetic English planters who, in the face of catastrophe, might see the shared Irishness of these settlers, rather than their varying rank and status, as constituting the least permeable of all social barriers.

The delicacy of this balancing act, and the skills its successful performance required, manifested itself in the careers of several colonists of Irish birth or descent who emerged as leading citizens of Montserrat during the final quarter of the seventeenth century. David Galway, a signatory to the 1668 remonstrance, had emigrated from Ireland to Montserrat in the 1660s and, assisted by his deep pockets and his supposedly "strong English sympathies," rapidly acquired both land and offices in the island. Galways, his plantation in the parish of St. Patrick, contained 1,300 acres of land and had all the machinery and outbuildings necessary for the operation of an active sugar estate, including a boiling house, a cattle mill, a windmill, and an assemblage of stair-stepped cisterns, as well as seventy-four African slaves.[39] In 1669, a year after Galway signed the petition, Governor William Willoughby placed him in charge of law enforcement in the southwestern region of the island, centering on his home parish of St. Patrick, in which the majority of the poorer sorts of Irish, primarily former servants, eked out an existence as subsistence farmers, landless laborers, or small artisans.[40] By the mid-1670s, Galway had attained two of the most distinguished positions available to a local planter, serving simultaneously as a major in the militia and as a member of the gubernatorially appointed island Council. Both of these offices were positions of considerable public trust and prestige, and appointment to the latter was contingent on the councillor's willingness to swear allegiance to the Church of England via the Test Act. Galway may indeed

---

traders to purchase it. By 1680, the aged Carmick owned a substantial estate on the island. See Egerton Mss. 2395, f. 54, "Mountserrat and Antigua Accounts," British Library, London, and Vere Langford Oliver, *The Monumental Inscriptions of the British West Indies* (Dorchester: Friary Press, 1927), 39.

[39] Lydia M. Pulsipher and Conrad M. Goodwin, "'Getting the Essence of It': Galways Plantation, Montserrat, West Indies," in Paul Farnsworth, ed., *Island Lives: Historical Archaeologies in the Caribbean* (Tuscaloosa: University of Alabama Press, 2001), 171.

[40] By the 1670s, St. Patrick's was apparently "full of Papists," who had established a large Roman Catholic burial ground there (Oliver, *Inscriptions*, 59).

have converted to Anglicanism, or he may have subscribed the test while maintaining a secret allegiance to the Church of Rome; he was said to have erected a Catholic church on his estate, but it is not clear whether it was for his use or for that of his Irish neighbors.[41] Whatever the case, neither national nor confessional identity appeared to have constituted an impenetrable barrier to his attainment of an elevated political, social, and economic rank, nor did it forestall the transmission of his wealth across several generations; a 1729 census shows another David Galway, probably the first David's grandson, continuing to enjoy the possession of his grandfather's thirteen hundred acres of land, "by far the largest holding in the entire island."[42]

Another signatory to the 1668 remonstrance, John Ryan, similarly illustrated the apparent metamorphosis of seemingly untrustworthy Irish Catholics into doughty defenders of Montserratian planting interests. Ryan had left Ireland either as a Cromwellian transport or to escape the Protectorate's penal laws, yet by 1678 he had risen to a level of prosperity that allowed him to be elected a member of the island's Assembly. It is interesting that, although Ryan was willing both to affix his name to the anti-Irish remonstrance and, as an assemblyman, to accept the provisions of the Test Act, his name was significantly missing from the list of those Montserratian assemblymen who in 1678 signed an address to Charles II congratulating him on having foiled the Popish Plot. Such an absence encourages one to speculate that Ryan might have been less negatively disposed toward the depredations of his fellow Catholics when such problems occurred at a more distant remove from the islands.[43]

The figure who is perhaps most emblematic of Irish Catholics' successful absorption within Montserratian society is Sir William Stapleton,

---

[41] Bishop Antoine Demets, *The Catholic Church in Montserrat, West Indies* (Plymouth, Montserrat: Privately printed, 1980), 26.

[42] Lydia M. Pulsipher, "Galways Plantation, Montserrat," in Herman J. Viola and Carolyn Margolis, eds., *Seeds of Change: A Quincentennial Commemoration* (Washington, DC: Smithsonian Institution Press, 1991), 142; Pulsipher and Conrad M. Goodwin, "A Sugar-Boiling House at Galways: An Irish Sugar Plantation in Montserrat, West Indies," *Post-Medieval Archaeology* 16 (1982), 21.

[43] In 1672, Parliament had passed the Test Act, which required all who held civil or military office at home or in the colonies to subscribe the "test" (Anglican Communion) and take the oaths of supremacy and allegiance. In Donald Akenson's words, "Some Roman Catholics could take [the oaths and test] without bruising their consciences, others could not" (Akenson, *If the Irish Ran the World*, 101). But even those Catholics who accepted the test and oaths with less than perfect sincerity were making a public performance of their loyalty to Crown and Church.

governor of the island from 1672 to 1678 and commissioner of the census examined in the preceding chapter. Despite his background – he was the scion of a family of "Old English" Tipperary gentry who had lost their estates to the Cromwellian confiscations – Stapleton, "tho' a Roman Catholick himself, did more for the Settlement and Support of the Church of England than all the Governors before or since his Time ... [except perhaps for] Colonel Christopher Codrington ... [and was] an active Well-wisher to Religion in general, and particularly to the Church of England."[44] Not only did Stapleton take decisive action to reform Montserrat's system of land tenure, regulate its currency, and increase its trade, but he was also responsible for erecting an Anglican church to replace that built by Anthony Briskett, which French invaders had destroyed some years earlier. Again, we see an Irish Catholic rising to the highest ranks of the island's elite and having done so by taking measures to support, rather than undermine, the foundations of English hegemony therein.

Throughout the 1670s and 1680s, the most pressing order of business for the members of Montserrat's elite, or for those who hoped to join it, was commerce. Writing at the beginning of the eighteenth century, the historian John Oldmixon opined that

in King Charles II, especially King James the IId's reign, the Papists drove a considerable Commerce to this Place; where Mr. Terrence Dermot, afterwards Sir Terrence Dermot, and Lord Mayor of London when King James was at Dublin, liv'd, and got an Estate; as did also Mr. Thomas Nugent, and other Roman Catholicks, that were originally of Ireland. When Col. Codrington was made Governour of the Leward Islands, Col. Blackstone [Irish Catholic Nathaniel Blakiston] was Governour of Montserrat.[45]

The French commentator Georges Butel-Dumont went further in emphasizing the importance of Irish-related commerce, claiming that during the later Stuart era nearly all of Montserrat's trade resulted from the endeavors of the Irish Catholic segment of its population. Such an assertion may

---

[44] Robert Robertson, *A Letter to the Right Reverend the Lord Bishop of London, from an Inhabitant of His Majesty's Leeward-Caribbee-Islands* (London: John Wilford, 1730), 45; J. R. V. Johnston, "The Stapleton Sugar Plantations in the Leeward Islands," *Bulletin of the John Rylands Library* 48 (1965), 176. Comparison to Codrington was high praise indeed, as this Leeward governor devoted years to the study of patristic writings and willed the bulk of his enormous fortune to the foundation of a theological college in Barbados.

[45] Oldmixon, *British Empire*, vol. 2, 193. Thomas Nugent was a member of the family of the earls of Westmeath (English, *Ireland's Only Colony*, 126).

be something of an exaggeration, but it is clear that during the 1670s and 1680s many Irish from the middle and upper classes emigrated to Montserrat, as well as to Barbados and the other Leeward Islands, and that, after they arrived, they succeeded in inserting themselves into the Galway-based network of commercial enterprise in the hope of cashing in on the "sugar revolution" that had swept Barbados and would later transform the Leewards.

Among the "several Irish adventurers [who] traded to this island, and made themselves fortunes" were the Blakes, one of the families who made up the Fourteen Tribes of Galway.[46] Hoping to restore the family's fortunes after the depredations of the Cromwellian era, Henry and John Blake, younger sons of a former mayor of Galway, emigrated to the West Indies in 1668. The brothers soon acquired an estate in Montserrat, which Henry oversaw while John established himself as a merchant in Barbados. The surviving letters between the Blake brothers and their relatives and friends in Galway depict Henry and John as struggling to succeed as merchants and planters, rather than making any attempt to create a network of Irish friendship and assistance beyond their preexisting connections with the West Indian cadet branches of the Frenches, the Bodkins, the Kirwans, and other "Tribal" families who were both their friends and their kin. In 1673, Henry wrote to his eldest brother, Thomas Blake of Galway, that the purpose of "my living here [in Montserrat] was to recruit [recoup] my great losses whereby I should be enabled to pay my debts at home."[47] By 1678, Henry had reaped sufficient profits to repay these debts, at which point he sold his share of the Montserrat property to John and returned to Galway, where he used his wealth to purchase estates there and in County Mayo. Frustrated by a run of unsatisfactory crops in Barbados, John resolved "to remove myself hence for Montserrat, and there to settle myself for some years, to the end I may in time gain something for to bring me at last home."[48] Unlike his brother Henry, John never reached his goal of a prosperous return to Ireland; although he attained a prominent local

---

[46] Barclay, *Traveller*, 293. See also Thomas N. Truxes, *Irish–American Trade, 1660–1783* (Cambridge: Cambridge University Press, 1988), and R. C. Nash, "Irish Atlantic Trade in the Seventeenth and Eighteenth Century," *William and Mary Quarterly* s3:42 (1985), 329–56.

[47] Gwynn, "Documents," 273. In 1653, Cromwell had deprived the Galway elite of their property and corporate authority and bestowed on them the contemptuous appellation the "Tribes," which they later adopted as a mark of distinction. See "A Brief Account of the Fourteen Ancient Families or 'Tribes' of the Town of Galway," in Blake, ed., *Blake Family Records*, 228.

[48] Henry Blake to Thomas Blake, July 22, 1673, in Blake, ed., *Blake Family Records*, 107.

position as speaker of the General Assembly of the Leewards, he died in
Montserrat in 1692, after having spent nearly a quarter of a century in
self-inflicted economic exile from Galway.[49]

What is particularly striking when one reads through the Blakes' letters is the absence of even a passing reference to any Irishman or -woman
outside of their Galway-based circle. Far from expressing the slightest
interest in supporting the Stuart cause or confederating with fellow Irish
and Roman Catholics in either Barbados or Montserrat, the brothers' letters are concerned almost entirely with issues of commerce, finance, and
estate management. The sole mention of the considerable population of
Irish indentured servants resident in both islands appears in a 1675 letter from John to Thomas, in which he referred to an Irish female servant
as "the whore" and stated that he kept her under "severe correction,"
though "I find her as yet most viciousless."[50] John went on to deplore the
necessity of employing such a woman in his household, but claimed that
he had no other options, his wife being too sick and weak to undertake
the tasks of "washing, starching, making of drink, and keeping the house
in good order," and closed his letter by stating that he "cannot be without a white maid … until [he can afford] a 'neger' wench."[51] Henry had
earlier expressed a desire to "bring all my children together to live with
some English mistress, for such of them as live in the country will want
schooling."[52] Clearly, the Blakes felt no sense of commonality with Irish
servants, based either on their shared nationality or on their religious
adherence; moreover, they attributed cultural authority to the English.
In 1744, a Blake descendant resident on Montserrat appeared in the
records of the Board of Trade as having entered into a passionate discussion with a neighbor, one William Fenton, on issues of Catholic doctrine,
such as transubstantiation and the invocation of saints, but John and
Henry appear to have been far more interested in matters of finance than
those of faith; in Howard Fergus's words, "John Blake did not come to
Montserrat to find free altars, he came to seek a fortune in canes and to
return home to enjoy it."[53] For the brothers Blake, their time in Montserrat

[49] George I. Mendes, "The Historical Notes of the Early Years of the Island of Montserrat,"
    Leeward Islands Review and Caribbean Digest 1 (1937), 12.
[50] John Blake to Thomas Blake, November 5, 1675, in Blake, ed., *Blake Family Records*,
    112.
[51] John Blake to Thomas Blake, July 28, 1676, in Blake, ed., *Blake Family Records*, 116.
[52] Henry Blake to Thomas Blake, July 22, 1673, in Blake, ed., *Blake Family Records*, 107.
[53] William Fenton to William Pym Burt, July 20, 1744, C.O. 152/26: Board of Trade,
    Original Correspondence, Leeward Islands, 1747–50, National Archives of Great Britain,
    Kew, London; Fergus, *Montserrat*, 57.

was not a new beginning, but a sojourn during which they strove to "find something to bring [themselves] home at last." They remained members of the Fourteen Tribes in the West Indies, as they had been in Galway, and they were no more concerned in the colonies than they had been in the metropole with sponsoring the progress of those they considered to be their social and economic inferiors. Although County Galway held a unique position in late Stuart and early Hanoverian Ireland as a region in which the Catholic gentry managed to retain a large degree of prestige and power, its sons and daughters who established themselves in the West Indies were far more interested in shoring up their own fortunes than they were in promoting the liberties of fellow Irish Catholics.[54]

The examples of Galway, Ryan, Stapleton, and the Blake brothers delineate the limits of Irish Catholic commonality and solidarity in post-Restoration Montserrat. Although all of these men were Catholics who had been born in Ireland, each of them attempted to balance their ascribed identity with the realities of the situation in which they lived. To gain prestige and prosperity, certain accommodations were necessary, among them at least a tacit endorsement of the processes of Anglicization at work in the island. The intensity of these processes increased after the Glorious Revolution, as did the pressure for ambitious Irish Catholics to accept them. After 1689, it was more crucial than ever that Irish Catholics differentiate themselves from those of their countrymen whom colonists and administrators alike might have considered to be, in the phrase of one Leeward governor, "dangerous tenants."[55]

Both colonial administrators and metropolitan officials feared that Irishmen in the American colonies might revolt in support of the deposed James II after news of the Glorious Revolution reached them, and these anxieties were not without grounds. In 1689, Leeward governor Christopher Codrington reported apprehensively to the Board of Trade that "the English are scarce three hundred [on Montserrat], and the Irish Papists upwards of eight hundred, men who of late have been very turbulent and rebellious." Fortunately for Codrington, in this instance forewarned was indeed forearmed. Some of the "Irish Planters and Inhabitants" proceeded to "declare for the late King [James II], and appeared in a Body of Seven or Eight hundred Men for that Interest,"

---

[54] Barnard, *Making the Grand Figure*, 149.

[55] On the colonial response to the Glorious Revolution, see Stephen Saunders Webb, *Lord Churchill's Coup: The Anglo-American Empire and the Glorious Revolution* (New York: Knopf, 1995), and Brendan McConville, *The King's Three Faces: The Rise and Fall of Royal America, 1688–1776* (Chapel Hill: University of North Carolina Press, 2006).

but they were stymied in their attempted rebellion by another Irishman, Colonel Nathaniel Blakiston, the island's governor, who

had raised what English men he could, to the number of Two hundred, with which he was resolved to attack them. But the Irish no sooner saw him appear with that unequal number of English, and to march towards them, but they all offered to lay down their Arms, and upon Articles promised to disperse, at which instant of time a Reinforcement of an Hundred and fifty Men arrived from Antego and seized the chief of the Irish, brought them up Prisoners from Antego, and solemnly Proclaim'd King William and Queen Mary, with all possible Demonstrations of Joy and Gladness.[56]

This passage implies that the Irish rebels surrendered because of their cowardice when confronted by a much smaller force. Although the broadside is tantalizingly vague in its description, one might infer that the Irish surrendered not because of any want of courage, but because the appearance of Blakiston, their fellow countryman and coreligionist, at the head of the Williamite forces made them realize that their plans would reap the opposition not only of the English planters, but also of an Irish elite anxious to preserve its hard-won privileges in the teeth of growing Protestant suspicions arising from the discovery of the Popish Plot of 1678.[57]

Relative stability soon returned to Montserrat and the rest of the Leewards after the unrest of 1689. Such calm resulted from a number of interlocking factors, particularly the strong, even domineering, leadership Governor Christopher Codrington exercised over the islands and the dramatic expansion of sugar cultivation throughout the Leewards, especially in Montserrat. The census of 1678 listed only 992 slaves on the island, but by 1707, on the eve of the French raids that would devastate it, this number had increased nearly fourfold, to a total of 3,580, indicating how far the colony had progressed in its "sugar revolution." Peace and prosperity, however, did not immediately ease island residents' fears regarding what many apparently believed to be the innate malevolence and untrustworthiness of Irish servants and former servants. In 1693, the Montserrat Assembly passed an act "encouraging the Importation of white Servants for the Strengthening and better Defence of their Majesties

---

[56] *A Full and True Account of the Besieging and Taking of Carrickfergus by the Duke of Schomberg, as also a Relation of what has lately pass'd in the Islands of Antego, Mevis, and Montserrat in the West-Indies, Where Their Majesties have been Solemnly Proclaim'd* (London: Richard Baldwin, 1689), 2.

[57] For comparable events on the American mainland, see Michael Graham, S.J., "Popish Plots in Early Maryland," *Catholic Historical Review* 79 (1993), 208–15.

Island, especially in this hazardous Time of War with the French," but these servants were only to be "able English, Scotch, or Welsh Men," a distinction echoed by the Kittitian planter Christopher Jeaffreson, who in 1677 informed an English kinsman that "Scotchmen and Welchmen we esteem the best servants; and the Irish the worst, many of them being ever good for nothing but mischief."[58] After the conclusive defeat of the pro-Stuart forces at the Battle of the Boyne in 1690, the only category of Irishmen whose importation to the West Indies was encouraged was that of convicted rebels, who were to serve as slaves for life rather than merely endure four- to ten-year terms of indenture. If many of the Irish who came to the Leewards in the late seventeenth and early eighteenth centuries were those adjudged to be felons or rebels, it is no surprise that Irishness would become ever more closely connected in the public eye to lawlessness and treachery. In 1745, writing at a moment of Jacobite resurgence as Bonnie Prince Charlie's army moved within striking distance of London, the Antiguan planter and current London resident Samuel Martin deplored the untrustworthy nature of "all papists." Although he admitted that "there are many good and faithful subjects among [them] ... who would not change their liberty, nor render their property precarious, by introducing tyranny, with their religion, into this country," he stated that "since these cannot be distinguished, by any certain criterion, from bigots of the Romish persuasion; and since none of that sect can, consistently with their avowed principles, give this government such testimonials of their allegiance as are required by its constitution, it is highly just and reasonable not to trust them with arms."[59]

In 1701, the Leewards were again embroiled in European hostilities, with the outbreak of the War of the Spanish Succession, as France and Spain fought England, the Netherlands, and Austria over the issue of whether a Bourbon or a Hapsburg would occupy the throne of Spain. In July 1712, a French fleet commanded by Admiral Cassart attacked, "landing in two places at Montserrat, carrying away about fourteen hundred Negroes, with abundance of other Booty."[60] Montserratian planters

---

[58] "An Act for Encouraging the Importation of White Servants," *Montserrat Code of Laws from 1688, to 1788* (London: J. Anderson, 1790), 19; John Cordy Jeaffreson, ed., *A Young Squire of the Seventeenth Century, from the Papers (A.D. 1676–1686) of Christopher Jeaffreson* (London: Hurst and Blackett, 1878), vol. 2, 207.

[59] Martin, *A Plan for Establishing and Disciplining a National Militia in Great Britain, Ireland, and in all the British Dominions of America* (London: A. Millar, 1745), 64. When Martin's beloved only daughter eloped with an Irish Catholic soldier in the Dutch army, Martin immediately disinherited her.

[60] English, *Ireland's Only Colony*, 76.

incurred losses to the extent of some £180,000, and the island and the great majority of its residents were reduced to a state bordering on destitution.[61] A list enumerating the losses reported by individual planters in the wake of the invasion implies that a number of Irish settlers, particularly those from the "Tribal" families, had had a lot to lose: David Bodkin reported a loss of £824; Thomas Blake, £909; Martin French, £1,500; Bartholomew Lynch, £2,675; Robert Skerrett, £2,325; John Kirwan, £1212; and Patrick Blake, nearly £10,000.[62]

For the rest of the decade, Montserrat's economy lay in ruins, and the island's planters, administrators, and clergymen forwarded a constant stream of petitions to London bemoaning their own and the island's poverty and requesting financial and material assistance from the mother country. "The humble Petition of David Bethun, Rector of the Parish of St. Anthony, and Jonathan Yate Gifford, Late Rector of the Parish of St. George" to Leeward governor Walter Douglas, lamented "the miserable Condition which we are brought to by the Invasion" and requested that Douglas "be pleased to recommend our sad circumstances to the consideration of the Lord Bishop of London, to the Society for the Propagation of the Gospel [SPG], and to what other well disposed Christians your Excellency shall think fit." Douglas sent the ministers' petition on to a Mr. Hoare of the SPG and added to the clerics' litany of affliction his assertion that "the only decent Church they had was much defaced by the Enemy, the few books Mr. Cockburn brought over to Antigua from whence I sent them to Mountserratt, were Stolen and Lost and the ministers Robb'd of all they were masters of."[63] The situation had not improved significantly by 1718, when William Gerrish, a leading Montserratian merchant, drew up a memorial to the Board of Trade on behalf of the "sufferers by the [a]cute Invassion and plundering the S[ai]d. Island by the ffrench."[64] A tax assessment of the town of Plymouth at the end of 1719 shows the poverty that continued to beset Montserrat; the house taxes for the entire town amounted to the paltry sum of £373. It is interesting that a significant number of those Plymouth residents assessed were Irishmen; the tabulation includes the names of Nicholas, Titon, Edward, and Robert Skerrett, Thomas, John, and Henry Blake, Patrick Browne, Patrick Goold,

[61] Fergus, *Montserrat*, 49.
[62] C.O. 152/16, Board of Trade: Original Correspondence, Leeward Islands, 1727–9.
[63] SPG: C/WIN/ANT 1, ff. 1a–1b, Society for the Propagation of the Gospel, Lambeth Palace Library, London. The church was that built in the 1670s by Stapleton.
[64] Memorial of Gerrish to Board of Trade, undated, C.O. 152/12: Board of Trade, Original Correspondence, Leeward Islands, 1717–19.

Martin and George French, Patrick and Arthur Lynch, and Mark and John Kirwan, all descendants of the Fourteen Tribes of Galway, as well as those of John Galway, son of David Galway of Galways Plantation, of the Irish-born merchant Gerrish, and of other Irish residents such as Em O'Gara, Dennis Daly, and Dennis Driscoll.[65] A number of these individuals appear to have been wealthy men, at least in comparison with their impoverished neighbors: William Gerrish's house was valued at £50, Martin French's at £25, John Lynch's, John Blake's, and John Kirwan's at £20 each, and George French's at £15.

By the 1720s, the island's commerce and agricultural productivity had begun to return to prewar levels, and by 1729 "a high degree of real and personal property concentration" marked Montserratian society, indicating that the island had proceeded far along the path toward sugar monoculture and its attendant socioeconomic stratification, a pattern that had emerged in the preceding century in the more precocious sugar colonies of Barbados and Nevis.[66] In 1729, Leeward governor, William Mathew, submitted to the Board of Trade a highly detailed census, the "Political Anatomy of Montserrat," which listed each head of household by name, occupation, number of dependents (both free and enslaved), and ownership of land, livestock, and sugar-refining facilities. The document depicts the existence of a sharp division between Montserrat's small elite and its far larger population of undercapitalized subsistence farmers, both groups of which included many individuals of Irish birth or ancestry.[67]

In 1729, the thirty largest landowners on Montserrat controlled 78.2 percent of the total land occupied and owned 60 percent of the slaves, three-quarters of the sugar mills, and the overwhelming preponderance of the livestock. Of these thirty planters, more than half were of Irish descent; the list includes such familiar Galway surnames as Kirwan, Blake, Lynch, Daly, and Galway, as well as various Farrells, Daniells, Fitz Denises, and so on. Although George Wyke, the island's largest landowner, was of English lineage, the rest of the top five landowners consisted of a Farrell, a Trant, a White, and a Roach, each of whom

---

[65] Lists of individual assessments and house taxes in Montserrat, October 2, 1719, C.O. 152/13: Board of Trade, Original Correspondence, Leeward Islands, 1719–21.

[66] Richard B. Sheridan, *Sugar and Slavery: An Economic History of the British West Indies, 1623–1775* (Baltimore: Johns Hopkins University Press, 1974), 172.

[67] The "Political Anatomy" is in C.O. 152/18: Board of Trade, Original Correspondence, Leeward Islands, 1730, and is reprinted in full in Vere Langford Oliver, ed., *Caribbeana* (London: Mitchell, Hughes, and Clarke, 1909), vol. 1, 302–11.

possessed between 300 and 370 acres of land and 150 to 225 slaves, as well as two or more sugar mills apiece. Among the "Tribal" families, the Lynches owned 121 slaves and 360 acres of land, and the Darcys 123 slaves and 350 acres. The Skerretts, who were merchants rather than planters, owned only a few acres of land, but the "Political Anatomy" listed them as holding nearly a hundred slaves, of whom many may have been destined for sale rather than constituting the permanent property of the family. The document is replete with the names of descendants of the Galway Tribes, who are invariably denoted as "Gents," "Planters," or "Merchants."

This largely Irish elite possessed cultural as well as financial capital. Leeward governor John Hart described these "Inhabitants of the Romish Religion" as being in "their behaviour ... very well towards the Government" of Montserrat and, by extension, toward that of Britain. They stood in sharp contrast, Hart claimed, to the aggressive, mostly English, residents of Nevis, many of whom were "most Obstinate and Perverse in their Nature and Manners [and] Inveterately disaffected to His Maj[es]ties Government."[68] Moreover, Irish Montserratians continued to be a mainstay of the commercial life of the island. London factors such as William Gerrish, Peter Hussey, and Nicholas Tuite, all of whom owned estates in Montserrat, represented the interests of island merchants and planters and facilitated trade between Montserrat, England, and Ireland. The island's merchants included Robert Skerrett, Joseph Lynch, John Daly, and, most important, Patrick Goold, who, as the scion of a powerful Cork mercantile family and the representative at Montserrat of the Bristol trading concern of Isaac Hobhouse & Co., managed the island's "West Indias & Ginny Trade" in African slaves.[69] The high status attained by members of the Irish plantocracy of Montserrat is exemplified by the names of the signatories to the proclamation of the accession of George II in 1727, which include a full complement of Frenches, Whites, Goolds, Blakes, and Dalys, among others.[70]

---

[68] John Hart to Lords of Trade, January 20, 1723, C.O. 152/14: Board of Trade, Original Correspondence, Leeward Islands, 1721–4.

[69] Truxes, *Irish–American Trade*, 60, 93, 101. Nicholas Tuite, descended from a powerful Westmeath family, was born on Montserrat in 1705 and appears in the "Political Anatomy" as the owner of 100 acres of land and 41 slaves. See Richard Sheridan, "An Era of West Indian Prosperity, 1750–1775," in Sheridan, ed., *The Development of the Plantations to 1750* (Bridgetown, Barbados: Caribbean Universities Press, 1970), 94.

[70] Proclamation of His Majesty George II, Montserrat, September 26, 1727, C.O. 152/16: Board of Trade, Original Correspondence, Leeward Islands, 1727–9.

Although Montserrat was widely known throughout the Atlantic world to be "possessed by the English, but mostly inhabited by the Irish," the "Political Anatomy" emphasized that by the 1720s only a relatively small percentage of the Irish segment of the population had much of a stake in the island.[71] At the opposite end of the socioeconomic spectrum from these Irish planters and merchants were the hundreds of Irish who resided in the rocky, infertile lands of St. Patrick's Parish in the south. The majority of these people were small artisans, wage laborers, and subsistence farmers, who possessed little or no land, held no slaves, and in many instances did not even own the small and primitive houses in which they lived.[72] Many of these Mulrains and Ryans, Sweenys and Barrys were not attributed a trade by the "Anatomy," but it is clear from their lack of land, slaves, and machinery that they were not cultivators of sugar. These impoverished islanders, marginalized within the political, social, and economic realms, had little to lose by openly professing their Roman Catholicism, and it was their behavior that the Anglican minister James Cruikshank deplored in a 1731 letter to the bishop of London. According to the disgruntled Cruikshank:

[T]here is and has been for those twenty years past Several Romish Priests entertained here. The two-thirds of the Inhabitants here and their Offspring are and have been Irish Papists, and sometimes they have had one, two, three and four Popish priests at one time, when at the same time but myself the only Clergyman of the Church of England.[73]

The Church of England's position in Montserrat, and particularly in St. Patrick's Parish, remained marginal throughout the middle decades of the eighteenth century, the high point of Montserrat's trajectory as a producer of sugar. In 1732, another disillusioned minister, one James Knox, informed the bishop that he was the island's sole Anglican cleric but that "how many Romish priests I know not" attended to the spiritual needs of the Catholic residents and that, "if my information is true, Mass is performed almost as publickly as the Service of the Church of England."[74] Things were not much different in 1746, when Governor William Mathew dolefully reported to the bishop that Montserrat still had only

---

[71] Patrick Gordon, *Geography Anatomiz'd: or, the Geographical Grammar* (London: J. and J. Knapton, 1730), 398.

[72] Robert V. Wells, *The Population of the British Colonies in America before 1776: A Survey of Census Data* (Princeton, NJ: Princeton University Press, 1975), 326, 331.

[73] Cruikshank to the Bishop of London, April 6, 1731, Fulham Papers: Gibson 2, 87.

[74] Knox to Bishop of London, April 18, 1732, Fulham Papers, Leeward 1, 211.

a single Anglican clergyman in residence, while the Catholic Church was sufficiently active that "they get proselytes daily."[75] It is difficult to discern the veracity of these complaints; as until the 1750s Catholic services and churches were prohibited by island law, and priests were forbidden to enter, any Catholic clergy must have arrived in secret and conducted clandestine ceremonies, most likely in private houses. But the perception of Anglican ministers that Montserrat was rife with Catholic observance is in itself a notable symbol of the continuing bifurcation between the wealthy Irish-descended planters who officially conformed to the Church of England and the far more numerous poor who openly maintained their Catholic faith.

Almost as soon as Montserrat had finished recovering from the invasion of 1712, the island suffered several new and substantial setbacks. In 1737, a particularly violent hurricane struck, which caused flooding severe enough to put much of Plymouth under water and to destroy several of the island's fortifications. Further storms in 1740 and 1744 were less destructive to the built environment but caused considerable damage to crops. Sugar production peaked in 1735, when Montserrat produced 3,150 tons of sugar; thereafter a combination of storm-related destruction, soil exhaustion, and poor economic planning precipitated the island into a slow but steady commercial decline.[76] Such economic difficulties, combined with lurid and often less than accurate accounts from the metropole of the Jacobite conflict of the 1740s, generated a revival of hostility and suspicion in Montserrat, which led to, among other things, an upsurge in anti-Irish Catholic sentiment, directed mostly toward the teeming poor of St. Patrick's but occasionally against members of the Irish elite as well, many of whom had maintained close ties over generations to Ireland and to Irish exiles on the Continent.[77] In 1744, William Wyke, who numbered among Montserrat's two or three most successful planters, reported to the Board of Trade that as he was

---

[75] Mathew to Lords of Trade, November 6, 1746, C.O. 152/25: Board of Trade, Original Correspondence, Leeward Islands, 1744–7.

[76] Fergus, *Montserrat*, 44–5, 227.

[77] In his 1724 will, Martin French bequeathed an annuity of £10 sterling to the "Poor of the Town of Gallway in Ireland ... payable by my brother Andrew French," and in 1750 Peter Blake of St. Kitts left £200 to his sister Mary in Dublin and 15 shillings to the poor of the parish of Knockmoye (Vere Langford Oliver, *The History of the Island of Antigua* (London: Mitchell and Hughes, 1894), vol. 2, 274; St. Christopher Deeds, Records, Book O, no. 1, pt. 1, Record Office, Basseterre, St. Kitts, 84–5.

passing by the House of James Ferrill [in Plymouth] ... [he] did see Edward Jessup ... in a Congregation met in the said house while Mass was said & Sung by a Popish Priest & that ... Jessup was then in the Middle of the Congregation and Seem'd to be very Attentive in a Posture of Devotion.[78]

More damningly, information soon came to light that in the preceding decade Colonel Jessup, normally resident on St. Kitts, had frequently visited and been "very Intimate" with the Jesuits at the English College at St. Omer, in France, and that his daughter was studying at a Catholic convent in preparation for taking her vows as a nun.[79] Immediately suspended from his seat on the St. Kitts Council, Jessup fled in disgrace to England, whence he sent the Board of Trade an impassioned defense of his character, in which he reminded the lords that he had lived in the Leewards for sixteen years, that he had "continued to Act there without reproach, in several Offices of Honour & Trust ... [and] was Constantly Chosen to Serve as a Representative of the People."[80] Jessup's punishment might appear to have been excessively harsh and arbitrary, but it seems likely that, had the incident occurred a few years later, more severe penalties might have followed. That the Jacobite rebellion galvanized support in the island among the Irish Catholics was suggested by Governor Mathew, who termed their behavior "very indiscreet." "Their Cheerfull Looks on the disapointment at Fontenoy they could not hide," wrote Mathew, and "they took no Pains to hide a Real Joy ... on the Affair of Preston Panns & Falkirk ... the Victory at Culloden has made every good Britton among us a Witness of their Melancholy Concern."[81]

These political and economic tensions devolved into open conflict as the Jacobite forces in Britain seemed poised on the edge of victory over the Hanoverian monarchy. The right of those wealthy and respectable

---

[78] Deposition of Wyke, April 16, 1744, C.O. 152/26: Board of Trade, Original Correspondence, Leeward Islands, 1747–50. Wyke's father, George, figured as Montserrat's wealthiest planter in the "Political Anatomy."

[79] Ibid. The English College at St. Omer, along with the seminary at Douai, trained the majority of Irish priests in the era of penal law. A 1701 act of the island of Nevis denoted a "Popish Recusant" to be anyone who had "due proof made against him or them, that he or they shall have been at Mass, or received the Eucharist according to the Church of Rome, or received Absolution from any Priest, Friar, or Jesuit, in Communion of the Church of Rome"; see *Acts of Assembly, Passed in the Island of Nevis, from 1664, to 1739, inclusive* (London: John Baskett, 1740), 35.

[80] William Mathew to Lords of Trade, November 6, 1746, C.O. 152/25: Board of Trade, Original Correspondence, Leeward Islands, 1744–7.

[81] Fontenoy was a crushing British defeat at the hands of the French, Prestonpans and Falkirk were Jacobite victories, and Culloden was the site of the collapse of Bonnie Prince Charlie's attempt to reestablish the Stuarts on the throne.

Irishmen who did not openly flaunt their Catholicism to "bear Arms, serve upon Juries, and to do their Country's service in all other respects the same with the Protestants" had long passed without any substantial challenge, and men of Irish descent, such as Anthony Fahie of St. Kitts, might be elected as members of or even serve as speaker of the individual islands' houses of assembly; their wealth, and their at least outward conformity with the Church of England, rendered them appropriate choices for office in small white societies in which the number of propertied men in residence was at any given time very limited.[82] But the latter half of the 1740s witnessed a breakdown of this unspoken consensus. The controversy began over "a Right the Roman Catholics Claim of Voting for Assembly Men," but soon dovetailed with a scandal over an alleged case of incest in the Farrell clan, one of the few families among Montserrat's Irish elite that openly professed an allegiance to the Church of Rome. The conclusive defeat of the Jacobite forces at Culloden, and the subsequent, if short-lived period of relative tranquility in European international relations before the outbreak of the Seven Years' War, eventually allowed the most violent hostilities among the Montserratian elite to dissipate, but suspicions of treachery, particularly in such a small society, were slow to fade. The physician Robert Poole, who made a tour through the Leewards in 1749, noted that after the Farrell family's intimate dysfunctions had been "made a Party Matter ... the amiable Bands of Union [between Catholics and Protestants] were broke, and have not since been united."[83]

These anxieties notwithstanding, the prospects of Irish settlers in the Leewards improved significantly over the course of the eighteenth century. The signing of the Treaty of Utrecht in 1713 brought to an end nearly half a century of active hostility between France and Britain, in the course of which the Leewards had been raided and ruined again and

---

[82] Smith, *Natural History*, 305; C.O. 241/2, St. Christopher's, Council and Assembly Minutes. Fahie's father, also Anthony, was listed in a 1712 document as owning 200 hundred acres of land and 90 slaves, and had married Elizabeth Molineux, daughter of an Anglican minister in Montserrat. The younger Anthony Fahie later became the judge of the St. Kitts Vice Admiralty Court, his son studied at the Middle Temple, and his grandson became a vice admiral and commander in chief of the Leeward naval station; see Oliver, ed., *Caribbeana*, vol. 4, 266.

[83] Poole, *The Beneficent Bee: or, Traveller's Companion* (London: E. Duncomb, 1753), 356. However, the Farrell family's disgrace was not permanent; in 1770, Francis Russell and Thomas Howe, respectively the author and publisher of *An Essay on the Reduction of Interest*, printed in Basseterre, St. Kitts, included the names of Dominick and Charles Farrell in the list of subscribers to the volume.

again. The cession to Britain of the French lands in St. Kitts at one stroke "removed the most irritating source of Anglo-French friction in the eastern Caribbean"; it also relieved the long-held fears of English planters that, in a time of war with the French, Irish Catholic servants and former servants would flock to the invaders' assistance.[84] At least as important, after approximately 1730 Montserrat began to undergo what Donald Akenson has called "the long wind down," as sugar production began a slow but steady decline, both in absolute terms and in relation to that of the other Leewards. In 1735, Montserrat shipped 63 common weight (cwt) of sugar to Britain, nearly 15 percent of the total sugar export of the Leewards, but by 1745 the figure had fallen to 32.9 cwt, just less than 10 percent of the complete Leeward shipment. Although a few years, notably 1749, 1755, 1760, 1761, 1764, and 1772, saw excellent harvests, in the four decades leading up to the American Revolution Montserrat's exports rarely exceeded 50 cwt a year.[85] As the island's productivity declined, and that of Antigua, St. Kitts, and, after 1763, the "Ceded Islands" of Dominica, Grenada, St. Vincent, and Tobago increased, halting economic calamity came to outrank maintaining distinctions of nationality and religion as a societal priority, and some of the longest-standing disabilities aimed at Catholics were removed: By 1756 Catholic priests were allowed to enter the island and openly dispense the sacraments, and by 1788 the property qualification for voting in Assembly elections was lowered from ten pounds to forty shillings, thus politically empowering at least some of the island's less affluent Irish residents.[86] In 1766, the Nevisian physician and poet James Grainger, author of the georgic epic *The Sugar-Cane*, stated that "in Montserrat, the Roman-catholics, who behaved well when our enemies attempted to conquer it, have many privileges." Among these privileges, apparently, was the tradition of holding a lavish public celebration on St. Patrick's Day, "which the Principal of the White Inhabitants, chiefly Irish, usually assemble together to commemorate."[87] In 1768, a number of the island's slaves seized on the festivities as a convenient time to attempt a rebellion, implying that the majority of whites, presumably including some individuals who were not Irish or Catholic, would be participating in the festivities and would be unable to keep the customarily strict watch over their bondspeople.[88]

[84] Dunn, *Sugar and Slaves*, 146–7.
[85] Akenson, *If the Irish Ran the World*, 154; Sheridan, *Sugar and Slavery*, 490–2.
[86] Akenson, *If the Irish Ran the World*, 157, 158.
[87] Grainger, *The Sugar-Cane: A Poem* (London: R. and J. Dodsley, 1766), 16.
[88] William Woodley to Secretary of State, April 22, 1768, C.O. 152/48.

The history of seventeenth- and eighteenth-century Montserrat illuminates the existence of a category of Irishness that was intimately
bound up with that of Roman Catholicism and with other undesirable
attributes. At the most basic level, Irishness denoted Catholicism, and
Catholicism Irishness, and both were connected in the public consciousness with rebellion and treachery.[89] The poorest and most disenfranchised
members of island society, epitomized by the hardscrabble small farmers
of St. Patrick's and by the struggling artisans and laborers who populated Plymouth and the impoverished and crime-ridden "Irish Town" of
Basseterre, St. Kitts, were far more likely to be designated "Irish" than
might a Blake, a Skerrett, or a Galway.[90] It was to these poor Irish that
Leeward governor Christopher Codrington referred in a conversation of
1697 with the French priest Jean-Baptiste Labat. In response to Labat's
query about whether the comte de Gennes, governor of the French sector
of St. Kitts, might be able to restore the depleted population of his territory with Irishmen, Codrington reminded the father that de Gennes had
earlier invented "a mechanical peacock, which walks about and picks
up corn with its beak which it swallows and digests." If the Frenchman
could construct such an elaborate toy, asked Codrington, would it not be
possible for him "to make five or six regiments of Irishmen in the same
way? He would have far less trouble making ugly brutes like them ...
and as he has infinite ingenuity M. de Gennes should have no difficulty
to make his mechanical Irishmen go through the necessary motions of
firing a musket equally well as real Irishmen."[91] In Codrington's opinion,
Irishmen were lower than many animal species; they were automaton-
like "brutes" whose only skill lay in warfare. As such, the poor Irish were
simultaneously a physical menace, a function of their allegedly aggressive nature, and a cultural nonentity. That the poorer inhabitants of St.
Patrick's chose to practice Catholicism was only to be expected. If, on
the other hand, a Colonel Edward Jessup, a member of the Council and

---

[89] On the intertwining in eighteenth-century Britain of ideas of poverty, criminality, and
Irishness, see Peter Linebaugh, *The London Hanged: Crime and Civil Society in the
Eighteenth Century* (Cambridge: Cambridge University Press, 1991), esp. ch. 9.

[90] A 1734 meeting of the St. Kitts Assembly approved "A Bill Entitled an Act for Obliging
the Churchwardens and Vestry Men of the Parish of St. George Basseterre to keep Watch
in ... Irish Town by Night and for preventing Robberies and Disorders that are frequently
committed therein"; Minutes of February 9, 1734, C.O. 241/3: Minutes of Council and
Assembly, St. Kitts, 1729–37; Sir Probyn Inniss, *Basseterre: The Story of a West Indian
Town* (Basseterre, St. Kitts: Privately printed, 1985), 14.

[91] Labat, *The Memoirs of Pere Labat, 1693–1705*, trans. John Eaden (London: Frank Cass,
1970), 213–14.

a leader of the militia, was a clandestine Catholic, his behavior constituted a threat because it showed his fellow members of the Montserratian
elite that papism could lurk behind the most respectable of facades.
Although Leeward governor William Mathew, writing in 1746, admitted that "there are many Roman Catholicks good Men among them," he
reminded the Board of Trade in the same letter that Irish Catholics were
nonetheless "Dangerous Tennants" on whose cooperation no governor
could rely and whose actions he must carefully monitor at all times.[92]
This dichotomy between "good men" and "dangerous tenants" was one
that troubled both the Irish colonists in the Leewards and their English
neighbors and administrators, even as the meanings of Irishness, "good"
and "dangerous" alike, shifted over the course of the century in both
metropole and colony.

"THE WORLD WAS MADE FOR SCOTS"

The negative stereotypes connected with Scots colonists differed in a
number of ways from those that Leeward islanders attributed to the Irish.
The Scots carried their own burden of prejudice, but outside of certain
exceptional circumstances "Scot" generally did not function, as "Irish"
usually did, as a term of opprobrium denoting an individual's poverty,
criminality, or disloyalty. The types of Scots who chose to settle in the
Leewards, and the shifting position Scots occupied in eighteenth-century
Britain, prevented English islanders from invariably labeling them as a
source of danger or disrepute. Moreover, the marked tendency of Scots
migrants to assist their friends and relatives in gaining employment and
other opportunities in the islands provides an example of what David
Hancock has termed the "destructive *and* constructive force of marginal
status."[93]

As a group, Scots did carry a certain amount of cultural baggage
deemed undesirable by English colonial society. Mrs. Amelia Flannigan,
an Irishwoman who married an Antiguan planter and composed the only
nineteenth-century work on the history of Antigua, emphasized the extent
to which Scots and their descendants had been and remained central to

---

92 Mathew to Board of Trade, November 6, 1746, C.O. 152/26: Board of Trade: Original
Correspondence, Leeward Islands, 1747–50.
93 Hancock, *Citizens of the World: London Merchants and the Integration of the British
Atlantic Community, 1735–1785* (Cambridge: Cambridge University Press, 1995), 69,
emphasis mine.

the island's commerce and society. In her description, Antiguan Scots fell
into two categories, those who were involved in commerce and those who
managed or owned plantations. She depicted the Scots businessmen as
"pale-faced, straight-haired clerks" who spent their lives in St. John's, the
Antiguan capital, "stand[ing] behind a counter and sell[ing] a few yards
of tape or a paper of pins" when not "busily employed in arranging their
incongruous goods to the best advantage."[94] This description recapitulates
the principal traits the English had long associated with the Scots, princi-
pally poverty, miserliness, and delusions of grandeur. Flannigan's words
hark back to seventeenth- and eighteenth-century English depictions of
Caledonians as ragged, aggressive hordes poised to follow a Scots leader,
such as James I or the earl of Bute, to London, where they would batten
upon a wealthy, unsuspecting Albion. A pamphlet issued just before the
Act of Union, vividly entitled *An English Ointment for the Scotch Mange*,
exemplified the sort of invective such migrations inspired, referring to
the Scots as "our Freckly Neighbours," "a parcel of Beggarly Male-
Contents," and a "Lousie Generation of Perfidious Wretches" who, over-
flowing "the Starving Limits of their own Barren Country," were spilling
into "the English Canaan that overflows with Milk and Honey."[95] Mrs.
Flannigan's rhetoric was somewhat milder than that of this pamphleteer.
She did not depict the inhabitants of St. John's mercantile "Scotch Row"
as having become "Cruel to others by their own Wants" and thus presenting any sort of threat to the social, political, or economic security of
Antigua.[96] Rather, she cast an amused and satirical eye on what she considered to be the ludicrous pretensions of these shopkeepers, who "ape
the man of fashion, call their haberdashery store a merchant's warehouse,
and forgoing the vulgar title of draper, take to themselves the loftier name
of merchant," perhaps in an attempt – in her eyes, a futile one – to connect themselves to the notably wealthy and influential mercantile community that had developed over the course of the eighteenth century in
Glasgow and other Scots port cities, particularly in the sugar and tobacco
trades. These pale-faced clerks, she asserted, did not limit their striving
to the realm of commerce, but were perpetually eager to "attend the governor's levees, play the amiable at a quadrille party, frequent the billiard
table, or perchance take wine with his excellency, and grin and bow with

[94] Flannigan, *Antigua and the Antiguans* (London: Saunders and Otley, 1844), vol. 1, 210,
212, 263.
[95] *An English Ointment for the Scotch Mange* (London: B. Bragg, 1705), 1–2.
[96] Flannigan, *Antigua*, vol. 1, 212.

approved precision." Flannigan's text here echoes Governor Codrington's description of the Irish as mechanical creatures, but it claims that Scottish automata act out the rituals of a sycophantic sociability rather than that of armed aggression.[97]

In addition to asserting themselves in inappropriately genteel forms of recreation, the Scotsmen, according to Mrs. Flannigan, took advantage of the limitations of the colonial social hierarchy and the paucity of venues for polite sociability in Antigua by setting their shops up to "provide an agreeable morning lounge for the superiors of the island, and in a glass of sangaree, or a flowing bowl of pepper-punch, the difference of grade between the entertainer and the entertained is overlooked." Again, Mrs. Flannigan did not describe the Scots as posing a threat to white society in any military sense, but she clearly conceived of them as upstarts who had taken advantage of the narrow social milieu of colonial Antigua to assert themselves in spheres that ought to have been far beyond individuals of their modest social and economic position.[98] Like the blacksmith's wife of seventeenth-century Barbados, whom a metropolitan observer had criticized for her violation of English sumptuary norms, dressing in flow-ered silk as if she were the wife of an aristocrat rather than of an artisan, these Scottish shopkeepers offended metropolitan observers with their refusal to know their places, an offense different in degree but similar in kind to a slave's unwillingness to accept a master's natural and obvious superiority.

If "our friends in 'Scotch-row'" incited Mrs. Flannigan's amused dis-dain, those Scotsmen involved in plantation agriculture were, in her opin-ion, still more deserving of ridicule. Scots plantation owners were, she claimed, the "descendents of those poor white persons, who in former years came to Antigua to act in the literal sense, as 'servants of servants,' but whose offspring, by dint of petty traffickings and small gatherings, amassed a sufficient sum of money to make them forget their origin."[99] Like the ambitious shopkeepers of St. John's, these strivers merited little respect from Mrs. Flannigan, who referred to them as "needy adventur-ers" who aspired, entirely inappropriately, to occupy positions of respect and prestige in Antiguan society. Her prototypical Scots overseer, after

---

[97] Ibid.

[98] Ibid. On loci of sociability in colonial British America, see David S. Shields, *Civil Tongues and Polite Letters in British America* (Chapel Hill: University of North Carolina Press, 1997), and Alan Karras, "The World of Alexander Johnston: The Creolization of Ambition, 1762–1787," *Historical Journal* 30 (1987), 63.

[99] Flannigan, *Antigua*, vol. 2, 265.

spending the day in the cane fields supervising the labor of the slaves, would in the evening comb "his straggling, sun-burnt locks, and exchanging his dirty white jacket for one of broad-cloth, or a coat whose cuffs and collar bore ample marks of time," and would appear "in the dining-room or hall, where a high stool or an education chair was placed for him near his master, at whose old jokes and worn-out tales he felt obliged to laugh, while he indulged in such luxuries as fowls' necks and odd ends of puddings, washed down by a single glass of wine." The humor of this situation, in the eyes of Flannigan and, presumably, her readers, was that such Scotsmen were either too proud or too unsophisticated to realize that they were ridiculous rather than dignified. Their lack of either humility or refinement blinded them to their failure to present a truly genteel appearance and prevented them from understanding that being seated on a stool and fed leftovers denoted their employers' sense of a vast gulf, both of nationality and of rank, separating the planter from the overseer.[100]

But in time, to Mrs. Flannigan's distaste, the paucity of white men in Antiguan society often allowed the uncouth "Sawney," a creature who had "left his mountain home, his trouty lochs, and oaten bannocks ... for the sake of siller," to advance to the position of manager or attorney to a resident or absentee planter, and perhaps even to acquire his own estate and marry his former employer's daughter. At this moment "Sawney," although he remained a "worthless grub," hastened to "put on the butterfly's painted wings and soar." Gaining "the pinnacle of his ambition," he soon forgot "his former lowly state and penniless pockets, and, with haughty brow and overweening pride," proclaimed "himself an aristocrat." "Sawney" signaled his transformation in status by purchasing a horse, a gig, a few bottles of wine, and a decent suit, and began "to make a show" and "ventured" to give a dinner-party to the "great people" of his neighborhood. He now considered himself to be "a man of family" and luxuriated in what he believed to be his newfound splendor, riding about the island in "a rattling, shaking, tumble-down carriage, drawn by a pair of spavined horses, and further graced by a shoeless coachman." Having presented this sardonic image of "Sawney's" triumph, Mrs. Flannigan abandoned this subject, but not before concluding with the barbed exclamation, "How very fast do mushrooms spring up!"[101]

---

[100] Ibid., 193–5.
[101] Ibid., 196–7. "Siller" is Flannigan's perception of the word "silver" filtered through a Scottish accent.

Throughout her text, Mrs. Flannigan subscribed to and promulgated a long-established image of the Scot as a penniless adventurer, an individual who was simultaneously servile and grasping, whose risible pretensions to gentility served only to underscore his lowly social and economic position, and whose failure or success alike made him the subject of mockery among his betters. Notably, though, her stingingly sarcastic portrait of "Sawney" depicted him as a figure of ridicule rather than one of menace. She lamented the fact that the scarcity of white residents in Antigua facilitated the emergence of Scots as potential employees, friends, and even spouses of elite Antiguan whites, but her principal objection was not that these ambitious young men might have conspired to seize control of Antigua's lands, wealth, or political offices, but simply that, in her opinion, their physical appearance, manners, and general presentation of self did little to ornament and much to blemish the complexion of local society.[102] Like mushrooms, they were unattractive and graceless, but nonetheless they appeared ludicrous rather than alarming; their principal failing, in Flannigan's eyes, was that their appearance and character failed to uphold her romanticized view of plantation society as chivalric or to live up to the feudal ideals reflected in the georgic visions of eighteenth-century visitors to the islands.

This disjuncture between derision and outright fear or disgust is a highly significant one with respect to ethnic relations in the British American colonies. It marks a space in which Scots could make their way in Leeward society and avoid having their nationality function as a marker of ineradicable and inimical difference. In this way, Scottishness followed a trajectory quite different from that of Irishness. The arrogance that allegedly typified Scots often appeared to the English as so inappropriate as to be ludicrous or even, in its ridiculousness, offensive, but the very fact that the Scots manifested such self-regard, even in the most difficult of circumstances, served to separate them from the Irish, not the proud Galway-based elite but the impoverished farmers of St. Patrick's, Montserrat, who seemed to English observers to be abject in their poverty and misery. As will be explored in Chapters 4 and 5, personal honor was one of the most important values in the colonial British American world. Although Scots' assertions of honor often provoked ridicule in white society, the fact that they saw themselves as meriting a place in the

---

[102] Londoners expressed similar sentiments about the Scots among them; according to David Hancock, Scots were "reviled by the English for their food, clothes, accent, financial and political connections, indeed their very success." See Hancock, *Citizens*, 45.

sphere of gentility and respect allowed them to emerge in the public eye with greater dignity than the Irish.[103] Mrs. Flannigan's work presented a number of instances in which West Indian Scots "forgot" their lowly position and aspired to count themselves among the local elite. Such forgetfulness might irritate the observer, but it also functioned as an assertion of selfhood and personal dignity, characteristics that society never attributed to the masses of poor Irish in Montserrat or St. Kitts.

Only in rare instances did Scottish identity serve as a marker of criminality or disloyalty, a fact that is particularly surprising when one considers that the first half of the eighteenth century saw two major Jacobite rebellions and an ongoing climate of hostility on the part of many Scots against England and the House of Hanover. Moreover, some of the Scots who settled in the Leeward Islands arrived there not by their own volition, but as political prisoners of the English government. A metropolitan observer described these Jacobite exiles as "the common Enemies of all Religion and Vertue" and as "a wicked people" who, if not subjected to close monitoring, would "go a Pyrating," but such pronouncements tended to carry little weight in the islands.[104] Had not previous transports, such as the "Monmouth Men," risen quickly to positions of wealth and prestige? Azariah Pinney, for example, had been exiled from England with only a Bible, a change of shirt, and a few shillings to his name, but he had founded a great "West-India fortune" and established a dynasty of Nevisian planters and Bristol merchants that lasted for generations.[105] Like Pinney, the son of a scholarly clergyman, many of the Scottish transportees were literate and numerate, due to Scotland's excellent system of public education. These attributes were in short supply and thus greatly valued in the West Indian colonies. Moreover, those very qualities – ambition, frugality, calculation – that an observer such as Mrs. Flannigan found most repugnant among the Scots appeared to Leeward planters to be excellent attributes in white employees, and it was this drive that allowed many Scots, even those relatively few who had arrived

[103] On Scots' alleged arrogance, see Robert Secor, "Ethnic Humor in Early American Jest Books," in Frank Shuffelton, ed., *A Mixed Race: Ethnicity in Early America* (New York: Oxford University Press, 1993).

[104] *The Substance of a Letter from One of the Prisoners who were Transported from Liverpool to the West-Indies* (London: n.p., n.d.), 2; *Elegy on the Mournful Banishment of James Campbel of Burnbank to the West-Indies* (Edinburgh: n.p., 1721), 1.

[105] The Pinney family's endeavors are detailed in Richard Pares, *A West-India Fortune* (London: Longmans, Green, 1950). See also Mark S. Quintanilla, "The 'Monmouth Men' in the West Indies" (Ph.D. diss., Arizona State University, 1993).

as political deportees, to overcome the obstacles of poverty and suspicion
and to rise to positions of real stature and influence in the Leewards. Not
only did this process yield to individual Scots many tangible benefits, but
it simultaneously worked to ensure that "Scot" did not become a byword
for poverty or turbulence, as "Irish" so often did.[106]

A career that epitomized Mrs. Flannigan's description of the progress
of the Scots "mushroom gentry," and one of which she may have been
aware while in the process of composing her history, was that of Walter
Tullideph. The son of a Presbyterian minister, Tullideph attended the
High School in Edinburgh, and after his graduation in 1718 he served
a term of apprenticeship to a local surgeon. Aware that his prospects
were not particularly bright at home, where men of good education
but little money outnumbered the opportunities available to them, he
opted in 1726 to relocate to Antigua, where several friends and relatives had already established themselves. Like many Scots of his generation, Tullideph hoped that Scotland's forfeiture of sovereignty by the
Act of Union might be offset by the opportunities that connection with
England opened to ambitious and well-educated Scots both at home
and in the colonies.

Drawing on both his professional skills and his personal connections, Tullideph soon succeeded in fitting himself into several niches in
Antiguan economic life. Because his elder brother had established himself as a merchant in London, Tullideph was able to use family ties to
set himself up as a factor, having his sibling send him textiles and other
dry goods, which he then sold to import-dependent Antiguan planters.
Simultaneously, his medical training placed him in considerable demand
within a largely underprofessionalized island society.[107] As Tullideph traveled from plantation to plantation selling the consignments of English
goods he received, first from his brother and soon from other merchants
in London and Scotland, he also provided medical care to the estates'
inhabitants, white and black alike, and several planters retained him to
serve on a contract basis at a fixed annual salary as physician and "Man-
Midwife" to their slaves.

Impressed by what they saw as Tullideph's trustworthy character, careful financial management, and strong work ethic, several Antiguan planters who planned extended sojourns in Britain appointed him to serve as

---

[106] Everett Wilkie, "The Image of the Scot as Colonizer" (paper presented to "The Scots in
the Atlantic World," John Carter Brown Library, Providence, RI, June 1994).

[107] On the paucity of professionals in the islands, see Poole, *Beneficent Bee*, 316–17.

their manager or attorney during their absences.[108] Although Tullideph, like most of his fellow Leeward residents, lacked formal legal training, his Edinburgh schooling placed him among the ranks of the best-educated men on the island. As he gained control, though not ownership, over the estates of a number of absentees, Tullideph entered into trade on his own, becoming a correspondent of his uncle William Dunbar, a London-based merchant who had spent some years resident at Antigua and retained connections there. This relationship enabled Tullideph to borrow substantial sums of money in exchange for the promise of the next year's consignments of sugar from the estates he managed. Seeing how chronically short of cash even the wealthiest planters often were, Tullideph used the funds he borrowed from Dunbar to provide loans to these men, frequently borrowing money at 5 percent interest and lending it out at 8 to 10 percent. In February 1728 he wrote to Hans Sloane, the famed naturalist and founder of the British Museum, that he was "in a pretty good way of living, haveing at present the manadgement of three pretty large plantations." So busy was Tullideph with his managerial responsibilities that "it enhances all my time during the Cropes, so it is a very great hindrance to me from prosecuteing my enquiries into Nature," the studies in relation to which he had entered into communication with Sloane.[109]

Such shrewd dealings allowed him to acquire the mortgages of several Antiguan estates when poor harvests prevented their owners from repaying the loans he had extended to them. By 1733, he had established himself as a respected member of the local commercial and financial community and was, as he wrote to Sloane, "endeavouring to get a moderate Fortune and have a good prospect in so doing."[110] By 1736, he had also

---

[108] Lord Adam Gordon, an officer of the 66th Regiment of Foot who was stationed in Antigua in the 1760s, wrote that "there are several large properties in the hands of Familys residing in Britain, who let them out to Managers, that pay them a certain agreed rent on the Exchange, and these Gentlemen generally make themselves great Fortunes." See "Journal of an Officer who Travelled in America and the West Indies in 1764 and 1765," in Newton D. Mereness, ed., *Travels in the American Colonies* (New York: Antiquarian Press, 1961), 375–6. Trevor Burnard has emphasized that "becoming the manager of a sugar estate, especially a large one owned by an absentee landlord, was a profitable alternative to striking out on one's own"; see Burnard, *Mastery, Tyranny, and Desire: Thomas Thistlewood and His Slaves in the Anglo-Jamaican World* (Chapel Hill: University of North Carolina, 2004), 59.

[109] Tullideph to Sloane, February 24, 1728, Sloane Mss. 4049, British Library, London.

[110] Richard B. Sheridan, "Letters from a Sugar Plantation in Antigua, 1734–1758," *Agricultural History* 31 (1957), 3; Sheridan, *Sugar and Slavery*, 198–9; Tullideph to Sloane, June 25, 1734, Letter-Book of Walter Tullideph, Ogilvy of Inverquharity Papers, GD205/53/8, Scottish Record Office, Edinburgh. I thank Baron Ogilvy of Inverquharity for permission to quote from these papers.

entered the ranks of Antiguan landowners as a result of his marriage to Mary Burroughs Tremills, "an agreeable Young Widow by whom I have gott Possession of a very fine Estate to which I am making additions & Improvements." This turn of events, he wrote to his brother Thomas, a professor of divinity at the University of St. Andrews, was his reward for "hav[ing] laboured very hard these ten years." It was also a symbol of the ways in which Scottish frugality and commercial acumen recuperated native-born West Indians' alleged propensity for mismanagement, as Tremills, "a Creole of this Island [was] a honest good natured man but his hospitality bordered on profuseness by which his Estate was mortgaged and ... sold to my mother in Law ... and by her conveyed to me and my heirs for ever" – perhaps the decisive factor disposing Tullideph to abandon his earlier intention to "keep myself for some rich Widow in Fife" and seek a spouse in the islands.[111] Tullideph might have been a striving newcomer who had arrived in Antigua with little capital other than the benefits of Scotland's system of public education, but within a decade he had both enriched himself and emerged as a suitable spousal choice for a wealthy widow, a path followed by other young Scotsmen, such as Alexander Fraser, "Surgeon of Dalzell's Regiment at Antigua," whose wife, Louisa, was the daughter of the Nevis chief justice and colonel of militia, William Pym Burt, and William McDowall and James Milliken of St. Kitts, both of whom acquired their first lands through advantageous marriages to plantation heiresses.[112] Tullideph's letters home display a sense that he saw himself as engaged in founding both a family and a fortune; in the same letter in which he first mentioned his marriage to his brother, he stated that his wife's mother, "the Old Lady ... has a great deal more in houses in the town [St. John's] & negroes and is dayly making money so that if I should have a little boy he will come in for a good deal more."[113]

Thus far, Tullideph's progress in Antigua matches closely that of Flannigan's prototypical "Sawney," even to his purchase of such

[111] Walter Tullideph to Thomas Tullideph, August 20, 1734, April 28, 1736, and June 11 1737, Letter-Book of Tullideph, 4, 40, 60. The Tremills estate had developed from the 300 acres that Mary's father-in-law, the carpenter William Tremills, had been granted in 1678 and from the further 136 acres purchased by her late husband, John Tremills; see Oliver, *History of Antigua*, vol. 3, 144.

[112] Milliken and McDowall soon became absentees; upon their return to Glasgow, they established the sugar-importing and -refining firm of James Milliken & Co., forerunner of Alexander Houstoun & Co., the leading Scottish West Indian house of the late eighteenth century (Hamilton, *Scotland*, 85).

[113] Tullideph to Thomas Tullideph, Letter-Book of Tullideph, 41.

accoutrements of gentility as a velvet sidesaddle with silk fringes and a silver-embroidered coat of arms. But Tullideph's subsequent career was very different from that of the ludicrous "mushroom," for Tullideph not only greatly increased his personal wealth (by 1757 his land in Antigua was valued at £30,000, and he had purchased the Scottish estate of Baldovan for the sum of £10,000), but became the key player in a network of patronage and assistance that connected Scots at home with those in Britain's West Indian colonies.[114] He became something of an informal employment agent to a crowd of young Scots possessed of education and ambition but lacking attractive prospects at home. His letter book is replete with references to his efforts to match employment opportunities in Antigua with suitable young men from Scotland. In 1735, he wrote to his uncle Dunbar in London to inquire "if you can agree with any Sober Young Surgeon who has been educated at Ed[inburg]h. (if possible) for three years ... to come out ... I will give him ye first year 30 pounds ye Second 40 & the 3d 50," in addition to "bed board & Washing."[115] By this point, seven years after his arrival at Antigua, Tullideph had become so preoccupied with his various commercial and managerial sidelines that he required the services of another medical practitioner to fulfill his commitments as a physician, and he was gratified when Dunbar succeeded in recruiting Dr. William Mercer to assist him. The following year, after his marriage and his acquisition of Tremills Estate, he requested of his brother Thomas that he and their brother David see "if any of our nephews will Study Physick and settle as a Planter. I can allow such a one £100 sterling p[e]r Ann[um] to manadge my Estate and take care of my negroes when I resolve to come home."[116] By such an arrangement, Tullideph replicated the pattern of behavior of the absentees whom he had served earlier in his career, filling the role of the successful planter eager to visit the metropole, while the younger men tried to follow his path from manager to landowner. Tullideph did not limit his patronage to members of his family, but also worked to help other recent arrivals from Scotland to set themselves up in Antigua. For several years, he wrote frequently of his attempts to assist the impoverished Charles Murray, by finding his young son a

---

[114] Tullideph to Martha Murray, November 8, 1735, Letter-Book of Tullideph, 39. By 1754, Tullideph had increased his holdings of land to nearly 600 acres and his number of slaves to 250; see Sheridan, "Letters," and Hamilton, *Scotland*, 60.

[115] Walter Tullideph to William Dunbar, March 24 1735, Letter-Book of Tullideph, 20.

[116] Walter Tullideph to Thomas Tulllideph, April 28, 1736, Letter-Book of Tullideph, 40.

suitable apprenticeship, and in 1740 he took a strong interest in the educational progress of Tom Trotter, a friend of his Scots relations, whom he hoped he might place as a physician in Antigua. He also urged his brother David to "bring Scotch Servants with you" on his next voyage to Antigua, as they were "the only kind wanted here."[117]

In many ways, Tullideph's patronage paralleled that of the great Antiguan planter Samuel Martin, who "for a quarter of a century ... provided a haven for young men who came to the West Indies to seek their fortunes."[118] The "loved and revered father of Antigua," and author of the widely circulated and frequently reprinted *Essay upon Plantership*, Martin, though not of Scots descent himself, was a keen admirer of Scottish Enlightenment "lecturers on the law of nature" and was sufficiently impressed by what he saw as the high quality of the Scots he encountered to become a source of support and preferment for many such young men.[119] Typical of Martin's pattern of patronage was a letter he sent to the London merchants (and kin to a prominent Antiguan planter family) Richard Oliver, Sr. and Jr., in which he offered to take "Mr Macdowells brother as an apprentice" under the following terms: "[I] will give Macdowell £20 Curr[ent]. money of Antigua p[e]r Ann[um] as wages and for his Cloathing ... pay his passage from Scotland to this Island, and for a Mattress a bolster a p[ai]r strong coarse sheets and a Blanket w[hi]ch must serve him at Sea or ashore ... also meat drink washing and lading and Physick according to the Customs of this Country and if he behaves as an honest diligent man, will teach him all the arts of plantership and prefer him at the End of his time as is his [Martin's] custom to all good Serv[an]ts."[120] Macdowell was not an isolated case of Martin's philanthropy toward Scots; the following year, Martin promised William Baird of Aberdeen that he would place the latter's son, Dr. Baird, formerly Martin's overseer at his estate on Barbuda, at Martin's customhouse or at "some easy employment in England, that will afford him a genteel maintainance and yet allow him time enough to follow his inclination to

[117] Walter Tullideph to David Tullideph, May 19, 1735, Letter-Book of Tullideph, 28.
[118] Richard B. Sheridan, "Samuel Martin: Innovating Sugar Planter of Antigua," 1750–1776," *Agricultural History* 34 (1960), 138.
[119] Quotation from Janet Schaw, *The Journal of a Lady of Quality*, ed. Evangeline Walker Andrews and Charles M. Andrews (New Haven: Yale University Press, 1923), 103; Martin, *A Short Treatise on the Slavery of Negroes in the British Colonies* (St. John's, Antigua: Robert Mearns, 1775), 5.
[120] Martin to Oliver and Oliver, October 27, 1759, Add. Mss. 41349: Martin Family Papers, British Library, London, vol. 4, 85.

books, for his Constitution is not nor ever has been robust enough, since I knew him, for the laborious life of a planter."[121] To replace the ailing Baird, Martin selected two other Scots, Dr. Grant and Colonel Home, to appraise and supervise his slaves and livestock at the Barbuda plantation.[122] Later that year, Martin informed absentee planter Benedict Willis, whose estate Martin was looking after, that he had selected another Scot, the "able planter" and "honest diligent good man" Dr. Robert Harvey, to serve as physician to Willis's slaves.[123]

Some years later, Martin was living in England, but he remained intent on looking out for his Scots friends; he praised a Dr. Malcolm for his "very particular care and tenderness of poor Sam" Rogers, an Antiguan friend, and because Malcolm refused to accept any financial recompense for his care of Rogers, Martin requested that his son, Samuel Martin, Jr., an assistant secretary of the Treasury, "obtain for Mr. Patrick Malcolm the Comptrolership of Parham Customhouse," on the northern coast of Antigua, by "recommend[ing] him to one of your acquaintance in the Treasury."[124] Considering the efforts of Martin and Tullideph, who numbered among the wealthiest and most influential planters on Antigua, in their attempts to assist a large number of Scots on the island, it is not surprising that many visitors to the island were struck by the extent to which "the greatest part of the estates ... are conducted by overseers, the most of whom are Scotsmen" who, "by their assiduity and industry, frequently become masters of the plantations, to which they came out as indentured servants."[125] As David Hancock has noted, the "marginal status" of Scots could be constructive as well as destructive: those Scots who succeeded as planters, merchants, and professionals were almost invariably willing, even eager, to assist their less favored kin and friends by finding them opportunities for employment and advancement in the Leewards.[126]

To many visitors, and as shown by Table 2.1, Scots' dominance of the social, economic, and political life of Antigua seemed almost hegemonic. By the 1750s, nineteen of the island's thirty-two medical professionals

[121] Martin to Baird, March 25, 1761, Martin Family Papers, vol. 4, 98.
[122] Martin to Samuel Redhead, Summer 1761 (undated), Martin Family Papers, vol. 4, 99.
[123] Martin to Willis, October 28, 1761, Martin Family Papers, vol. 4, 118–19.
[124] Martin to Martin Jr., April 26, 1769, Add. Mss. 41348, Martin Family Papers, vol. 3, 44. Parham was "a port of entry, consisting of two or three houses or stores, a custom-house, and church," and was considered "very safe and good ... for the loading of ships"; see Daniel McKinnen, *A Tour through the British West Indies* (London: J. White, 1804), 59.
[125] Poole, *Beneficent Bee*, 320.
[126] Hancock, *Citizens*, 68, 69.

TABLE 2.1. *Classification of Gentry Families of Antigua, 1707–75*

Name	Nationality	Acreage	Assembly	Council
Gordon/Brebner	Scots	1,891	Yes	Yes
Delap/Halliday	Unknown	1,655	Yes	No
Grant	Scots	1,288	No	No
Harvey	Scots	1,196	No	No
Leslie/Livingston	Scots	885	Yes	Yes
Dunbar	Scots	846	Yes	Yes
Willock	English	824	Yes	No
Brooke	English	821	Yes	Yes
Redhead	English	740	Yes	No
Young	Scots	655	Yes	Yes
Gaynor	Irish	643	No	No
Sydserfe	Scots	570	Yes	No
Tullideph	Scots	536	Yes	Yes
Douglas	Scots	510	Yes	Yes
Maxwell	Scots	461	Yes	No
Doig	Scots	320	Yes	No
Webb	English	320	Yes	No
Mathews	English	315	Yes	Yes

Adapted from Richard B. Sheridan, "The Rise of a Colonial Gentry: A Case Study of Antigua, 1730–1775," *Economic History Review* s2:13 (1961), 356.

were either Scottish-born or Scottish-educated, and a lodge of Freemasons of the Scottish Rite had been established in St. John's; by the time that John Luffman visited the town in 1789, local gentlemen were performing in amateur theatricals in order to raise money for the construction of a new and more elaborate lodge building.[127] The Scots traveler Janet Schaw, who visited Antigua shortly before the outbreak of the American Revolution, was similarly impressed by the "Scottishness" of Antigua, as represented by "the sheer numbers of Scots she encountered ... Duncans, Millikens, Blairs, Bairds, Hallidays, Tullidephs, Mackinnons

[127] Hamilton, *Scotland*, 114; Edward Thompson, *Sailor's Letters: written to his Select Friends in England, during his Voyage and Travels in Europe, Asia, Africa, and America, from the Year 1754 to 1759* (London: T. Becket, 1766), vol. 2, 12; John Luffman, *A Brief Account of the Island of Antigua* (London: T. Cadell, 1789), 99, 119; William Shervington, *A Sermon Preached before the Free and Accepted Masons in the Town of St. John's, Antigua, on the 24th June, 1754* (St. John's, Antigua: Benjamin Mecom, 1754), unpaginated. In 1746, Grand Master Lord Caernarvon had appointed William Mathew, as provincial grand master of the Leewards; see James Anderson, *The History and Constitutions of the Most Ancient and Honourable Fraternity of Free and Accepted Masons* (London: J. Robinson, 1746), 195.

and Malcolms" and the "many Scotch names" she noticed on the graves in the island's churchyards.[128] Of the eighteen great Antiguan planter families that emerged between the passage of the Act of Union and the outbreak of the American Revolution, eleven can be clearly identified as having come from Scotland.

Not only did the Gordons, Grants, Dunbars, Douglases, Maxwells, et al. possess estates whose acreage numbered in the hundreds or thousands and own several hundred slaves apiece, but nine of these families had members who were elected to serve in the Assembly, and six of these nine contributed members to the appointed Governor's Council. The first William Gordon arrived as a penniless doctor, but his son James became chief justice of St. Kitts, served on the Council of Antigua, and died possessed of the Moor Place estate in Hertfordshire and of lands in his father's native Aberdeenshire, while William's stepson, James Brebner-Gordon, served as an Antiguan councillor and as the chief justice of the newly Ceded Islands in 1761, earning the praise of the usually censorious Leeward governor George Thomas as "a Man of Understanding, and possessed of a considerable Landed Estate in this Island."[129] Andrew Leslie, another Aberdonian, gained his fortune from his post as victualer of His Majesty's West Indian Fleet, served as a councillor and colonel of militia, and in 1763 sold his 450-acre estate to another Scot, William Livingston.[130] Livingston by 1767 owned 885 acres and more than 250 slaves, and in his 1774 will disposed as well of "jewels, plate, furniture, chaises, and horses," tenements and wharves in St. John's, and a 200-acre estate on Dominica.[131] Alexander Brodie came to Antigua in 1760 as a merchant, acquired an estate in St. Mary's Parish, which he named Windyhills after his Scottish birthplace, married Ann Kidder, daughter of the bishop of Bath and Wells, and saw his son Alexander become chaplain to the prince of Wales.[132] Walter Tullideph himself occupied the offices, successively, of parish vestryman, justice of the peace, assemblyman, and councillor, positions marked by increasing degrees of status and public trust.[133] The traveler Robert Poole, who visited Antigua in 1749, stayed with

---

[128] T. M. Devine, *Scotland's Empire and the Shaping of the Americas, 1600–1815* (Washington, DC: Smithsonian Books, 2003), 241.

[129] Oliver, *History of Antigua*, vol. 2, 22, 27.

[130] Ibid., 180, 178.

[131] Ibid., 181, 197.

[132] Oliver, *Caribbeana*, vol. 1, 98.

[133] Richard B. Sheridan, "The Rise of a Colonial Gentry: A Case Study of Antigua, 1730–1775," *Economic History Review* s2:13 (1961), 356; Sheridan, *Sugar and Slavery*, 199–200.

Colonel Leslie and was impressed by the elegance of his country house at Bermudian Valley; fifteen years later, the naval officer Adam Gordon described the Brebners, Maxwells, Hallidays, and Grants as being "of Note on the island ... all good people."[134]

Considering how spectacularly a notable proportion of Scots migrants to Antigua succeeded, it is not surprising that some observers might resent their luck and express themselves, not with Mrs. Flannigan's tone of gentle mockery, but with considerable bitterness. Edward Thompson, a lieutenant of the British navy, visited Antigua in 1756 and was sufficiently perturbed by the preeminence of Scots, only a decade after the debacle of Culloden had seemed to have crushed "Sawney" forever, that he penned a stinging set of verses in which he compared Scots unfavorably to Negroes. Africans, however repugnant Thompson and other white visitors might find them, bore no responsibility for their presence on the island, as they had been "forced in chains from Gambia's shore / But should we ask, How came MacDuggle here?" In Thompson's formulation, the Scotsman, "obnoxious to the law for some damn'd crime / He flies from England to some savage clime / Shame, like a whirlwind, swallow up your pride / Or Heaven, from better men, your clan divide."[135] William Shervington, a Church of England clergyman in Antigua, caricatured Scots in his "Dialogues on Duelling, and other Subjects," supplementing "MacDuggle" with "Doctor Keneth Macgrewel", a "North Briton" who challenged Shervington to a duel after the parson had turned down his offer to lend him a pair of gloves, "for fear of infection," perhaps from the "Scots Mange" described in the invective of a previous generation.[136] Writing from Jamaica in 1762, the overseer Thomas Thistlewood expressed his belief that Scots were concerned only with looking after their own; when a Scot gained the post of island secretary, Thistlewood was convinced that "no Englishman will be permitted to hold a place under them."[137]

Thompson, Shervington, and Thistlewood were not alone in professing contempt and mistrust for Scots, as we can see from the words and images with which English journalists of the early 1760s depicted those Scots who, they claimed, followed the newly elected prime minister, Lord

[134] Poole, *Beneficent Bee*, 307, 318; Gordon, "Journal," in Mereness, ed., *Travels*, 376.

[135] Thompson, *Sailor's Letters*, vol. 2, 45–6.

[136] Shervington, "Dialogues on Duelling, and other Subjects," in *Miscellanies* (St. John's, Antigua: Edward Hughes, 1763), 93.

[137] Burnard, *Mastery*, 89.

Bute, to England, or "Money-Land," in search of their fortunes, or from William Hogarth's famous image of *The Gate of Calais*, better known as *The Roast Beef of Old England*, which contrasts the strapping English soldier with his huge side of meat with the scrawny, tartan-clad Scotsman seated on the ground and gnawing on an onion.[138]

But why, then, do we observe relatively few traces of the same prejudice in the Leewards, where small white societies might logically have felt quite threatened by the presence of so many Scotsmen in an era of considerable popular anxiety over the possibility of Jacobite revolts? The fact is that the cultural baggage that Scots brought with them to the Leewards, though considered by some to mark them as grasping and coarse, served two functions in smoothing their path in the islands: Not only did their alleged ambitiousness and frugality benefit them directly, but these same qualities, which emerged as the stereotypical hallmarks of Scottishness, made them attractive as employees and trusted associates among the established planters. Scotsmen might be parvenus, but Leeward society generally lacked the pretensions to aristocracy that characterized eighteenth-century Barbados or Virginia, and the fact that a man had recently acquired his wealth did not mark him as socially undesirable. If a "Monmouth Man" such as Azariah Pinney could rise to the top of the heap, how much more acceptable might a literate, hard-working, ambitious Scotsman be to local society, particularly if he possessed the legal or medical training so needed in the Leewards but rarely found there?[139] Scots were also far less provocative to English religious sensibilities than were the Catholic Irish; although the Presbyterian Church made significant inroads in the Leewards in the period following Emancipation, for the great majority of the Scots of the earlier period "the practice of religion was relatively unimportant," and "proclaiming Presbyterianism as an alternative to Anglicanism was not an issue."[140] Janet Schaw, a staunch proponent of the Kirk of Scotland, expressed her disappointment that in the course of her stay on Antigua she could worship only

[138] Karras, *Sojourners*, 15–18.
[139] By the mid-eighteenth century, Edinburgh had established an international reputation for medical education. The universities of Glasgow, St. Andrews, and Aberdeen also boasted medical schools, and the Royal College of Physicians in Edinburgh and Glasgow and the Royal College of Surgeons in Edinburgh also issued diplomates and licentiates in medicine, of the sort Walter Tullideph received. See Richard B. Sheridan, *Doctors and Slaves: A Medical and Demographic History of Slavery in the British West Indies, 1680–1834* (Cambridge: Cambridge University Press, 1985), 56–7.
[140] Hamilton, *Scotland*, 49.

in a church "which performs the English service. ... You know I am no bigoted Presbyterian, and as the tenets are the same, I was resolved to conform to the ceremonies, but am sorry to find in myself the force of habit too strong, I fear, to be removed." Yet she was quick to praise the building and its congregation, writing that "tho' the outside is a plain building, its inside is magnificent. It has a very fine organ, a spacious altar, and every thing necessary to a church which performs the English Service. The church was very full, the Audience most devout. I looked at them with pleasure."[141]

Not only were the majority of Scots willing to conform, albeit sometimes grudgingly, to Anglican practice, but they were in some cases even less tolerant of the alleged menace of the Church of Rome than English Protestants were. As Douglas Hamilton has noted, "The commitment to British views of the Crown, liberty, and Protestantism demonstrates the perception among West India Scots of their part in a Greater Britain," a part they appeared eager to play.[142] Although few Scots in the Leewards could match the dramatic success of Walter Tullideph, the minister's son who returned to Scotland so wealthy that he was able to purchase a great estate and marry his daughters into the aristocracy, few experienced the persistent poverty, and therefore gained the reputation for turbulence, criminality, and treachery, that many people associated with Irishness and that Montserratians in particular, including many who were themselves of Irish birth or descent, projected onto those who appeared to constitute a threat to the social order.

At least as important, Scots migrants to the Leewards, like those elsewhere in the West Indies and in North America, were a relatively homogeneous group. Whereas the ranks of the Montserrat Irish included "Catholics (native Irish, and Old English) and Protestants (mostly New English, and a few Ulster-Scots)," the Scots who emigrated to the Leewards were overwhelmingly Lowland Presbyterians, often urban and generally well educated.[143] It is a hoary cliché, and was so even two centuries ago, that Scots are noteworthy for their "clannishness," but like many clichés, it is rooted in truth. As Douglas Hamilton and Alan Karras have described in detail, Scots migrants, whether in Antigua or Virginia, Jamaica or Philadelphia, spun "webs of patronage" within an individual British American colony, between colonies, and between

---

[141] Schaw, *Journal*, 93.
[142] Hamilton, *Scotland*, 165.
[143] Akenson, *If the Irish Ran the World*, 26.

colony and metropole. In North America, these "webs" were represented by the St. Andrew's Society, named for Scotland's patron saint, which was first organized in 1749 in Philadelphia and which by the outbreak of the American Revolution could be found throughout colonial British America, from Nova Scotia to Savannah.[144] That no such group arose in the West Indies is, according to Hamilton, a symbol of the strength of less formal Scots networks, based both on actual blood kinship and on "the practicalities of geographical proximity and upon more pragmatic alliances of common interest."[145] Although Thomas Thistlewood's disgruntled assertion that, once a Scot gained a position of influence, he would dispense patronage exclusively to men of his own nationality should probably be taken with a grain of salt, the records of the eighteenth-century Leewards, particularly those of Antigua, show the extent to which Scots did look out for one another, whether in commerce, in political office, or in marital alliances. Because of this relative homogeneity, Leeward Scots were able to work together in a way that Irish migrants could or would not.

Finally, the fact that the majority of Irish settlers arrived in the Leewards during the seventeenth century and that most of the Scots came in the eighteenth is in itself quite significant.[146] By the time the Act of Union came into effect, Leeward society had moved beyond the era of white servitude and into that of African slavery, sugar semi-monoculture, and the consolidation of plantation landholdings within a small white elite. The types of white settlers the islands needed were not laborers, artisans, or small farmers, as in the seventeenth century; instead, planters needed attorneys, overseers, and managers, "competent and trustworthy people to man and supervise the operations."[147] They also needed medical men to attend both to themselves and their families and to their slaves, particularly innovative practitioners such as Thomas Fraser, whose experiments with inoculation against smallpox kept slaves healthy without necessitating the purchase of expensive medicines, or "persons of good Learning, strong natural Parts, and untainted Veracity" like Dr. Paten of Nevis, whose medical education at the University of Aberdeen was supplemented by the experience he had gained in the course of several

---

144 Karras, *Sojourners*, 118; Hamilton, *Scotland*, 48.

145 Hamilton, *Scotland*, 26.

146 See Elizabeth Mancke, "Another British America: A Canadian Model for the Early Modern British Empire," *Journal of Imperial and Commonwealth History* 25 (1997), 1–36.

147 Hancock, *Citizens*, 150.

voyages he had made to India as a ship's surgeon.[148] Many opportunities existed for men who possessed some degree of education and who would populate the middling ranks of white society as professionals and clerical workers. Scotland had only too many men such as Walter Tullideph who were willing and able to occupy these positions, and after the Act of Union removed most of the obstacles to Scottish participation in the empire, they flocked to the West Indian colonies. Scots, therefore, generally entered Leeward society at a level above that of Irish who lacked "Tribal" affiliations or who were otherwise able to establish fortunes early in their tenure in the islands. Clearly, some Leeward residents saw the Scots among them as avaricious and crude, but they did not consider them to be like the Irish, a "riotous and unruly lot" given to drunkenness, violence, and rebellion.

As much as the Leeward colonies had changed over the course of the seventeenth century, the empire had changed still more. Throughout most of the seventeenth century, the French were England's principal foe both at home and overseas, but after 1713, with the conclusion of the War of the Spanish Succession and the signing of the Treaty of Utrecht, the French were considerably weakened, particularly in terms of their ability to make war on England's West Indian possessions. The dissipation of the French threat in the Caribbean eased many tensions among Leeward settlers and made them somewhat less anxious about the presence of non-English Britons and potential Francophile Catholic fifth columnists in their communities. Much of the prejudice islanders directed against the Irish, particularly those of the lowest classes, stemmed from a pervasive anxiety that these individuals, many of whom had little stake in upholding the status quo, would join their fellow Catholics in attacking English plantations. By the time that the Act of Union brought a much larger number of Scots into the Leewards, the diminution of the French menace encouraged planters to concentrate on building their fortunes rather than fending off invaders. Under these circumstances, Scottish settlers seemed to be not part of the problem, as many had characterized the Irish, but part of the solution. Even in the wake of the Jacobite uprising of 1745, it was Irish Catholic settlers, not Scots migrants, whom Leeward planters labeled as potential rebels. Robert Poole, visiting Antigua in the spring of 1749, described the "high Festival" he attended "in Remembrance of the Duke [of Cumberland]'s Victory over the Rebels at the Battle of Culloden" as an event celebrated with an "elegant Entertainment" during

---

[148] Hamilton, *Scotland*, 123; Smith, *Natural History*, 19.

which "at every Health [to the royal family], by a signal to the Fort, the Guns were fired." Poole's hosts at this event were the island's governor, councillors, and assemblymen, many of whom were of Scots birth or parentage, and the venue was the Freemasons' lodge, a prime site of Scots sociability.[149] Even as the Antiguan elite celebrated the House of Hanover's deliverance from the forces of an exiled Scottish prince, it incorporated, seemingly without question, Scots migrants whose personal and corporate qualities seemed beyond suspicion. Similarly, while the events of "the Forty-Five" inspired in Samuel Martin considerable anxiety about the trustworthiness of "bigots of the Romish persuasion" among Irish settlers, notwithstanding the presence among them of "many good and faithful subjects," the march of Jacobites toward London in no way dissuaded him from continuing to train young Scots migrants as estate managers and to "prefer [them] at the End of [their] time as is his custom with all good Servants."[150]

CONCLUSION

At the end of the eighteenth century, the Jamaican planter and historian Bryan Edwards offered readers of his *History, Civil and Commercial, of the British Colonies in the West Indies* an arresting image of social relations between white men in the English islands in the Caribbean. According to Edwards:

The poorest White person seems to consider himself nearly on a level with the richest, and, emboldened by this idea, approaches his employer with extended hand, and a freedom, which, in the countries of Europe, is seldom displayed by men in the lower orders of life towards their superiors. It is not difficult to trace the origin of this principle. It arises, without doubt, from the pre-eminence and distinction which are necessarily attached even to the complexion of a White Man, in a country where the complexion, generally speaking, distinguishes freedom from slavery.[151]

At first glance, Edwards's pronouncement may not seem to accord with the picture that has emerged thus far of relations between English, Scots, and Irish colonists in the Leeward Islands. We have seen that the Irish Catholic former servants of St. Patrick's, Montserrat, were viewed as a "riotous and unruly lot" not only by English settlers, but by the more

[149] Poole, *Beneficent Bee*, 327–8.
[150] Martin, *A Plan*, 64; Sheridan, *Sugar and Slavery*, 380.
[151] Edwards, *History*, vol. 2, 403.

prosperous and established planters of Irish descent. The distaste that commentators such as Mrs. Flannigan felt for the Scottish "mushrooms" is unmistakable, as is the ongoing perception on the part of island and metropolitan authorities of the need to carefully enumerate and monitor the activities of those who stood outside the norms of Englishness and Protestantism. But at the same time, it can be argued that many people of Scots and Irish descent were in some instances able to rid themselves of the stigma of their nationality, to stave off prejudice or persecution, and to rise as far as they chose in terms of wealth, ownership of land and slaves, occupation of significant local offices, and intermarriage within the island's elite. Richard Sheridan's study of the formation of the eighteenth-century colonial Antiguan elite, for example, shows that, in the period between the Act of Union and the onset of the American Revolution, only five of the eighteen most prominent Antiguan families were of English origin. These thirteen Scots and Irish families not only were successful in acquiring land and slaves, but also gained cultural capital by being elected or appointed to the Council or Assembly.[152]

Church of England ministers lamented that "two-thirds of the Inhabitants here [at Montserrat] and their Offspring are and have been Irish Papists, and sometimes they have had one, two, three and four Popish priests at one time, when at the same time but myself the only Clergyman of the Church of England."[153] In 1744, the Reverend Mr. Byam complained to the bishop of London that "the increase of Papists in these Islands must give every good Christian and Englishman a sensible concern," as such people "grow very daring and insolent and I am told in Montserrat have Mass as publickly said as in any of the Roman Catholic Countries; they have performed in some private houses in this Island Antigua]."[154] Yet Colonel Hart, governor of the Leewards in the 1720s, informed the Board of Trade that, although Montserrat had "many Inhabitants of the Romish Religion, yet their behaviour is very well towards the Government," contrasting them to the settlers of Nevis, whom he viewed as orthodox in their religion but disorderly in their politics.[155] And despite the evidence presented earlier that hostility against Catholics often moved from rhetorical to physical violence, it is noteworthy that no tradition of Pope's Day arose in Montserrat as it did

---

[152] Sheridan, "Rise of a Colonial Gentry," 345, 356.
[153] Cruikshank to Bishop of London, April 6, 1731, Fulham Papers: Gibson 2/87.
[154] Byam to Bishop of London, June 16, 1744, Fulham Papers, 275.
[155] Hart to Board of Trade, January 20, 1723, C.O. 152/14.

throughout the mainland colonies of British America. In the latter colonies, it emerged as an imperial ritual through which colonists affirmed their opposition to Catholicism, often represented by the figure of Guy Fawkes, and their support of English Protestant values, symbolized by processions and bonfires that centered on ritual combat and the destruction of papal effigies. Popeshead Street in St. John's, Antigua, supposedly recalls the presence of a defaced pontifical figure, but on the whole the situation of the islands' Irish Catholics was marked more by grudging acceptance than by overt hostility.[156] Those Irish who were willing to cast off the external markers of allegiance to Rome might hope to be as successful as the eighteenth-century Scots settlers in gaining access to the lands, slaves, local offices, and wealthy spouses that were the markers of social, political, and economic success in their small societies; those whose poverty rendered them socially and economically marginal and encouraged them to retain their Catholic faith had by the middle decades of the eighteenth century emerged as people who could largely be ignored rather than feared. Lines of nationality and religion were strongly marked, but they were not immutable. As Trevor Burnard has observed, "If there is anything that unified colonial British Americans, it was ... their overwhelming desire to be judged according to British values. Anglicisation, far more than ethnicity, seems to have been a crucial shared value for colonials ... ethnicity must be measured against other social processes like Anglicanisation and metropolitan/periphery tensions that capture more accurately the major preconditions of colonial existence."[157] The following chapter will explore the processes of Anglicanization, along with the experiences of those who were neither Anglican nor Catholic – Jews, Quakers, and Huguenots. It will also examine the ways in which these religious minorities negotiated their place in Leeward society and, like the ethnic minorities analyzed in this chapter, became socially integrated to an extent that might initially seem surprising but was in fact quite consonant with Leeward settlers' desire to judge others and to be judged themselves by the depth to which they and their communities reflected what they considered to be the most fundamental norms, practices, and values of Englishness.

---

[156] McConville, *The King's Three Faces*, 56–63; Benjamin J. Kaplan, "Fictions of Privacy: House Chapels and the Spatial Accommodation of Religious Dissent in Early Modern Europe," *American Historical Review* 107 (2002), 1057–9.

[157] Burnard, "Ethnicity in Colonial American Historiography: A New Organising Principle?" *Australasian Journal of American Studies* 10 (1992), 10, 11.

3

Managing Religious Diversity

INTRODUCTION

Throughout the period under study, metropolitan observers were on the whole highly critical of the state of the Church of England in Britain's American colonies, particularly in relation to the plantation-based settlements of the mainland south and of the islands. The clergyman-philosopher George Berkeley spoke for many of his fellow church members when he wrote in 1725 that "there is at this day, but little sense of religion, and a most notorious corruption of manners, in the English colonies settled on the continent of America, and the islands." To Bishop Berkeley, this unhappy state of affairs could best be remedied by sending more and better qualified clergy "to reform morals, and soften the behaviour of men," as in his view the Anglican churches throughout the colonies were nothing more than "a drain for the very dregs and refuse" of British clergy. To Charles Leslie, whose account of his experiences in Jamaica was published in 1740, the fault lay at least as much with the men who constituted the island's elite; although there were "indeed here several Gentlemen that are well acquainted with Learning ... these are few; and the Generality ... love a Pack of Cards better than the Bible."[1] The physician and evangelical Christian Robert Poole, who traveled throughout the Leewards in the late 1740s, complained repeatedly that the various churches he encountered were "thinly visited and carelessly attended to," which he interpreted as a sign of the settlers' irreligious nature, as corroborated by

---

[1] Quoted in Michal J. Rozbicki, "The Curse of Provincialism: Negative Perceptions of Colonial American Plantation Gentry," *Journal of Social History* 63 (1997), 732, 733.

the fact that "many of those who call themselves Christians, [were] keeping open Shop, with their Goods publickly exposed to Sale" on Sunday, and that even those who attended services "by their Behaviour, seem'd pretty great Strangers to the Duty of worshipping God with Decency and Reverence."[2]

Such criticisms notwithstanding, it would be inaccurate to conclude that most Leeward colonists were either hostile or indifferent to the practice of Anglican religion. These settlers prided themselves on their English heritage and believed that they had done as much as they could to transform these distant tropical islands into, if not "little Englands," than at least colonial outposts that upheld recognizably English ideals and practices in matters of church and state. Moreover, even those individuals who were themselves apathetic in spiritual matters, or who might have begrudged payment of the taxes necessary to erect and maintain churches or pay clergy, would have identified the Anglican Church as a principal source of English national identity. They would also have seen at least tacit conformity with the Church as a line that definitively separated the trueborn Englishman from a variety of feared or despised "others" – from the Spanish, England's original enemy in the settlement of the Americas, and the French, their principal opponent from the mid–seventeenth century until the end of the Napoleonic Wars; from the Irish at home and abroad; from commercially useful but culturally alien groups such as the Jews; from the Protestant sects – Quakers, Congregationalists, Muggletonians, and others – who symbolized the extremism of the Cromwellian era; from Indians; and from slaves. Even the least enthusiastic communicants of the Church of England were aware that their religion was something that differentiated them from those they saw as their natural enemies or inferiors, that it afforded them a privileged legal and political status in colony and metropole, one that allowed them to acquire property, wield authority, and play a part in the governance of the community. Although the governors of the Leewards might be willing to overlook their subjects' apathy toward the Church or, as we have seen in the preceding chapter, to grant certain rights and privileges to wealthy settlers who were probably covert Catholics, as long as they outwardly conformed to Anglicanism, they were also keen to prove to metropolitan authorities that "God Almighty [was] devoutly and duly served

---

[2] Poole, *The Beneficent Bee: or, Traveller's Companion* (London: E. Duncomb, 1753), 353, 330, 315.

throughout [their] Government."[3] In so doing, it was crucial that they monitor carefully the behavior of religious minorities in the Leewards and that they find ways either to keep such minorities on the margins of the social order or to find methods by which to incorporate them within a society whose identity was rooted in allegiance to the Church of England.

Of course, these concerns were not unique to the Leeward Islands. No British American colony, even in New England, was without its complement of inhabitants whose faith diverged from the established Church, or of nominally Anglican settlers who displayed scant interest in attending services or subsidizing the building of churches or the salaries of ministers. Indeed, many of the mainland colonies endured considerably greater doctrinal tension in the era of the Great Awakening than was experienced within the Leewards. However, understanding the ways in which the Leeward Church, faced both with a considerable amount of religious heterodoxy and with a perhaps understandable reluctance on the part of many residents to devote much money or effort to sustaining the Church, succeeded in upholding a reasonable degree of spiritual authority offers important insights not only into the religious strategies of Leeward society, but into broader patterns of confessional allegiance throughout the British Atlantic world.

THE CHURCH OF ENGLAND IN THE LEEWARD ISLANDS

Numerous challenges presented themselves to those who hoped to create in the Leewards a fully functioning Church of England. The first order of business was the creation of parishes; as the Stapleton census of 1678 shows, fifty years after the origin of English settlement in the islands the military unit of the division had yet to be replaced throughout all four islands with the ecclesiastical one of the parish. St. Kitts had made this transition by 1655, and two parishes had been created in Montserrat and four in Nevis by 1676, while Antigua retained its divisions until 1681.[4] But the creation of parishes was the beginning, not the end, of the process of creating a religious infrastructure in the Leewards; once an island had been placed under the Church's aegis through the establishment of

---

[3] "Instructions for our Trusty and Welbeloved Daniel Parke Esqr," June 18, 1705, Shelburne Papers, William L. Clements Library, University of Michigan, Ann Arbor.
[4] Donald B. Cooper, *The Establishment of the Anglican Church in the Leeward Islands* (Stillwater: University of Oklahoma Press, 1966), 15.

these units of religious authority, it was necessary that each parish be provided, by the combined efforts of colony and metropole, with churches and clergymen. As we shall see, neither buildings nor ministers were easily acquired or maintained.

Some of the first Anglican churches in the Leewards appeared before parishes were established, as was true of the church of St. Thomas Lowland, St. Kitts, erected in 1640.[5] The French raids of 1666–7 saw the destruction of three English Kittitian churches and both of those that had been erected on Montserrat. When Stapleton assumed the governorship in 1672, he informed the Board of Trade that there were four Anglican churches in Nevis and two each in Antigua, Montserrat (they had been rebuilt after 1667 but were destroyed again in an earthquake that struck the island on Christmas Day, 1672), and St. Kitts, perhaps reflecting the spurt of activity referred to by his predecessor, Charles Wheeler, who had noted in the preceding year that "the islands have made liberal provisions for the maintenance of clergy, and are everywhere erecting churches and chapels."[6] Wheeler reported himself appalled by the fact that the "near 10,000 Christian Subjects" of the Leewards relied for their spiritual well-being on "but two in Holy Orders, both scandalous livers, and one a notable schismate." He petitioned Charles II to "command Dr Turner, master of St John's College, Cambridge, to be consecrated Bishop of Nevis and the other Leeward Islands, to settle the government of the Church and answer the most earnest cries of the people," hoping the new bishop would found a college there that would train local men as clergy and would have the authority to ordain its graduates rather than send them to England for such service. But the king made no such provision, and when Stapleton made his report in 1673, he claimed that, although Nevis had "some few Ministers," there were no others anywhere in the Leewards.[7]

These complaints would be heard again and again over the next hundred years. Governors bemoaned the lack of clergy and the perceived

---

[5] George F. Tyson, Jr., and Carolyn Tyson, *An Inventory of the Historical Landmarks of St. Kitts–Nevis*, rev. ed. (St. Thomas, Virgin Islands: Island Resources Foundation, 1974), 11; Arthur Charles Dayfoot, *The Shaping of the West Indian Church, 1492–1962* (Gainesville: University Press of Florida, 1999), 94.

[6] Cooper, *Establishment*, 20, 21; Egerton Mss. 2395, British Library, London, 528; petition of Wheeler to Charles II, July 20, 1671, in W. Noel Sainsbury et al., eds., *Calendar of State Papers: Colonial Series* [hereafter C.S.P. Col.], *1669–1674* (London: HMSO, 1889), 109.

[7] Egerton Mss. 2395, British Library, London, 528; petition of Wheeler to Charles II, July 20, 1671, in *C.S.P. Col.*, *1669–1674*, 243; Cooper, *Establishment*, 94.

shortcomings of those who appeared, and ministers were infuriated by the lack of churches, or their smallness and dilapidation, and the paucity of attendees at services. Meanwhile, individual islanders often resented, and resisted, paying taxes for the support of the Church. This was not always the case; in the last quarter of the seventeenth century, visitors to the Leewards remarked on both the quality and the quantity of the religious buildings therein. By the mid-1680s, Montserrat apparently had rebuilt at least one of its churches, which the cartographer Richard Blome described as "very fair ... of a delightful Structure ... the Pulpit, Seats, and all the rest of the Carpenters and Joyners Work, being framed of the most precious and sweet-scented Wood," while in St. Kitts "the English have erected five fair Churches, well furnished with Pulpits, and Seats of excellent Joyners work of precious Wood." By the early 1690s, Nevis boasted three churches, and even Antigua, still the least settled of the four islands, had erected a small, rectangular, steeple-less building on the site of what would become the Cathedral of St. John's, a building that was most likely the storehouse of the hundred pounds' worth of books the Anglican minister Thomas Bray had sent to support the endeavors of the Church's ministers in that island.[8] But this rapid development of the ecclesiastical landscape was undercut by the effects of ongoing warfare between the Leeward settlers and their French neighbors, particularly in the course of Queen Anne's War. In 1712, the church of St. Thomas Lowland, Nevis, the oldest in the Leewards, was burned by the French; that of St. Anthony on Montserrat "was much defaced by the Enemy, the few Books ... Stolen and Lost and the ministers Robb'd of all they were masters of," to such a degree that David Bethun, the rector, begged the bishop of London in 1715 to send him some books, ornaments, Bibles, and prayer books to replace those the French had destroyed.[9] In 1720, the Anglicans of Basseterre, in the formerly French part of St. Kitts, had no place for worship but "a small hired room belonging to a private house not sufficient to contain but a third part of the audience and so extremely hot by reason of its narrowness and lowness of the roof that

---

[8] Blome, *The Present State of His Majesties Isles and Territories in America* (London: T. Milbourn, 1686), 134, 47; Robert Morden, *Geography Rectified* (London: Robert Morden and Thomas Cockerill, 1693), 573; A Layman, *Antigua: The Story of the Cathedral and Parish Church of St. John, 1678–1932* (Privately printed, 1933), 10; Gregory Frohnsdorff, "'Before the Public': Some Early Libraries of Antigua," *Libraries & Culture* 38 (2003), 3.

[9] Governor Walter Douglas to Mr Hoare, April 5, 1714, SPGL C/WIN/ANT1L, Rhodes House Library, Oxford; Bethun to Bishop, Fulham Papers, General Correspondence: Section B-WI, vol. 19, Leeward 1, 1681–1749, Lambeth Palace Library, London.

several persons every Sunday are ready to faint away and be carried out whereby you may easily guess how stifling the heat is upon him that performs Divine Service," in this instance the Reverend John Anderson. Anderson found particularly galling the contrast between this stifling room and the nearby ruins of the French church, which he claimed had been "one of the fairest and best in all the West Indies, and it appears to have been so from the walls and ruins yet remaining"; unfortunately for his congregation, this church had been burned in the course of the English conquest of French territory in 1712 and "in all appearance will never be rebuilt without a contribution from England," an award that was not forthcoming.[10]

Even in times of peace, Leeward colonists were often reluctant to tax themselves in order to build new churches or repair existing ones. In 1720, for example, Antiguans expressed a deep unwillingness to pay for the erection of a church in the parish of St. Philip, as "there was already a Church and a Chappel of Ease, both in very good repair," and "it was unreasonable to build a new church for the convenience of eight or ten people, who were the only men that contended for building the same, when the majority of the inhabitants were against it."[11] Those who supported the construction of the new church claimed that, as much of the parish's population had moved inland, the old church by the sea at Willoughby Bay was no longer conveniently located, but their opponents won the day, retaining the seaside church and promising to improve the chapel of ease for the use of those residing on the far side of the parish. A few years later, when the new parish of St. George was separated from that of St. Peter's, Antigua, the residents of the former elected not to construct a new house of worship, but to use the small chapel at Fitch's Creek as their place of worship.[12]

It would be easy to interpret this unwillingness to devote public funds to the building and rebuilding of churches as an indication of the low value Leeward colonists placed on religious observance. But as we have seen, between 1666 and 1713 the Leewards were raided and ruined on numerous occasions by French attack, and were at all times subject to hurricanes, earthquakes, and other natural disasters, in the course of

---

[10] C.O. 241/2, July 15, 1720.

[11] *Journal of the Commissioners for Trade and Plantations, from January 1722–3 to December 1728* (London: HMSO, 1928), 20.

[12] Vere Langford Oliver, *The History of the Island of Antigua* (London: Mitchell and Hughes, 1894), vol. 1, xcvi.

which the built environment was repeatedly devastated. To many settlers, it made little sense to devote a large share of local tax revenues to the erection or repair of elaborate church buildings if they were likely to be destroyed within a few years; low wooden structures were far more likely to survive hurricanes and earthquakes than were taller ones built of stone. Unlike, for example, colonial Virginians, Leeward planters did not conceive of "the house of God [as] the residence of the greatest gentleman in the neighbourhood"; as Robert Poole noted, they seemed no more or less willing to attend service in a small church "almost destroyed by Time and Negligence" than in one that boasted "a very neat Altar-Piece" and "ornamental Gilding and Painting."[13] Moreover, individual residents often made generous gifts to their parish churches. St. Thomas Lowland, the Leewards' first church, was the beneficiary in 1679 of the will of Sir Francis Morton, president of the island's Council and colonel of its militia, who left twenty thousand pounds of sugar for the maintenance of the church and the purchase of Communion plate. In 1703 Henry Carpenter of Nevis left the sum of £200 sterling to St. Paul's parish, Charlestown, for the purchase of books on history and divinity "to found a Library ... for the encouragement of Piety and Learning." St. John's Church in Antigua had by the mid–eighteenth century acquired a fairly impressive set of Communion silver, as well as the life-sized lead figures of Saints John the Baptist and the Divine, apparently a prize seized from a French ship from Martinique at the beginning of the Seven Years' War.[14] The Reverend William Smith, who served as rector of St. John's, Nevis, in the 1730s, pronounced himself delighted by the "Good-nature and Generosity" of his parishioners, who "offered me what present Money I had occasion for, and farther assure me, that they would give me Thirty pounds per Annum above the Salary due by Law; which promise they most honourably kept to the last hour of my stay," while in Montserrat, public accounts record the Council's provision of bread and wine for all the island's Anglican churches during the Christmas season.[15]

---

[13] Dell Upton, *Holy Things and Profane: Anglican Parish Churches in Colonial Virginia* (New Haven: Yale University Press, 1986), 164; Poole, *Beneficent Bee*, 363, 30.

[14] William Smith, *A Natural History of Nevis, and the rest of the English Leeward Charibee Islands in America* (Cambridge: J. Bentham, 1745), 213–14; Vere Langford Oliver, *The Monumental Inscriptions of the British West Indies* (Dorchester: Friary Press, 1927), 108; Oliver, *Caribbeana* (London: Mitchell, Hughes, and Clarke, 1909–19), vol. 4, 289; A Layman, *Cathedral*, 28, 31.

[15] Smith, *Natural History*, 212; Public Accounts of Montserrat, 1719, C.O. 152/13: Leeward Islands, Original Correspondence, 1719–20.

The quantity and quality of clergy remained a vexing issue in the Leewards throughout the period under study. Charles II had commanded the bishop of London to supply ministers to the island colonies, and William III directed the bishop to apply to the Treasury for funds to cover the costs of these clergymen's passages.[16] In 1681, the Church Act passed by the Assembly of Antigua ordered that each of the island's parishes grant "the Sum of Sixteen Thousand Pounds of Sugar or Tobacco, as a constant yearly Salary for the Support and Maintenance of every Minister, to be paid them at the Feast of St. John Baptist," and the rest of the islands followed suit by 1705, when the General Assembly of the four islands approved "An Act to secure the Payment of Ministers Dues."[17] By this act, the governor of the Leewards was designated by the bishop of London as his ordinary, "a sort of lay bishop" who was given the responsibility of appointing individual clergymen to the various island parishes, but in such a situation, a governor who was indifferent to religion or preoccupied with other matters was unlikely to devote much effort to locating appropriate candidates. Moreover, few clergymen were keen to commit to even a relatively short term of service in the Leewards, as many of the reports submitted to the bishop by those who made the voyage described their experiences in highly negative terms. Not only were the individual churches frequently in a serious state of dilapidation, but from a financial standpoint life in the islands could be very difficult. The stipend of sixteen thousand pounds of sugar might have seemed substantial in 1681, but it was not increased for more than a century, and its value was subject to considerable fluctuation. In 1705, the Reverend Francis Le Jau, who had served for five years as Montserrat's only Anglican cleric, reported to the newly founded Society for the Propagation of the Gospel (SPG) that "everything there, particularly cloathing ... [was] three times as dear as in England," that his parishioners had provided him with "a house built with wild canes, thacht, but never finished," and that they had never made good on their promise to pay him an annual supplement of £60 sterling; he claimed that, without the financial assistance provided by Governor Christopher Codrington and a few others, "he must have perished through want."[18] In 1720 John Anderson, formerly a grammar

---

[16] Gerald Fothergill, *A List of Emigrant Ministers to America, 1690–1811* (Baltimore: Genealogical Publishing Company, 1965), 1.

[17] Dayfoot, *Shaping*, 95; C. F. Pascoe, *Two Hundred Years of the S.P.G.: An Historical Account of the Society for the Propagation of the Gospel in Foreign Parts, 1701–1900* (London: Society for the Propagation of the Gospel, 1901), vol. 1, 211.

[18] Quoted in Pascoe, *S.P.G.*, 211.

school teacher in Lambeth, made similar complaints about the financial limitations under which he and other St. Kitts clergy labored, claiming that ministers "have had no other settlement but voluntary contributions ... which is the reason this place has had more ministers ... than I can well remember to reckon up, the incumbent being required to shift for himself by going to some Colony as soon as any considerable arrears became due to him." It was for this reason, Anderson claimed, that the parish of Trinity Palmetto Point "even when it was in a flourishing condition never was able to maintain a minister by itself only, and it is now in a manner desolate the inhabitants coming to live in Basseterre."[19] James Cruikshank, who was Montserrat's only Church of England minister in 1731, informed the bishop that his church had no Bible or Books of Common Prayer other than those that Stapleton had donated more than half a century earlier, and in 1717 Charles Porter, living in Antigua, complained of the difficulties of obtaining his salary, which he attributed to the fact that "the People here have almost to a man a disesteem for our Function."[20] As the Reverend Henry Pope wrote from Nevis to Bishop of London Edmund Gibson in 1723, "Your Lordship may plainly perceive there is little encouragement for clergymen to waste themselves in this scorching climate; for after many years we are but where we were, tied down to a poor stipend which will scarce find us meat, drink, and clothes." He implored Gibson to find him a living in Britain, "resolving rather there to accept of the smallest thing in your Lordship's gift, than to live miserably here."[21]

These difficulties notwithstanding, the quality of the Leeward clergy, in contrast to their quantity, appears to have been relatively high. Francis Le Jau had received a doctoral degree from Trinity College, Dublin, and had been made a canon of St. Paul's Cathedral, a comfortable and prestigious post he chose to leave in favor of ministry in the Leewards and, later, in South Carolina.[22] The clergy of Montserrat included Rees Daly, Lewis Gaillard, and Richard Molineux, all of whom had matriculated at Oxford; in Nevis, William Smith and John Langley were Oxford graduates, Edward Thomas and William Scott held master's degrees,

---

[19] John Anderson to Board of Trade, July 15, 1720, C.O. 241/2: Sessional Papers, St. Kitts and Nevis, 1713–18.

[20] Cruikshank to Bishop, April 6, 1731, Fulham Papers: Gibson 2; Porter to Bishop, September 20, 1717, Fulham Papers, General Correspondence: Section B-WI, vol. 19, Leeward I, 1681–1749, Lambeth Palace Library, London.

[21] Quoted in Cooper, *Establishment*, 10, 28.

[22] Ibid., 20.

and Thomas Powers had been a fellow of Trinity College, Cambridge. In Antigua, four eighteenth-century ministers held master's degrees, and Kittitian clergy included Walter Thomas (MA Oxon.), the Reverend John Merac, who gained a law degree from Cambridge, Thomas Paget, a fellow of King's College at the same university, and James Ramsay, a former naval surgeon who would by the 1770s become a celebrated proponent of abolition and the author of the influential *Essay on the Treatment and Conversion of African Slaves in the West Indian Colonies* (1784).[23] Moreover, at least some of these clergy attained positions of political as well as spiritual authority in the Leewards. Walter Thomas and Andrew Perrot served on the governing council of St. Kitts and Francis Byam on that of Antigua, and Charles Rose was judge advocate of Antigua's vice admiralty court.[24]

The comments of Leeward clergy regarding the progress of the Church in the islands must be interpreted with a degree of skepticism. On the one hand, ministers who regaled the bishop and the SPG with accounts of great success might have hoped to advance their metropolitan careers; on the other, those whose letters were replete with details of their poverty and of the settlers' irreligion may have been attempting to justify their lack of success or to convince sympathetic readers to find them positions in England. Others may have suffered initial disappointment when faced with low attendance at services or popular ignorance of Anglican doctrine, but may have adjusted their expectations. Robert Robertson, who served as minister at St. Paul's, Nevis, from 1707 to 1737, appears to have accepted the prevailing opinion among the island's white population that "[they] thought they did pretty well in keeping the Face of Religion amongst themselves on the Lord's Day," although he was sad to note that, whereas he had at the time of his arrival attracted 150 or more persons to his Sunday services, by 1724 the number had dropped to 60 or 70, which he attributed to "the strange decay" of Nevis in the face of warfare and natural disaster. He wrote wryly that "most people here are fond enough of frequent preaching ... they would have the Minister go to church, but will not do so themselves, and none are louder this way than some that never go to church."[25] William Smith claimed that Leeward

[23] Oliver, *Monumental Inscriptions*; Margaret Deanne Rouse-Jones, "St. Kitts, 1713–1763: A Study of the Development of a Plantation Colony" (Ph.D. diss., Johns Hopkins University, 1977), 160.

[24] Rouse-Jones, "St. Kitts," 171; Cooper, *Establishment*, 27.

[25] Robertson, *A Letter to the Right Reverend the Lord Bishop of London, from an Inhabitant of His Majesty's Leeward-Caribbee Islands* (London: John Wilford, 1730); Oliver, *Caribbeana*, vol. 3, 322.

planters were not innately irreligious, but instead were frustrated by the fact that, rather than choosing their own clergymen, they were reliant on those chosen by the governor or the bishop, most of whom were not "West India Clergymen" but "Great Persons Sons, Relations, and Dependants."[26] Even the generally censorious physician Poole, who so harshly criticized the unimpressive churches and small congregations he encountered in the Leewards, found some reasons for optimism regarding the settlers' commitment to the Church; at Parham, on Antigua's northern coat, "the Congregation was pretty large, considering the Place, and we had a very excellent Discourse, by an old Gentleman." He praised the women he saw at services in Montserrat, noting that, rather than using religious services as a venue in which to show off the latest fashions, a criticism frequently lodged in London and the southern colonies, "they go in a decent Matron-like Manner, regarding Dress but little, after the Manner of true Housewives, whose Minds are occupied in something more noble."[27]

As Donald Cooper has noted, Leeward settlers throughout the period under study were "not anti-religious as such" and "were willing to give lip service to the church so long as it did not oppose them."[28] The Anglican Church of the Leewards developed a "latitudinarian philosophy" in the face of the limited availability of clergy and the general lack of religious fervor among its white residents. Yet it was also a church that "complemented a slave-owning society with its emphasis on hierarchy, authority, and obedience."[29] Until the nineteenth century, it was almost exclusively the church of the islands' white residents. On rare occasions a slave or free person of color, usually female and often of mixed race, might be included: Poole saw a "young Negro Woman receive the holy Sacrament" on Easter Sunday in Antigua, and the minister of St. John's Fig-tree Church, in Nevis, baptized in the summer of 1763 Eve an "Adult Mulatto the property of Frances Brodbelt." But from the beginning of slavery in the English colonies, the perceived clash between making a bondsperson a Christian and holding him or her as chattel encouraged slave owners to aggressively oppose the conversion of their slaves to Anglicanism, and any such attempts by Church of England ministers were met with a heated response. Francis Le Jau, for one, claimed that

---

[26] Smith, *Natural History*, 212.
[27] Poole, *Beneficent Bee*, 327, 361.
[28] Cooper, *Establishment*, 35.
[29] Andrew Jackson O'Shaughnessy, *An Empire Divided: The American Revolution and the British Caribbean* (Philadelphia: University of Pennsylvania Press, 2000), 31.

the real reason masters refused to allow the conversion of their slaves was that they would then be forced "to look upon 'em as Christian brethren and use 'em with humanity."[30] While the Moravians, who arrived in the Leewards in the 1750s, and the Methodists, whose theology was introduced to Antigua in 1760 by a prominent convert, the planter Nathaniel Gilbert, were both keen to include slaves and free people of color in their services, most Leeward clergymen appear to have upheld the color bar, often, like William Smith, sharing their parishioners' anxiety that "a Slave … once Christened, conceits that he ought to be upon a level with his Master, in all other respects." When James Ramsay adopted an abolitionist stance and began to give religious instructions to St. Kitts's slaves, his actions inflamed local opinion to the extent that the Kittitian planters attacked him in print, refused to attend services at his church, and caused him to flee to England for his own safety.[31]

Throughout the seventeenth and eighteenth centuries, the Church of England struggled to find its footing in the Leewards. It was frequently short of cash, of churches, of clergymen, and, perhaps most importantly, of public enthusiasm. Yet Anglicanism in and of itself was an important source of identity at both the individual and the communal level. To be an Anglican was to be part of an Atlantic community centered on a Protestant vision of empire, one that was in the process in this period of eclipsing its "papist" rivals, Spain and France. The Church located colonists and colonies within a "Great Chain of Being" that linked them to God, the monarch, Parliament, and the English people, and endowed them with a set of rights and responsibilities that they believed granted them a degree of political and spiritual liberty unique in early modern Europe and its empires. Within the colonies, it differentiated between white and black, master and slave, as well as between people who could claim the right to full participation in the political realm and those who could not. By examining the various experiences of Jews, Quakers, and Huguenots in the Leewards, we can gain an understanding of the lines of inclusion and exclusion within these island communities and of the ability, and desire, of these minority groups to accommodate themselves to the norms of these communities.

---

[30] Oliver, *Caribbeana*, vol. 4, 23; C. S. S. Higham, "The Early Days of the Church in the West Indies," *Church Quarterly Review* 92 (1921), 127; Pascoe, *S.P.G.*, 211. See also Higham, "The Negro Policy of Christopher Codrington," *Journal of Negro History* 10 (1925), 150–3.
[31] O'Shaughnessy, *Empire*, 31.

"BROTHER ISRAELITES"

Alexander Hamilton is undoubtedly the most famous scion of the island of Nevis and the most prominent West Indian colonist in the history of the early national United States. In actuality, Hamilton's residence in Nevis was brief, limited as it was to the period between his birth in 1755 and his mother's relocation to the Danish island of St. Croix a decade later. Few documentary materials exist relating to his life on the island, but a tantalizing fragment remains in the form of an anecdote regarding his early education. Hamilton's mother, Rachel Faucette Levine of St. Kitts, had run away from her allegedly abusive husband but was unable to obtain his consent to a divorce. Although her subsequent liaison with James Hamilton, a physician and the kinsman of a Nevis family of aristocratic Scots lineage, was of long standing, and although most white Nevisians apparently regarded the relationship as legitimate in a social if not a legal sense, the couple's two children, Alexander and James, Jr., were, in the eyes of the Church of England, bastards.[32] As such, the boys were barred from attendance at Nevis's only school, which operated under the auspices of the Church, so five-year-old Alexander received his earliest formal education at a Jewish school in Charlestown, which appears to have been a sort of dame school run by an elderly Jewish woman. Not only did Alexander master the rudiments of reading and writing at this "Jews' School," but he also apparently learned some Hebrew there, and within a few months of his enrollment had memorized and could recite the Decalogue in that language.[33]

It may seem surprising that an island colony as small in terms of its physical size and white population as Nevis could have been home to a Jewish community large enough to support its own school. However, Jews were a constant presence in the West Indian colonies from the middle of the seventeenth century to the later decades of the eighteenth, a period that saw the beginning and rapid expansion of the sugar industry in these islands. The economic and social development of the Caribbean, particularly in the islands settled by the English and Dutch, was greatly influenced by the diaspora of Jewish settlers from Brazil in the middle

---

[32] On the unconventional Levine–Hamilton ménage see Natalie A. Zacek, "Sexual Transgression and Social Control in the English Leeward Islands, 1670–1763," in Merril D. Smith, ed., *Sex and Sexuality in Colonial America, 1492–1800* (New York: New York University Press, 1998), 190–214.

[33] Samuel M. Wilson, "Caribbean Diaspora," *Natural History* 102 (1993), 55; Forrest McDonald, *Alexander Hamilton: A Biography* (New York: Norton, 1979), 8.

of the seventeenth century. In 1654, Portuguese forces gained control of the Dutch colony of Recife, the center of the sugar industry of northern Brazil. Among the first signs of the new imperial order was the arrival of a group of Jesuits, whose appearance encouraged the settlers to believe that the Portuguese intended to institute the Inquisition among them. Many of these colonists were Jews who had settled in Recife to take advantage of both the economic opportunities and the religious freedom offered by the Dutch administration. Their ancestors had been drawn to the Netherlands after the *reconquista* of 1492 and the subsequent expulsion of non-Christians from Spain, but within a few generations the Jewish community of Amsterdam had become overcrowded with Iberian refugees, as well as by Ashkenazim who had fled poverty and persecution in Poland and Lithuania, and many chose to look for better opportunities in the New World.[34] With the possibility of inquisitorial persecution looming, these Jewish colonists abandoned Brazil and settled elsewhere in the Atlantic world. The Spanish and Portuguese colonies clearly offered no haven to Jewish refugees, and the increasing hostility of Louis XIV's France toward non-Catholics both at home and in its overseas possessions forestalled resettlement anywhere in *la Nouvelle France*.[35] The only places that offered Jews a refuge from religious persecution were the English and Dutch settlements in the Americas, particularly those in the Caribbean, in which the displaced Recifeans' expertise in the cultivation and commerce of sugar would, they hoped, enable them to reestablish their families and fortunes.[36]

Seventeenth-century English attitudes toward Jews, though considerably more accommodating than those of Europe's Catholic powers, were not particularly welcoming. For Englishmen, metropolitan and colonial alike, religious tolerance fell far short of a willing acceptance of alien groups such as Jews. Many Englishmen and -women might have found farfetched William Hughes's assertion, made in a tract published

---

[34] Michelle M. Terrell, *The Jewish Community of Early Colonial Nevis: A Historical Archaeological Study* (Gainesville: University Press of Florida, 2005), 17.

[35] In Article 1 of the *Code Noir* of 1685, Louis XIV instructed French colonial officials "to expel from our islands all the Jews who have settled there; to them, as declared enemies of Christianity, we command to leave within three months from the publication of this edict, on pain of loss of liberty and property" (reprinted in F. R. Augier and S. C. Gordon, *Sources of West Indian History* [London: Longman, 1962], 92).

[36] Richard Dunn asserts that Recifean expertise enabled first Barbados and then the rest of England's West Indian colonies to begin large-scale sugar cultivation; see Dunn, *Sugar and Slaves: The Rise of the Planter Class in the English West Indies, 1624–1713* (Chapel Hill: University of North Carolina Press, 1973), 60–2.

in 1656, that Jews "make it their annual practice to crucifie children" and that they perpetually "conspire against City and people," and they would probably have viewed Shakespeare's Shylock as a less than naturalistic theatrical representation of Jewish masculinity. However, they might have deemed more convincing the warning of another pamphleteer, Thomas Papillon, that Jews, though not necessarily a threat to national security, were so culturally and socially alien that it would be impossible to assimilate them into the mainstream of English society.[37] After a royal decree of 1190 had expelled them, Jews were rarely encountered in England until Oliver Cromwell allowed them to resettle there after 1655. A seventeenth-century Englishman or -woman was more likely to have met a Muslim, or "Moor," than to have had a personal encounter with a Jew, and in this instance unfamiliarity bred, if not contempt, at least suspicion.[38] By the beginning of the early modern era, the figure of "the Jew" had emerged within English culture as a symbol of immutable alterity, a fetish that allowed Gentiles to construct and partake in *communitas* through the deployment of this pejorative image. In his posthumously published *Second Part of the Institutes of the Lawes of England* (1642), the influential jurist Edward Coke described Jews as "wicked and wretched men" who used "cruell" means to enrich themselves and "shewed no mercie" to the trueborn Englishmen to whom they owed "debts of cruelty." Although Coke, who died in 1634, probably never encountered a Jew – the very few who lived in England before 1655 presented themselves publicly as Spanish or Italian Catholics and practiced their faith in secret – he was convinced that Jewish nature was eternal and unchangeable, and that it was not necessary to be personally acquainted with Jews in order to know – and despise – their character.[39]

English distaste for Jews after their readmission is evident from a number of anonymous broadsides of the early eighteenth century, which attempted to defame the Scots by comparing them to Jews. A 1721 verse

---

[37] Frank Felsenstein, *Anti-Semitic Stereotypes: A Paradigm of Otherness in English Popular Culture, 1660–1830* (Baltimore: Johns Hopkins University Press, 1995), 40; Daniel Statt, *Foreigners and Englishmen: The Controversy over Immigration and Population, 1660–1760* (Newark: University of Delaware Press, 1995), 82.

[38] Nabil Matar, *Turks, Moors, and Englishmen in the Age of Discovery* (New York: Columbia University Press, 1999), 3–4.

[39] Holly Snyder, "'Usury, to the English Mind': The Image of the Jewish Merchant in the British Atlantic World" (paper presented to the Ninth Annual Conference of the Omohundro Institute of Early American History and Culture, New Orleans, June 2003), 1–2.

that satirized the "Caledonian Clans" opened by inquiring of the reader, "Was you ne'er, in a Cabbin / Confin'd like a religious *Rabbin?*" and went on to compare the Jewish clergyman to "a Monkey ('Tis all by Way of Simile) / Imprison'd in a Cage)."[40] Still cruder in its satire was an earlier screed against the Scots, which claimed that the Caledonians were "down-right Egyptians by the[ir] Lice" but that their allegedly miserly nature branded them simultaneously as "right Jews in their Hearts."[41] In the popular imagination, Jews and Scots, though represented by the very different physical stereotypes of the swarthy, hunched Semite and the freckled, gangly Caledonian, both served as representatives of the undesirable qualities of miserliness, avarice, and general untrustworthiness, particularly in the context of commerce and finance.

Seventeenth- and eighteenth-century Scots and Jews tended to be both educated and unlanded, attributes that encouraged their participation in the world of trade and speculation as the sorts of "sophisters, economists, and calculators" whom Edmund Burke would later deplore as bringing about the end of "the age of chivalry."[42] Of course, Scots were, in the eyes of most Britons, far less foreign and more assimilable than Jews; both groups might have suffered as subjects of frequent ridicule, but only the latter had their civil rights abridged by law and custom. Popular distaste toward Jews was a constant in seventeenth- and eighteenth-century England, and although this hostility might remain dormant for years, it could easily flare up at moments of public anxiety, as it did in the summer of 1753. When Parliament passed the Jewish Naturalization Bill, which gave foreign-born Jews the right to own land and ships and to engage in commerce with Britain's colonies, its members were surprised by the tremendous popular furor it evoked. Pamphlets and sermons poured forth depicting Jews as "money grubbing, dishonest, cunning interlopers" who were "blasphemous, clannish, and traitorous," and Jewish peddlers were attacked in the streets of London.[43] Fearing a loss of public order, Parliament quickly repealed the bill, accepting with reluctance that the

---

[40] "To ******** *******, Esq.," in Samuel Keimer, ed., *Caribbeana* (Millwood, NY: Kraus Reprint Co., 1978), vol. 2, 54–55, emphasis in original.

[41] *Caledonia; or, The Pedlar turn'd Merchant: A Tragi-Comedy, as it was Acted by His Majesty's Subjects of Scotland, in the King of Spain's Province of Darien* (London: n.p., 1700), 9. In early modern English parlance, "Egyptians" denoted gypsies.

[42] Quoted in Michal J. Rozbicki, *The Complete Colonial Gentleman: Cultural Legitimacy in Plantation America* (Charlottesville: University of Virginia Press, 1998), 124.

[43] Dana Rabin, "The Jew Bill of 1753: Masculinity, Virility, and the Nation," *Eighteenth-Century Studies* 39 (2006), 157, 158.

British public was not yet willing to extend to Jews the rights of liberty and property that were synonymous with the name of Englishmen.

Despite the presence of such powerful undercurrents of anti-Semitism, England was from the time of the Restoration until the latter half of the nineteenth century "probably the freest European country a Jew could find," and its West Indian colonies, lacking the resources and in many instances the desire to establish a strong Church of England presence therein, appeared to be a potential haven to the Recifean exiles.[44] Nonetheless, the governments of several of the English islands imposed substantial disabilities on their Jewish inhabitants. In 1661, only a few years after the onset of the Brazilian Jewish diaspora, a delegation of the merchants of Barbados, at that time the wealthiest colony in English America, petitioned the Lords of Trade and Plantations to bar Jews from participation in island commerce, pleading that "the Jews are a people so subtle in matters of trade ... that in a short time they will not only ingross trade among themselves, but will be able to divert the benefit thereof to other places," presumably by constructing tightly knit networks of their coreligionists throughout the Americas.[45] Although the majority of Jewish migrants to the Caribbean had taken considerable pains to acquire letters patent of denization, which granted them the status of English subjects and thus the right to engage in trade without violating the provisions of the Navigation Acts, they were subject to still stricter controls in Jamaica, where they not only were obligated to pay heavy additional taxes but were excluded from holding public office and from serving in the militia, principal venues of masculine prestige and patronage in island society.[46] In addition to accepting these disabilities, the Jews of Jamaica felt it necessary to propitiate the local authorities from time to time by presenting

---

[44] David Brion Davis, *Slavery and Human Progress* (New York: Oxford University Press, 1984), 100.

[45] Report of the Council for Foreign Plantations to the King [Charles II], July 24, 1661, in *C.S.P. Col., 1661–1668* (London: HMSO, 1880), 49. As Nuala Zahedieh has observed, "The skill with which Jewish merchants managed to comply with English [trade] regulations, and their success at commerce, combined to cause resentment" on the part of non-Jewish English colonists; see Zahedieh, "The Capture of the *Blue Dove*, 1664: Policy, Profits, and Protection in Early English Jamaica," in Roderick A. MacDonald, ed., *West Indies Accounts* (Barbados: University of the West Indies Press, 1996), 45.

[46] Frank Wesley Pitman, *The Development of the British West Indies* (New Haven: Yale University Press, 1917), 27. See also Samuel J. Hurwitz and Edith Hurwitz, "The New World Sets an Example for the Old: The Jews of Jamaica and Political Rights, 1661–1831," *American Jewish Historical Quarterly* 55 (1965), 37–56, and Snyder, "Usury," 14. On the aristocratic and prestigious nature of island militias see Richard Pares, *War and Trade in the West Indies, 1739–1763* (London: Frank Cass, 1963).

them with what Christian islanders called "Jew pies," pastry crusts filled with coins, which they hoped would yield them improved treatment, or at least prevent their situation from worsening.[47]

It was attitudes such as these, in combination with increasing restriction on trade with their friends and kin in the Netherlands and its American and Caribbean colonies, that encouraged Jewish settlers in Barbados and Jamaica, such as the Abudiente, Senior, and Levy Rezio families, to try their luck in the Leeward Islands.[48] But these smaller communities, although they made no serious attempts to block Jewish immigration, were not initially particularly welcoming to Jews; in 1694, the Antiguan House of Assembly approved a bill that attempted to relegate Jewish islanders to a second-class legal and economic status by forbidding them to engage in trade with slave peddlers and by licensing magistrates to try Jews suspected of criminal activities by using "any such evidence as the said Justices shall judge sufficient in their own judgments and consciences."[49] Even in Nevis, home to the largest Jewish population in the Leewards, Jews were the subject of punitive legislation as "evil-minded Persons, intending nothing but their own private Gain, and the Ruin of the Poor," who were known to "ingross and buy whole Cargoes of Provisions at a cheap Rate, and to retale them again at excessive Prices, thereby forestalling the Market." They were also accused of profaning the Christian Sabbath by "trading with Negroes ... on the Lord's Day," participating in the semi-illegal markets that slaves carried out on Sundays, their only days free from labor.[50] These misdeeds appeared to threaten both the stability of the institution of slavery and the security

---

[47] Jacob R. Marcus, *The Colonial American Jew* (Detroit: Wayne State University Press, 1970), vol. 1, 108.

[48] Mordechai Arbell, *The Jewish Nation of the Caribbean: The Spanish–Portuguese Jewish Settlements in the Caribbean and the Guianas* (Jerusalem: Gefen Publishing House, 2002), 214, 217. The Abudientes, Portuguese *marranos* who in the early 1600s emigrated to the Netherlands in order to practice Judaism openly, were described by Lucien Wolf as having "ancient lineage, authority in Jewry, literary eminence, financial power, social rank, [and] a posterity distinguished in politics, the army and the Church." Rowland Abudiente, a London merchant who relied on his West Indian kin for cargoes, was in 1697 "the first Jew to obtain the freedom of the City of London." See Wolf, "The Family of Gideon Abudiente," in Wolf, *Essays on Jewish History* (London: Jewish Historical Society of England, 1934), 171–2.

[49] Quoted in Mindie Lazarus-Black, *Legitimate Acts and Illegal Encounters: Law and Society in Antigua and Barbuda* (Washington, DC: Smithsonian Institution Press, 1994), 25.

[50] *Acts of Assembly, Passed in the Island of Nevis, from 1664, to 1739, inclusive* (London: John Baskett, 1740), 11, 12. As Karen Fog Olwig has noted, Jews in Charlestown, Nevis, "were alleged to deal with slaves who sold them stolen goods and thus to practice unfair

of an import-dependent economy, the very foundations of life in these island colonies, leading some Nevisians to accuse their Jewish neighbors of "taking the Bread out of the Christians' mouths."[51]

Burdened as they were by legal proscriptions and popular prejudices, Jews nonetheless flourished in the English West Indian colonies. The Recifean exiles and their descendants constructed and participated in an extensive network of contacts that connected them with their core-ligionists elsewhere in the Caribbean, in the Dutch colony of Surinam, and in the Netherlands, as well as throughout British North America, particularly in New York and Newport. Their extensive experience in the business of sugar cultivation and their familiarity with the languages and commercial practices of the Dutch, Spanish, and Portuguese empires allowed them to function as conduits of information, finance, and commerce across the imperial boundaries of the Atlantic world.[52] In addition to these valuable skills and networks, Jews also possessed the advantage of their white skins; as the ratio of black slaves to white settlers rose steadily, Jews' very complexion became a badge of their comparative trustworthiness to their fellow islanders. Their enforced cosmopolitanism might be regarded by English authorities as a worrying rootlessness, but at the same time it ensured their loyalty to the English crown and prevented them from falling victim to colonial anxieties regarding ethnicity and nationality.[53] By 1740, the passage of the Naturalization Act by Parliament exempted Jews in the colonies, though not in the metropole, from the need to take the oaths of supremacy and allegiance, and provided for the naturalization of foreigners who had lived in Britain's American colonies for seven years, allowing both English- and foreign-born Jews to attain a greater degree of inclusion within colonial society.[54]

---

trade. Similar accusations were made against Jews throughout the West Indies and seem to have been occasioned by the fact that they controlled a large part of the trade on several islands." See Olwig, *Global Culture, Island Identity: Continuity and Change in the Afro-Caribbean Community of Nevis* (Chur, Switzerland: Harwood Academic Publishers, 1993), 63.

[51] Eli Faber, *A Time for Planting: The First Migration, 1654–1820* (Baltimore: Johns Hopkins University Press, 1992), 97.

[52] Angus Calder, *Revolutionary Empire* (New York: Dutton, 1981), 317.

[53] On the relationship between racism and anti-Semitism, see Pierre Pluchon, *Negres et juifs: Le racisme au siècle des Lumières* (Paris: Tallandier, 1984). See also David Lowenthal, *West Indian Societies* (New York: Oxford University Press, 1972), 195, and Marcus, *Colonial American Jew*, 97.

[54] Holly Snyder, "Rules, Rights and Redemption: The Negotiation of Jewish Status in British Atlantic Port Towns, 1740–1831," *Jewish History* 20 (2006), 147–70.

It is difficult to pinpoint the origins of Jewish settlement on Nevis. A few Jews were resident on the island in 1678, as shown in the Stapleton census, which described a handful of Nevisians as "Jewes": Isaac, Senior, Abraham Rezio, Solomon Israel, Daniel Mendez, and Rachel Mendez and her three children. A few other individuals whom the census enumerated as slave owners were most likely Jews, including John Isaac and his wife, Judeh, who possessed three slaves, and Solomon Hayman or Hyman, who owned seven. Rowland Gideon and Abraham Abudiente are listed among the passengers on the *Phoenix*, which sailed from Barbados to the Leewards in November 1679. From these few scattered individuals, we can observe the origin of what was to become a sizable community. By 1688, the number of Jews resident on Nevis was sufficient to support a synagogue, a building that has long since disappeared but whose grave-yard survives and the tombstones of which provide evidence of the sub-stantial growth of the island's Jewish population in the late seventeenth and early eighteenth centuries.[55]

In 1724, the Reverend Robert Robertson, a Church of England min-ister resident for many years on Nevis, estimated that the island's white population consisted of "about seventy householders with their families, being in all (children included) some three hundred whites of which one-fourth are Jews."[56] Although scholars of Jewish life in the West Indies have accepted uncritically Robertson's estimate, which implies that approximately seventy-five Jews were resident in Nevis by the 1720s, the island census of 1707 lists only six Jewish households, and only that of the Israel family persists from the 1678 census. But as Mordechai Arbell has emphasized, census data rarely yield a complete picture of reality; in this instance, "the census took into account only permanent residents and property owners ... [whereas] the Jewish population fluctuated, shifting between Barbados and Nevis ... [and] the existence of a Jewish ceme-tery ... and perhaps a synagogue ... show that the Jewish population was much larger than that indicated."[57] Ten of the twenty-five families whose names appear on the tombstones of the Nevis burial ground had

[55] Cardozo de Bethencourt, "Notes on Spanish and Portuguese Jews," *Publications of the American Jewish Historical Society* 29 (1925), 37–8. Zvi Loker states that Nevis's first synagogue was established by 1671; see Loker, *Jews in the Caribbean: Evidence on the History of the Jews in the Caribbean Zone in Colonial Times* (Jerusalem: Institute for Research on the Sephardi and Oriental Jewish Heritage, 1991), 352. My thanks to Philip Morgan for referring me to this work.
[56] Quoted in Wilson, "Caribbean Diaspora," 57; Richard Pares, *A West-India Fortune* (London: Longmans, Green, 1950), 24–5.
[57] Arbell, *Jewish Nation*, 219, 220.

Barbadian connections, and Jewish names occur regularly in the lists of Nevisians resettling on the island after fleeing French attacks from 1708 to 1711, which implies that some Jews not listed as resident in the census nonetheless owned land or businesses there.[58] Fragmentary evidence suggests that these aforementioned families had known one another in Barbados and had emigrated to Nevis as a group, connected not only by their religion, but more specifically by mercantile links to the great Hanseatic port of Hamburg.[59]

Although the Jews of Nevis had by the end of the seventeenth century established a number of institutions, including a synagogue, a burial ground, and a school, for their exclusive use, they did not constitute a completely segregated subculture, but participated in the wider white social and commercial life of Nevis.[60] In the absence of significant descriptive sources produced by or about members of this community, it is in legal and commercial documents, primarily wills and inventories, that evidence of the social and business networks of Nevis's Jews can be discerned. The will of Haim Abinum de Lima, for example, depicts this Nevisian Jew as being enmeshed in a network of personal and commercial relationships with Jews and non-Jews alike that crossed colonial and imperial boundaries. De Lima was open in his profession of Judaism, as is indicated by his wish "to be buried after the rites of the people called Jews," by his philanthropic activity in connection with the Mikve Israel synagogue in the Dutch island of Curaçao, and by his bequests of a "Little Sepher for Sr Eustacia Rodes for the Kaal, [and] the great Sepher for my cousin David the son of Ab[raha]m Piza, senior."[61] But his identity as an observant Jew did not forestall the development of close contacts, and even friendship, with Christian islanders. None of the three men who served as witnesses to his will – William Liburd, John Burke, Sr., and

---

[58] On November 10, 1712, those taking oaths to resettle at Nevis included Abraham Bueno de Mesqueta, Sarah Lobatto, Maher Shahel Hashbeth Heath, Isaac Pinheiro, Shakerly and Catherine Israel, Hananiah Arrobas, Raphael Abenduna, Deborah Lobatto, Ephraim Mesqueta, Solomon Israel, and Jacob Senior. See *Journal of the Commissioners for Trade and Plantations, February 1709 to March 1715* (London: HMSO, 1925), 383; Arbell, *Jewish Nation*, 217.

[59] Terrell, *Jewish Community*, 143.

[60] Ongoing archaeological excavations suggest that Nevis's synagogue was constructed in the late 1670s or early 1680s; see "The Official Homepage of the Nevis Synagogue Archaeology Project," http://www.tc.umn.edu/~terreo11/Synagogue.html.

[61] Will and codicil of Haim Abinum de Lima, June 27, 1765, and December 2, 1765, "Abstracts of Nevis Wills in the P[rivy]. C[ouncil]. C[ollections].," in Oliver, *Caribbeana*, vol. 2, 158–9. The term "Sepher" or "Sefer" refers to any of a number of Jewish sacred books, most commonly the Torah.

Adam Brodie – were Jews. This situation might be considered axiomatic; in many instances island law barred Jews, like other nonjurors, from acting as witnesses to any kind of legal transaction. But Liburd, Burke, and Brodie were men of considerable property and prestige in Nevis, and their apparent willingness not merely to witness de Lima's will but also to accept the responsibility of carrying out its provisions and bequests indicates a significant degree of Anglo-Jewish amity. Such a responsibility was not a trivial one, particularly in cases such as that of de Lima, who chose to distribute his property among a large number of heirs in St. Kitts, Barbados, and Curaçao, and whose estate was therefore complicated and time-consuming to administer.[62]

That Haim de Lima's personal contacts were not restricted to the circle of his fellow Jews becomes still clearer from a codicil to his will, which a lawyer drew up while de Lima was visiting London in December 1765. From this document, we learn that de Lima was a merchant or, as he called himself, a "shopkeeper" in Nevis and that the majority of his clients were non-Jews and included members of some of the island's wealthiest and most socially prominent families, the prime market for the luxury items he imported from Europe. De Lima's principal concern in this codicil was that, should he die before returning to Nevis, as he indeed did, his customers would receive the items that he had ordered at their request and for which they had made payment in advance. These items included such ornate and expensive articles as "a gold watch and salt cellars belong[ing] to Mr Chaulenger," a more modest "Pinchbeck watch" belonging to John Springett, "a box with pewter for James Bradlett, esq.," "a pair of stone [i.e., jeweled] earings for Eliz[abe]th Barnes," and "a mahogany case ... 1 silver ladle, knives, etc." for John Scarborough.[63] Both the nature of the goods ordered and the names of de Lima's customers show that his clientele was not restricted to the community of his fellow Jews, but included some of the wealthiest residents of Nevis.[64]

Considerably more elevated than Haim Abinum de Lima in both the economic and social realms was the Pinheiro family. The family's progenitor, the prosperous merchant and rum distiller Isaac Pinheiro, was born in Spain and became a freeman of New York in 1695, but maintained

---

[62] Ibid., 159.

[63] Ibid., 158.

[64] A 1722 inventory of the household goods belonging to the wealthy Pinney family of Nevis listed similar items, including "four silver salts," "one large saucespoon," and "one dozen of ivory hafted knives"; see C.O. 186/1: Minutes of Assembly, Nevis, 1722.

Charlestown, Nevis, as the headquarters of his rapidly expanding mercantile network.[65] Isaac Pinheiro and his family appeared in the 1708 census of Nevis, which listed him as the head of a household containing two white men, four white women, six black men, and three black women.[66] Based on information derived from Isaac's will, which was drawn up the following year, we can identify the white members of his household as his wife, Esther, their daughters, Sarah, Rebekah, and Judith, and their son, Moses.[67]

Nothing in Isaac Pinheiro's life became him like the leaving of it, insofar as documentary evidence relating to his familial connections, commercial relationships, and material possessions has survived. Pinheiro died in 1710 in the course of a visit to New York, to which he may have traveled in order to carry out his responsibilities as commercial agent to Abraham Bueno de Mezqueta, another Jewish resident of Nevis and the patriarch of a wealthy family whose business interests extended throughout colonial British America.[68] Perhaps sensing the approach of death and doubting that he would survive the long voyage back to Nevis, Isaac drew up a new will in New York, the provisions of which reveal

[65] Marcus, *Colonial American Jew*, vol. 1, 99.

[66] Oliver, *Caribbeana*, vol. 1, 173. Ownership of slaves was not uncommon among Jewish settlers in the West Indies; Reverend Robert Robertson of Nevis observed that "many [Jews] ... in the two former islands [St. Kitts and Nevis] are Owners of a Number of Slaves" (Robertson, *Letter*, 102), but on the whole Jews in the English West Indies were far more likely to reside in town than on plantations, and few owned large complements of slaves (Eli Faber, *Jews, Slaves, and the Slave Trade* [New York: New York University Press, 1998], 104).

[67] "Jews of Nevis" (unattributed typescript, Nevis Historical and Conservation Society, Charlestown, Nevis), 7. See also Malcolm H. Stern, *First American Jewish Families: 600 Genealogies, 1654–1977* (Cincinnati: American Jewish Archives, 1978), 250.

[68] "Jews of Nevis," 3. De Mezqueta appears in 1692 as "Mr Abraham Buino Demesquieta," one of nine Barbadian Jews possessed of "houses and plantations on the island"; see Frank Cundall et al., "Documents Relating to the History of the Jews of Jamaica and Barbados in the Time of William III," *Publications of the American Jewish Historical Society* 23 (1915), 29. Isaac Pinheiro's voyage to New York may have been occasioned by the death of Abraham's brother Joseph, whose estate was valued at several thousand pounds and included "plate ... rings, jewels, necklaces ... [and] Five Books of the Law of Moses in parchment with the ornaments of plate belonging thereto." Isaac Pinheiro appears to have purchased this Pentateuch from Joseph's heirs; it appears in the inventory of his estate, valued at the vast sum of £150. See Lee M. Friedman, "Wills of Early Jewish Settlers in New York," *Publications of the American Jewish Historical Society* 23 (1915), 149, and Leo Hershkowitz, "Original Inventories of Early New York Jews," *American Jewish History* 90 (2002), 317. Benjamin, another de Mezqueta brother, or perhaps Abraham and Joseph's father, had died in 1683 and was buried at the Chatham Square Jewish cemetery in Manhattan; see *The Jewish Community in Early New York, 1654–1800* (New York: Fraunces Tavern Museum, 1980), 13.

the extent of both his wealth and his affective relationships. Isaac's wife, Esther, was his principal legatee, inheriting "all the Houses and Land in Charles Towne," but his resources were large enough to allow him to make sizable bequests to his five adult children and to leave annuities to his father Abraham and sister Rachel in Amsterdam and to his sister Sarah Mendes Goma in Curaçao.[69] To serve as "Trustees and Overseers of this my Will," Isaac selected two Nevisians. One was Solomon Israel, a prosperous merchant and a leading figure in the Jewish community; the other was Captain Samuel Clarke, a prominent planter and the commander of the island's militia.[70] The relationship between Pinheiro and Clarke appears to have been an intimate one; not only did the former refer to the latter as "my Loving Friend," but he also bequeathed to him the sum of "Tenn pounds currant Money of this Island … to buy … a Mourning Sute," the custom of wearing mourning clothes being reserved for the family and intimate friends of the decedent.[71] No less eminent a person than New York governor Rip Van Dam, whom Esther Pinheiro named as "my friend," served as one of two "special attorneys" to assist the widow in her role as executor.[72]

After Isaac's death, Esther assumed his place at the head of his commercial network, maintaining and expanding the family's business interests, primarily through the acquisition of a small fleet of merchant vessels that traveled between New York, New England, Britain, and the Leewards, with an occasional stop at Madeira to take on casks of the wine so popular among West Indian planters.[73] Between 1716 and 1718, Esther herself made a series of voyages to the ports of New York and Boston in her twenty-ton sloop, the *Neptune*, exchanging cargoes of sugar, molasses, and other island commodities for New England timber and provisions and European manufactured goods.[74] By 1720, Esther was the owner of

---

[69] Will of Isaac Pinheiro, in Leo Hershkowitz, *Wills of Early New York Jews, 1704–1799* (New York: American Jewish Historical Society, 1967), 21–4; Stern, *American Jewish Families*, 250.

[70] Ibid., 24. Solomon Israel also served as a witness to the wills of the vintner George Richardson and the merchant Azariah Pinney; he is notable for being perhaps the only Jew in the English West Indian colonies to have been permitted to serve as a juror, a responsibility restricted by law and custom to members of the Church of England.

[71] Marcus, *Colonial American Jew*, 99. I thank Patrick H. Butler IV for his information regarding the customs and meanings related to mourning garb.

[72] Friedman, "Wills," 158.

[73] See David Hancock, "Commerce and Conversation in the Eighteenth-Century Atlantic: The Invention of Madeira Wine," *Journal of Interdisciplinary History* 29 (1998), 197–220.

[74] C.O. 187/1 and 187/2, Naval Office Returns, Nevis, 1720–9.

another vessel, the sloop *Samuel*, a twenty-five-ton ship with a crew of five, which made several voyages each year between Boston and Nevis from 1720 to 1722. The *Samuel* ceased to appear in Nevis's Naval Office records after 1722, implying that it had been lost at sea or sold to someone off the island, but by the beginning of 1724 it had been replaced in the Pinheiro fleet by the brigantine *Esther*, a sixty-ton vessel that the eponymous Mrs. Pinheiro owned in partnership with Jonathan Dowse of Charlestown, Massachusetts, where the ship had been built the preceding winter. Initially, the *Esther* appears to have replaced the defunct *Samuel* on the Boston–Nevis route, but by 1728, when Ebenezer Hough, another Bostonian, had replaced Dowse as the ship's co-owner, it began to make far more ambitious transatlantic voyages between Nevis and the ports of London and Cork. Around this time Esther acquired yet another ship, the *Abigail*, a small brig of thirty-five tons, which plied the route between Nevis, London, and Madeira.[75] The Pinheiro shipping concerns were not large or lucrative in comparison with those operated by such great eighteenth-century trading houses as, for example, that of Perry of London.[76] What makes the Pinheiro business notable is the fact that it comprised, in its time, the single largest group of vessels owned by any individual resident of Nevis. Even the wealthy and commercially influential Pinneys of Nevis and Bristol owned during the 1720s only a single ship.[77] As a participant in both local and transatlantic commerce, Esther wielded influence that stretched beyond the spheres of both her family and Nevis's Jewish community. Her entrepreneurial activities assured her a place of importance in the mercantile community in which she lived and further allowed her to integrate her family into Nevisian society and, beyond, into the economic life of New England's shipping industry.

The appearance of Samuel Clarke, who, as a substantial planter and commander of the militia, was a pillar of island society, as coexecutor and principal mourner of "his loving Friend" Isaac, suggests that the Pinheiro family held a position of respect within the larger white planter society of Nevis. This assertion gains further support from the text of William Smith's *Natural History of Nevis*, the only local history of the island to be published during the eighteenth century. In the first of the eleven

---

[75] C.O. 187/1 and 187/2.

[76] In 1719, for example, the Perrys imported tobacco from Virginia to England on fifty vessels in which the firm held shares in various proportions; see Jacob M. Price, *Perry of London: A Family and a Firm on the Seaborne Frontier* (Cambridge, MA: Harvard University Press, 1992), 41–2.

[77] Pares, *Fortune*, 128.

letters to Cambridge don Charles Mason which comprise the volume, Smith described a recreational outing that took place "in the Month of July, 1719," at which time "Mr Moses Pinheiro a Jew and myself, went to angle in Black Rock Pond," a body of water "situate[d] a quarter of a mile or better Northwards from Charles Town our Metropolis or Capital, and about thirty yards distant from the Sea."[78] In this anecdote, we observe a Nevisian who is a Jew engaging in social intercourse with a local resident who was not merely non-Jewish, but a member of the clergy of the Church of England. Smith lived in Nevis from 1719 to 1724, serving as rector of the Anglican parish church of St. John's Fig Tree, outside Charlestown, before returning to England to take up the well-endowed living of St. Mary's, Bedford.[79] As the island's principal clergyman, Smith possessed considerable social capital; his letters to Mr. Mason were replete with references to his active social life among the island's elite, including his friendships with two wealthy dowagers, Mrs. Akers and Lady Stapleton, and with Archibald Hamilton, whose lineage connected him both to the governor of the Leewards and to the Scots laird of Cambuskeith.[80] That Reverend Smith, who mingled in the best society Nevis could afford, would choose not only to count a practicing Jew among his friends but to admit openly to such a friendship shows, as much as the names of Haim de Lima's clientele and executors or as Esther Pinheiro's position in the island's business community, that the Jews of Nevis, despite their consistent endogamy and their sustaining of transcolonial and transatlantic networks of their coreligionists, were not barred from social or economic participation in the life of the white community of Nevis. Rather, they were linked by ties of commerce and friendship to many of the most prominent local Christian families.

"Linked," though, is a relative term, as are "ties" and "connection." The small world that Jews constructed for themselves on Nevis existed largely parallel to, rather than intertwined with, that of Gentile islanders. The examples presented earlier make it clear that Jews held a place in the commercial and social life of the Leeward Islands and that they were

---

[78] Smith, *Natural History*, 10. Moses was the only son of Isaac and Esther Pinheiro.

[79] Elsa V. Goveia, *A Study on the Historiography of the British West Indies* (Washington, D.C.: Howard University Press, 1980), 34.

[80] Smith, *Natural History*, 62, 111, 191; John Chester Miller, *Alexander Hamilton and the Growth of the New Nation* (New York: Harper and Row, 1964). Lady Stapleton was the widow of a baronet and the daughter-in-law of the former Leeward governor William Stapleton, and Mrs. Akers was a member of a prominent and well-connected merchant and planter family of St. Kitts, Nevis, and London.

received with a degree of acceptance and even amity on the part of some local Christians. But what is striking is the extent to which Nevisian Jews lived, by choice or by necessity, in a closed community.[81] The Jews of Nevis were entirely endogamous; they married other members of their community or looked to the Jewish enclaves of the Dutch Antilles, Barbados, or the North American mainland colonies for spouses. Endogamy was desirable from the perspective of religious adherence and cultural persistence, but it prevented Leeward Jews, unlike Scots, Irish, Quakers, or Huguenots, from reaping the many benefits that could be gained through intermarriage, such as the possibility of acquiring land, money, and political influence through participation in the kinship networks of the "great tangled cousinry" that constituted the white elite of Nevis and of colonial British America.[82] It is noteworthy that Solomon Israel, the only Nevisian Jew to sit on a jury, and therefore claim the legal and political rights of an Englishman, had married a Christian, an action that encouraged "his disassociation from the faith … and his ability to move within the upper social, political, and economic classes of Nevis."[83] Moses Pinheiro might have gone fishing with an Anglican clergyman, but when he came to take a wife, he chose a Barbadian Jewish woman named Lunah.[84]

Clearly, endogamy did not prevent Nevisian Jews from attaining wealth; individuals such as Isaac Pinheiro and Abraham Bueno de Mezqueta acquired property and business interests that spanned the Atlantic and were both a cause and an effect of their involvement in their own "tangled cousinry" in Europe, North America, and the West Indies.[85] It did, however, ensure that Jews would remain outside the formal and informal spheres, those of officeholding and of kinship, that presented those who settled in the Leewards with their most promising opportunities to rise in influence and esteem within local white society.

---

[81] Harmannus Hoetink has found a similar pattern in Jewish–Christian relations on the Dutch island of Curaçao; see Hoetink, *The Two Variants in Caribbean Race Relations*, trans. Eva M. Hooykaas (Oxford: Oxford University Press, 1967), 114.

[82] The phrase is that of Bernard Bailyn in "Politics and Social Structure in Virginia," in James M. Smith, ed., *Seventeenth-Century America* (Chapel Hill: University of North Carolina Press, 1959), 111.

[83] Terrell, *Jewish Community*, 147.

[84] Stern, *American Jewish Families*, 250.

[85] For example, the families of Abudiente, Abinum de Lima, Arrobas, Israel, Levy Rezio, Mendes, and Pinheiro, recorded as residents of Nevis in the 1708 census, all had kin buried in the graveyard of the synagogue at Bridgetown, Barbados; see E. M. Shilstone, *Monumental Inscriptions in the Jewish Synagogue at Bridgetown, Barbados, with Historical Notes from 1650* (Barbados: Macmillan, 1988).

Even the wealthiest Jew could not sit on the Governor's Council or in the Assembly, or even serve as a juror, a justice of the peace, or a member of the militia, despite the fact that propertied white men were so few in number on Nevis that the island administration often found it difficult to fill these offices. In times of war, Jews were encouraged to "assist and defend Your Majesty's said Charibbee Islands with the utmost of their Power, Strength, and Ability," but in less fraught moments, the sole civic responsibility entrusted to them was "to behave themselves fairly and honestly amongst us."[86] In this light, even William Smith's jovial mention of his fishing expedition with Moses Pinheiro looks a bit disingenuous; his description of Moses as a Jew brands his companion with the mark of alterity and inclines the reader to see Smith's anecdote as displaying either his broad-mindedness in his selection of companions or the exotic nature of Nevisian society.

Nevisian Jews' prosperity, coupled with their apparent willingness to accept a fairly marginal position, allowed them to overcome the force of the most negative stereotypes and to develop some connections of trade and companionship with local Gentiles, but these connections were limited and provisional in their nature and extent. The cosmopolitan nature of Jewish identity in the Atlantic world allowed Jews to develop networks of kinship that stretched over thousands of miles and across imperial boundaries, benefited their participants in their search for marital and commercial opportunities, and allowed the small number of synagogues in the eighteenth-century Americas to flourish in financial and cultural terms and to function as nodes of support and cultural survival. But Judaism marked a boundary more definite than that of even the most radical and alarming deviations within Protestantism, as is evident from the trajectory of Quaker and Huguenot settlement and social integration in the Leewards. As we shall see, Huguenots and Quakers could, and did, eventually distance themselves from their suspect heritage through intermarriage with Anglicans and at least outward adherence to Anglican practices. Jews, in contrast, neither desired nor were encouraged to marry outside their faith, and the stamp of otherness marked even those who were less than entirely committed to their religion. Alternative Protestant identities were permeable to processes of Anglicization and Anglicanization in a way that could never be true of Jews in the Leeward colonies. Jacob

---

[86] "An Act to repeal a certain Act against the Jews," *The Laws of the Leeward Islands,* in *Acts of Assembly Passed in the Island of St. Christopher; From the Year 1711, to 1769* (St. Christopher: Daniel Thibou, 1769), 11.

Marcus, the pioneering historian of Judaism in the Americas, claimed that "the typical colonial Jew was true to his heritage because he was not pressed to be untrue to it," but nor was he in any way encouraged to connect himself to a more general sense of Englishness.[87]

The apparently rapid dissolution of the Jewish community of Nevis reflects the tenuous nature of the relationship between the Jewish population and the wider local community. As the sugar trade began to decline in the final decades of the eighteenth century, as the onset of the American Revolution disrupted British Atlantic patterns of shipping and commerce, and as a series of hurricanes devastated the eastern Caribbean, Jewish islanders, at least some of whom had family connections in Nevis that stretched back over a century, quickly abandoned the colony in favor of other Anglo-American settlements.[88] By 1772, there were no longer enough Jews on Nevis to support an actively functioning synagogue. In her recent study of the Nevis synagogue site, historical archaeologist Michelle Terrell hypothesizes that the Torahs, or "Sefers," mentioned in Haim Abinum de Lima's will of 1765 were those that had previously been housed in the Nevis synagogue and that their dispersal symbolized the congregation's disappearance.[89]

"THE PEOPLE CALLED QUAKERS"

The pattern of Quaker settlement and persistence in the Leewards is strikingly different from that of the Jews. Throughout the seventeenth century, Leeward officialdom viewed Quakers with considerable fear and distaste, considering them inherently destabilizing elements in settlements that already labored to cope with numerous challenges to the social order. Persecution waxed and waned according to the inclination of individual officials, but any administrator or clergyman who chose to attack the Friends could draw on a reservoir of general mistrust and hostility toward these dissenters among the local public.[90] By the beginning of the eighteenth century, though, Quakerism had shed much of its negative baggage, and as Friends grew richer and more respectable, they also became more circumspect in the practice of their faith, two tendencies that erased public awareness of and antipathy to Quakerism, much in the

[87] Marcus, "The American Colonial Jew: A Study in Acculturation" (B. G. Rudolph Lecture in Judaic Studies, Syracuse University, 1968), 19.
[88] Arbell, *Jewish Nation*, 221.
[89] Terrell, *Jewish Community*, 129.
[90] A Layman, *Antigua*, 8.

way that the acquisition of wealth and land had effaced the Catholicism of some of the Irish inhabitants of Montserrat.

Throughout the Interregnum, the staunchly royalist Leeward settlers were alarmed and affronted by the presence of Quakers in their midst. In 1655, Nevis governor Peter Lake informed the Lords of Trade that the island was experiencing difficulties in relation to an aggressive faction of "Annebaptests."[91] Far more troubling to island authorities was the advent, under the Protectorate and throughout the early years of the Restoration, of a small but steady stream of Quaker visitors to the Leewards. The first Friends to arrive were Peter Head, John Rouse, and Mary Fisher, who came to Nevis in 1656 as the guests of a local planter, Humphrey Highwood (or Heywood).[92] The local authorities, angered that Highwood had neglected his legal obligation to apprise them of the arrival of strangers, committed the planter to jail, at which time Highwood announced that he, like his guests, was a Quaker and that he therefore refused either to bear arms or to serve in the militia, both of which were mandatory duties for all able-bodied adult white male settlers. Highwood's intransigence earned him a lengthy sojourn in the Charlestown jail and served as a goad to the Nevis Assembly to pass immediately an act empowering the island's marshal to examine all new arrivals and to deport instantly any they believed to be Quakers. Among those banished under this law was Justinian Hollyman, soon to be a founder of the Quaker community in Antigua.[93]

In the early 1660s, four Quaker families, those of Hollyman, Samuel Winthrop, Jonas Langford, and William Hill, settled in Antigua. These four families served as the basis of the only Quaker community of any substance to develop in the Leewards, and they took advantage of the

[91] Babette M. Levy, *Early Puritanism in the Southern and Island Colonies* (Worcester, MA: American Antiquarian Society, 1960), 287. The Anabaptists, also known as the Familists, were one of many radical Protestant sects that sprang up in the era of the English Civil War. Anabaptists were proponents of adult baptism and viewed the Church of England as a voluntary congregation rather than a national church; they refused to tithe to the Church or to swear oaths, and the more radical among them preached in favor of the abolition of private property. As a general term, "Anabaptist" denoted opposition to the existing social and political order. See Christopher Hill, *The World Turned Upside Down: Radical Ideas During the English Revolution* (New York: Viking Press, 1972).

[92] Fisher, with her companion, Hester Biddle, went on to visit St. John's, Newfoundland, in 1659, where the women "managed to convert several shipmasters"; see Peter E. Pope, *Fish into Wine: The Newfoundland Plantation in the Seventeenth Century* (Chapel Hill: University of North Carolina Press, 2004), 294.

[93] Harriet Frorer Durham, *Caribbean Quakers* (Hollywood, FL: Dukane Press, 1972), 35.

fact that the island, the largest of the Leewards in physical terms, was significantly underpopulated and thus unlikely to turn away potential white settlers simply because they were Friends, particularly while Christopher Keynell, Oliver Cromwell's handpicked representative, remained in power as the island's governor; indeed, according to Langford, Keynell "treated him kindly and gave him Liberty to Live where he saw Meet."[94] Langford, the first Friend to settle in Antigua, was a merchant and planter who, at the time of his death in extreme old age in 1712, had long held the privilege of styling himself "esquire" and was the owner of the Popeshead and Cassada Garden plantations, which numbered among the island's greatest estates.[95]

Winthrop, a merchant and commercial agent and the son of John Winthrop, the founder of the Massachusetts Bay Colony, soon attained a position of prominence in the island; between 1664 and 1671, he was a member of the Council, and for two of those years he served as its president and frequently used his house, Groton Hall, as the venue for the group's meetings.[96] Between 1668 and 1671, Winthrop also held the office of lieutenant governor of Antigua, and many Antiguans believed that he might be selected as their next royal governor.[97] However, for Winthrop and his fellow Friends on Antigua, the numerous metropolitan and colonial disturbances Britain experienced in the late 1660s and early 1670s, particularly the disastrous war with the French and Dutch in the Caribbean, created a climate of hostility and suspicion in which any non-Anglican settler became a potential enemy.

Winthrop had never attempted to hide his Quakerism and had made his house a center not only for local government, but also for proselytizing. During the 1671 visit to Antigua of the "Quaker Apostle," William Edmundson, Winthrop's house became the missionary's base of operations, at which he held "great meetings, [where] many were convinced and turned to the Lord; several justices of the peace, officers and chief men came to meetings, and confessed to the Truth, which we declared

---

[94] Joseph Besse, *The Sufferings of the People Called Quakers* (London: L. Hinde, 1753), vol. 2, 370; Langford, *A Brief Account of the Sufferings of the Servants of the Lord called Quakers, from their first Arrival in the island of Antegoa, under the several Governours; from the Year 1660, to 1695* (London: T. Sowle, 1706), 5.

[95] A Layman, *Antigua*, 8. Cassada Garden passed through Langford's daughter Mehitabel into the Redwood family, prominent Rhode Island Quakers who in 1747 founded Newport's Redwood Library.

[96] Larry D. Gragg, "A Puritan in the West Indies: The Career of Samuel Winthrop," *William and Mary Quarterly* s3:50 (1993), 775.

[97] Ibid., 775.

in the power of God."[98] In the wake of this triumph, Edmundson and Winthrop sailed to Barbuda, "where we made a little Stay, and had some Service for Truth," and to Nevis, where they hoped to find similar enthusiasm, but although "several honest tender Friends" among the Nevisians welcomed them, they also attracted the attention of Leeward's governor, Sir Charles Wheeler, an ardent royalist and former commander in Charles I's army.[99] Horrified by the arrival of the Friends, Wheeler dispatched the Nevis militia to the harbor "with strict command, that none of us [the Quakers] should go ashore, or any come from shore to speak with us, upon penalty of a great fine." Wheeler then forced the ship's captain to pay a deposit in the amount of £1,000 that he would immediately return these unwelcome visitors to Antigua. As Edmundson noted in his journal, when the Friends returned to Antigua, they were "received with gladness, and had great service, many of all sorts flocked to meetings, and generally confessed to the Truth."[100] However, once Wheeler became aware of their success, he began to make inquiries about the situation in Antigua, and when he "found a Quaker President of the Council," a man who "refused the oaths of allegiance & supremacy," he removed Winthrop from office and commissioned Colonel Philip Warner as governor in his stead.[101]

Wheeler's hostility toward Quakers was due in part to his ardent royalism, but it stemmed at least as much from concerns over local security as it did from differences in political ideology and religious doctrine. The principal menace the Society of Friends presented in the Leewards, and throughout colonial British America, was not that Quaker beliefs were heretical or sinful, although many settlers and administrators believed they were both, but that Quaker pacifism, both in theology and in practice, encouraged its adherents to refuse to "watch and ward" against internal or external threats, to bear "Carnal Weapons," or to "learn War and Fighting" and engage in any kind of military activity, even that undertaken in self-defense.[102] A principal tenet of Quakerism was to

98 William Edmundson, *The Journal [Abridged] of William Edmundson: Quaker Apostle to Ireland and the Americas, 1627–1712*, ed. Caroline N. Jacob (Philadelphia: Religious Society of Friends, 1968), 44; *A Journal of the Life, Travels, Sufferings, and Labour of Love in the Work of the Ministry, of that Worthy Elder, and Faithful Servant of Jesus Christ, William Edmundson* (London: J. Sowle, 1715), 53.

99 Gragg, "Puritan," 782; Edmundson, *Journal*, 54.

100 Edmundson, *Journal*, 45–6.

101 "Sir Charles Wheler's Account of the Present State of the Leeward Islands," December 14, 1671, in Oliver, *History of Antigua*, vol. 1, xlviii.

102 Vincent K. Hubbard, *Swords, Ships, and Sugar: A History of Nevis to 1900* (Placentia, CA: Premiere Editions, 1991), 17; Langford, *Brief Account*, 4. For example, in 1673 four

"disapprove of War, as inconsistent with the Nature and Perfection of the Gospel," but for a colony such as Antigua or Nevis, both of which possessed a very small number of able-bodied adult white males and lived in perpetual fear of attacks by rival European powers and of slave uprisings, a man's failure to carry out his military duties, even in the name of religious conviction, was intolerable.[103] When Edmundson and a party of Friends attempted to hold a meeting on Montserrat, they were met by "an Officer and Soldiers ... with strict Charge, that none of them should go on shore, nor any come from shore to speak with them, on Penalty of a great Fine.... we hear that since your Coming to the Caribbee-Islands, there are seven Hundred of our Militia turned Quakers and the Quakers will not fight, and we have Need of Men to fight, being surrounded with Enemies."[104] Because many island residents resented militia duty as a time-consuming and tedious chore, and often took advantage of any opportunity to avoid fulfilling these unwanted responsibilities, officials feared that the presence of even a small number of visible Quaker conscientious objectors could touch off a more general resistance to military service among the wider Nevisian population, a situation that could easily lead to a security disaster for the island. Quakers were widely considered to be "a peaceable, frugal, industrious people, and upon these accounts valuable members of society," but they were simultaneously seen as "holding obstinately to the principle of non-resistance, [by which] they resign every social blessing to the first bold invader" and were thus potentially "injurious to society," as "if a government is ruined, it matters not by what hands, whether by foreigners unresisted, or by subjects ill affected."[105] As C. S. S. Higham pointed out, "Persecution of the Quakers ... was neither

Antiguan Quakers, John Atkins, Thomas Darlow, Henry Graydon, and Edward Martin, "were commanded by Capt. Jeremiah Watkins to the Place appointed for Alarms, but because they refused to bear Arms, he caused them to be sent to Prison, and detained there nine days" (Oliver, *History of Antigua*, vol. 1, xlix). In 1676, Friend William Boone of Antigua was beaten and imprisoned for refusing to carry out his military duties; in 1684, he was "sent to the Fort for not appearing in arms" (ibid., 69). But George Fox, the founder of Quakerism, asserted in an "Epistle to Friends in Nevis" that it was acceptable for Quaker men to "watch in your own Way, without carrying Arms"; see *A Collection of Some Writings of the Most Noted of the People called Quakers, in their Times* (Philadelphia: W. and T. Bradford, 1767), 12.

[103] John Randall, *A Brief Account of the Rise, Principles and Discipline of the People call'd Quakers, in America, and elsewhere* (Bristol: Samuel Farley, 1747), 17.

[104] Dunn, *Sugar and Slaves*, 124, 135–6; Oliver, *History of Antigua*, vol. 1, xlv.

[105] Samuel Martin, *A Plan for Establishing and Disciplining a National Militia in Great Britain, Ireland, and in all the British Dominions of America* (London: A. Millar, 1745), 66.

a fanatical outbreak nor a regular organized attack; it was rather the constant collision between authority and 'passive resisters'" brought about
by the "inherent impossibility of a conscientious pacifist like the Quaker
fitting in to the life of a frontier state, the basis of whose organization was
essentially military."[106]

Similarly, the Quakers' unwillingness to pay "priests' wages" or
"forced Maintenance of Church Ministers," taxes in support of the
Church of England, threatened to spark a similar refusal among other
islanders, many of whom, as has been discussed, were little more enthusiastic about financing the Church than were the Friends.[107] As an ecclesiastical historian of the Leewards has written, "Civil obedience was
the understood basis of both political and religious toleration, and the
Quakers, having deliberately broken this agreement, had to accept the
consequences."[108] In 1679 Nevis Quaker John Brown, abetted by two
associates, disrupted the Anglican service at St. George's Church in the
parish of Gingerland, rising to his feet at a moment of silent prayer and
accusing the minister, John Lawson, of being a "man of iniquity" who
would not preach unless he had been paid to do so. For this breach
of sacred and secular order, Brown and his comrades were placed in
the stocks, then jailed. Brown, as the apparent ringleader, was the subject of a governor's order that he be banished from Nevis and forcibly
embarked on the ship *Hope*, to be taken "to the island of Long-Island
or any other place where there are Quakers." As he was led from his cell
to the docks, the island's provost marshal, Caesar Rodney, "beat [him]
with a great cane," a painful and deeply humiliating punishment associated with slave status, which showed onlookers how seriously the island
administration took Brown's offense and how harshly any such actions
would be treated in the future.[109]

Passive as well as active resistance to local political and religious
practice on the part of Quakers met with a highly unsympathetic public
response. The Friends' refusal to take any sort of civil oath, as "they also
think those Words of Christ Swear not at all, amount to a Prohibition
of solemn, as well as profane Swearing," marked them not only as defi-
ant of local law but also as standing outside of a community in which
a man's word was his bond.[110] Through their refusal to swear oaths,

---

[106] Higham, "Early Days," 124.
[107] Durham, *Caribbean Quakers*, 34; Langford, *Brief Account*, 4.
[108] Cooper, *Establishment*, 38.
[109] Hubbard, *Swords*, 18–19.
[110] Randall, *Brief Account*, 18.

Quakers placed themselves beyond the bounds of patriarchy and legal personhood, and thus constituted themselves as the sorts of masterless men who seemed to threaten social order in the metropole and the colonies alike.[111] At least as troubling to island authorities was the Friends' admission of slaves and free people of color to their meetings; as an act of the Barbados legislature stated, should black people be "Hearers of their Doctrine, and taught in their Principles," presumably referring to their belief in spiritual equality across barriers of race, gender, and social status, "the Safety of this Island may be much hazarded."[112] George Fox, the founder of the Society of Friends, maintained that people of all races had the right to hear the good news of their salvation, and "that which we have spoken to them is, to exhort and admonish them ... to love their masters and mistresses, and be faithful and diligent in their masters' service and business." Popular belief, however, claimed that Friends' comparatively egalitarian ideology and willingness to acknowledge the spiritual claims of "negroes," as shown by Quaker missionary Joan Vokins's holding meetings "with White People and Blacks" in the course of her 1681 stay in Antigua, was in and of itself a dangerous precedent to set.[113] Even the refusal by Quaker men to obey the rules of manly honor by removing their hats in court represented a silent but infuriating refusal to obey basic societal rules, as the doffing of the hat represented a willingness to hear and obey a superior's commands.[114] This intransigence provoked a heavy-handed response from the Nevis authorities, who ordered that "whosoever for the future should come into any Court with his Hat on, should pay a Fine of 500 lb. of Sugar, or suffer a Month's Imprisonment."[115] A man's failure to remove his hat in the presence of his putative superiors, whether secular or ecclesiastical, was a challenge to norms of behavior and ideology that could not be permitted to pass without challenge and, taken in combination with the several other ways in which male Friends flouted long-established

---

[111] Ibid., 18.

[112] *Acts of Assembly, Passed in the Island of Barbadoes, from 1648, to 1718* (London: John Baskett, 1732), 94.

[113] S. D. Smith, *Slavery, Family and Gentry Capitalism in the British Atlantic: The World of the Lascelles, 1648–1834* (Cambridge: Cambridge University Press, 2006), 27; Fox et al., "Letter to the Governor of Barbados, 1671," in John L. Nickalls, ed., *The Journal of George Fox* (Cambridge: Cambridge University Press, 1952), 604; Joan Vokins, *God's Mighty Power Magnified* (London: Thomas Northcott, 1691), 61.

[114] C. Dallett Hemphill, *Bowing to Necessities: A History of Manners in America, 1620–1860* (New York: Oxford University Press, 1999), 14, 16.

[115] Quoted in Dayfoot, *Shaping*, 83–4.

norms of gender and race, signified their apparent refusal to comply with societal rules.[116]

Quakers might insist, as George Fox did in the course of a visit to Barbados, that their creed neither "den[ied] God, and Christ Jesus, and the Scriptures of truth" nor encouraged Friends to "teach the negroes to rebel," but their insistence on both their doctrinal orthodoxy and their absolute commitment to truthfulness convinced few island residents, who persisted throughout the seventeenth century in seeing Quakers as undesirables and troublemakers.[117] The Lords of Trade instructed Sir Charles Wheeler's successor, Sir William Stapleton, that "no man be molested in the exercise of his religion," but throughout the 1670s and 1680s a particularly aggressive civil or religious leader might frequently push the boundaries of "molestation" by haranguing local Quakers from the bench or the pulpit.[118] Throughout the final quarter of the seventeenth century, persecution of Quakers waxed and waned according to the whims of individual governors and most commonly involved fining Friends for holding meetings, working on fast days, or refusing to bear arms or pay ministerial taxes. In 1684, for example, Jonas Langford, Antigua's leading Quaker settler, was fined nearly nine thousand pounds of sugar in lieu of the "Priest's Wages" he had refused to pay; a few months later, the island's constables seized another thousand pounds from him for what he described as "the pretended dues of William Jones Priest," and other Quaker colonists were relieved of wool, hogs, horses, and tobacco for similar offenses. Frustratingly for the authorities, island Quakers clearly preferred to pay their fines rather than alter their conduct, not least because by this time they were on the whole sufficiently prosperous to afford these charges.[119]

By the end of the seventeenth century, attitudes toward Quakerism had mellowed in the Leewards, as they had in many parts of colonial British America in the wake of the Act of Toleration of 1689. Memories of the sectarian crises of the mid–seventeenth century were by then several

[116] Penelope J. Corfield, "Dress for Deference and Dissent: Hats and the Decline of Hat Honour," *Costume* 23 (1989), 64. See also Michael J. Braddick, "Civility and Authority," in Braddick and David Armitage, eds., *The British Atlantic World, 1500–1800* (New York: Palgrave Macmillan, 2003).
[117] Fox et al., "Letter to the Governor of Barbados, 1671." See also Steven M. Shapin, *A Social History of Truth: Civility and Science in Seventeenth-Century England* (Chicago: University of Chicago Press, 1994), 95.
[118] A Layman, *Antigua*, 8–9.
[119] Oliver, *History of Antigua*, vol. 1, lxvi, lxix; Durham, *Caribbean Quakers*, 34.

decades old, and the popular image of the Friend now owed less to the menacing specter of the Ranter or the Leveller than to the reassuring vision of the hardworking and austere man of business. The development of the colony of Pennsylvania and the rise of a wealthy and law-abiding mercantile elite in Philadelphia made Quakers appear less likely to favor a "world turn'd upside down," and recast them in the popular eye as worthy members of colonial society and active and valuable participants in Atlantic commerce. In 1705, the nagging issue of oath-taking was resolved, as the Leeward legislatures, led by Nevis, passed acts stating that "the Solemn Affirmation and Declaration of the People called Quakers, shall be accepted instead of an Oath in the usual form." This "beneficial Law" was "an encouragement to Trade and a Means to further the Settlement of these Colonies." It also legally removed the last significant barrier to Leeward Quakers' full participation in local administration and society.[120] Throughout the eighteenth century, self-proclaimed Friends held elective and appointive offices throughout the Leeward Islands. By 1711, the Quaker George French of Antigua had served successively as the island's treasurer, then as the king's escheator, and finally as a member of the Assembly, and his son Nathaniel proved agreeable to "serv[ing] in the corps of Carabineers." Richard Oliver, also an Antiguan, became an assemblyman, a speaker of the Assembly, a justice of the peace, and a councillor. Many of their descendants followed in their footsteps or married those who did. John Humphreys had been "imprisoned as a Quaker" in 1669, but his son Nathaniel was a captain in the island militia, and Nathaniel's daughters were baptized in the Anglican church at St. John's. Samuel Winthrop might have been displaced from the presidency of the governing Council, but his three sons, prominent planters all, held positions of high rank in the Antiguan militia and the Assembly, and his daughters made successful matches with wealthy non-Quaker planters of Antigua and Nevis.[121]

In the early decades of settlement, ties between the small population of Quakers remained sufficiently close that Leeward Friends intermarried extensively. The Oliver family, who established a great trading concern in London and whose descendant was lieutenant governor of Massachusetts on the eve of the American Revolution, were connected by marriage to the Langfords, whose progenitor was Jonas Langford, Antigua's first Quaker

---

[120] *Acts of Assembly, Passed in the Island of Nevis, from 1664, to 1739, inclusive* (London: John Baskett, 1740), 55.
[121] Gragg, "Puritan," 786.

settler.[122] The Langfords also intermarried with the Lovells, Antiguan and Philadelphian Quaker merchants, and with other Friends from Pennsylvania.[123] But by the early decades of the eighteenth century, most Antiguan Friends had begun to look beyond the circle of their coreligionists for suitable spouses and in many instances chose to attend Anglican services. Whether intermarriage with non-Quakers was the cause or the result of adherence to the Anglican Church, what is apparent is that a situation of greater public tolerance of Quakerism resulted in an effacement, rather than an efflorescence, of Quaker practice. Eighteenth-century Antiguan parish registers recorded the births, marriages, and burials of Boones, Humphreyses, Langfords, Lovells, Olivers, and Winthrops, all of whom descended from Quaker families, and the Anglican Cathedral of St. John's received its magnificent silver Communion service as a gift from John Otto Baijer, a descendant of Friends.[124] The children of Antiguan Quakers married into the locally prominent families of Warner, Lavington, Blizard, Byam, Williams, Hodge, and others, and thus became part of that "tangled cousinry" that provided over decades the political, economic, and social leadership of the Leewards.

Little evidence exists to show that sectarian Quakerism continued to flourish in the islands. Friends Edmund Peckover and Daniel Stanton, who visited Nevis in the 1740s, found the meetinghouse abandoned and in a ruinous state, and around the same time the Anglican minister Francis Byam reported to the bishop of London that there were "but two or three Quakers in the whole island"; according to the journal of another Friend, Thomas Story, the last meeting had taken place in 1709 and had attracted fewer than a dozen congregants. In 1744, Byam informed the bishop of London that there were "but two or three Quakers in the whole Island."[125] As Richard Sheridan has posited, it is possible that orthodox Quakers chose to leave the Leewards and the rest of the English island colonies in disgust with "compulsory militia service, the slave system,

[122] Richard B. Sheridan, "Planters and Merchants: The Oliver Family of Antigua and London, 1716–1784," *Business History* 13 (1971), 104–5.

[123] Will of Jonas Langford, 1710, HM. 41725, Henry E. Huntington Library, San Marino, CA. J. Hector St. John de Crevecoeur noted Quakers' "fondness for their own mode of worship, for be they ever so far separated from each other, they hold a sort of communion with the society, and seldom depart from its rules" (quoted in Susan S. Forbes, "Quaker Tribalism," in Michael Zuckerman, ed., *Friends and Neighbors: Group Life in America's First Plural Society* [Philadelphia: Temple University Press, 1982], 145).

[124] A Layman, *Antigua*, 31; Sheridan, "Planters and Merchants," 105.

[125] Byam to Bishop, June 16, 1744, Fulham Papers, General Correspondence: Section B-WI, vol. 19, Leeward I, 1681–1749.

and the laxity of morals ... [which] were incompatible with the tenets of the faith," but those who remained had clearly "relinquished strict Quaker principles."[126] By the beginning of the eighteenth century, as John Miller has noted, "the element of 'difference' between Quakers and their neighbours was reduced to a tolerable level," and the Friends were "as fully integrated into their communities as they were ever likely to be."[127] Indeed, so complete was this integration, and so minimal these differences, that Leeward Quakers, once they were no longer under communal pressure regarding their practices, found it paradoxically easy to gradually abandon them in favor of an easy rapprochement with an Anglican establishment that demanded relatively little of its nominal adherents.

"A FRENCHMAN BORN"

The position that Huguenots occupied in the society of the Leewards was simultaneously more and less secure than that held by Jews or Quakers. As people of French heritage, the Huguenots were inherently suspicious characters. As Linda Colley has argued, British national identity developed and was deployed throughout the eighteenth century in polar opposition to France and the French; "men and women came to define themselves as Britons ... because circumstances impressed them with the belief that they were different from those beyond their shores, and in particular different from their prime enemy, the French."[128] England's West Indian colonists had still greater reason to hate and fear the French in the second half of the seventeenth century; as Spain's power in the Caribbean waned, the English and French competed for territorial and commercial mastery, leading them into warfare again and again, most notably in 1666–7, in 1689, and in the decade-long War of the Spanish Succession (1702–13).

But although Huguenots were French subjects, they were also Protestants, many of whom had encountered real persecution in France and its overseas possessions, particularly throughout the long reign of Louis XIV, whose increasing hostility to their beliefs had by 1685 led to the revocation of the Edict of Nantes. Although there is no evidence

[126] Sheridan, *Sugar and Slavery: An Economic History of the British West Indies, 1623–1775* (Baltimore: Johns Hopkins University Press, 1974), 366.
[127] Miller, "'A Suffering People': English Quakers and Their Neighbours, c. 1650–c. 1700," *Past and Present* 188 (2005), 103.
[128] Colley, *Britons: Forging the Nation, 1707–1837* (New Haven: Yale University Press, 1992), 17.

that any French colonist who "spoke against the Catholic religion was ... punished by having his lips split, and for subsequent offenses, the tongue was to be pierced with a hot iron, or ... torn out, with perpetual banishment from the Islands," the situation of Huguenot settlers became precarious in French colonies.[129] Under certain circumstances, these colonists came to view their interests as better served through confederation with English imperial authorities.

Rapprochement between Huguenots and English settlers was both facilitated and complicated by the fact that for nearly a century the island of St. Kitts was shared by England and France. Anglo-French combat was not confined to the lands and seas of Europe; it flared up thousands of miles away in the West Indies, where the two nations' colonies engaged in hostilities as their metropoles' proxies. St. Kitts was particularly vulnerable during these outbreaks of warfare: Not only did it occupy the awkward position of a joint settlement, but its location to the leeward of Martinique, the locus of French power in the Caribbean, placed it directly in the pathway of French incursions. According to Richard Pares, this accident of geography made it inevitable that the island would "be lost or ruined again and again," an observation borne out by the anguish resonating throughout the settlers' repeated appeals to Parliament deploring the loss of their estates, slaves, and fortunes.[130] To force the French to cede all of their lands on the island, as stipulated by the Treaty of Utrecht in 1713, would have been sweet revenge to the repeatedly dispossessed English Kittitian colonists.

The English, however, were not the only group to lay claim to the French lands. "The French" as an imperial power might have been forced to abandon the island, but "the French" as individuals had not all followed suit. Although the majority of French settlers "removed from thence into their other islands," resettling in Martinique, Saint-Domingue, and elsewhere in the Caribbean basin, a significant number of French colonists petitioned the British crown to allow them to retain their landholdings in St. Kitts on the basis of their alleged English sympathies and Protestant beliefs.[131] For example, the widow Elizabeth Renoult made a "humble Peticon" to retain her husband's "Considerable Estate," on the grounds

---

[129] DuBois Schanck Morris, Jr., "Aspects of Toleration and Tribulation in the West Indies," in Peter Steven Gannon, ed., *Huguenot Refugees in the Settling of Colonial America* (New York: Huguenot Society of America, 1985), 275.

[130] Pares, *War and Trade*, 232.

[131] John Campbell, *Candid and Impartial Considerations on the Nature of the Sugar Trade* (London: R. Baldwin, 1763), 13.

that "he was of the Protestant Religion ... and did ... Swear Allegiance to the [English] Crown," and Alletta de la Coussaye requested that she and her children be granted the two-hundred-acre plantation of her father, Captain Vandelbourg, in Capisterre, as he had suffered persecution by the French authorities on account of his Huguenot faith.[132] Another widow, Elizabeth Salenave, petitioned for the reinstatement of her claim to the four hundred acres held by her late husband, Jordain, supporting her credentials as a friend of English interests by noting that her spouse was "a Protestant and a great friend to the English Nation" and that her niece was married to Lieutenant Robert Cunningham, an officer of the St. Kitts militia, whose "great zeal to your Majesty and your Royal Family is notoriously known."[133] The English commentator John Campbell, writing at the end of a later Anglo-French conflict, noted that "it is certain that some of the best [French] families remained" on the island, correlated by the appearance of Ozea Guithen, Jacob Lagourge, Francis Dechamps, Francis Duplessy, Stephen Palissier, Anthony Duroy, and various de Marsals, Bourryaus, Brisacs, and Soulegres in the "Account of Grants for Land in the former French Part" in 1716.[134] The West Indian planter-historian Bryan Edwards concurred, remarking that "some few of the French planters, indeed, who consented to take the oaths, were naturalized, and permitted to retain their estates," an assertion corroborated by the list of signatories to a 1727 petition to Governor William Mathew from the residents of the former French lands, of which such French names as de Brissac, Dumoulin, Dupuy, and Perreau make up nearly a quarter.[135] The legislative records of St. Kitts in the first half of the eighteenth century contain many instances in which individuals whose names are clearly of French provenance were allowed to become naturalized as British subjects. The island's Assembly passed a series of private acts to naturalize people such as Francis Amedeus de Fontaines, John Lespeir, "John Duquesne Doctor in Physick," and "Mary Magdalen

---

[132] "The humble Peticon of Elizabeth Renoult Widdow" and "The Humble Petition of Alletta De La Coussaye of St. Cristophers," in C.O. 152/10: Board of Trade: Original Correspondence, Leeward Islands, 1713–16.
[133] C.O. 239/1: Leeward Islands: Original Correspondence, Secretary of State; Oliver, *Caribbeana*, vol. 1, lxxxvii.
[134] Campbell, *Candid and Impartial Considerations*, 43; C.O. 152/11/3: Board of Trade: Original Correspondence, Leeward Islands, 1716–17.
[135] Bryan Edwards, *The History, Civil and Commercial, of the British Colonies in the West Indies* (London: John Stockdale, 1801), vol. 1, 461; C.O. 241/1: St. Christopher's: Council Minutes, June 29, 1727.

the Wife of the Hon. Stephen Payne, Esquire."[136] In 1733, twenty years after the Treaty of Utrecht, an act of the St. Kitts Assembly "for erecting into Parishes those Parts of this Island formerly belonging to the French" listed among those parishes' greatest landowners such Huguenot families as those of Bourryau, Marsal, Duport, Guichard, Guinilat, Audain, Dupee, Soulegre, Gullien, and Therould.[137]

French Huguenot families who had succeeded in retaining their estates and gaining naturalized status followed the pattern of the Quakers rather than that of the Jews in relation to the issue of exogamy. Within a generation of the Peace of Utrecht, marital alliances between English colonists and their Huguenot neighbors had become commonplace, particularly in St. Kitts and in its near neighbor, Nevis. The aforementioned Mary Magdalen (or Marie-Madeleine) had wed the prominent planter Stephen Payne, and Matthew Mills, one of St. Kitts's wealthiest men, had chosen as a spouse Cornelia Soulegre, whose father was a Huguenot from Languedoc who had become naturalized after the war and whom Leeward governor Hart described as "not only the wealthyest man" on the island, but "in all respects a worthy and discreet person."[138] Sophia Spooner, whose father, John, owned four plantations in St. Kitts, married Zachariah Bourryau, whose obituary in London's fashionable *Gentleman's Magazine* referred to him as "an eminent West India merchant," and Henry Brouncker, son of St. Kitts's deputy collector, wed Susannah Feuilleteau; after his death, she married John Stanley, solicitor general of the Leewards from 1771 to 1781. Charles Pym Burt, whose father was Nevis's chief justice and colonel of militia, took as his wife Hester Duport.[139] "One of the Nevis grandees," whose estate, "one of the largest in the island, was worked by 255 slaves, and yielded an annual income of £12,000," was John Latysionere Jefferys; his name manifested his and his parents' pride in their kinship to the family of Le Toissonier, whom a Jefferys descendant described as "an old Nevis family related to us."[140] This Huguenot descendant's home

[136] *Acts of Assembly, Passed in the Charibbee Leeward Islands, from 1690, to 1730* (London: John Baskett, 1734), 181; *Acts of Assembly Passed in the Island of St. Christopher*, 124, 134, 166; Kathleen Manchester, *Historic Heritage of St. Kitts, Nevis, Anguilla* (Privately printed, 1971), 18, 26.
[137] *Acts of Assembly, Passed in the Island of St. Christopher; from 1711, to 1739, inclusive* (London: John Baskett, 1739), 144–7.
[138] Hart to Lord Carteret, December 3, 1723, *C.S.P. Col.*, *1722–1723*, 381.
[139] Oliver, *Caribbeana*, vol. 5, 91.
[140] "John Latoysonior" appears in the records of the Assembly of Nevis in 1732, at which time William Stewart "examined [him] in physic and surgery" and found him qualified to practice (C.O. 186/1, Minutes of Council and Assembly of Nevis, February 18, 1732).

was apparently "a centre of Nevis social life, much frequented by officers of the navy. Captain Horatio Nelson was a visitor whenever the fleet was in those waters and was the godfather of one of Jefferys's sons."[141] In the Leewards, as in Charleston, South Carolina, the primary locus of Huguenot settlement in North America, marriages purely between individuals of French descent were a rare event by the middle decades of the eighteenth century, and such Anglo-French marital alliances appear to have raised neither opposition nor comment.[142]

Why were the Huguenots not merely accepted, but in some instances welcomed into Leeward white society? The reasons are several and inter-related. The Huguenots were less likely than either the Quakers or the Jews to appear to be uninvited interlopers in the islands; clans such as the Allaires, Pintards, and L'Hommedieus numbered among the earliest white inhabitants of St. Kitts, and their arrival long predated that of most of the English colonists. At least as important, they were considered by many English settlers to be something of a "model minority"; seventeenth-century English writers were impressed by their "work ethic of Calvinism and by their industriousness and dependability," as well as by their aptitude at "adjust[ing] to dissimilar life-styles and disparate cultures."[143] They did not share with the Friends a commitment to pacifism or an insistence on divisive matters of social practice, such as the refusal of "hat honor," nor were they similar to the Jews, who practiced strict endogamy and whose dietary and social habits barred them from sustained social intercourse with those outside their community of faith. These matters were far from trivial in societies that contained only a few hundred or thousand white men; by constituting themselves as potential comrades in arms, drinking partners, or spouses to English colonists, these French Protestants rendered themselves welcome to their neighbors.

They were also valuable in financial and commercial terms. The revocation of the Edict of Nantes served the Huguenots as the Portuguese conquest of Brazil did the Jews: It produced a cosmopolitan diasporic community stretching across national and imperial boundaries, creating ties of kinship and friendship that resulted in the construction of an

---

[141] Edward Miller Jefferys, *Jefferys of Worcestershire, Nevis, Philadelphia* (Philadelphia: Privately printed, 1939), 7–8.

[142] R. C. Nash, "Huguenot Merchants and the Development of South Carolina's Slave-Plantation and Atlantic Trading Economy, 1680–1775," in Bertrand van Ruymbeke and Randy J. Sparks, eds., *Memory and Identity: The Huguenots in France and the Atlantic Diaspora* (Columbia: University of South Carolina Press, 2004), 227.

[143] Morris, "Aspects," 276, 277.

extensive and flexible network of commercial relationships. J. F. Bosher has termed this network "the Protestant International" and has traced its connections between France, Switzerland, England, and the mainland and island colonies of the Americas.[144] The St. Kitts families of Therould and Allaire were imbricated in the web of trade spun by the D'Harriette family, which extended from the Huguenot stronghold at La Rochelle to the French settlements at Acadia and Martinique, from Amsterdam to New York, and from London and Bristol to New England. The Allaires were also kin to the far-flung Faneuil family, whose members resided in France, Ireland, the Netherlands, London, Saint-Domingue, New York, and Boston, and whose ranks included not only numerous merchants, but also a bookseller in London's Strand, a subscriber to the Bank of England, and an attorney at Cap Français.[145] David Hancock has illuminated the extensive business networks established in St. Kitts by one Augustus Boyd, nephew of André Thauvet, a Huguenot who had not only gained naturalization but had been made a captain in the island militia. Twenty-year-old Boyd ventured to St. Kitts in 1700, fleeing the poverty and ignominy his family's Jacobite sympathies had brought upon them; within a decade, he had rented four dozen slaves and a substantial sugar plantation, and by 1720 he had purchased an estate of 150 acres, consolidated his mercantile connections with nearby islands, and married Lucy, daughter of John Peters, a wealthy planter who had served as speaker of St. Kitts's Assembly.[146] At the time of his death in 1765, Boyd was possessed of an estate worth more than £50,000, a fortune acquired over his long life through decades of hard work, but also from his ties of kinship and friendship to Kittitian Huguenot clans such as the Bourryaus and the Duports, who "brought him cargo and clients" that enabled him to acquire such lucrative properties as the 180-acre Castle and 214-acre Stones Fort plantations, which, in conjunction with his lands in St. Croix, yielded the impressive income of £9,000 per year.[147]

The incorporation of the Huguenot colonists into the English societies of the Leewards did not occur entirely without controversy. The English Kittitian Roderick Mackenzie complained in his *General Survey*

---

[144] Bosher, "Huguenot Merchants and the Protestant International in the Seventeenth Century," *William and Mary Quarterly* s3: 52 (1995), 77; Nash, "Merchants."

[145] Bosher, "Protestant International," folding charts between pp. 80 and 81.

[146] David Hancock, *Citizens of the World: London Merchants and the Integration of the British Atlantic Community, 1735–1785* (Cambridge: Cambridge University Press, 1995), 46, 47.

[147] Ibid., 48, 383.

of that Part of the Island of St. Christophers, Which formerly belonged to France (1722) that "some pretended French refugees, who (as pretended Sufferers for their Religion) lay Claim to several Thousand Acres ... as their pretended former Possessions." To Mackenzie, these settlers were not true Protestants, but instead had been "sometimes Protestants, and sometimes Papists; changing always their Religion, or rather the Profession thereof ... as they found the same suit best." He called on the local authorities to look carefully upon "the Titles and Merit of all such Pretenders," adding in a footnote that Huguenot soldiers serving the Crown in Ireland were in some cases carrying on their persons "their Crucifixes and other Popish Trinckets" and ended their lives "trussed up ... on a Triple Tree ... as Deserters to the Irish Army."[148] Similar prejudices appear to have played a leading role in the case of Captain Alexander Delavaux, who in the summer of 1741 found himself under suspicion of espionage in St. Kitts. Delavaux, a British military surveyor who was stationed at Brimstone Hill, the island's principal fortification, had spent an evening drinking in company with Nathan Crossley, supervisor of the works on the hill, in the course of which "there happened to arise a long Argument upon the knowledge of English and fforeign Mathematicians Engineers and Soldiers," in which Delavaux "insisted so strenuously on the Superior skill and knowledge of fforeigners ... that he used severall Expressions ... derogatory of the Honour of the British Nation."[149] Such provocation could not pass without challenge; although Delavaux was a "Brother Officer" and a "Gent who merited the highest confidence," the fortress's commander, Captain Harris, ordered that he be "Confin'd there as a Prisoner of State," believing that the former's aggressive defense of French technological expertise and his avid interest in the workings of the fortress betrayed him as a spy for the French. The intervention of the island's lieutenant governor brought Delavaux his freedom by the autumn, but the "Poor Man! Unhappy Martyr to St. Kitts and his Inclination to the British Service," once released, left St. Kitts for Dutch-controlled Surinam, where he was "well treated ... having been found innocent of every charge."[150]

---

[148] Mackenzie, *A General Survey of that Part of the Island of St. Christophers, Which formerly belonged to France* (London: J. Roberts, 1722), 24, 25.

[149] Deposition of James Latimer, Professor of the Mathematicks, St. Christophers, July 16, 1741, Beinecke Lesser Antilles Collection, Burke Library, Hamilton College, Clinton, NY, M77a.

[150] Deposition of James Paterson, Esq., July 16, 1741, Beinecke Collection, M77c; Complaints from Gilbert Fleming against William Mathew, April 14, 1742, Beinecke Collection, M79.

But despite the writings of Mackenzie and the actions of Harris, attitudes among Leeward settlers toward Huguenots were better reflected by an Antigua act of 1702, which welcomed the settlement of "Protestant Aliens," provided that "upon examination it shall be judged that the said person is what he pretends to be, and not a spy or disguised papist," and that "no Alien ... shall be enabled to Serve as a Counsellor or Assembly Man, Justice of the Peace, or Courts, or in the Militia as a Field Officer." We see in the language of this act a lingering suspicion of these "Protestant Aliens," requiring that they be "examined" to ensure that they were indeed sympathetic to English interests and barring them for the immediate future from taking on significant military or civilian duties. But the act also allowed the children born to these colonists to hold these offices, establishing them as full participants in the adopted community of their parents, as epitomized by the experience of the Losack family of St. Kitts. "Lewis de Lansac," apparently the son of Antoine de Lussac, comte d'Eran, was made a free denizen in 1685; his son James Losack became speaker of the island's Assembly in 1744, and James's son Richard was president of the Council in 1770.[151] In a manner similar to that of Quakers, and distinct from that of Jews, Huguenots were able to overcome the taint of communal suspicion and attain full membership in English Leeward society. For them, as for the islands' Quaker descendants, their confessional alterity was a matter of practice rather than of character, and as such could eventually be completely effaced in the eyes of their community.

CONCLUSION

The apparent assimilability of Quakers and Huguenots offers an interesting contrast to the continued distinctiveness of Jews in Leeward society. All three groups encountered significant opposition and even persecution in seventeenth-century England, wracked as it was by every kind of political and religious disorder, and in its empire, yet all succeeded in creating niches for themselves in Leeward society by the early decades of the eighteenth century. Jews, however, remained a self-contained enclave

---

[151] "An Act for the further encouraging the Settlement of this Island," *Acts of Assembly, Passed in the Charibbee Leeward Islands, from 1690, to 1730* (London: John Baskett, 1734), 126; John Henry Howard, *The Laws of the British Colonies, in the West Indies and Other Parts of America, concerning Real and Personal Property and Manumission of Slaves* (Westport, CT: Negro Universities Press, 1970), vol. 1, 409; Oliver, *Caribbeana,* vol. 5, 241, 242.

centered on Charlestown, Nevis. They participated in island commerce and, to a certain extent, in neighborly rituals, but unlike the Quakers and Huguenots, they appear almost never to have intermarried with Anglican settlers. Nor did they gain a role in the political or military establishments that were a principal source of local prestige and patronage.

The divergent fates of Leeward Jews, Huguenots, and Quakers resulted from both the willingness of local society to admit outsiders and the intensity of these outsiders' desire to seek such admission. It stands to reason that the greater assimilability of the Quakers and Huguenots was the result of the lesser degree of alterity that either community offered to English planter society, in comparison with that presented by the Jews. But it is also important to recall that it was Quakers and Huguenots, not Jews, who represented an actual challenge to authority in the Interregnum and the early years of the Restoration. Quakers might be English and Protestant, but they were also rebels against religious and political authority throughout several decades of England's imperial expansion. Huguenots were Protestant, but French rather than English, representatives of England's greatest enemy in Europe and the colonies in the seventeenth and eighteenth centuries. Certainly Huguenots and Quakers were on some levels far more assimilable than Jews into the mainstream of Leeward white society, but this assimilability was at least in part a result of their apparent willingness to become part of the larger society, a tendency that few if any Leeward Jews seem to have shared. As the preceding chapter's discussion of the Irish and Scots presence in the Leewards has emphasized, societal inclusion resulted from the combination of the *ability* of a group or an individual to accommodate itself to certain norms and its *willingness* to do so. In other words, inclusion in a community was the result, not of a completely autonomous decision on the part of one side or the other, but of a negotiation between the two. In the end, the Jews of Nevis, and of other English West Indian colonies, might under certain circumstances be *integrated* into the wider community, but they would not be *assimilated* into it. The persistence of anti-Jewish sentiment among seventeenth- and eighteenth-century Englishmen dovetailed with the communal and self-enclosed tendency of Jewish islanders to create a subtle yet strong sense of cultural distance that both groups were willing to enforce through law and custom alike. In the end, the Jews of Nevis were prototypical pioneers in the early modern Americas, moving between islands and mainland and across imperial boundaries, and leading lives characterized by fluidity and mobility; perhaps only those who were laid to rest in the Jewish cemetery on Nevis can be described as permanent residents of this small place in the Atlantic world.

The experiences of these various non-Anglican groups also highlights the flexibility of religious practice in the Leewards. Throughout the period under study, the leaders of these islands struggled to uphold the authority of the Church of England in the face of scarce financial resources, a paucity of clergymen and churches, and significant popular apathy toward attendance at services. Yet it is misleading to conclude that these limitations reflected the Church's overall weakness and its lack of relevance to the lives of Leeward colonists. On the contrary, it was the largely undemanding nature of the Church's presence that allowed it to maintain its hold in the islands: One could consider oneself a loyal member of the faith without being called on to make a significant financial commitment to its support, to alter one's personal behavior to suit the dictates of ecclesiastical courts, or even to make regular appearances at services. The Church offered its members something desirable – allegiance to a central component of English identity – without expecting very much in return. On the one hand, its spiritual monopoly as an established religion allowed it to separate its communicants from the adherents of less favored belief systems. On the other, its lack of zeal for persecution of these others forestalled the continuance of doctrinal hostilities inherited from the Old World, thus allowing the islands to reap economic and social benefits from the presence of Jews, Quakers, and Huguenots without encouraging a polarization of religious opinion that could have been so disruptive to the functioning of these small societies. The management of a doctrinally heterodox population was a delicate balancing act, and as such provides further evidence of the improvisatory nature of sociocultural development in the Leewards and of the settlers' adaptability and resilience in matching English ideals to tropical realities.

4

Sex, Sexuality, and Social Control

INTRODUCTION

Perhaps the most prevalent image of the English West Indian colonies in the era of sugar and slavery is of these islands as places of sexual license, in which white settlers enjoyed boundless opportunities for sensual gratification both with one another and with their slaves. In the absence of church courts and other sacred and secular institutions that aimed to regulate sexual behavior in the metropole and in the North American colonies, West Indian colonists supposedly devoted themselves to the pursuit of sexual pleasure, often across racial boundaries, and simultaneously failed to create the sorts of stable families that might have become the foundations of a recognizably English society. As Maaja Stewart has observed, eighteenth-century narratives about the West Indies, fictional and factual alike, are replete with "images that represent the breakdown of the nuclear family," such as instances of "adultery, bigamy, incest, and illegitimacy."[1] In the eighteenth-century Anglo-American popular imagination, the morality of the island colonies was undermined by several interrelated factors. The first was environmental, as it was easy to associate a sultry tropical climate with sensual excess; William Pittis, the author of The Jamaica Lady (1720), had his character Pharmaceuticus, a ship's surgeon, assert that the very air of the West Indies "so changes the constitution of its inhabitants that if a woman land there chaste as a vestal, she becomes in forty-eight hours a perfect Messalina."[2] Many

---

[1] Stewart, "Inexhaustible Generosity: The Fictions of Eighteenth-Century British Imperialism in Richard Cumberland's The West Indian," The Eighteenth Century 37 (1996), 46.
[2] Pittis, The Jamaica Lady, or, The Life of Bavia (London: Thomas Bickerton, 1720), 35.

seventeenth- and eighteenth-century pamphleteers claimed that the social atmosphere of the islands was as inimical as the physical to the development of good morals, that "a rogue in England will hardly make a cheater here," and that a whore, if attractive, might hope to attain a position of wealth and respectability by marrying a rich planter. The eighteenth-century historian and travel writer Thomas Salmon, who visited the islands early in the eighteenth century, went so far as to claim of the colonists that "they take as many Wives as they please ... their Governors are esteemed according to the Number of their Wives; and those who fight valiantly may have as many as they will, for none whom they court refuses them."[3] Some of the blame for these apparent moral failings was attributed to the allegedly low origins of the early settlers, whom the parliamentarian soldier Henry Whistler described as "rogues and whores and such like people," who swarmed to this "dunghill whereupon England doth cast its rubbish." The pamphleteer Edward Ward claimed that white West Indian women were "such as have been Scandalous in England to the utmost degree, either Transported by the State, or led by their Vicious Inclinations; where they may be Wicked without Shame, and Whore on without Punishment."[4]

It is important to note that many of these and similar criticisms were made while the English colonies in the West Indies, particularly the Leeward Islands, were at an early stage of their social and cultural development, when a small number of planters were struggling to "hew a fortune out of the wild woods" and when the male/female ratio among the settler population was seriously unbalanced. In 1678 there were 176 white men to every 100 white women in the Leewards, but by 1720 the ratio had become 108 to 100, and by 1756 it was 104 to 100, a dramatic rebalancing caused by the termination of the islands' "frontier stage," in which immigrants were overwhelmingly single men, and by the tendency of men in the islands to die more rapidly than women.[5] As marriage to a white woman became a possibility for the majority of white West Indian men, these potential wives and mothers underwent a cultural reevaluation by locals and visitors alike; "creole" women were now described

---

[3] Salmon, *A Critical Essay Concerning Marriage* (London: C. Rivington, 1724), 333–4.

[4] Whistler, "An Account of Barbados in 1654," in N. C. Connell, "An Extract from Henry Whistler's Journal of West Indian Expedition under the Date 1654," *Journal of the Barbados Museum and Historical Society* (1938), 5; Ward, *A Trip to Jamaica: With a True Character of the People and the Island* (London: J. How, 1700), 16.

[5] Robert V. Wells, *The Population of the British Colonies in America before 1776* (Princeton, NJ: Princeton University Press, 1975), 218.

not as lustful strumpets, but as angelic figures whose immaculate characters upheld both the purity of the white race and the legitimacy of colonial authority. For example, the Anglican minister and poet William Shervington, who attended the Antigua Governor's Ball of July 1746, described the "sparkling charms of th'Antigonian fair" in relation to the young women's modesty and innocence; he reserved special praise for Delia, who "smil'd so innocently gay," and Florimel, whose "unaffected innocence ... unlook'd-for conquest gains," rather than imply that he experienced any kind of sexual excitement at the sight of such "Beauties."[6] The author's scant references to the women's physical appearances and his substitution of pseudo-classical cognomens for their given names emphasize the idealized nature of his description of the young women and their removal from the arena of casual sexual conquest or even of voyeuristic desire. But in order that white women be placed on such a pedestal, black and mixed-race women, both enslaved and free, had to assume the blame for all varieties of sexual immorality, to be denigrated universally as libidinous creatures whose innate depravity lured white men to fall into "dissipation's dear delightful downy lap" and who inevitably gave rise to "a slaveish sooty race" of mulattoes.[7] Even Janet Schaw, a well-educated and socially progressive Scotswoman who visited Antigua and St. Kitts on the eve of the American Revolution, was keen to contrast the "excellent wives, fond attentive mothers, and ... amiable creoles" she encountered among the women of the local elites with the "young black wenches [who] lay themselves out for white lovers," a process in which, she concluded with dismay, "they are but too successful."[8]

Over generations, many scholars of the West Indies have reified the contrast between a sexually restrained early modern England and its licentious West Indian colonies, a distinction that has been considerably overdrawn. But as Michel Foucault asserted in the first volume of his investigation of the history of sexuality, sex is an "especially dense transfer point for relations of power" and as such can never be monolithic,

---

[6] W.S.A.B., *The Antigonian and Bostonian Beauties: A Poem* (Boston: D. Fowle, 1790), 2; an earlier version, "The Antigonian Beauties," appears in Shervington's *Occasional Poems* (St. John's, Antigua: T. Smith, 1749), 30–9.

[7] J. B. Moreton, *Manners and Customs of the West India Islands* (London: W. Richardson, 1790), 78; Governor Daniel Parke, quoted in Richard S. Dunn, *Sugar and Slaves: The Rise of the Planter Class in the English West Indies, 1624–1713* (Chapel Hill: University of North Carolina, 1973), 145.

[8] Schaw, *The Journal of a Lady of Quality*, ed. Charles Andrews and Evangeline Walker Andrews (New Haven: Yale University Press, 1923), 112, 113.

even within a single society, creating a significant disjunction between the prescribed social and sexual order of any society and the actual behavior of individuals in that society.[9] Moreover, the centrality of slavery to the social, political, economic, and cultural life of the West Indian colonies renders questions of sexual behavior important not only in the spheres of morality and religion, but also in the areas of property, inheritance, and legal personhood. As Hilary Beckles has noted, "The entire ideological fabric of the slave-based civilization was conceived in terms of sex, gender and race."[10] Because laws in force throughout the Anglo-American plantation colonies from the late seventeenth century onward decreed that all infants followed the condition of the mother, that is, into slavery or freedom, regardless of the father's racial or legal status, issues of sexual morality and behavior were subject to constant negotiation, and breaches of law or custom could attract not merely communal condemnation but also legal scrutiny. Moreover, white colonists were quite aware of metropolitan discourses and attitudes regarding the alleged tendency of islanders toward "creolean degeneracy," to the threat of cultural as well as physical miscegenation by which "the Anglo-Saxons in the West Indies showed a tendency to decay" and "good white blood was continuously lost to the white race." Under these circumstances, they frequently considered it imperative to police certain behaviors whose prevalence might suggest that the islands' whites were undergoing an "uncontrolled mimesis" in relation to their constant interactions with slaves and free people of color.[11] Under such circumstances, the perceived sexual license of the colonies was not necessarily greater, and in some cases may have been significantly less, than that experienced within the metropole.

In so many historical contexts, sexual behavior is perhaps the most mysterious and least penetrable realm for the historian. These difficulties

[9] Foucault, *The History of Sexuality: An Introduction*, trans. Robert Hurley (New York: Pantheon Books, 1978), 103.

[10] Beckles, "White Women and Slavery in the Caribbean," *History Workshop Journal* 36 (1993), 66. See also Kathleen M. Brown, *Good Wives, Nasty Wenches, and Anxious Patriarchs: Gender, Race, and Power in Colonial Virginia* (Chapel Hill: University of North Carolina Press, 1996); Jennifer L. Morgan, *Laboring Women: Reproduction and Gender in New World Slavery* (University of Pennsylvania Press, 2004); and Carol Barash, "The Character of Difference: The Creole Woman as Mediator in Narratives about Jamaica," *Eighteenth-Century Studies* 23 (1990), 406–24.

[11] Frank Wesley Pitman, "The West Indian Absentee Planter as a Colonial Type," *Proceedings of the Pacific Coast Branch of the American Historical Association* (1927), 121; Kathleen Wilson, *The Island Race: Englishness, Empire, and Gender in the Eighteenth Century* (New York: Routledge, 2003), 154.

are exacerbated in the context of the late seventeenth- and eighteenth-century Leewards because of the relative paucity of surviving collections of planters' personal papers and the fact that at most times before the 1770s these islands lacked newspapers or other documentary representations of the public sphere in which issues relating to individual or communal norms of sexual behavior might have been discussed, whether these tenets were observed or ignored.[12] Moreover, the very nature of a plantation society ensured that the people who almost certainly were the most aware of the private activities of members of the white community were black slaves, who were almost universally illiterate and were prevented by local law from presenting any testimony regarding sexual incidents that could give rise to legal actions.[13] A reading of the islands' law codes in conjunction with legislative records, anecdotes reported by visitors to the Leewards, and scattered church records leads to a far from complete picture of the ideals and practices of sociosexual behavior in these islands. Nonetheless, from these fragments we can at least begin to discern the ways in which Leeward society accommodated particular deviations from metropolitan mores while resisting others, displaying the same sense of improvisation that characterized their responses to other challenges to social stability.

MAKING MARRIAGES AND FAMILIES

In his *Critical Essay Concerning Marriage* (1724), Thomas Salmon described the "Marriage Rites in the Caribbee and Leeward Islands" in terms echoing the classical trope of the rape of the Sabine women: Not only did West Indian colonists apparently "take as many wives as they please," but "the only Ceremony is for the Man to carry her home."[14] Although Salmon's claim that creole men routinely practiced polygamy can be dismissed as fantasy, it is easy to understand why he might have

[12] Neither Montserrat nor Nevis boasted a newspaper before the second half of the nineteenth century. In Antigua, issues of the *Gazette* were published sporadically between 1753 and 1756, and the *Mercury* began publication around 1769; the St. Kitts *Charibbean and General Gazette* first appeared around 1768 (Howard S. Pactor, ed., *Colonial British Caribbean Newspapers: A Bibliography and Directory* [New York: Greenwood Press, 1990], 1, 2, 88).

[13] Trevor Burnard, "'A Matron in Rank, a Prostitute in Manners': The Manning Divorce of 1741 and Class, Gender, Race and the Law in Eighteenth-Century Jamaica," in Verene A. Shepherd, ed., *Working Slavery, Pricing Freedom: Perspectives from the Caribbean, Africa, and the African Diaspora* (New York: Palgrave, 2002), 138.

[14] Salmon, *Critical Essay*, 333.

believed that Leeward marriages were solemnized simply by a man bringing a woman to live under his roof. As described in the preceding chapter,
the Leewards suffered from a scarcity of clergymen throughout the century under study; at any given moment an island might have no clergy at
all in residence, or the sole Anglican minister might be stationed a considerable distance away from many of his putative parishioners. Under such
circumstances, the governments of the individual islands were obligated
to "take into their serious Consideration the great Scarcity of Ministers"
in order to "prevent the manifold Sins of Incontinency" that might
develop in the absence of personnel authorized to conduct marriages.
Although, as these various acts made clear, the ideal marriage was one
that had been solemnized by an Anglican clergyman, in the absence of
such a man a justice of the peace might unite a couple "in the holy Estate
of Matrimony." A 1678 act of Montserrat was aimed at ensuring that the
children of all such couples would be "legitimate, and capable to receive
all such Privileges as are usually appertaining to Children lawfully begot-
ten." But if an "Orthodox Minister" was on hand, the Assembly refused
to "authorize or confirm any Marriages had or solemnized" by anyone
other than a member of the clergy.[15]

If a parish possessed an incumbent minister, a couple's decision to
marry became a matter for both sacred and secular authorities, as well
as for the wider community. Acts passed in Montserrat and St. Kitts
expressed anxiety about "clandestine Marriages ... whereby Parents have
been deprived of their Children without Consent or Approbation, to the
great Injury and Inquietude of Families," and called on the local clergy
to forestall the "irregular Practices" of "evil-minded Persons" by setting
out strict rules about the circumstances under which islanders might be
joined in matrimony. The two options consisted of banns and license. In
the former case, the names of the prospective spouses would "be duly
called in the Church ... where one of the Parties shall reside for Three
Sundays or Holy-days, successively, during the Time of Divine Service,"
and in the latter, the couple would visit the office of the island secretary
to procure a marriage license, which would be signed by the governor in
his capacity as ordinary of the Church of England.[16] In general, as was

---

[15] "An act about contracting Marriages," *Montserrat Code of Laws from 1668, to 1788*
(London: R. Hindmarsh, 1790), 11–12; "An Act for the confirming all Marriages had and
Solemnized by any Justice of the Peace or other Magistrate within this Island," *Acts of
Assembly, Passed in the Charibbee Leeward Islands, From 1690, to 1730* (London: John
Baskett, 1734), 45.

[16] "An Act for preventing clandestine Marriages in the Island of Montserrat," *Montserrat
Code of Laws*, 73; "An Act for preventing clandestine Marriages in the Island of St.

true in England, the poorer settlers chose to be married by banns, and the wealthier opted for the license; for example, when the extremely wealthy Henry Brouncker, the deputy collector of St. Kitts, married Susannah, the daughter of the rich Huguenot planter Lewis Feuilleteau, at Basseterre in 1761, their nuptials were conducted by license.[17] But neither type of union was likely to be enacted in a church or chapel; John Luffman, who visited Antigua in 1786, averred that, according to a local tradition of long standing, "marriages are always solemnized in the houses, as also are baptisms, and the churches are very thinly attended but on funerals, and on particular public occasions."[18] To a visitor such as Thomas Salmon, such small, private ceremonies might easily give the impression that islanders had dispensed with all of the formalities associated with marriage and had adopted a practice by which creole men simply "carried home" their chosen women.

In the eyes of both civil and religious authorities, all white children in the Leewards should ideally have been the offspring of parents who had been legally married to one another; the children of unmarried couples were bastards or "base" children in the eyes of both sacred and secular authorities. However, the fragmentary parish records remaining from all four islands include baptismal entries for many children whom the clergyman described as being "base" or "bastard." In most instances, the names of both of the child's parents are given, as with "Ann the base child of Sarah Garner and John Donell" and "Thomas the base child of Joseph Pheasant and Elizabeth Martin," but in some cases only one parent's name is given, as with "James the base child of Jane Donaldson" or "Eleanor, a bastard of Timothy Sheas."[19] These scattered records stand as evidence of the variety of marital and familial strategies pursued by Leeward colonists. Several women are listed as having given birth to more than one "base" child; in St. Kitts, the widow Ann Corbett's son Allen was baptized on December 6, 1734, and buried only days later, and her son William was baptized on February 12, 1738, while Elizabeth

---

Christopher," *Laws of the Island of St. Christopher, from the Year 1711, to the Year 1791* (Basseterre, St. Kitts: Edward Luther Low, 1791), 81.

[17] Vere Langford Oliver, *The Monumental Inscriptions of the British West Indies* (Dorchester: Friary Press, 1927), 47; Oliver, *Caribbeana* (London: Mitchell Hughes and Clarke, 1914), vol. 3, 355. So wealthy was Brouncker that in his marriage settlement of 1761 he promised to leave Susannah £25,000 should she survive him and made bequests to the extent of £35,000 to other relatives.

[18] Luffman, *A Brief Account of the Island of Antigua* (London: T. Cadell, 1789), 37–8.

[19] Register of Trinity Palmetto Point, St. Kitts, in Oliver, *Caribbeana*, vol. 6, 28; parish records of St. Anthony, Montserrat, in ibid., vol. 1, 44.

Martin had a son by Joseph Pheasant in January 1738 and a daughter by James Keige nearly fifteen years later. In Montserrat, Grace Bass had an illegitimate daughter in 1722 by John Daly Fitz John and another five years later by Charles Daly, presumably a kinsman of her first partner. Some unwed couples had several children together, implying the existence of a sustained partnership, although one not solemnized by marriage. Katherine Shoghro and Richard Cooke's son George was baptized in St. George's parish, Montserrat, in June 1725, and his brother John in St. Anthony in October 1727, and John George and Ann Brown had two sons, one baptized at St. John's Fig Tree, Nevis, in January 1764 and the other in April 1766.[20]

Particularly noteworthy are the numerous baptismal and burial entries that hint at the existence of mixed-race children. In some instances, the reference is simply to a slave, such as "Valentine, a Slave of John Legayes," or "Edward, a Slave of George Underwood," both baptized in Montserrat in the spring of 1726. It is difficult to evaluate such entries, or those relating to individuals such as Johnny, "a Mulatto, the property of Henry Herbert," buried in Nevis in September 1763.[21] These individuals may well have been the illegitimate sons of their owners, born to enslaved women, but it is conceivable that they were simply slaves whom their owners favored because of their light skin or their apparent Christian piety and to whom these owners were thus inclined to extend the religious rights, and rites, usually reserved for whites. Other entries, however, are far more direct in their mention of interracial sex; in May 1742, the incumbent of St. Mary Cayon, St. Kitts, baptized two "mulatto child[ren] of John Whites," a man who also fathered an illegitimate child by a Mrs. Thomas in 1745, while the mid-eighteenth-century records from Nevis's St. John Fig Tree parish are replete with entries reflecting sexual relationships between black and white residents. In each instance, only the name of the white father is given, as with "Mary a Mulatto daughter of George Ashby," baptized in March 1752, or "Anne base born D[aughter]. of William Wilkinson by a Negro Woman," baptized in February 1769, and it is not clear in which cases the children's fathers were also their owners. A couple of records bear witness to more overt interracial relationships. At Nevis in December 1759 was recorded the burial of "Anne a free Negroe wife of Richard Lindley," and presumably the mother of Lindley's "free Negro daughter," another Anne, who had died in 1752 at

---

[20] Oliver, *Caribbeana*, vol. 1, 44, 88, 378.
[21] Ibid. 43, 378.

the age of 22; in the same parish was recorded the marriage in 1752 of "Samuel Styles a free Mulatto and Mary Frost." Because Lindley's and Frost's names were recorded without reference to their race, it is probable that both were whites who had taken the unusual step of solemnizing their relationships with free persons of color.[22]

Although the church records of the Leewards have survived only in fragments, making it difficult either to construct a narrative of development over time within an individual island or to draw significant comparisons between all four, what remains offers tantalizing glimpses of the mores and methods that governed the marital and reproductive choices of white, black, and mixed-race residents. Of particular note is the fact that irregular relationships, including interracial unions and the bearing of children outside of wedlock, involved some of the wealthiest and most prominent members of white society. Colonel John Molineux, an Oxford graduate whose military title attests to his position of leadership in Montserrat, fathered a "bastard Son" by Alice Sweeney in 1726, and his fellow colonel of militia Richard Cooke had two out-of-wedlock sons with Katherine Shoghro in the same decade. Both male and female descendants of the elite Irish "Tribal" families were the parents of "base" children, as mentioned earlier. Grace Bass was the mother of illegitimate children by two men of the Daly family, "an Ancient Irish family in the County of Galway," and Anne Daly had a "bastard Son" by William Anderson in 1724. In Antigua, the 1709 will of the wealthy planter Thomas Trant mentioned his "mulatto children," Ben and Nanny. In Nevis, men from the Herbert family pursued an apparently active sexual life with white and black women alike: William Herbert's "Mulattoe children" William and Mary were baptized in December 1751, and Henry Herbert's "base children" Joseph and Charlotte in September 1752, followed in November 1756 by Elizabeth, another "base daughter," while Christmas Day 1758 saw the baptism of Emilia, "base daughter" of Joseph Brown Herbert. None of these peccadilloes prevented another Herbert brother, John Richardson, from being appointed to the island's Council in 1752; three decades later Admiral Nelson, who was about to marry Herbert's widowed niece, Frances Nisbet, described him as being "very rich, and very proud."[23] The Herberts' fellow Nevis grandees Thaddeus

---

[22] Ibid., 299, 324, 325, 376; vol. 2, 165.

[23] Ibid., vol. 1, 44, 88, 325; Richard B. Sheridan, *Sugar and Slavery: An Economic History of the British West Indies, 1623–1775* (Baltimore: Johns Hopkins University Press, 1974), 169; Antigua Film Project (http://www.candoo.com/genresources/antiguafilms.htm), 8.

Bridgewater and Samuel Clarke, the latter a justice of the court of King's Bench and Common Pleas, also fathered, respectively, an illegitimate daughter and a mixed-race son in 1764. In Antigua, some of the island's most prominent men are recorded as having fathered children by women described in the records of St. John's parish as "curtizans"; in the years between 1713 and 1725, approximately 5 percent of the sixty-five baptisms recorded in this parish were of the offspring of "curtizans." Among those so listed were the sons and daughters of such important men as George Lucas, who served variously as a captain in the 38th Regiment of Foot, as the island's treasurer, and as the speaker of its Assembly. Lucas was described by Leeward governor John Hart in 1724 as a "gentleman of a worthy character and heir to one of the best estates in Antigua," and in the following decade he became a leading planter in the South Carolina Low Country and the father of the widely known agricultural innovator Eliza Lucas Pinckney. The 1775 will of the leading planter Francis Delap appointed guardians of his "reputed naturall children by Mary Shippen, a free woman, dec'd, viz: Sarah, Robert, Eliz. & Francis Delap," as well as of Arthur Delap, "son of Fanny, the house-wench"; he not only publicly acknowledged these mixed-race children, but gave them names shared by his white kin.[24]

At first glance, these entries may seem to confirm at least some of the lurid contemporary and modern conceptions of the sociosexual lives of these West Indian colonists, specifically that many settlers carried on extramarital sexual relationships, both with slaves and free people of color and with one another. Clearly, some degree of miscegenation was prevalent throughout Leeward plantation society in this period. Contemporary white male commentators almost universally conceived of the black woman, whether free or enslaved, as predestined by virtue of her race and gender to be subordinate, and therefore sexually available, to all white men. Many of these writers claimed that such women entered into temporary or long-term sexual relationships with white men not because they were coerced by the latter, or because they hoped to gain their freedom, if enslaved, or money and valuable gifts, if free, but primarily because they were inherently lustful and thus eager for sex with any man. Rather than considering black women to be doubly burdened by their gender and race, Janet Schaw viewed them as seeking to gratify their lust and greed; they "wear little or no clothing ... and they are

24 Carol Walter Ramagosa, "Eliza Lucas Pinckney's Family in Antigua, 1668–1747," *South Carolina Historical Magazine* 99 (1998), 249, 245; Oliver, *Caribbeana*, vol. 1. 196.

hardly prevailed on to wear a petticoat," the better to "lay themselves out for white lovers" rather than "marrying with their natural mates," that is, black men.[25] Since the overwhelming majority of people of African descent in the Leewards were slaves, relations between white men and black women required no greater degree of community surveillance or legal regulation than would the man's management of his livestock or his other chattels; antimiscegenation laws are conspicuous by their absence from the legal codes of the islands, except for that of Antigua, in which acts of 1644 and 1672 fined ministers who performed interracial marriages the sum of fifty pounds and dictated that a person who espoused a slave was obligated to pay his or her owner twenty pounds.

For a white man to engage in sexual relations with, or even father children by, a black woman was in no way forbidden. It might not be a topic of open discussion or a source of public approval, and newcomers to the islands often deplored the "ubiquity of black concubinage among European men of all ranks, married and unmarried," but long-term residents appear to have accepted such relationships as a matter of course.[26] When a white man was publicly criticized for his sexual relations with black women, the accusation usually functioned as an additional source of opprobrium against someone whose behavior in other respects had antagonized members of his community. Daniel Parke accused Christopher Codrington, his predecessor as Leeward governor, of "keeping a slave seraglio and fathering four or five bastards," but the impetus for this charge lay not in Parke's outraged morality – as will be discussed later in this chapter, his own sexual behavior was most accurately described as libertine – but in his suspicion that the extremely wealthy, well-connected, and imperious Codrington was attempting to foment discontent against the new governor, and thus the taunt was aimed at humiliating and discrediting the former to both the local public and the Board of Trade. Indeed, Parke also claimed that Codrington had carried on an extramarital relationship with a white Antiguan woman named Kate Sullivan, who had "layed two Bastards to him, but she giving him the Pox he turned her off."[27] When John Bramley, a member of the Montserrat Assembly, appeared in the 1750s before the Court of Grand Sessions in order to perform his service as a member of a grand

---

[25] Schaw, *Journal*, 112.

[26] Wilson, *Island Race*, 45.

[27] Vere Langford Oliver, *The History of the Island of Antigua* (London: Mitchell and Hughes, 1894), vol. 1, 169.

jury, George Frye, president of the Council, objected to Bramley's attire, as the juror was apparently "very meanly clad with a white cap on."[28] Presumably Frye felt that Bramley's casual dress was inappropriate for a man engaged in serious public business; the informality of the cap was especially troubling to him because a gentleman generally appeared in public wearing a wig, a hat, or both. When Frye scolded him for his slovenly appearance, Bramley defended his right to dress as he pleased, at which point an outraged Frye suggested that "since he was so fond of a white cap, he would advise him to wear one on his p—k, and not keep a seraglio of negroes."[29] Like Parke, Frye deployed sexualized insults as a weapon with which to embarrass and discredit those who angered or intimidated him; he responded to an "ill-spelt" insult carved into a tavern table by recommending that the writer "learn to spell of his aunt, or couzin, it being dubious which of the two she was (for it is to be noted that her mother had lain with White's grandfather and uncle, and could not tell to which of them to lay the child)," and claimed of another opponent that "his aunt had been f—d by a humpback'd Scotchman." In a different register, in 1766 the Antiguan planter Samuel Martin dismissed an overseer, Mr. Pooley, who, he claimed, "lay in Bed every Morning till 9 a Clock with a negro whore." Although Martin was a devout Christian and a strict moralist, it is doubtful that he would have rid himself of an effective overseer solely due to his having availed himself of what many white plantation employees considered to be one of the major perks of their jobs. In this instance, Pooley's moral lapse was compounded by the fact that, according to Martin, he had "used my poor Negroes with moroseness and severity, & neglected them when sick, by which means I lost 14 Negroes, & many of them valuable."[30]

Clearly, interracial sex was far from uncommon in the Leewards, but it is extremely difficult to determine just how prevalent it was. Censuses taken of the individual islands employed only "white" and "black" as racial categories, and they aggregated within the ranks of "blacks" slaves, free people of color, and free and enslaved individuals of racially mixed heritage. Daniel Parke, for one, asserted that the "unnaturall and monstrous lusts" of the planters had given rise to a "slaveish sooty race" of

[28] Frye, *The Case of George Frye, President of the Council of the Island of Montserrat* (London: n.p., 1754), 48.

[29] Ibid. See also Penelope J. Corfield, "Dress for Deference and Dissent: Hats and the Decline of Hat Honour," *Costume* 23 (1989), 68.

[30] Martin to Pooley, March 6, 1766, Add. Mss. 41350, Martin Family Papers, vol. 5, British Library, London, 23.

mixed-race children, and Janet Schaw complained that white Leeward men gave themselves "indulgence ... in their licentious and even unnatural amours, which appears too plainly from the crouds of Mullatoes, which you meet in the streets, houses, and indeed every where." John Luffman warned his readers that, should they visit Antigua, they would encounter everywhere free or enslaved "mulattoes, mestees, and quarteroons, and the two latter mentioned, are frequently as fair as Englishmen ... having blue eyes and flaxen-hair, and complexioned equal almost to any on your side the water." Like Schaw, he reserved particular distaste for mixed-race women, claiming that they "are generally prostitutes" who "dress in a very ridiculous manner, assuming the name of their keeper for the time being, and laying it aside when turned off." Luffman expressed his disgust that "publickly cohabiting with them, is considered here merely as a venial error" that "strikes at the root of honourable engagements with the fair, prevents marriage, and is, thereby, detrimental to the increase of legitimate population."[31]

But these comments ought not to be accepted entirely at face value. Schaw and Luffman were visitors to the Leewards and newcomers to colonial British America, and may thus have been prone to exaggerate the prevalence of miscegenation, either from their shock at first confronting a tropical colonial society or to provide their readers, whether they were a family circle or a wider public, with exotic tales of creole decadence. Parke's comments were made shortly after his arrival in the islands and were no doubt influenced by his bitterness at being passed over for the governorship of his native Virginia and instead being dispatched to what he saw as a colonial backwater. Moreover, as a Virginian of the late seventeenth century, he was the product of an English colonial society that, in the wake of Bacon's Rebellion, sought to increase racial solidarity among white settlers of disparate social and economic status, a goal whose success rested on maintaining in every sphere of life the supremacy of all whites over all blacks. To achieve this objective, sexual mixing of the races had to be prevented, or at least kept to a minimum, toward which goal the House of Burgesses had in 1691 passed an act that criminalized marital and sexual relationships between whites, blacks, and Native Americans.[32] Parke would hardly have been unaware of interracial sex

---

[31] Parke, quoted in Dunn, *Sugar and Slaves*, 145; Schaw, *Journal*, 112; Luffman, *Brief Account*, 115.

[32] Edmund S. Morgan, *American Slavery, American Freedom: The Ordeal of Colonial Virginia* (New York: Norton, 1975), 335.

before his arrival in the Leewards, but like Luffman nearly a century later, he may have been surprised by its frequency, by its assessment as merely a "venial error," or both. As he was greatly aggrieved about his appointment to what he considered a thankless post in a highly undesirable location, he may have chosen to exaggerate the prevalence of interracial relationships among his new subjects in order to blacken their reputations among imperial authorities, and thus to legitimize the increasingly aggressive tactics he employed in what he described as an attempt to bring the Leewards into closer conformity with English standards of governance and morality.

Why were the white residents of the Leewards seemingly so prone to engage in extramarital or interracial relationships? In the absence of personal papers that might have illuminated some of these individual decisions, any answer must remain speculative. In the first place, the fragmentary nature of the records of baptisms, marriages, and burials makes any attempt at generalization difficult. Almost no records have survived from the period before the Treaty of Utrecht in 1713; as noted in the preceding chapter, the various Anglican churches in the Leewards were damaged or destroyed by natural disasters and by Anglo-French warfare, and their records with them. The relative scarcity of clergymen in the islands dictated that at any given moment there might be no one on hand to baptize a baby, marry a couple, or inter a corpse, or to keep records of these activities. Even when an Anglican cleric was available, many individuals might have dispensed with his services, because they were not members of the Church of England, because they lacked or begrudged the sums of money he would charge for these services, or because such an event occurred at an inconvenient time, such as during hurricane season or in the course of the cane harvest. Moreover, it is difficult to evaluate the accuracy or completeness of these records; although the ministers were asked to provide the governor with lists of baptisms, marriages, and burials in their respective parishes, some produced exact transcripts while others gave only the bare figures. Finally, there is always the specter of "the dog that did not bark": of births, marriages, and deaths that individuals might have wished to conceal from their neighbors, particularly from clergymen and, by extension, from local and imperial authorities.

Beyond these caveats, the most obvious answer to the question of why at least some white Leeward residents made what might be termed irregular choices in their romantic and sexual lives is that they lived in a colonial society in which these choices were not just possible, but to some degree overdetermined. In relation to the issue of interracial sex, although the sex ratio among Leeward whites evened out over the course of the eighteenth century, the uneven distribution of the white population among the four islands and the significant rate of at least temporary absenteeism meant that there was no guarantee that every white man could easily find a white woman to take as his wife. Significantly more single white men than women emigrated to the islands, epitomized in the eighteenth century by the steady stream of Scottish doctors, attorneys, and overseers, and the daughters of the elite were in many instances given in marriage to men drawn from their family's commercial and social networks in Britain. Although some of the eighteenth-century Scots migrants, epitomized by Walter Tullideph, were seen as good spousal choices by affluent local women, due to their relatively high degree of education and professional success, those who started out on the lower rungs of the occupational ladder, such as bookkeepers, found themselves less favored as potential husbands of white women.[33] And because so many Leeward men considered themselves likely to leave the West Indies either permanently or frequently, what they sought in the Leewards might not be marriage or the production of legitimate heirs, but impermanent relationships, particularly with women of color. Although seventeenth-century English commentators had on the whole evaluated the physical appearance of women of African descent in highly unflattering terms, as a supposedly hideous foil to the pale-skinned, flaxen-haired ideal of English beauty, the eighteenth century saw the promulgation of an alluring image of black beauty, the "Sable Venus." John Luffman may have exaggerated when he wrote that "many of these gentlemen-managers, as well as the overseers under them, contribute to a great degree, to stock the plantation with mulatto and mestee slaves," the products of their relationships with enslaved women, but Trevor Burnard's study of the "Anglo-Jamaican world" of the eighteenth-century overseer Thomas Thistlewood offers evidence that untrammeled access to female slaves as coerced or willing sexual partners was seen by many white men in the West Indies as one of the principal benefits of plantation life.[34]

It is difficult to gain a definite sense of the emotional and physical valence of slaveholding, but clearly at least some individuals who wielded

[33] Cecilia A. Green, "Hierarchies of Whiteness in the Geographies of Empire: Thomas Thistlewood and the Barretts of Jamaica," *New West Indian Guide* 80 (2006), 15.
[34] Luffman, *Brief Account*, 37; Burnard, *Mastery, Tyranny, and Desire: Thomas Thistlewood and His Slaves in the Anglo-Jamaican World* (Chapel Hill: University of North Carolina Press, 2004.

authority over their or another's bondspeople conceived of the relationship in absolute terms, of supreme power and utter powerlessness, and
in many, if not all, instances "the threat of sexual violence pervaded the
master–slave relationship."[35] As epitomized by Thistlewood's journal, in
which notes on his individual sexual encounters with enslaved women
are juxtaposed with his descriptions of his physically and emotionally
damaging punishments of other slaves, the ownership or management of
slaves allowed white men to do as they pleased with their bondspeople's
bodies, to enact physical or sexual violence, or a combination of both,
upon them, and at least some Leeward settlers chose to exert that authority in the sexual sphere. Although, as far as we can discern, local society
did not praise such behavior, neither did it execrate it; men who carried
on temporary or long-standing liaisons with free or enslaved black or
mixed-race women faced no significant social or political censure for so
doing.

But if interracial sex was a pleasure in which white men in the Leewards
might engage without serious censure, it appears that the islands' white
women were not granted similar privileges. Sexual relationships between
white women and black men are by far the least understood area within
the history of race relations in colonial British America. Although clear
evidence exists that such relationships, as well as marriages, existed
throughout the North American colonies, the stakes were far higher in
the West Indies, particularly in the eighteenth century, when the ratio of
black to white residents in an island might be 8 or 9 to 1, and the overwhelming majority of blacks were slaves. Not only would such relationships "severely undermine white claims to superiority" and "tarnish the
cherished ideals of white womanhood," giving the lie to the idea of white
women as "superior to the arts of seduction," but they would undermine
the social order should they result in the birth of children who would follow their mothers' status into freedom, even if their fathers were slaves.[36]
The dire consequences that could befall a white West Indian woman who
was even suspected of having sexual relations with a black man are illustrated by a Jamaican case of 1741, in which Elizabeth Manning, the wife
of a wealthy Kingston merchant and member of the island's Assembly, was
accused by her white former maidservant of allowing black men to enter

---

[35] Kirsten Fischer, *Suspect Relations: Sex, Race, and Resistance in Colonial North Carolina*
(Ithaca, NY: Cornell University Press, 2002), 164.
[36] Cecily Forde-Jones, "Mapping Racial Boundaries: Gender, Race, and Poor Relief in
Barbadian Plantation Society," *Journal of Women's History* 10 (1998), 19; Luffman,
Brief Account, 37.

her bedchamber, where the servant apparently overheard them "kiss and smack." Although Mr. Manning was already agitated by rumors that his wife was engaged in an affair with Ballard Beckford, another high-status white man and Manning's close friend, it was these further allegations that appear to have motivated his decision to petition the Assembly for an absolute divorce, the only case of this type in the history of prerevolutionary Anglo-America. As Trevor Burnard has noted, although Manning clearly was galled that his wife had conducted an affair with a white man, the thought that she had done the same with one or more black men, and that she might give birth to a mixed-race child, was far beyond bearing. Manning eventually reconciled with Beckford and went on to become a "major political power-broker" in Jamaica, later serving as speaker of the Assembly, the most powerful post in the colony other than that of governor. His reputation suffered neither from the separation from his wife nor from his long-term liaison with a free woman of color with whom he had two daughters. By contrast, Mrs. Manning, having fled her husband's estate in the wake of a violent argument with her spouse, was not mentioned in the wills of her former lover Beckford, of her estranged husband, or of her brother and cousins; as one who was "a matron in rank" but publicly deemed "a prostitute in manners," she "vanishes from the historical record as if she were invisible."[37] Such was the price a white woman might pay for even the suggestion that she had engaged in sexual relations with men of color.

In circumstances in which a white woman's sexual contact with a black man was likely to result in social ostracism for the former, it is not surprising that, while the church records of the Leewards include numerous references to either obvious or implied relationships between white men and black women, none relate to those between white women and black men, with the single exception of the 1752 marriage in St. Kitts of the "free Mulatto" Samuel Styles and the presumably white Mary Frost. This exception, however, probably proves the rule. Styles was not a dark-skinned slave but a freeman of mixed race, perhaps even one of the light-complexioned, blue-eyed "mulattoes, mestees, and quarteroons" observed by John Luffman, and it is possible that Frost might also have

---

[37] Burnard, "Matron," 146. In contrast, another eighteenth-century Anglo-Jamaican matron, Ann Gallimore Tharp, survived the exposure of her affair with her daughter's husband "with her social networks intact"; see Sarah M. S. Pearsall, "'The late flagrant instance of depravity in my Family: The Story of an Anglo-Jamaican Cuckold," *William and Mary Quarterly* s3:60 (2003), 571.

been of mixed race, albeit sufficiently fair skinned that she might pass for white, at least to the extent that the minister chose to omit mention of her race. Of course, this argument from silence does not mean that no instances existed in which a white woman chose a black or mixed-race man as a temporary or long-term partner, but it does imply that, if such relationships existed, they were kept secret by the participants in order to avoid social censure, or at the very least that even those clergymen who included in their parish records evidence of extensive extramarital sexual activity between white men and both white and black women were not willing to do so with regard to relationships between white women and black men.

We might, then, wonder why a society that upheld a double standard for white men and women in relation to interracial sex seems to have countenanced white women becoming "curtizans" and bearing out-of-wedlock children with white partners. But it is important to understand that, well into the eighteenth century, ecclesiastical and common law in Britain and its colonies was confused and contradictory on the question of what constituted a marriage. Although, according to Lawrence Stone, in the late seventeenth and early eighteenth centuries "both the laity and the clergy came increasingly to regard the wedding in church as the key ceremony," the civil lawyers who ran the courts continued to recognize spousals (exchange of promises) before witnesses as a legitimate basis on which to consider a couple to be husband and wife; only with Lord Hardwicke's Marriage Act of 1753 was the church wedding recognized as the sole basis of an officially recognized marriage.[38] If many English couples before the approval of the Marriage Act preferred the informality of spousals to marriage by banns or licence – and Stone asserts that "perhaps not much more than half the population were being married strictly according to the rules of canon law" – so much more might West Indian colonists, whose access to ministers and churches was far more limited. The Antiguan records that describe the partners of high-status white men and the mothers of their heirs as "curtizans" may have been written by clergymen who sought to express their disapproval of couples whose marital arrangements were sanctioned by civil law but not by the canons of the Anglican Church. A similar attitude is displayed in the records of St. Anthony and St. George parishes, Montserrat, in the 1720s, in which an infant baptized in January 1728 is described as "Mary

---

[38] Stone, *The Family, Sex, and Marriage in England, 1500–1800*, abridged ed. (New York: Harper and Row, 1979), 37.

a Bastard of Richard Finch & Eleanor Gilbert his Wife," and another in June 1725 as "William Bastard S[on]. of Wm Frye Junr Esqr & Sarah his Wife."[39] The fact that these registers denominate other children as "bastards" without referring to their mothers as wives (as with "John bastard S. of John Cooper by Catharine Biggs") implies that the incumbents of these parishes recognized the existence of a gray area in relation to marital practices, wherein a couple's union might carry communal and legal legitimacy, yet would fail to conform to clerical ideals or canon law.

CHALLENGING PATRIARCHAL CONTROL

Thus far, we have observed a society that allowed white colonists, particularly men, a considerable degree of latitude in terms of their sexual relationships. It displayed a recognition of the realities of a tropical plantation society by accepting, though not explicitly valorizing, sex between white men and black women, while upholding English ideals of womanhood by censuring sex between white women and black men. Although the incidence of nonmarital sexual relationships, as indicated by the number of "base" or "bastard" children whose baptisms and burials are listed in the islands' parish registers, may seem high in relation to the contemporary and modern conception of sexual restraint in the theocratic communities of Puritan New England, such relationships were far from uncommon either in England or in its American colonies, particularly in the period before Hardwicke's standardization of marriage practices. Should a man and a woman choose to cohabit and to produce children without observing all, or even some, of the formalities that would transform the woman from a "curtizan" to a wife, or should otherwise unattached adult women and men engage in brief affairs, their actions might trouble no one, whether parent, spouse, or wider community, and thus attract no controversy. As Sarah Pearsall has shown in her study of the letters of the Tharp family of Jamaica, in the latter half of the eighteenth century the combination of the increasing incidence of absenteeism, particularly among the wealthiest West Indian planters, and the rise of the "culture of sensibility" among elite Anglo-Americans might allow even a flagrantly unfaithful wife such as Ann Gallimore Tharp to survive, in both social and financial terms, the exposure of her infidelity with her son-in-law. Not only was her husband far away in London, but he, in contrast to Edward Manning, chose to overlook her actions in order to

[39] Ibid., 34, 35; Oliver, *Caribbeana*, vol. 1, 86, 88.

spare himself and their children, including the daughter with whose husband Mrs. Tharp had committed her adultery, the public embarrassment that a separation action would have precipitated.[40]

But it would be a mistake to conclude that irregular sexual relationships could always escape public notice or censure. As Trevor Burnard has observed, "Sex and sexual jealousy could lead to a deterioration in relations between whites, thus weakening the fabric of white solidarity."[41] This deterioration was particularly marked in cases in which a white man, particularly one of relatively high social and economic status, believed that his authority as a husband or father had been undermined by the sexual behavior of a female member of his family or by another man's offering a sexual insult to such a woman. Even in the latter half of the eighteenth century, as new discourses of sensibility and sentimentality began to inflect familial relations, English men and women, including those in the American colonies, continued to frame their society in terms of hierarchy and patriarchy. Ideally, the male head of a household was expected to know about and control the behavior, particularly the sexual conduct, of everyone resident beneath his roof, including both family members and servants, and sexual or sexualized acts that occurred against his wishes or without his knowledge undermined his authority both within and beyond the household.[42] It was particularly difficult to ignore such challenges in the inescapably intimate colonial communities of the Leewards, in which the white population, particularly as rates of absenteeism increased in the later eighteenth century, numbered only in the hundreds. As Henry Hulton, a Liverpudlian who spent several years in Antigua as deputy collector of customs in the 1750s, noted, when the marriage between the son of Colonel Leslie, president of the Council, and the daughter of Stephen Blizard, the chief justice, went sour, "the unhappiness of this marriage caused a breach between the families ... and it was difficult in so small a society to maintain an intercourse with both of them."[43] Under such circumstances, it was inevitable that particular

40 Pearsall, "Cuckold," 572.
41 Burnard, "Thomas Thistlewood Becomes a Creole," in Bruce Clayton and John A. Salmond, eds., *Varieties of Southern History* (Westport, CN: Greenwood Press, 1996), 112.
42 Susan Dwyer Amussen, *An Ordered Society: Gender and Class in Early Modern England* (Oxford: Basil Blackwell, 1988), 37–8; Mary Abbott, *Family Ties: English Families, 1545–1920* (London: Routledge, 1993), 1–2; Brown, *Good Wives*, 15–17.
43 Hulton, "Account of Travels," Codex. Eng. 74, John Carter Brown Library, Providence, RI.

sexually transgressive acts would precipitate public uproar and would require some form of communal action. In their attempts to maintain social order to the greatest possible degree, island authorities felt it imperative to regulate and, in some cases, to punish severely those offenses that they believed directly undermined patriarchal dominance within the family and society. Nonetheless, force of circumstance obligated them to allow certain transgressions to pass without overt censure.

These small, delicately calibrated societies were in some instances able, if not especially happy, to accommodate themselves to a range of sexual behaviors, particularly miscegenation between white men and black women, which would have been far less acceptable to metropolitan sensibilities. Nevertheless, the islanders deemed it necessary to resist those expressions of sexual activity that explicitly threatened the ideals of masculine honor and patriarchal order on which the Anglo-American colonial enterprise centered. In order that some semblance of order might persist in a difficult and frequently threatening physical and cultural environment, the basic rules of social and sexual behavior had to remain fluid, yet at least in some sense meaningful. The case of Daniel Parke provides a useful illustration of what Leeward society considered to be the limits of tolerable sexual conduct. Parke was appointed governor of the Leewards in 1705, arrived in the islands the following year, and had served a scant four years when an angry mob of Antiguan residents murdered him on December 7, 1710. The assassination of a Crown official by his subjects was a shocking and treasonous event, one that would not be repeated even in the course of the American Revolution, and many observers in the mother country saw it as proof that the West Indian colonies were degraded and chaotic places in which the rules of English life and law had fallen into complete disarray.[44]

As will be discussed further in the following chapter, Parke was in many respects a highly unsatisfactory head of government for the Leewards and probably would have been a problematic leader of any of the Anglo-American colonies. Having hoped to return as governor to his native Virginia, he was intensely dismayed to be posted instead to what he saw as a remote and undesirable place of exile.[45] From the moment of his arrival, he wasted no time in alienating his new subjects, first by antagonizing the powerful and domineering Christopher Codrington, a former

[44] Dunn, *Sugar and Slaves*, 46.
[45] Helen Hill Miller, *Colonel Parke of Virginia: "The Greatest Hector in the Town"* (Chapel Hill, NC: Algonquin Books, 1989), xvii.

governor with a huge fortune and many influential friends in London, then by raiding the islands' Treasury to build the opulent and much-resented Government House in St. John's. He cemented his ill repute by attempting to establish complete control over the process of making appointments to public office in the islands. However, as much as Parke's political actions alarmed and angered Leeward residents, they were not the only offenses that led to his murder. After all, as we have seen, an early governor of Montserrat, Roger Osborne, had allegedly murdered Samuel Waad, who was both his brother-in-law and the island's leading merchant, yet succeeded in keeping not only his life but his office. As Chapter 5 describes, over the century under study Leeward colonists had accused nearly all of their governors of various abuses of power.[46] At least some of the aggravating factors in Parke's case, however, related to his sexual behavior in the islands.

As his most recent biographer, Helen Hill Miller, has observed, Daniel Parke "had all the vices of a Restoration rake," qualities that had been apparent to observers long before his appointment as governor of the Leewards.[47] Having spent some years in London in the 1680s and 1690s, this "complete sparkish Gentleman" returned to Virginia with an English mistress, a Mrs. Berry, whom he had apparently "conveyed away from her husband" and by whom he had a son. When he returned to England in 1697, Parke abandoned his wife, Jane Ludwell Parke, and their two legitimate daughters, Frances and Lucy, along with his and Mrs. Berry's son, Julius Caesar Parke, and brought Berry, whom he attempted to pass off as his widowed "Cousin Brown," with him to London.[48] His relationship with Mrs. Berry did not pass without comment in England and Virginia, but paled in comparison with his behavior in the islands. There Parke, having apparently abandoned his mistress, quickly became involved in a series of liaisons with married women, most notably with Catharine, the wife of Edward Chester, a member of the Assembly of Antigua and the factor of the Royal African Company for the Leeward Islands.[49]

Parke's affair with Catharine Chester, which the governor made no effort to keep from public knowledge, was guaranteed to provoke

---

[46] F. G. Spurdle, *Early West Indian Government* (Christchurch, New Zealand: Whitcomb and Tombs, 1963), 11.

[47] Miller, *Colonel Parke*, xviii.

[48] Parke Rouse, Jr., *James Blair of Virginia* (Chapel Hill: University of North Carolina Press, 1971), 105, 107.

[49] Algernon E. Aspinall, "The Fate of Governor Parke," in *West Indian Tales of Old* (New York: Negro Universities Press, 1969), 30.

outrage and controversy among members of white Leeward society. Public sympathy overwhelmingly supported Edward Chester, particularly when he caught Parke "skulking behind the Door of a Room adjoining to Mrs. Chester's bed-chamber." Chester attempted to throw both his erring spouse and her lover out of his house, but when Parke threatened the unarmed cuckold with a sword, the aggrieved Chester was forced to "take in his Wife again, whom he had turned out of doors upon this Occasion."[50] Parke's behavior in this altercation showed an utter lack of respect for Chester. His actions made it clear not only that Parke was carrying on a sexual relationship with Chester's wife, literally taking her husband's place in the marital bed, but that Parke was not sufficiently committed to Catharine to try to remove her from her husband's house and bring her into his own bachelor household. By forcing Chester to recognize that he was being cuckolded and then obliging him through force of arms to continue to live with and financially support an obviously unfaithful wife, Parke displayed absolute contempt for Chester as a man and as a husband, attacking him in his public and private roles as a head of household.

Chester gained even more reason to detest Parke when, in 1710, the governor drew up a new will, in which he bequeathed "all my estate in these islands, both land and houses, negroes, debts, and so forth ... for the use of Mistress Lucy Chester, being the daughter of Mistress Katharine Chester."[51] Parke directed that, should Lucy die before her twenty-first birthday, this bequest would pass to Catharine Chester, but that if Lucy were to live to the age of her majority, she was to "take my name & use my coat of arms which is yet of my family of the co[unty]. of Essex."[52] The child in question was clearly a newborn, as "she is not yet christened." Yet Parke had already gone to considerable lengths to make it clear both to Edward Chester and

---

[50] *Some Instances of the Oppression and Male-Administration of Col. Parke, late Governor of the Leeward Islands* (London: n.p., 1713), 10. The unknown author may have intended that the term "Male-Administration" serve as a double entendre referring to Parke's sexual behavior in the Leewards.

[51] Aspinall, "Fate of Parke," 247. Lucy Chester Parke was to inherit only Parke's property in the Leewards, as his legitimate children inherited his holdings in Virginia and England.

[52] *Antigua. Lucy Chester Parke, Widow, Appellant. Charles Dunbar, Esq; and John Doe his Lessee, Respondents. The Appellant's Case* (London: n.p., 1740), 1. Catharine Chester died in 1715, but Lucy, who died at the age of sixty in 1770, obtained possession of "Gambles," Parke's Antiguan estate, in 1723 and not only called herself Lucy Chester Parke before her marriage, but convinced her husband, Thomas Dunbar, to join their surnames, with the result that their children were called Daniel Dunbar Parke and Elizabeth Dunbar Parke.

to the entire community, including the several locally prominent men who served as witnesses to the document, that he, not Catharine's husband, was the infant's father.[53] By making the child his heiress, the namesake of his mother, and his legitimate daughter, Parke brought her to public attention as the living symbol of his adulterous affair with Catharine Chester; the child thereby served as a constant reminder to Edward Chester, and to his community, of Catharine's infidelity with Parke.

No documents have survived that might have illuminated the affective nature of the relationship between Parke and Mrs. Chester, but it seems possible that Parke embarked on his affair with Catharine at least in part to impugn her husband's authority. As the Royal African Company's representative in the Leewards, Chester controlled the price and availability of slaves to the islands' planters. His position brought him both influence and wealth; he was said to have taunted Parke by informing him that his annual salary from the company was twice that which the Crown paid the governor. Moreover, this position of power, combined with a talent for clandestine operations, had enabled him to reap still greater profits as a smuggler, trading illicitly with the Dutch colonists on the nearby island of St. Eustatius.[54] Chester was an obvious threat to Parke's authority, both as a man and as the islands' governor. What better way could there be to symbolically unman and publicly demean him than by cuckolding him and impregnating his wife? The Chester imbroglio, after all, would not have been the first instance in which Parke had chosen to strike at a rival through his wife; in Virginia, having quarreled bitterly with the influential Williamsburg minister James Blair, commissary of the bishop of London, Parke publicly undermined Blair's authority as a husband by seizing Blair's wife by the arm and dragging her from her pew in Williamsburg's Bruton Parish Church in the middle of her husband's Sunday sermon.[55] Although nothing in the historical record implies that Parke was in any way sexually involved with Sarah Blair, his public manhandling of another man's wife was a sexualized form of assault, even a symbolic rape, and as such brought shame on a husband who had failed to protect his spouse from such abuse.

---

[53] Miller, *Colonel Parke*.

[54] Ibid., 192, 196.

[55] Ibid., xvi. As a clergyman, Blair was immune to challenges to duel, a standard method by which man-to-man conflicts in the genteel classes were resolved. Parke had made several attempts to induce Blair's friend and ally, William Nicholson, governor of Maryland, to engage in a duel, and Nicholson's repeated refusals led Parke to seek satisfaction from Blair by humiliating his wife (Rouse, *James Blair*, 105–6).

A man could choose to overlook lesser insults without a complete loss of face, but an undisguised and deliberate assault on his wife, particularly one of a sexual nature, could not pass unchallenged, especially in a small and competitive society such as that of early eighteenth-century Antigua. A man's sexual relationship with the lawful wife of another called into question not only the woman's virtue but also her husband's mastery over her, epitomized by his complete control over and sole access to her sexuality and the paternity of her offspring. Under some circumstances, a wife's infidelity might be allowed to pass without her husband's or her community's censure; as we have noted, John Tharp gave at least the outward impression of having forgiven his wife Ann's affair with their son-in-law, Richard Phillipson, and Edward Manning's divorce action was probably precipitated by his suspicion that his wife had had sexual relations with black men rather than by her alleged affair with his friend Ballard Beckford. In neither case had the alleged adultery been observed by individuals beyond the household, nor did Phillipson or Beckford force the evidence of the affairs into the cuckolds' faces or otherwise make it public knowledge. It is hardly surprising that Governor Parke's openly conducted sexual relationship with Catharine Chester, and with other married Antiguan women, combined with the host of fiscal and political grievances locals held against him, would goad the Antiguans into rebellion against and even murder of a royal official.[56] Edward Chester had apparently been overheard to have sworn that he "would gladly lie seven years in Hell to be avenged" against Parke. Such a desire for personal vengeance, when combined with white islanders' various other grudges against Parke and their conviction that he did not hold them in the esteem they considered befitting their status as white Englishmen, encouraged Antiguans to turn to violence at least partly in order to punish the governor for actions that not only insulted Edward Chester, but challenged cherished ideals regarding social and sexual order.

Local society judged the married Antiguan women who had consorted with Daniel Parke nearly as harshly for their sexual misconduct as they did Parke, although their punishments were less drastic than his. Lucia French, the wife of Parke's close friend and pamphleteering apologist George French, was publicly whipped for her "lewd" and "infamous" behaviour as one of Parke's lovers, a traditional public punishment for unfaithful wives but one rarely applied to women of the elite classes.[57]

---

[56] George French, *The History of Colonel Parke's Administration* (London: n.p., 1717), 1.
[57] Miller, *Colonel Parke*, 203; Stone, *Family*, 317; French, *Parke's Administration*, 1.

Despite the fact that her husband continued to maintain both her innocence and that of his friend Parke, the anger and discomfort that the
governor's behavior had generated in the community required that Mrs.
French suffer a physically painful and humiliating punishment for her
alleged part in the imbroglio. Elinor Martin escaped physical punishment, but Antiguan society shunned her completely for "having been a
known assistant to [Parke] in his lewdness" and damned her further by
accusing her of having debauched her own daughter by allowing Parke to
deflower her, a stratagem by which Mrs. Martin allegedly hoped to prevent Parke from seeking his pleasure elsewhere.[58] What is significant in
these cases is that these "Persons of lewd profligate Lives, and infamous
Characters" were wives; as such, their conduct brought disgrace not only
on themselves but also, and perhaps more importantly, on their husbands
and, by extension, on white society itself. Such women did not need to
fear for their lives or their freedom, but they instead suffered a kind of
social death, epitomized by their disgrace and exclusion from participation on the highest levels of their society.[59]

As has been discussed previously, extramarital sexual behavior was
not always in itself an object of censure. The memoirs of the Anglo-Irish
adventuress Laetitia Pilkington, a friend of Jonathan Swift and Samuel
Richardson, include an anecdote about an aristocratic but impoverished
Frenchwoman, presumably a Huguenot, who had served as a lady-in-
waiting to the wife of the deputy governor of St. Kitts and who, upon
her mistress's death, had replaced her both as the governor's hostess
and as his lover. Although the man died before his intended marriage
to his paramour, the woman in question apparently attracted no public
opprobrium for her unmarried state; she inherited her lover's entire estate
and received proposals of marriage from a number of eligible islanders,
who may well have wished to wed her in order to inherit the mantle of
her former partner's authority, as well as his substantial fortune.[60] The
Frenchwoman's behavior may have been unorthodox, but because she
was an unmarried woman lacking family in the islands her conduct did
not reflect negatively on a husband, father, or brother, and as such did not
merit the sort of punishment meted out to Daniel Parke's married lovers.

[58] Miller, *Colonel Parke*, 203.
[59] *Some Instances*, 3.
[60] Pilkington, *Memoirs of Mrs. Laetitia Pilkington, 1712–1750, Written by Herself*
(London: George Routledge and Sons, 1928), 354–5. See also Lynda M. Thompson,
*The 'Scandalous Memoirists': Constantia Phillips, Laetitia Pilkington, and the Shame of
'Publick Fame'* (Manchester: Manchester University Press, 2000).

The sexual transgressions of an unmarried woman could sometimes be overlooked; those of a wife could never be.

The story of Rachel Faucette Levine Hamilton presents an interesting contrast to that of Daniel Parke and his various mistresses. Rachel, the mother of the American statesman Alexander Hamilton, was the daughter of a French Huguenot family of Nevis; her father's skills as a physician and his naturalization as a subject of the Crown lent the family a reasonable degree of social standing, despite the financial reverses they suffered shortly after Rachel's birth.[61] In 1745 Rachel, aged about sixteen, paid a visit to her married sister, Ann Faucette Lytton, in the Danish West Indian colony of St. Croix, where she met the merchant John Michael Levine.[62] Convinced by Levine's "peacock wardrobe" that he was a man of wealth, Mary Uppington Faucette, Rachel's mother, urged her daughter to marry the man, despite his being far older than she and apparently having an unappealing personality and appearance.[63]

The Levines' marriage quickly devolved into disaster. One of Alexander Hamilton's many biographers claims that the problem was simply that "Levine was sedate and elderly," whereas Rachel was "hot-blooded and young," while another asserts that "Rachel's stubborn nature ran against Levine's desire to dominate and utterly control his wife." Hamilton himself claimed that Levine was "a fortune hunter … [who] paid his addresses to a handsome young woman having a snug fortune" and that he became increasingly dissatisfied with his marriage when he found that Rachel's family was considerably less wealthy than he had believed.[64] Whatever the sources of discord may have been, they were sufficiently powerful that Levine took advantage of a Danish law against unfaithful wives and swore out a formal complaint that Rachel had "twice been guilty of adultery," a claim that resulted in her being confined briefly in the jail of St. Croix's Christiansted Fort.[65] Levine may have meant merely to intimidate

---

[61] Gertrude Atherton, *The Conqueror* (New York: Macmillan, 1902), 3–5. "John Fauset" is listed in 1712 among the "sufferers at Nevis and St. Christopher's" in the wake of French raids in Queen Anne's War; see *Journal of the Commissioners for Trade and Plantations from February 1708–09 to March 1714–15* (London: HMSO, 1925), 384.

[62] Jacob Ernest Cooke, *Alexander Hamilton* (New York: Scribner's, 1982), 1.

[63] Forrest McDonald, *Alexander Hamilton: A Biography* (New York: Norton, 1979), 6; Noemie Emery, *Alexander Hamilton: An Intimate Portrait* (New York: Putnam, 1982), 15.

[64] Nathan Schachner, *Alexander Hamilton* (New York: Appleton-Century, 1946), 6; Emery, *Hamilton*, 15; Ron Chernow, *Alexander Hamilton* (New York: Penguin, 2004), 10.

[65] Cooke, *Hamilton*, 1; Broadus Mitchell, *Alexander Hamilton: Youth to Maturity, 1755–1788* (New York: Macmillan, 1957), 7.

Rachel into giving up what he saw as "her ungodly mode of life" and to bend her to his will, but his stratagem backfired; as soon as her husband agreed to her release from prison, Rachel abandoned him and their young son, Peter, and, after a brief sojourn among friends in Barbados, returned to her mother's home in Nevis.[66]

Shortly after her arrival at Nevis, Rachel, while visiting friends in St. Kitts, met and became romantically involved with James Hamilton, a younger son of the Scottish peer Alexander Hamilton, laird of Grainge in Ayrshire, who had come to stay with his kinsman William Leslie Hamilton, a prosperous planter and attorney and a member of the island's Council, hoping that this successful relative would assist him in setting up as a merchant.[67] But marriage was not an option for the pair; Rachel was still married to Levine, and no laws existed in the Leewards for divorce, nor were there ecclesiastical courts through which a petitioner might request a separation.[68] The only lawful route to divorce was via a private act of the Assembly and its subsequent approval by Parliament, a course of action requiring far more money and metropolitan influence than either Rachel or Hamilton possessed.[69] Recognizing the impossibility of legally resolving this predicament, Rachel and Hamilton chose to live together as common-law husband and wife, and their relationship eventually produced two sons, Alexander and James, Jr. The majority of their fellow islanders accepted the couple's relationship and treated Rachel and Hamilton as man and wife de facto, if not de jure. They appear in the records of the neighboring island of St. Eustatius as "James Hamilton and Rachel Hamilton his wife," having stood as godparents to the son of their friends Alexander and Elizabeth Fraser.[70] The only recorded instance of communal disapproval occurred when Alexander was of age to begin his education; his legal status as a bastard proscribed him from enrolling at Nevis's only school, which existed under the auspices of the Church of England.

[66] McDonald, *Hamilton*, 7.
[67] Neil Wright and Ann Wright, "Hamilton's Sugar Mill, Nevis, Leeward Islands, Eastern Caribbean," *Industrial Archaelogy Review* 13 (1991), 122; Rosane Rocher and Michael E. Scorgie, "A Family Empire: The Alexander Hamilton Cousins, 1750–1830," *Journal of Imperial and Commonwealth History* 23 (1995), 191.
[68] Allan McLane Hamilton, *The Intimate Life of Alexander Hamilton* (New York: Scribner's, 1911), 10; Burnard, "Matron," 138.
[69] Schachner, *Hamilton*, 8. By contrast, the Jamaican Manning was a man of sufficient wealth and political authority that he was able to gain parliamentary assent to his divorce from his unfaithful wife.
[70] Mitchell, *Hamilton*, 11.

How did Rachel, legally a married woman, manage to avoid the censure of her neighbors for living openly with and bearing children by a man who was not her husband? Several factors facilitated her acceptance. First, Rachel's husband, Levine, was not a resident of the Leewards; he had been born in Europe and had spent only a few months in Nevis before moving to Danish St. Croix, where he had met and married Rachel. Had Levine been a permanent member of their community, the Nevisians might have reacted quite differently to his wife's behavior; the presence on the scene of an angry, cuckolded husband might have brought forth the same kind of public reaction Parke encountered in his entanglement with Edward and Catharine Chester. However, Levine was out of sight and therefore, it seems, out of mind. Furthermore, he was a foreigner, English neither by parentage nor by naturalization, and believed by many to be Jewish, and therefore alien to Christian practices and European ideals of masculinity.[71] Those few Nevis residents who had met Levine apparently considered him to be "a coarse man of repulsive personality," a man devoid of personal honor, and this evaluation mitigated the sympathy they might have felt for a husband whose wife had abandoned him and their child and taken up with another partner with whom she had what Levine called her "whore-children."[72] Indeed, it seems that Rachel's most fervent champions were not the women of Nevis, who might have identified with her struggle to escape an unhappy marriage and to find a more congenial partner of her own choice, but rather the island's men, who, instead of identifying with a cuckolded and abandoned husband, chose to see themselves as the champions of a young, attractive, and, in their opinion, mistreated woman.[73] The sort of "patriarchal rage" that might have encouraged Nevis's white male elite to scorn or punish such an openly unfaithful wife was transmuted into sympathy for Rachel, a probable consequence of their admiration for her apparent beauty and intelligence, and of a desire to see justice done by freeing her from a loveless and abusive marriage.[74]

---

[71] Although it is clear that Levine was not English, scholars have reached no consensus about his background; he may have been a German or a Dane, and perhaps a Jew. Even his surname is a matter of argument; it appears variously as Levine, Lavine, Lavien, Levein, Lawein, and Lavion.

[72] Schachner, *Hamilton*, 11; Chernow, *Hamilton*, 20.

[73] Mitchell, *Hamilton*, 6–7.

[74] On misogyny and gynophobia among elite men in colonial British America, see Kenneth A. Lockridge, *On the Sources of Patriarchal Rage: The Commonplace Books of William Byrd and Thomas Jefferson and the Gendering of Power in the Eighteenth Century* (New York: New York University Press, 1992).

The comparative social acceptance of Rachel and Hamilton's unorthodox ménage might also have reflected their secluded and relatively impoverished existence, one lived outside the usual round of elite Nevisian social life. Their neighbors did not see them as flaunting their unconventional lifestyle, nor did they use their connections to well-respected local and metropolitan families in order to demand acceptance into or precedence within the highest echelons of white society. It may be that Rachel's apparent personal unwillingness or financial inability to compete for a preeminent position within local society prevented her from becoming an object of dislike to Nevis's white women. Instead, her apparent willingness to withdraw from the elite and move down the social ladder made it clear to her neighbors that her unorthodox personal life did not threaten the local social order. Rachel escaped the full weight of public censure for her extramarital sexual behavior because her husband, unknown to or disliked by most members of her community, failed to mobilize public opinion against her in defense of his own honor and because her transgressions could be viewed as stemming either from her spouse's alleged mistreatment of her or from his generally unappealing character. Rachel's actions may have been a source of considerable gossip and at least some disapproval in her community, but they were sufficiently unthreatening to the values of local society to avoid encountering significant opposition.[75]

Montserrat was the site of an interesting case that illustrated the early modern English adage "A man's honesty and credit doth depend and lie in his wife's tail."[76] In this instance, what was at issue was not a wife's chastity, but the fact that a man other than her husband drew attention to her sexuality by exposing himself to her in front of her husband, thus implying that her spouse did not hold complete control over her sexuality

---

[75] Many years later, when the adult Alexander was involved at the highest level of American politics, his opponents' invective frequently made reference to the unorthodox circumstances of his birth and upbringing and the allegedly immoral characters of his parents, especially his mother. John Adams called Hamilton "the bastard brat of a Scotch pedlar," and a widely circulated lampoon described him as "the son of a camp-girl." Even Thomas Jefferson, usually relatively tolerant of unconventional modes of life, thundered that it was "monstrous" that a "foreign bastard" should rise to a position of such great power in the virtuous postrevolutionary world of the United States. These barbs, however, were aimed at an ambitious and much feared political rival; there is no evidence that the people among whom Rachel and James Hamilton lived spoke or thought of them in such negative terms. See Claude G. Bowers, "Hamilton: A Portrait," in Jacob Ernest Cooke, ed., *Alexander Hamilton: A Profile* (New York: Hill and Wang, 1967), 2, and Robert Warshow, *Alexander Hamilton: First American Business Man* (Garden City, NY: Garden City Publishing Company, 1931), 3.

[76] Thomas Wythorne, cited in Stone, *Family*, 317.

and that, like Parke's Reverend Blair, he was unable to protect her from an actual or symbolic assault. This volatile situation arose in 1750 when one William Dyett approached George Frye, president of the Council of Montserrat, "under pretense of asking leave to fish in his private pond." Dyett apparently "came up to him [Frye] stark naked when he [Frye] was riding with his wife"; later the same day, Dyett, by now presumably clothed, appeared at Frye's house and told him that "the pond in which he had asked leave to fish was not his [Frye's] own but a publick pond, and that he [Dyett] would fish in it in spite of him."[77] At this point, the furious councillor ordered his overseer to whip Dyett, who endured a few lashes and then ran off.[78]

One might assume that the incident would have ended there, but instead its repercussions were felt for the next several years. As late as 1753, petitions and depositions were flying back and forth between Montserrat and London regarding this seemingly trivial event, and the rhetoric in these various communications became in some instances extremely heated. Frye asserted that Dyett had appeared before him and his wife "naked, and with his obscene parts uncovered," while Dyett charged that Frye had ordered his overseer not merely to whip him but to "Kick him in the Ass" and to set dogs upon him. To add to the indignity, Dyett informed Mr. Molineux, the speaker of the Montserrat Assembly, that Frye had ordered Dyett to be whipped not only by the white overseer, but also by several of Frye's slaves, an appalling degradation in a society in which whites were empowered to strike blacks, but the reverse was unthinkable and would ordinarily result in the offending slave's execution.[79] Perceiving himself to be the object of a grievous sexual slur, Frye had responded in what he hoped was an equally shaming manner, by making Dyett the recipient of an appalling racial insult. Simultaneously, Frye asserted his position at the apex of a hierarchy of white employees, black slaves, and animals by using these various dependents and chattels literally as weapons against someone who dared to challenge his authority.

What becomes apparent from an examination of the documents relating to the case of Frye and Dyett is that their confrontation was not the cause, but rather the result, of a climate of hostility in Montserrat, in which President Frye was at odds with many of the people over whom he held authority. William Dyett was not the only local resident with whom Frye

---

[77] Frye, *Case of Frye,* 12–13.
[78] Ibid., 12–13.
[79] C.O. 152/28/21, 26, 29.

had quarreled; he apparently had also publicly insulted another councillor, Michael White, and had come into conflict with members of such
locally prominent families as the Skerretts and the Trants, descendants of
the Fourteen Tribes of Galway.[80] Dyett, whether of his own volition or
prompted by other complainants, chose to confront the widely disliked
Frye, and to do so in the most insulting manner possible, by exposing his
"obscene parts" to Mrs. Frye in the presence of her husband. Such an act
affronted Frye's manhood and dignity and called his status as a husband
into question, because in theory the only adult male who possessed the
right to appear unclothed before a white woman was her spouse. Such an
offense was not strictly illegal, as Montserrat's law codes mentioned no
such eventuality, but the action served to question not only Frye's manliness but also his capacity to hold public office. If the man could not shield
his wife from Dyett's symbolic assault, how could the public rely on him
to maintain the island's security and prosperity? The fact that Dyett, a
small farmer, was of a socioeconomic status inferior to that of the Fryes
compounded the insult. Interpreted in such a light, Dyett's actions seem
as deliberately provocative and as dangerous as Daniel Parke's open
cuckolding of his enemy Edward Chester. Like Parke, Dyett entered into
a figurative male-to-male conversation that putatively focused on the
body of another man's wife but that in reality struck at his opponent's
prestige and symbolically unmanned him. Even the language Dyett used
to describe his desire to gain access to Frye's pond was charged with sexual meaning. His original taunt can be interpreted as expressing a desire
to enter not Frye's pond, but his wife, and his subsequent claim that the
pond was not really Frye's property, but actually "publick" implied that
Frye held no dominion over his wife and that therefore she was open
to sexual use by the public, as represented by Dyett. Given the gravity
of such a challenge, it is not surprising that Frye reacted so violently to
this symbolic attack, though his behavior was considerably less extreme
than that by which Chester and his comrades chose to avenge themselves
against Parke's amours with their wives. Frye's many time-consuming
efforts to obtain a judgment against Dyett show how deeply his sense of
honor had been damaged by what he clearly saw as a shocking breach of
community norms of social deference and respect for the rights of husbands over their wives.

A final case of sexually transgressive behavior that became a matter
of significant public concern relates also to Montserrat, predating by a

---

[80] C.O. 152/28/28–9.

few years the conflict between William Dyett and George Frye. In this instance, "about the year 1743 ... one *James Farell*, and his sister, children of a *Roman* Catholick family in the island, were detected in the commission of the horrid crime of incest."[81] Not surprisingly, the siblings' parents were apparently horrified by their discovery of the nature of their son and daughter's relationship, and intended to deal with the situation by placing the girl in a European convent and sending the boy into military service in a Continental army. One might imagine that the Farrells' fellow Montserratians would be pleased to see such troublesome youngsters leave the island. Incest, after all, made a travesty of the ideal of the orderly patriarchal household; not only were the children engaging in sexual behavior without their parents' knowledge or approval, but they were also ignoring the laws of consanguinity, or closeness of blood relationship. Consanguinity was a source of such alarm within English metropolitan and colonial culture that it was one of the very few legal grounds for the granting of a divorce decree of *a vinculo matrimonii* ("[freedom] from the chains of matrimony"), the only legal proceeding that allowed previously wed individuals to remarry within the Church of England.[82] One would also think that the inhabitants of such a small white settler society as that of Montserrat, where spousal choice was in many cases quite limited, would not mourn the loss of residents who were publicly known to have violated the societal taboos against incest, thus striking a shattering blow against the moral and physical health of the nuclear family.

The events that followed the discovery of James Farrell's sexual relationship with his sister and their parents' decision to send both children away from one another and from the island, though, unfolded rather differently from what one might have expected. As a contemporary observer wrote, "Several of the Protestant families [of Montserrat], and even a majority of the council, hearing of the affair, prevailed on the son and daughter to turn Protestants, under a notion that as such the son might lawfully dispossess his own father of his inheritance."[83] The island establishment, far from scorning the young pair, championed them against their parents, despite the fact that the elder Farrells had behaved in a manner that upheld both the legal and religious ideals on which Anglo-American colonial society rested. Supporters of James and his sister "not

---

[81] Frye, *Case of Frye*, 9, emphasis in original.
[82] Stone, *Family*, 309.
[83] Frye, *Case of Frye*, 9.

only maintained the son and daughter, and encouraged and received them into their houses," but even succeeded in convincing Sir William Mathew, the Leewards' governor, to appoint James commander of the island's militia, a signal honor for which residents competed jealously, and one ordinarily quite unlikely to have been granted to a Catholic.[84] Equally surprising is the fact that "when the chief justice of the island granted a warrant for the apprehension of the daughter (a girl under age) in order to deliver her up to her parents ... the marshal ... refused to execute it; threats were publickly given out, that any attempt to put it in execution should be opposed by force; and the chief justice himself, for granting it, was personally threatened and insulted in the streets, and forced to fly to his own house for shelter."[85] Although local authorities attempted to uphold the seemingly sacrosanct principle of parental authority over children, an ideal enshrined in the island's act forbidding "clandestine Marriages," a significant element within the island's white community claimed that the elder Farrells' failure to have prevented their children from developing an incestuous sexual relationship, a cardinal duty in preserving order within a household, should cause them to forfeit the privileges of parenthood, which would now devolve onto those who styled themselves as the champions of these young people.

Why would the residents of Montserrat, including a majority of the members of the island's legislature, overlook the unlawful and, in the eyes of most observers, immoral behavior of the Farrell siblings, to such an extent that they not only financially supported the pair but openly flouted all attempts to bring the youngsters under the control of the law and their parents? The Farrell affair, it appears, was an instance in which entrenched ideals of approved sexual conduct came into direct conflict with political realities and in which the latter imperatives won out. As discussed in Chapter 2, some Irish Catholics, particularly wealthy families such as the Farrells, were able to rise to positions of high socioeconomic status in Montserrat, particularly after the Treaty of Utrecht dissipated the threat of French attack and the resulting anxiety that Irish islanders might ally with their fellow Catholics. But at a time when metropolitan and colonial anxieties regarding the resurgence of Jacobitism were on the rise, an opportunity such as that presented by the Farrell case was too good for at least some Protestant Montserratians to ignore; if they should succeed in persuading James Farrell to join the Anglican Church,

[84] Ibid., 9–10.
[85] Ibid., 11.

he could by virtue of island law dispossess the Catholic father he now hated of his property. Such an action would be a classic quid pro quo; James would be able to assert his emotional and financial independence from his father, and the English camp would have the satisfaction of seeing the estate of the island's most affluent openly Catholic family fall into Protestant hands. Toleration of an act of incest, or at least forgiveness of its participants, might seem a very high price for such an achievement, but it was one many residents of Montserrat were apparently willing to pay. Accustomed as they were to a steady diet of lurid invective against the allegedly immoral and shameless "Papists," the English Protestant interest may have felt that this tolerance set no dangerous precedent regarding violations of the incest taboo. Could society not assert that incestuous behavior was yet another example of the abhorrent practices of Catholics?

Patriarchal authority and its control over dependents' sexuality might have been a touchstone of colonial society, but that society found it far easier to ignore the furious protests of those individuals it despised, such as the Catholic Farrell parents or the unappealing foreigner John Michael Levine, than the rancor of such a prominent member of local society as a George Frye or an Edward Chester. These inconsistencies are pointed up by public response to the elopement in 1765 of Margaret, the nineteen-year-old daughter of Leeward governor George Thomas, with Arthur Freeman, a member of the Antigua Council. Thomas was enraged by this turn of events; he disapproved of a match between his daughter and a man more than twice her age, and moreover was humiliated by the fact that Freeman, who up to that point had been "his most intimate companion," had "in defiance of the laws of Great Britain and of this Island, in contempt of the respect due to him as his Majesty's Governor ... and in violation of the laws of hospitality [had] basely and treacherously seduced his daughter ... by prevailing upon her to make a private elopement." So distraught was the governor that not only did he punish Freeman by suspending him from the Council, but he himself resigned his post and went to England, where he made an unsuccessful attempt to prevent the Privy Council from restoring Freeman to his Council seat.[86] Although Thomas, unlike many of the islands' royal governors, was a native of the Leewards, local opinion was generally sympathetic to Freeman. He may have encouraged Margaret to engage in an

[86] Schaw, *Journal*, 102; Andrew J. O'Shaughnessy, ""The Stamp Act Crisis in the British Caribbean," *William and Mary Quarterly* 53:51 (1994), 220.

unlawful "clandestine marriage," but she was of legal age to marry, and most people within the Antiguan elite deemed Freeman a most desirable husband. He had traveled widely throughout Europe, voyaging as far as Constantinople in search of Greek manuscripts, was considered to be "a very sensible, well accomplished man," and owned a large plantation that Janet Schaw described as an "earthly paradise." By contrast, Thomas was described even by the generally straitlaced Henry Hulton as "a character rather respected, than beloved," due to his being "severe and proud, haughty and distant." Although Hulton's memoir of his experiences in Antigua indicates his disapproval of children who went against their parents' wishes, even he admitted that Freeman, whom he had first met in Brunswick in 1752, was a man of "liberal endowments and captivating talents" and that, if Thomas had failed to imagine that his daughter would become infatuated with such a man, he must have been "ignorant of human nature."[87] No doubt at least some Antiguan parents understood the governor's anger at what he saw as a betrayal by both his daughter and his best friend, but most white Antiguans considered the former's response to be a considerable overreaction; not only did Freeman marry Margaret, albeit without her father's permission, but in so doing she was joined to a man for whom the local community had only respect and admiration.

CONCLUSION

Clearly, correct sexual behavior was not a monolithic construct within Leeward society, as local whites were in many instances willing to overlook words and actions that violated legal injunctions and societal rules alike. The pressing need to adapt to local circumstances meant that certain behaviors were tolerated, particularly those connected to miscegenation, but islanders' sexual behavior was far from uncontrolled. White society in the Leewards was willing, if not always pleased, to accommodate certain forms of sexual license, particularly those that resulted from uneven sex ratios, but it fervently resisted and punished others. Those sexual transgressions that infringed on the honor of established men who possessed a deeply rooted sense of their own reputation and dignity could not pass without censure and, in some instances, violent retribution, because such challenges threatened the position and authority not only

---

[87] Schaw, *Journal*, 102; Hulton, "Account," 68–70.

of the aggrieved individual, but also the ideals on which colonial British American society based its authority. Leeward society clearly possessed both the ability and the willingness to modulate the tenor of its official and private responses between the varied types of sex-related offenses with which it was obligated to deal. In so doing, the Leeward colonists were confident that their communities on the whole conformed to recognizably English norms of sexual behavior, and that they had no reason to fear that the effects of a tropical climate and of plantation slavery had corrupted their morals or made them anything other than staunchly English in their social values.

5

Political Culture, Cooperation, and Conflict

INTRODUCTION

From the onset of English settlement until 1670, the Leeward Islands were governed by Barbados – essentially as a colony of a colony – and they achieved their independence as a result of years of lobbying, during which they claimed that the Barbadian colonists were concerned only with their own security and prosperity, to the disadvantage of that of their fellow English settlers in the Leewards. Should the latter be granted the right to govern themselves, the argument ran, Antigua and Montserrat, Nevis and St. Kitts would be bound together in harmony, and the four islands would work together to their mutual benefit. But although Barbadian governor William, Lord Willoughby, pronounced himself pleased to be rid of these additional responsibilities, his pessimistic prediction was that the Leeward colonists would soon find themselves as dissatisfied with each other as they had been with the Barbadians and that before long they would fall to squabbling among themselves rather than look out for one another's best interests. The separation of the Leewards from Barbados, Willoughby claimed, would "put every island upon its particular guard" and thus "enfeeble the strength of the whole," and therefore the Leewards were "acting the part of him that saws off the bough on which he sits."[1] Not surprisingly, most Leeward settlers dismissed Willoughby's comment as the "sour grapes" attitude of a royal

---

[1] Willoughby to Council, October 29, 1670, and to Codrington, November 7, 1670, in W. Noel Sainsbury, ed., *Calendar of State Papers, Colonial Series* [hereafter C.S.P. Col.], *1669–1674* (London: HMSO, 1889), 119–20, 127.

governor who had begun his administration in charge of five islands and would end it in command of just one, but within a few decades his warning would appear all too prescient regarding the challenges of governing the "wayward Leewards."

As has been discussed in Chapter 1, throughout the period under study the Leewards faced a host of challenges to their political, economic, social, and physical stability, threatened as they were by natural disasters, slave uprisings, and foreign attack. Strict limitations characterized their natural and human resources: These already tiny islands included significant areas of land unsuited to any sort of cultivation, and the white population, particularly that of adult males, was undercut by the prevalence of short- or long-term absenteeism and declined over the course of the eighteenth century both in absolute terms and in relation to the enslaved population. The same observations could, on the whole, have been made in relation to Barbados or Jamaica, or about the French, Spanish, or Dutch colonies in the Caribbean basin. The Leewards, however, labored under an additional set of difficult circumstances in relation to their administrative and political structure. Because Antigua, Montserrat, Nevis, and St. Kitts had each been founded as a separate English colony, the independent Leeward Islands were simultaneously one polity and four. As such, they were an anomaly in colonial British America with which Whitehall struggled to deal; one historian has described the islands as having "the oddest governmental arrangement in British America."[2] The royal governor of the Leewards served as the monarch's personal representative and as the military commander in chief of all four islands, but each island had its own lieutenant governor as well as its own Council and Assembly. Although the ongoing threats posed by warfare, slave rebellion, and natural calamities demanded that the islands cooperate with one another, both physical and political factors often discouraged them from doing so. Inter-island communication was rapid and easy between St. Kitts and Nevis, which were separated only by the Narrows, a two-mile strait of usually calm waters, but trade wind patterns were such that it might take several days for people, goods, or news to travel from Antigua, forty miles east of Nevis, to any of the other three islands (Montserrat is twenty-five

---

[2] Michael Watson, "The British West Indian Legislatures in the Seventeenth and Eighteenth Centuries: An Historiographical Introduction," in Philip Lawson, ed., *Parliament and the Atlantic Empire* (Edinburgh: Edinburgh University Press, 1995), 92; Kenneth Morgan, *The Bright–Meyler Papers: A Bristol West-India Connection, 1732–1837* (New York: Oxford University Press, 2008), 583.

miles southwest of Antigua and thirty-five miles southeast of St. Kitts and Nevis), and such a passage would be still slower, or entirely impossible, in times of warfare or extreme weather.[3]

At least as important, all four islands clearly exhibited a desire to retain as much independence from one another as possible. Although, as Ralph Payne, who served as governor of the Leewards between 1771 and 1775, noted, "it is perfectly impracticable to carry on the very laborious Business of my Government, without a ready and easy communication with every District of it," royal governors often found it difficult to convince the legislatures of the four islands to grant them sufficient funds for the purchase or hire of a sloop by which to make these rounds.[4] Moreover, even at moments when the number of white men who met the qualifications to serve in an island's Assembly or Council was so low that the unexpected death, absence, or refusal to take office of one or two men threatened to leave the house without a quorum by which to carry out its business, no island was willing to cede sovereignty by establishing a joint legislature with another.[5] This particularism was so ingrained in the individual Leewards that councillors and assemblymen insisted that no act passed by one island's legislature could be taken automatically to apply to any of the other islands. Sir William Stapleton, the second governor of the Leewards, frustrated by what he saw as the inefficiency of this aggressive localism and its literal insularity, attempted to simplify administrative structures by creating a general assembly to which all of the Leewards would send delegates and that would create a uniform set of laws for the entire colony, as well as organize common measures for its defense. But although Stapleton was a well-established local planter, one who gained his constituents' praise for his "Loyalty, Courage and fidelity, Mixt with military prudence [which] hath ... made us happy and flourishing under his well Regulated Government," his federalist plan

---

[3] C. S. S. Higham, "The General Assembly of the Leeward Islands," *English Historical Review* 41:162 (1926), 191.

[4] Quoted in Andrew Jackson O'Shaughnessy, *An Empire Divided: The American Revolution and the British Caribbean* (Philadelphia: University of Pennsylvania Press, 2000), 100.

[5] For example, in 1738 Governor William Mathew informed the Board of Trade that the Antigua Council "from the many absent in Europe, often meets to do its business but in vain. Col. Morris from a bad state of health, Col. Frye from age and having about twenty miles to ride each council day, and Col. Crump from age and sickness very often are uncapable of attending. These circumstances make it fit I should apply to you for orders to the absent councillors to return or for leave to name others here unless H.M. please to name them at home" (*C.S.P. Col., 1738* [London: HMSO, 1969], 229).

attracted little support from the big planters of the individual islands.[6] At the first meeting of the General Assembly in 1681, the delegates refused to approve the governor's proposal to replace the London agents for each island with one man who would represent the interests of the entire colony, although such a measure would save them a significant amount of money. In the next year's session, Stapleton urged that "all laws be alike in the respective islands ... we being under one government, and the like constitutions and circumstances." The assemblymen responded that such a plan "will not stand with the advantage and profit of the islands," and by 1683 the Kittitians used their sharing of their island with the French as a basis on which to be "excused from General Assemblyes and from the laws enacted by the authority thereof."[7] The governorship of Stapleton's successor, the elder Christopher Codrington (1689–98), coincided with an extended period of Anglo-French warfare, a situation in which the need for a united military command temporarily overcame most colonists' reluctance to cede any element of self-government, but as will be discussed later in this chapter, Governor Daniel Parke's machinations brought the General Assembly into disfavor, and in the wake of his murder in 1710 it was dissolved, never to be revived.[8] Later governors, though, were less inclined to place all of the blame for the General Assembly's decline on Parke; as Governor John Hart opined in 1722, "There is in all these people a certain indolence and indifference to all commands that do's not immediately relate to their own interest."[9]

If the inhabitants of the Leewards displayed little enthusiasm for the creation of trans-island structures of political authority, this skepticism was also at work within each of the islands in relation to the development of local mechanisms of governance. Until the final decades of the eighteenth century, none of the four islands had erected permanent structures in which to transact government business. This reluctance to invest in public building stemmed from several sources: The Leewards

---

[6] Council of Nevis to Lords of Trade and Plantations, February 14, 1684, BL 358, Blathwayt Papers, Henry E. Huntington Library, San Marino, CA.

[7] Higham, "General Assembly," 196.

[8] The Leeward Islands General Assembly was convened again after many years in 1798 to work on a slavery amelioration act for all of the islands. See David Barry Gaspar, "Ameliorating Slavery: The Leeward Islands Slave Act of 1798," in Robert L. Paquette and Stanley R. Engerman, eds., *The Lesser Antilles in the Age of European Expansion* (Gainesville: University Press of Florida, 1996), p. 242, and C.S.S. Higham, "The General Assembly of the Leeward Islands," Part II, *English Historical Review* 41:163(1926): 366–388.

[9] Hart to the Council of Trade and Plantations, July 11, 1722, C.S.P. Col., *1722–1723* (London: HMSO, 1934), 109.

had been captured, sacked, and recaptured multiple times in the course of Anglo-French hostilities between 1666 and 1713, and those residents who remained were more concerned with rebuilding their estates than they were with erecting imposing meeting places for the Council and Assembly or a stately residence for the royal governor. Although the threat of French invasion waned after the signing in 1713 of the Treaty of Utrecht, throughout the eighteenth century the Leewards were, even more than the other English colonies in the West Indies, subject to natural disasters, hurricanes, and earthquakes, which devastated town and country alike and which were particularly destructive of the more ambitious public and private buildings. Under these circumstances, the construction of dedicated government buildings was rarely a priority.

A deeply rooted skepticism about the nature of state power underlay the Leeward colonists' reluctance to invest in what Francis Dodsworth has termed "the fabrication of the administrative state in a prominent, permanent and symbolically significant form."[10] In many instances the Councils, Assemblies, and law courts held their sessions in a tavern or private home in the islands' capital cities. Although these venues were unlikely to include such accoutrements as the "2 dozen cane or leather chairs, 2 oval tables each big enough for 16 people, [and] 2 green carpets for tables" that were requested by the Council of St. Christopher's at the beginning of the eighteenth century, taverns might be fitted with special furnishings, such as platforms for trials, or might include a separate room decorated with symbols of royal authority, such as "the King's arms."[11] The minutes of a 1722 session of the Assembly of Nevis include a request that "Mrs. Olivia Williams be paid and allowed by the Publick for the Use of her house for a Court Hall for One Year ... Twenty five pounds"; in 1739, that island's Council noted that a local man, Robert Thompson, had kept a tavern in his house "for many years past ... for the Entertainment of the Council and Assembly and the several Courts of Law."[12] A decade later, the island government still lacked a building of its own, and the Council opted to rent two rooms in the house of John Canty to be used for Council and Assembly meetings and court

---

[10] Dodsworth, "*Virtus* on Whitehall: The Politics of Palladianism in William Kent's Treasury Building, 1733–6," *Journal of Historical Sociology* 18 (2005), 199.

[11] C.O. 241/4: St. Christopher's; Council Minutes, September 19, 1704; Martha J. McNamara, *From Tavern to Courthouse: Architecture and Ritual in American Law, 1658–1860* (Baltimore: Johns Hopkins University Press, 2004), 22.

[12] C.O. 186/1: Minutes of Nevis Council and Assembly, April 25, 1722; C.O. 186/3: Minutes of Nevis Council and Assembly, March 8, 1739.

sessions.[13] Across the strait in St. Christopher's, the situation was similar; in 1758, the Assembly remitted Alexander McCabee's tavern license fee with the understanding that "he shall furnish the Council and Assembly with Two Convenient Rooms to Sitt in and provide proper entertainment for both houses" and that he would also "provide dinner for the Judges of the Courts of Law and the Officers and Gentlemen that attend them."[14] Another contender for the government's patronage was a woman named Ann Titley, who requested exemption from licence fees for retailing strong liquors, "provided she do furnish the Council and Assembly with Two Convenient Rooms ... [and] proper Entertainment."[15] Two years later, the Assembly formed a committee "to hire for one year only a proper and Convenient House in the Town of Basseterre in which the Council and Assembly may hereafter meet and the Courts of Justice be held," and within a few weeks they had agreed with William Smith that "they might rent his house to this purpose for £125 a year."[16] By the summer of 1760, the public of St. Christopher's had finally agreed to finance a new public building in Basseterre, but in the course of its construction the island government relocated temporarily to the smaller town of Old Road, where "there not being a proper place ... for the Meeting of the Council and Assembly," a Mrs. Elizabeth Franks "proposed to this Board to open a Tavern there and provide such a place for the meeting of both Houses provided she can have a Licence granted her and the Tax imposed on Tavern keepers remitted," requests to which the Council agreed.[17] In Montserrat, it was not until 1769 that the Assembly voted in favor of raising funds to purchase "a proper and convenient Building ... for the Purpose of holding Courts of Judicature, and for other public Uses," and that structure was not custom-built for government business, but was instead a private home purchased from the lawyer Terry Legay.[18] Even in St. John's, the administrative and commercial center not only of Antigua, but of the whole Leeward colony, as late as 1764, at a time when the island's Assembly was beginning to challenge parliamentary privilege by

---

[13] Ibid., May 30, 1749.

[14] C.O. 241/7: St. Christopher's, Minutes of Council and Assembly, March 21, 1758.

[15] Ibid.

[16] C.O. 241/8: St. Christopher's, Minutes of Council and Assembly, January 4, 1760, February 20, 1760.

[17] C.O. 241/8, July 29, 1760.

[18] "An act for raising a sufficient Sum of Money to pay Terry Legay, Esquire, for the Purchase of his House sold to the Public of this Island," *Montserrat Code of Laws: from 1668, to 1788* (London: R. Hindmarsh, 1790), 174.

protesting aggressively against newly levied revenue acts, the island still lacked a "Publick Court House" and met

in such a House or Building as now is or can be rented by the Publick of this Island for those Purposes; and the same Inconveniencies always did and must follow the holding such Meetings in private Buildings, none of which are contrived properly for such Purposes, being generally much too small; so that all Persons, who are obliged to attend on such Occasions, suffer great Overheatings and Expence of Spirits, which there is good Reason to think has occasioned much Sickness, and even to have caused the Death of many Persons; and besides there are no Conveniencies in such private Buildings for the Grand Juries and Petty Juries to be in or withdraw to separately, but they have been forced often to retire to Taverns, and other Houses adjacent, while the Courts have been sitting.[19]

Antigua had boasted an imposing government house earlier in the century, erected at the behest of Governor Daniel Parke, but the Antiguans considered the building needlessly expensive and extravagant in its design, and soon came to view it as symbolic of what they considered to be Parke's tyranny. It became the site of his murder at the hands of the Antiguan colonists, and it was pillaged and left in ruins shortly thereafter as a symbol of the Antiguans' distaste for what they saw as excessive imperial interference in local affairs.

But if the Leeward colonists feared and resented the outward forms of governance, they were on the whole unable to avoid involvement in local politics. As Cecil Headlam has observed, "The Leeward Islands were overprovided [by metropolitan command] with administrative and legislative machinery," with the result that nearly all propertied white men would have been expected at some point in their lives to serve on the Council, in the Assembly, or as a lieutenant governor, judge, or justice of the peace in their island of residence. As an Antiguan planter and speaker of the island's Assembly, Samuel Martin, informed the readers of his *Essay upon Plantership*, if a man was "born to a large estate, or has acquired it by industry, he must expect to be a member of the legislature."[20] In Headlam's evaluation, "In such petty communities family connections and ties of interest bound together the few men of substance into cliques," and because

[19] "An Act for erecting a Publick Court House upon the Place commonly called the Market Place, in the Town of Saint John in Antigua, and appropriating the same Court-House, when built, to certain publick Uses," *Acts of Antigua* (London: John Baskett, 1764), 49.

[20] Martin, *An Essay upon Plantership* (London: A. Millar, 1765), ix. According to Michael Watson, "Assemblies in the Leeward Islands had ratios of one representative for fewer than 20 white males during the eighteenth century, by far the lowest in British America" (Watson, "British West Indian Legislatures," 93).

"practically all the other offices were served by deputy, and the deputies being necessarily resident and receiving only small returns for their works, [they] were dependents of the ruling oligarchy."[21] In order to vote or hold office, a Leeward male colonist had to be at least twenty-one years old, to be a native or naturalized British subject, and to have the freehold of ten acres of land or of real estate that incurred ten pounds a year in taxes, and metropolitan officials expressed the hope that all officeholders would be "Men of Good Life & well Effected to our Government and of Good Estates & abilities and not Necessitous Persons or so much in Debt."[22]

Trevor Burnard has suggested that white West Indian colonists, particularly those of sufficient wealth and social standing to reach the upper ranks of local politics, "found it difficult not to be tyrants in all of their relationships," surrounded as they were by people whose inferior social and legal status was written all too clearly on their bodies. Many governors of the Leewards, and of Britain's other sugar colonies, asserted that the islands' leading planters, those who filled the seats of the Assembly and the Council in each island, were on the whole "Obstinate and Perverse in their Nature and Manners: Inveterately disaffected to his Maj[es]ties Government: And that a person has been Esteem'd as the Most Couragious amongst them, who rejects everything propos'd by their Governours."[23] Until the middle of the eighteenth century, the majority of Leeward governors were either strangers to the islands or local men who had spent many years pursuing opportunities in the metropole. Crossing the Atlantic, usually leaving their families in England, and taking command of a colony they had never seen or from which they had long been absent, these men soon became aware that, although on paper they possessed extensive powers, in reality their unfamiliarity with local practices, their lack of kin and friends in the islands, and the small salary that forestalled them from dispensing patronage placed them in a difficult position in the face of local officeholders who, like many other colonial British Americans of this era, "saw every governor as a potential

[21] Headlam, "Introduction," *C.S.P. Col., 1726–1727* (London: HMSO, 1936), xxxviii.

[22] "An Act for preserving the Freedom of Elections; and appointing who shall be deemed Freeholders, and be capable of electing, or being elected Representatives," *Laws of the Island of St. Christopher, from the Year 1711, to the Year 1791* (Basseterre, St. Kitts: Edward Luther Low, 1791), 30; Instruction to Governor Hart from the Board of Trade and Plantations, C.O. 186/1, October 20, 1730.

[23] Burnard, "Theater of Terror: Domestic Violence in Thomas Thistlewood's Jamaica," in Christine Daniels and Michael V. Kennedy, eds., *Over the Threshold: Domestic Violence in Early America* (New York: Routledge, 1999), 244; Governor Hart to Board of Trade, January 20, 1722, C.O. 152/14: Board of Trade: Original Correspondence, Leeward Islands, 1721–4.

reincarnation of Charles I and James II."[24] Yet at the same time that the islands' Assemblies aggressively upheld what they considered to be their rights, asserting that their houses possessed privileges analogous to those of the British Commons, they also feared the broad powers the governor theoretically possessed, including the right to call or dismiss the Assemblies, to appoint or remove judges and other officers of the law, and to veto acts passed by the Council and Assembly. In situations in which both governor and governed were perpetually anxious about the nature and limits of one another's authority, it was easy for each side to convince itself of the other's malevolence and for rising tensions to explode into verbal or physical violence.

As difficult as the relationship between governors and the Assemblies could be, it was not the only source of political tension in the Leeward Islands. When a governor's frequent absences or his willingness to employ a light touch in his dealings with local officeholders removed one source of friction, island legislators might be moved to abandon the unity they had found in their opposition to the governor and fall to feuding among themselves. As Andrew O'Shaughnessy has observed, there existed within the Leewards "a strong predisposition to interpret virtually all political conflicts as struggles between prerogative and liberty." Taken in combination, these circumstances rendered the administrative and political life of the late-seventeenth- and eighteenth-century Leewards inherently unstable and overdetermined the outbreak of vitriolic conflict whenever even one member of the governing elite chose to upset the applecart – and in the first three quarters of the eighteenth century, many appeared to be willing, even eager, to do so.[25]

This chapter explores the formation of a core of political ideology and practice among Leeward white settlers through which they articulated a strong sense of British identity and an "overwhelming desire to be judged according to British values."[26] It examines a variety of instances in which they resorted to verbal, physical, and even murderous attacks against individuals they believed were attempting to undermine what they considered to be their natural rights as Englishmen. Again, we see a spirit of improvisation and adaptability at work: It was an audacious act to imagine that four varied islands could work together as a colony,

---

[24] O'Shaughnessy, *An Empire Divided*, 117.
[25] Ibid., 118.
[26] Trevor Burnard, "Ethnicity in Colonial American Historiography: A New Organising Principle," *Australasian Journal of American Studies* 10 (1992), 10.

and once established, the individual Leewards and their officials found themselves called on again and again to develop creative solutions to unforeseen challenges, while simultaneously negotiating constantly shifting and often highly individualized ideas of what it meant to create a recognizably English, and then British, colonial society in a world of tropical plantations.

"ARBITRARY POWER AND PRACTICES"

The four Leeward islands, like the mainland settlements of colonial British America, had by the latter half of the seventeenth century developed political institutions that were "based upon the principle of the British Constitution" and intended to replicate those of the mother country. Each of the islands had its own Council, which, in principle, functioned as a miniature version of the House of Lords, and Assembly, which filled the role of the Commons, while the governor served as the monarch's representative. As in Parliament, both houses had to approve an act, as did the governor, before it could become law, and any law that was in force for more than twelve months had to be confirmed by the Board of Trade, a subcommittee of the Privy Council.[27] Members of the Council and Assembly were drawn from among each island's inhabitants, while the governor was appointed by the monarch. The men of the Council also obtained their seats via the royal mandamus, but the selection process did not rest exclusively under metropolitan control; in many instances, it was the governor who proposed the appointment of Council members, based mostly on their wealth and their perceived loyalty to the Crown's interests, and requested the monarch's approval via that of the Board of Trade. Members of the island elites either enlisted the assistance of their governors or colonial agents, or wrote themselves to the Board of Trade or to friends in Parliament or at court requesting that they or their friends and associates be considered for open seats on the Council.

---

[27] Cecil A. Kelsick, "The Constitutional History of the Leewards," *Caribbean Quarterly* 6 (1960), 181; "The Leeward Islands: Their Past and Present Condition," *Proceedings of the Royal Colonial Institute* 12 (1881), 29. In the early 1660s, the Privy Council was aided in its administration of the colonies by the Council for Foreign Plantations, and in 1675 these responsibilities passed to the Lords of Trade, a subcommittee of the Privy Council; this group was in 1696 renamed the Lords Commissioners of Trade and Plantations and was generally known as the Board of Trade (Susan Dwyer Amussen, *Caribbean Exchanges: Slavery and the Transformation of English Society, 1640–1700* [Chapel Hill: University of North Carolina Press, 2007], 110).

Lacking firsthand knowledge of the local population, the monarch was in many instances willing to make these appointments on the basis of recommendations of his or her advisers or those of the Leewards' governor. No governor could remove a councillor without sufficient cause, and any such removal had immediately to be reported and justified to the monarch, again via the Board of Trade. This practice allowed councillors to acquire legitimacy simultaneously as representatives of their communities and as participants in imperial politics.[28] Moreover, although the governor, as the monarch's representative, in theory possessed considerable authority, he had to gain the cooperation of the Council in carrying out many of his responsibilities, including the primary duties of establishing courts, granting lands and confirming titles, calling the Assembly into session, and regulating the fees charged for various administrative and judicial procedures. Although the governor had the authority to dismiss uncooperative councillors, this power could be used only sparingly, as the number of suitable replacements was at any time very limited, and the small white elite classes of the Leewards were so heavily intermarried that a governor would in many situations be hard pressed to find an appropriate candidate who lacked close ties to his predecessor.[29]

In the Leewards, as throughout colonial British America, the interests of the royal governor frequently came into conflict with the desires of the Council and the locally elected Assembly; the history of these islands in the period under study is notable for the "ever-present tendency for the islands to assert themselves against the general authority of the governor."[30] Such a system of checks and balances was, of course, precisely the goal of many seventeenth- and eighteenth-century English constitutional theorists and politicians, who tended to view discord among the various elements of the "mixed constitution" as inevitable and relied on the carefully calibrated balance of power among the various branches of government to prevent the tyranny of any single group or individual. In the wake of the Glorious Revolution, Britons were filled with pride by what they saw as the ability of monarch, House of Lords, and House of Commons to forestall one another's potential abuses and excesses, and they believed, with some accuracy, that they were the freest and

[28] Kelsick, "Constitutional History," 181.

[29] F. G. Spurdle, *West Indian Government* (Christchurch, New Zealand: Whitcomb and Tombs, 1963), 34; Elsa V. Goveia, *Slave Society in the British Leeward Islands at the End of the Eighteenth Century* (New Haven: Yale University Press, 1965), 72.

[30] G. H. Guttridge, *The Colonial Policy of William III in America and the West Indies* (Cambridge: Cambridge University Press, 1922), 131.

best-governed people one could find anywhere in Europe and, by extension, throughout the globe. At the same time, though, they were convinced that their liberties were constantly under threat and that a central element of political life was the inevitable struggle between the defenders of English liberty and its attackers, both internal and external.[31] In the West Indian colonies, and particularly in the Leewards, an increasingly confident political elite had by the end of the seventeenth century come to believe that "the rights and privileges of Englishmen should apply to colonial subjects" and that implicit in the settlement of 1688 was the right of the Assemblies to all of the privileges and powers of Parliament.[32] In a 1689 letter to the Lords of Trade, the first Governor Christopher Codrington, urged that the Leewards' "subjection to and dependence on" Crown authority be strongly "asserted and further explained," as at least some of the colonists had shown "almost the vanity to fancy these Colonies independent states" and believed their "little assemblies" possessed authority comparable to that of the mother of parliaments.[33] But this colonial self-confidence was undermined by an awareness that it was the governor who had the ear of the Board of Trade and who thus held the power to influence imperial policy, as well as the more immediate authority to call, prorogue, and dismiss the Assemblies, to advise the Lords of Trade on nominations to the islands' Councils, and to veto any act of legislation approved by the Council and Assembly. When a governor chose to take an aggressive stance toward local pretensions, Leeward colonists were quick to become angry and fearful, believing that they lay at the mercy of a potential tyrant who could oppress them at home and slander them in the mother country.

On their own side, many of these governors felt that their office forced them into the impossible position of having to serve two masters, one of whom was far away in London and the other of whom was all too nearby. In principle, they wielded substantial viceregal authority, but in reality, they could assert their own initiatives only in minor matters and

---

[31] Jack P. Greene, "Empire and Identity," in P. J. Marshall, ed., *The Oxford History of the British Empire*, vol. 2, *The Eighteenth Century* (Oxford: Oxford University Press, 1998), 210.

[32] Stephen Conway, "From Fellow-Nationals to Foreigners: British Perceptions of the Americans, circa 1739–1783," *William and Mary Quarterly* s3:59 (2002), 76.

[33] William Laws, *Distinction, Death and Disgrace: Governorship of the Leeward Islands in the Early Eighteenth* Century (Kingston: Jamaican Historical Society, 1976), 66; Codrington to Lords of Trade, November 11, 1689, *C.S.P. Col., 1689–1682* (London: HMSO, 1901), 177.

were expected to follow to the letter the instructions issued by the Board of Trade. They might, for example, approve an act of one of the island legislatures or of the General Assembly in order to maintain cordial relations with local elites, but then faced the humiliating possibility that the board would disallow the act because it contradicted metropolitan law, damaged imperial economic interests, or encroached on the royal prerogative; should such a circumstance arise, the governor would lose face both with the board and among those he governed.[34] Of course, the same was true throughout colonial British America, but no other royal governor faced the prospect of dealing with four sets of Councils and Assemblies, as well as a federal one, all of which were noted for their aggressiveness toward imperial administration. Moreover, the governorship of the Leewards rewarded its incumbent with prestige but not with riches; for decades it offered the lowest salary of any governorship in the first British Empire. Metropole and colony alike expected a royal governor to dispense a considerable degree of hospitality and liberality in his person and household; one English visitor to mid-eighteenth-century Antigua claimed that a governor could not gain the respect and cooperation of local planters unless he could "not only keep an hospitable table, but be the jolly companion." But such a responsibility was difficult to fulfill if one lacked significant personal resources.[35] Moreover, the governor was dependent on the Assembly for payment of his salary, and it often suited the latter to keep the former "dependant on their favours from year to year," despite the difficulties inherent in "supporting the dignity of a Governour, in a place where all the necessarys of life are at a most extravagant price."[36]

As William Laws has noted, successful performance as a West Indian colonial governor "demanded that the incumbent be a first-class administrator, chancellor, probate judge, vice-admiral ... local head of the

[34] Laws, *Distinction*, 57.
[35] Henry Hulton, Comptroller of Customs at St. John's, Antigua, in the 1750s, described the Leeward governor George Thomas as "respected but not beloved," because although he was a native of Antigua and had a reputation among his subjects as a sensible and honest man, he was also "considered as parsimonious, and not living equal to his rank" (Hulton, "Account of Travels," Codex Eng. 74, 69, John Carter Brown Library, Providence, RI). On early modern Anglo-American ideals of hospitality, see Michal J. Rozbicki, *The Complete Colonial Gentleman: Cultural Legitimacy in Plantation America* (Charlottesville: University Press of Virginia, 1998), 157–61, and Lawrence Stone, *The Crisis of the Aristocracy, 1558–1641* (New York: Oxford University Press, 1967), 256–7.
[36] Hart to Board of Trade, April 4, 1722, *C.S.P. Col., 1722–1723*, 36.

Church of England, diplomatist, commander-in-chief ... strategist, [and] military engineer ... and above all a go-between in metropolitan–colonial relations," and that he be able to fulfill these diverse responsibilities in a situation in which "it was hardly possible for him to avoid trouble either with London or with the colony."[37] Some Leeward governors were successful in carrying out this delicate balancing act, but others enraged island residents by committing actions that the islanders saw as threatening both their liberty and their property. In 1690, the merchant and writer Dalby Thomas claimed that "the great discouragement those [West Indian] Collonies lye under, is the Arbitrary Power and practices of their Governours there ... which some have to their undoing felt and all are liable to," a complaint Leeward residents made again and again over the course of the late seventeenth and eighteenth centuries. These colonists were unshakable in their belief that "the Greatest and Best of Kings never gave any one of his Subjects Authority to oppress the rest," as when "a Person whom he imploys to take Care of them ... shall by Virtue of that Authority ... assume a Power of doing such Things as will only answer Purposes diametrically opposite to those his Duty obliges him to Promote."[38] When such a governor appeared to pose a threat to the security of their persons and property, colonists drew on the concept of the right to resistance that was explicit in the rhetoric of the Glorious Revolution and remained implicit in the settlement generated by that revolution. The combination of such strong convictions with the "intense ardor, [and] the unbounded ferocity of politics" in this era made conflict between the governors and the governed unavoidable.[39] In a struggle between official prerogative and local practice, the stakes were high, and in a political culture that tended to valorize individual honor and self-assertion over cooperation and compromise, the results could be devastating.

THE "MALE-ADMINISTRATION" OF COLONEL DANIEL PARKE

Chapter 4 examined in some detail the sexual depredations committed by Daniel Parke while he served as governor of the Leewards from 1706

[37] Laws, *Distinction*, 1.
[38] Thomas, *An Historical Account of the Rise and Growth of the West-India Collonies* (London: John Hindmarsh, 1690), 42; "Standing Up for the Liberties of my Fellow Subjects," in *The Barbadoes Packet* (London: S. Popping, 1720), 3.
[39] Patricia U. Bonomi, *The Lord Cornbury Scandal: The Politics of Reputation in British America* (Chapel Hill: University of North Carolina Press, 1998), 7.

to 1710. These misdeeds have played the largest part in the development of Parke's posthumous notoriety; as the preceding chapter emphasized, Parke's sexual behavior inflamed Leeward public opinion because it challenged entrenched ideals of masculine honor, feminine virtue, and patriarchal order. But these transgressions were only one element of Parke's bad reputation in life and after death, and represented just one aspect of his apparent contempt for the people he governed. While Parke deliberately flouted conventional morality relating to sexual behavior, he simultaneously persisted in violating what his subjects viewed as their rights as Englishmen. Although his sexual activities clearly angered and alarmed many Leeward colonists, particularly those whose wives or daughters numbered among the governor's many conquests, it was Parke's abuses of political authority that inflamed public opinion against him and led directly to his death at the hands of those he governed.

Parke would probably have been an ill-advised choice for the governorship of any British American colony. He had spent his youth in the pursuit of dissipation and had developed a reputation both in his native Virginia and in England as "a complete sparkish Gentleman," one whose "quick resentment of every the least thing that looks like an affront or Injury" made him "the greatest Hector in the Town," whether that town was Williamsburg or London.[40] Not only was Parke apparently a womanizer and a spendthrift who appeared to have little concern for the public humiliation or financial difficulties to which he subjected his wife and daughters, but he was sufficiently hot tempered to have taken a horsewhip to Francis Nicholson, the governor of Maryland, when the latter publicly accused him of lying.[41] Outbursts such as these made Parke highly unpopular in Chesapeake society and encouraged him to leave Virginia and to seek his fortune and pleasure in England, where, after an unsuccessful attempt to gain a seat in the House of Commons, he joined Queen Anne's army, which was then embroiled in the War of the Spanish Succession.[42] Parke became aide-de-camp to John Churchill, duke of Marlborough, and found his great opportunity in 1704, when Marlborough dispatched him to the queen with the welcome news of

---

[40] James Blair, quoted in Parke Rouse, Jr., *James Blair of Virginia* (Chapel Hill: University of North Carolina Press, 1971), 105.

[41] Ibid., 106.

[42] Parke took a seat in the House of Commons as a member for Whitchurch, Hampshire, where he owned an estate, but was expelled soon after his arrival on a charge of bribery; see Vere Langford Oliver, *The History of the Island of Antigua* (London: Mitchell and Hughes, 1894), vol. 1, 2.

the duke's victory at Blenheim. So enthused was Anne by the report of this triumph that she rewarded Parke with a purse containing the vast sum of a thousand guineas, as well as a miniature portrait of herself, encrusted with diamonds. Apparently the queen was also taken with Parke's physical attractiveness and his ability to display considerable charm when it was in his interest to do so. When the post of governor of the Leeward Islands came open some months after the battle of Blenheim, upon the death of Sir William Mathew, she appointed Parke to the position.[43]

Neither Parke nor the planters of the Leewards viewed this turn of events with particular enthusiasm. For the better part of twenty years, the islands had been dominated by two governors named Christopher Codrington, father and son, who had angered many of the settlers with what struck them as an arrogant and high-handed style of rule. The planters' tempers had been piqued over the course of many years in which the Codringtons had continually frustrated them by transacting most of their political business through the General Assembly, which represented all four islands, thus essentially ignoring the four local Assemblies. Both father and son had been accused of arbitrary use of their power in relation to the liberty, and particularly the property, of individual islanders; in 1701 William Freeman, a Kittitian planter, laid charges in the House of Commons against the younger Codrington, whom he claimed had dispossessed him and several other planters of their legitimately held estates.[44]

But however unhappy the Leeward colonists had been under the leadership of the Codringtons or under Mathew's brief administration, few in the islands welcomed the arrival of any new governor, and Daniel Parke's personal history encouraged many to dislike him long before they met him and, on the whole, confirmed their negative impressions. Unlike Mathew and the Codringtons, who at least were natives of the West Indies, Parke was a Virginian by birth and a Londoner by preference. The circumstances of his promotion were also suspect in the eyes of many of his new subjects, who failed to discern in him any personal qualities of intellect, courage, or leadership that might render him worthy of his office. They

---

[43] Richard Dunn, *Sugar and Slaves: The Rise of the Planter Class in the English West Indies, 1624–1713* (Chapel Hill: University of North Carolina Press, 1973), 144.

[44] See *A Copy of the Petition of William Freeman, Esq., in behalf of himself, Mr Mead, and others, owners of several tracts of land in the Charibbee Islands in America against Colonel Codrington, Governor of the Leeward Islands, presented in the House of Commons, with remarks thereon* (London: n.p., 1702).

might have welcomed the appointment of a fellow colonial rather than a Westminster placeman to the post, but they also resented the fact that a man from what they considered to be the far less economically and strategically valuable colonies of the North American mainland, rather than another West Indian, should be given such a position. Parke's reputation as a ladies' man obsessed with personal advancement suggested to many that he owed his success to Queen Anne's having developed something of a passion for him. Although even the most scurrilous gossips constrained themselves from accusing the matronly, middle-aged, and generally popular monarch from having entered into any kind of sexual relationship with Parke, some feared that the latter's charisma had clouded Anne's judgment, and they were equally skeptical of Parke's connection with John and Sarah Churchill, the duke and duchess of Marlborough, who many British subjects at home and abroad thought wielded far too much influence in Parliament and at court.[45] The colonial public, like that of the metropole, tended to be suspicious of those who occupied the position of royal favorite and resented such individuals' reaping what they considered to be undeserved rewards in the political as well as the financial and social spheres.

Parke's connection with the Marlboroughs and the suspicious nature of his relationship to Anne, combined with his reputation as a spendthrift and a rake, as well as his reported attempt to bribe his way into a seat in the Commons, made him suspect to those Leeward residents whose metropolitan connections had informed them of his history before his arrival in the islands. Those who were particularly well versed in the politics of Britain's North American colonies would probably have been troubled to learn that Parke had in his youth been a protégé and a great admirer of Edmund Andros, who had served variously as governor of New York, of the short-lived Dominion of New England, and of Virginia, and had been recalled from each of these posts, at least in part because of his imperious and arbitrary style of governance, in which he repeatedly picked quarrels with important local figures and attempted to place strict limits on the powers of the colonial assemblies. For his own part, Parke was less than enthused about becoming governor of the Leewards, an office with a low salary in a remote locale. Parke had hoped that Anne might appoint him governor of Virginia, perhaps imagining himself returning home in triumph to rule over old adversaries. Instead, he resented finding himself

[45] Bonomi, *Lord Cornbury*, 109–10.

in the position of an "unfortunate Divel here to be roasted in the sun, without the prospect of getting anything."[46]

When Parke landed at Antigua in July 1706, the islands were suffering the ongoing effects of the War of the Spanish Succession: The French had recently ravaged Nevis and St. Kitts and threatened to attack again, and privateers lurked in the waters around the islands and rendered shipping hazardous. Many islanders were convinced that England was doing far too little to assist its colonies in the course of a war that had resulted from European politics rather than local inclinations.[47] John Johnson, lieutenant governor of Nevis and acting governor of the Leewards in the period between Mathew's death and Parke's arrival, claimed that many people were "very much dispirited, not to say despairing," and that they contemplated leaving the Leewards to seek a more secure settlement elsewhere in British America. At the same time, the islands struggled to cope with a series of natural disasters: Antigua, always dry, was in the throes of a severe drought, fever was epidemic on Nevis for the second time in a decade, and all four islands had been significantly damaged by a recent hurricane.[48] At such a difficult time, assertiveness on the part of the governor would not necessarily have been unwelcome. But Parke's actions, though decisive, almost immediately alienated the majority of his constituents, including Christopher Codrington the younger, who had succeeded his late father as governor from 1700 until 1704 and who had unsuccessfully lobbied the Board of Trade to regain the position after the death of his successor, Mathew. Codrington resented Parke, viewing him as an upstart who had gained his post illegitimately, and Parke, realizing that "that Machiavell" Codrington was an implacable and powerful opponent, decided to preempt any malfeasance on the latter's part by striking at him first.[49] Not only did Parke confiscate Codrington's enormous estate on St. Kitts, but

---

[46] Quoted in Dunn, *Sugar and Slaves*, 144. Parke claimed that "the Duke [of Marlborough] promised me the Government of Virginia at the Battle of Blenheim, but for some Reasons of State that was given to my Lord Orkney"; see Oliver, *History of Antigua*, vol. 1, lxxviii.

[47] Nevis was the capital and thus the residence of the Leeward governor from 1671 until 1698, at which point its population and prosperity had so declined in comparison with the far larger island of Antigua that the seat of government was moved to St. John's (Keith Mason, "The World an Absentee Planter and His Slaves Made: Sir William Stapleton and His Nevis Sugar Estate, 1722–1740," *Bulletin of the John Rylands Library* 75 [1993], 108).

[48] Laws, *Distinction*, 10.

[49] Algernon E. Aspinall, "The Fate of Governor Parke," in *West Indian Tales of Old* (New York: Negro Universities Press, 1969), 25; Higham, "General Assembly," 206.

he challenged "by what authority, he the said Codrington did hold the island of Barbuda" and brought suit to force Codrington to give up the substantial amount of prize money he had acquired during the early years of the war against France.[50] Parke also missed no opportunity to defame Codrington; he accused him of erring in respect to Colonel Johnson, an allegedly illiterate former bricklayer, by successively honoring him with the positions of major, lieutenant colonel, and lieutenant governor of Nevis. According to Parke, Codrington thus favored Johnson because the latter had brought him a "store of black cattle during the war."[51] He also claimed that Codrington, whose public reputation was that of a devout Christian whose preferred leisure activity was reading patristic texts, had fathered a child by a low-status white woman, only to break with her after she infected him with a venereal disease. By making these charges against Codrington, Parke publicly denounced his opponent as having conducted himself basely as a governor, as a planter, and as a man, three interconnected roles that constituted Codrington's claim to an honorable status in the Leewards and the mother country alike.

Parke made a serious miscalculation when he chose to attack Codrington. He may have believed that harassing Codrington would not only subdue his principal opponent but would win him favor among the islanders, many of whom had resented what they considered the latter's high-handed and self-serving ways during his governorship; they had not been displeased when the Board of Trade recalled him in 1704. Ardent royalist that he professed himself to be, Parke may also have thought that by attacking Codrington he would demonstrate the power of the monarch, as employed by her representative, to prevent overmighty subjects from aggrandizing themselves at the expense of their less powerful neighbors or of royal prerogative. In reality, though, Parke's assaults on Codrington encouraged many Leeward residents to alter their opinion of the latter and to view him less as a fallen tyrant than as a fellow sufferer at the hands of the new governor. If Parke could use his position to attack a man such as Codrington, with his title, his thousands of acres of land, his hundreds of slaves, his Oxford education, and his connections within the highest echelons of English political and cultural life, who

---

[50] Aspinall, "Fate," 34; Dunn, *Sugar and Slaves*, 145. Barbuda, a 68-square-mile coral island twenty-five miles north of Antigua, had been leased by the Crown to the elder Christopher Codrington and his brother John in 1685, at a rent of "one fat sheep yearly, if demanded"; in 1705, Queen Anne had renewed the lease for another ninety-nine years, at the same rent.

[51] Oliver, *History of Antigua*, vol. 1, lxxvi.

could consider themselves safe from the governor's aggression? Parke's attempts to divest Codrington of his lands in St. Kitts and Barbuda were particularly alarming to island residents because they implied that this new governor was willing to call into question even long-held titles to landed property, the most powerful symbol of an individual colonist's status and independence. Through his treatment of Codrington, Parke brought about a situation in which his subjects were inclined to view him as the tyrannical oppressor and Codrington as his hapless victim.

Parke might have been able to subdue Codrington without aggravating public opinion against him had he not simultaneously embarked on a program that he claimed was one of much-needed administrative reform but that appeared to many islanders to be a blatant attack on what they considered their right to govern themselves. Within a few months of his arrival in the Leewards, Parke began to reshuffle the lieutenant governors of the four islands and also undertook to fill the islands' Councils beyond their prescribed limits; he carried out both endeavors in order to place his supporters in positions of authority, particularly so that they might aid his efforts to stamp out the illegal but highly lucrative trade that many colonists carried out with the nearby Dutch and French islands.[52] The Board of Trade reprimanded him for these actions, which ran contrary to their instructions, but reluctantly gave their assent to the appointments, hoping that Parke would restrain himself in the future.[53]

No such restraint was forthcoming, either from the governor or the governed. It was Parke's misfortune to have taken command of the Leewards at a moment when the islands' Assemblies were in a mood to test their authority by claiming ever greater powers, most of which were at the expense of the Crown and its representative, the governor; it was equally unfortunate, from the colonists' point of view, that they had been placed at such a challenging moment under the control of a man so intent on upholding royal authority over local wishes. In the summer of 1708, tensions flared between Parke and the Assembly of Antigua over a bill "for ascertaining ... the rights, powers, authorities and priviledges" of the latter. The assemblymen demanded that veto power over acts of legislation lie with the speaker of the Assembly, rather than with the governor, or even with the Crown, and that the Assembly be allowed to act as a court of judicature. Parke was equally incensed by both

---

[52] Charles Royster, *The Fabulous History of the Dismal Swamp Company: A Story of George Washington's Times* (New York: Knopf, 1999), 17.
[53] Spurdle, *Early West Indian Government*, 39; Oliver, *History of Antigua*, vol. 1, lxxvi.

measures; he wrote to the Board of Trade that, had he agreed to lodge veto power with the speaker, he himself "ought to have been hanged" and that the Assembly's demand for judicial powers stemmed from its desire to "imprison and fine anyone that should reflect on anyone of their House," including himself, the island's lieutenant governor, or the members of the Council. When he refused to approve a bill of such an "extraordinary nature," one that, had he accepted it, would undoubtedly have been disallowed by the Board of Trade, the Assembly drew on its power of the purse and denied him funds for his rental of a house in St. John's. As the legislative session moved to its adjournment, Parke attempted to soothe the assemblymen's tempers, apologizing that "my administration is not pleasing to you" and explaining his veto by claiming that "I cannot comply with what You have desired; it being contrary to my Instructions."[54]

Parke's conciliatory tone impressed the Board of Trade far more than it did the Antiguans. The first set of formal complaints against the governor reached London in the summer of 1708, along with Parke's responses to these charges. Upon consideration, the board found Parke's statements, and the glowing testimonials he had gathered from some of the islands' councillors and from officers in the royal regiments then stationed in the Leewards, more convincing than the statements of his opponents, which they deemed to be "false," "irregular," and "scandalous." The members of the board were troubled by what they saw as the dangerous pretensions of the Antiguan Assembly in its demands for "unwarrantable priviledges"; they concluded that Parke's governorship had been marked by "great zeal for H[er].M[ajesty's]. service" and that he had displayed "great care and diligence for the good and security" of the islands.[55] But the board's dismissal of these charges increased tensions rather than, as it had hoped, lessening them. While his exoneration by the board, and its praise of his performance, encouraged Parke to continue to stand fast against his disgruntled public, his opponents, frustrated by their failure to bring about his rebuke or recall, committed themselves to an all-out campaign against him in colony and metropole alike. At the beginning of 1709, they drew up twenty-two articles against the governor, in which they requested that Queen Anne recall Parke in light of his misgovernment, and dispatched the merchant William Nevine to London to present their grievances to the colonial

[54] Laws, *Distinction*, 59, 60.
[55] Ibid., 73, 74.

agent for Antigua, Richard Cary, and to the monarch and the Board of Trade.[56] During the months between Nevine's departure for England and the royal response to his representation, tensions rose still higher between Parke and the Antiguans, and a number of islanders responded to this charged atmosphere with intimations of violence. In February 1709, the brothers Barry and John Tankerd, who had long been among Parke's staunchest opponents, armed some of their slaves and posted guards on paths running through their estates in order to forestall the governor's ability to execute any warrant against them. A few weeks later, Barry Tankerd organized a meeting of prominent Antiguan citizens, "who were all armed ... [and] all inimical to Parke."[57] The summer hurricane season passed tensely but without violence, but this peace was shattered in September when Sandy, a slave belonging to John Otto-Baijer, who with his brother Bastian was one of Parke's most ardent opponents, shot Parke in what was clearly an assassination attempt, leaving the governor alive but with a shattered left arm and a renewed determination to block his subjects' increasingly desperate attempts to rid themselves of him by fair means or foul.[58]

In March 1710, news arrived from London that most Leeward residents greeted with joy; on February 5 the Privy Council had issued an order demanding that Parke return to England to answer the charges his subjects had presented against him, and on February 25 the Crown had revoked Parke's commission as governor and ordered him to resign immediately in favor of Colonel Walter Hamilton, the lieutenant governor of St. Kitts.[59] Considering how strongly the Board of Trade had backed Parke in response to the earlier complaints against him, why might they have turned against him so quickly thereafter? Taken on an individual basis, none of the twenty-two original articles of complaint, or the nine that were submitted slightly later, was exceptionally damning. Many of them focused not on Parke's actions, but on his words. The first one claimed that Parke "did frequently and publickly declare, That he had assurance from my Lord High-Treasurer of *England*, and the Dutchess of *Marlborough*, that he should be supported and protected, let him do what he would."[60] Other articles asserted that Parke "hath

[56] Aspinall, "Fate," 38; Oliver, *History of Antigua* vol. 1, lxxix.
[57] Oliver, *History of Antigua*, vol. 1, lxxix, lxxx.
[58] Ibid., lxxxi; Bonomi, *Lord Cornbury*, 186.
[59] Aspinall, "Fate," 40; Oliver, *History of Antigua*, vol. I, lxxxi.
[60] The articles and Parke's responses are in C.O. 152/8, and are reprinted in George French, *The History of Colonel Parke's Administration* (London: n.p., 1717), 90–172. All

frequently declar'd his high and severe Resentment against a great many Persons who voted for such Men [the Antigua Assemblymen] to be their Representatives," that he had announced that "he would be guided by no Laws or Precedents whatsoever, in making his Decrees" in the Antigua Court of Chancery," and that he "has several Times threaten'd to displace and turn out Judges of the Common Law."[61] Still others seem more indicative of petty jealousies in the islands than of active malevolence on Parke's part, such as the article claiming that "he has made and appointed Justices of the Peace of the meanest and lowest Rank, and most wretched Character" or that he "hath appointed one of his Creatures [Michael Ayon], who came over a private Man in the Regiment now station'd in the Leeward Islands, Provost Marshal" of Antigua. According to William Laws, the board was to blame for many of the problems that grew up between Parke and the Leeward colonists, as it had failed to provide the governor with regular instructions or to take seriously the earlier rumblings of discontent from the islands. In addition, although the board had apparently promised Parke that he would be allowed to read and respond to all complaints against him before it made any decision regarding his future, it failed to notify him of the nature of the charges against him before ordering him back to London to answer these charges. It seems likely that at least part of the board's sudden turn against Parke stemmed from the waning power of the duke of Marlborough and a desire of John Churchill's opponents to speed his political demise by striking at his protégé. In any case, it was clear to Parke that his options consisted of "either staying here ... to seem thereby to faile in my regard to H[er]. M[ajesty's]. Order, or to appear before Her covered with crimes."

Faced with these unappealing options, Parke chose to remain in Antigua, hoping that he might profit by cultivating the friendship of the new secretary of state, Lord Dartmouth, whom he thought might resolve the difficult situation in the Leewards by offering the embattled governor a comfortable appointment in England. But Parke appeared to have underestimated the depth of hatred many Leeward colonists, particularly the Antiguans, felt for him; if he believed that they had vented their frustrations in the articles of complaint and thus achieved a degree of catharsis toward his administration, he was entirely mistaken. In March 1710, he called a meeting of the General Assembly of the

references are to French's volume; emphasis in original. The lord treasurer was Sidney Godolphin, a close associate of the Marlboroughs.

[61] French, *History*, 119–20, 131, 145.

Leewards for the first time since his arrival in the islands. In so doing, he may have taken a leaf from the Codringtons' book, bypassing the individual Assemblies, particularly that of Antigua, with the intention of diluting the influence of disaffected individuals therein. But here, as in Antigua, Parke's determination to minimize the legislature's powers ran up against that body's desire to expand these powers. After listening to the governor's request for their approval of a substantial program of legislation, the members of the General Assembly clashed with him on the issue of who held the privilege of appointing the clerk of the Assembly. According to the assemblymen, it was they, not Parke, who held this right, as such was the practice in the individual Assemblies of the four islands. The governor saw the issue very differently; after all, as he informed the General Assembly, the House of Commons itself lacked the power to select its own clerks, and "he would accept no argument from antiquity, for the few decades of existence of the local assemblies could not be weighed against the hoary customs of parliament, on whose procedure he gave a lengthy disquisition."[62] The assemblymen, however, were on the whole unconvinced by Parke's lecture and, led by the delegates from Antigua, retorted that, should they be refused the right to appoint their own clerk, they would do no further business, at which point the governor felt that he had no option but to dissolve the session by proclamation.

In the wake of the dismissal of the General Assembly and of Parke's refusal to return to England, the Antiguans despaired of liberating themselves of their hated governor. After several years of relative calm, the French naval threat suddenly intensified, causing Parke to request funds for the island's defense. Frustrated by their inability to rid themselves of him, the General Assembly invoked its power to refuse to vote the governor supplies, despite the rumored approach of a French fleet. As tempers frayed, Parke made his most audacious strike yet against the liberties of his subjects by admitting a party of grenadiers into the Assembly's chambers in Government House at St. John's and ordering the soldiers to disperse the legislators at the point of their bayonets.

At this moment, the situation passed from tense to lethal. The dismissed assemblymen and their supporters spent the next several days roaming the streets of St. John's, making speeches, stockpiling weapons, and organizing a demonstration by which they hoped to serve Parke with

---

[62] Higham, "General Assembly," 206–7.

"such a pill ... as he should not digest" and to attack him "by such a force ... as would drive him and his grenadiers to the devil!"[63] In the face of this turmoil, Parke withdrew from public view and sequestered himself with a small band of his supporters in Government House, which he garrisoned with his seventy grenadiers and armed with five cannons that had earlier been brought from Nevis in the face of the threat of French attack. On the morning of December 7, a mob estimated to have consisted of four to five hundred men, many of whom had recently made their way to St. John's to confront the governor, surrounded Government House and demanded that the governor dismiss his soldiers, resign his post, and leave the island immediately. When Parke refused to "quit the Government with which he had been entrusted by his Royal Mistress," his opponents formed two assault squads. Captain John Piggott and his men attacked the governor's mansion from the front, and those com-manded by Captain Painter advanced on it from the rear.[64] Parke ordered that the soldiers fire on the attackers, but the mob, which outnumbered the defenders by at least 6 to 1, soon overwhelmed the grenadiers and broke into the house, where they found that Parke had locked himself in his bedchamber. Piggott and his men broke down the door, at which point Parke shot and killed Piggott, but was almost immediately felled by a bullet wound to his leg.

Hereafter, the story becomes murky. The relatively sober accounts assert that Parke's wound was mortal and that Piggott's men permitted some of the governor's defenders to transport him to the nearby house of a Mr. Wright, where Gousse Bonnin, a Huguenot physician, bandaged the wound, but these ministrations came too late to prevent the governor's death from blood loss.[65] However, a number of alternative versions claim that Parke's end was far more violent. One account concurs that Parke died in Wright's home under the care of Dr. Bonnin. The same account states, however, that after Parke was wounded the crowd did not imme-diately permit his friends to remove him, but instead stripped him of his clothes "with such violence that only the wrist and neckbands of his shirt were left on him" and dragged him down the steps of Government House and into the street. There, his assailants, after getting their fill of insulting and reviling him, left him to die of his wounds and of thirst in the heat of the afternoon, at which point Wright and Bonnin were able to ease his

[63] Aspinall, "Fate," 42.
[64] Ibid., 44.
[65] Oliver, *History of Antigua*, vol. 1, lxxxi.

end.[66] Other variations of the story depict the attackers as rending apart not only Parke's clothes, but his body; they "dragged him by the members about his house, bruised his head, and broke his back with the butt end of their pieces."[67] Another version of the story is still gorier, maintaining that after Parke was felled by his leg wound he was "then torn into pieces and scattered in the street."[68]

To discern which, if any, of these versions represents the reality of Parke's death is impossible; the fighting was close, and the witnesses, both Parke's supporters and his opponents, had ample motivation to exaggerate or to minimize the seriousness of his injuries. However, the final version of the story, the one claiming that the mob mutilated Parke's body, perhaps while he was still alive, is the one that has captured the imaginations of both contemporary pamphleteers and modern historians. Part of the anecdote's interest stems directly from its luridness and its uniqueness in the history of colonial British America; no other royal governor suffered such a fate, even in the course of the American Revolution. But at the same time, the story of dismemberment continues to resonate because it fits so well with how contemporaries and scholars alike conceived of Parke and the threat he appeared to pose to the integrity of the Leeward body politic. The idea that Parke's body natural was destroyed, cut or torn into pieces, at the hands of a crowd representing the body politic has a kind of poetic justice. As Lorna Clymer has observed:

Fragmenting the living body of one who dared to challenge the integrity of the body politic was a common means of British punishment for treason and sedition. Heads and the body parts generated by the execution method of drawing and quartering were commonly displayed during the sixteenth and seventeenth centuries on London's gates and public buildings. Several of the forty-one identified as regicides were executed in the fall of 1660 according to what were already standard forms of punishment for treason: they were first hung, their members were cut off, their bowels removed through abdominal incisions, and the various quadrants of their bodies were drawn and then displayed throughout the city.[69]

---

[66] Aspinall, "Fate," 45–6.
[67] Quoted in Dunn, *Sugar and Slaves*, 146.
[68] Edwards, *The History, Civil and Commercial, of the British Colonies in the West Indies* (Philadelphia: J. Humphreys, 1806), vol. 2, 166.
[69] Clymer, "Cromwell's Head and Milton's Hair: Corpse Theory in Spectacular Bodies of the Interregnum," *Eighteenth Century* 40 (1999), 97.

Of course, it is impossible to verify the account of Parke's dismemberment. The importance of the story lies not in its veracity, but in its appearance and reappearance in different accounts of the governor's death. To George French, Parke's staunchest defender, the dismemberment testified to the "turbulent Spirits and Loose Principles" of the "fomenters in the Rebellion," and French invoked the mutilation of Parke's body as an appeal to Parliament to mete out severe punishment to the guilty.[70] To the Jamaican planter-historian Bryan Edwards, writing nearly eighty years later, on the other hand, the destruction of Parke's physical body was a harsh but necessary response on the part of the long-suffering Antiguans; "it was as lawful to cut him off by every means possible as it would have been to shoot a wild beast that had broke its limits and was gorging itself on human blood."[71] The fact that the anecdote appears in the writings of French, Parke's principal apologist, and of Edwards, who execrated him, does not prove that it accurately describes Parke's fate. What it does demonstrate is that many people considered such a punishment to have been entirely appropriate in light of Parke's offenses.

In response to this act of high treason, Lieutenant Governor Walter Hamilton of St. Kitts, now acting governor of the Leewards, summoned a meeting of the General Assembly in St. John's to aid him in his inquiries into the murder. To his great frustration, Hamilton found that the Antiguan public, to a man, professed complete ignorance of the circumstances of the late governor's death, despite the fact that several hundred white Antiguan men (of a population of approximately 700 adult white males) – "all or ... most of Her Majesty's subjects" on the island – had participated in the attack on the governor's mansion, and those who had not taken an active role in the assault were almost certainly aware of what had transpired.[72] Queen Anne, distraught at the violent death of her onetime protégé, sent General Walter Douglas, a professional soldier, to Antigua to serve as the Leewards' new governor, in the hope that a strong-arm military man might be able to resolve the situation. To Anne's distress, Douglas had no more success than Hamilton in bringing Parke's murderers to justice, as "the feeling against Parke was so strong that he dared not punish those implicated in the murder."[73] To arrest every adult

[70] French, *History*, 1, 86–7.
[71] Edwards, *History*, vol. 2, 166.
[72] Higham, "General Assembly," 207; Carol Walter Ramagosa, "Eliza Lucas Pinckney's Family in Antigua, 1668–1747," *South Carolina Historical Magazine* 99 (1998), 243.
[73] Aspinall, "Fate," 47.

white male in Antigua was impossible, and although some Antiguans publicly professed themselves to be disgusted by the fact that Parke's murder symbolized an act of treasonous rebellion against the Crown, few were willing to risk incurring their neighbors' wrath by naming those involved in the plot.

At Anne's behest, Douglas issued a general pardon to the Antiguans but attempted to find "not fewer than three nor more than six" ringleaders of whom he might make an example. Douglas fulfilled this order by imprisoning William Hamilton, John Kerr, John King, and John Painter in St. John's, while Dr. William Mackinen and Samuel Watkins, who had traveled to London in the wake of Parke's death, were arrested upon their arrival and imprisoned at Newgate.[74] The men's imprisonment, however, did not last long, and the Antiguan elections of 1711 made clear the public's feelings about the killing of Parke; the voters returned all of the members of the previous rebel Assembly to their seats.[75] Antiguans were in retrospect shocked and somewhat cowed by the savagery with which they had resolved the problem of Parke, and some were willing to admit that they had participated in "an act for which they must ever begg God's pardon and Her Majesty's mercy." In the same breath, though, they maintained that the "desperate proceedings ... and aggravating circumstances" of Parke's rule were the first cause of their actions and that the late governor's depredations had "deprived [them] of their reason and ... wrought [them] up by despair and revenge," circumstances in which their only recourse was the drastic exigency of destroying Parke before he could destroy their English liberties. Although some participants in Parke's murder may well have felt a degree of regret for their actions, on the whole the Leeward colonists believed that they had behaved justly and

[74] Ibid., 47. Painter had been one of the leaders of the attack on Parke's house, and Kerr had allegedly threatened to cut the governor's throat when the grenadiers had broken up the Assembly. In his account of Parke's murder, George French described Mackinen as "one of the most criminal" in relation to Parke's death (French, *History*, 67).

[75] Mackinen and Watkins were released under the provisions of the Act of Grace issued by George I upon his accession to the throne in 1715, as noted by Mackinen's descendant Daniel McKinnen in his *Tour through the British West Indies, in the years 1802 and 1803* (London: J. White, 1804), 74. In 1791, Sir William Young, governor of Dominica, encountered on St Vincent an ancient slave named Granny Sarah, who had spent her childhood on Antigua, and informed Young that "she remembers perfectly well the rejoicing on the Sacra's (white men's) being let out of gaol, who had killed Governor Park" (Young, *A Tour through the Several Islands of Barbados, St. Vincent, Antigua, Tobago, and Grenada in the Years 1791 and 1792* [London: John Stockdale, 1801]). Thanks to Simon Smith for this reference.

that they had escaped communal and individual punishment for Parke's murder because they had succeeded in convincing the Crown and the Board of Trade that Parke had far overstepped his rights as governor, and thus was a danger to the political integrity of colony and metropole alike. This view was reflected and promulgated by West Indian historical writers throughout the next century.[76]

According to Richard Dunn, "The murder of Governor Parke ... was not an isolated or accidental event. It summed up many long years of life on the tropical firing line."[77] In Dunn's view, Parke's murder was just another example, albeit an exceptionally bloody one, of the "disastrous social failures" of the West Indies, as precipitated by the supposedly violent and uncivilized people who populated them.[78] In reality, though, the murder *was* in important ways an isolated event in the history of the English West Indian colonies. As we have observed, Leeward colonists, though certainly replete with prejudices, dislikes, and insecurities, were in many instances willing and able to incorporate into society various representatives of initially suspect groups and individuals, including Irish Catholics, Scots, Sephardic Jews, Quakers, unmarried couples, participants in interracial sexual relationships, and others, at least to a certain degree – that is, as long as these people did not overtly challenge the norms and ideals Leeward residents most valued, particularly in terms of what they considered to be their innate Englishness and the natural rights they viewed as an integral component thereof. What was notable in Leeward politics, and thus problematic in relation to Daniel Parke, and what led directly to his death was that he appeared to many people in the Leewards to be bent on denying them many of the rights of Englishmen, especially those connected to the security of their persons and property. By ridding themselves of Parke, Leeward whites were not expressing their un-English

---

[76] For example, the Church of England minister Robert Robertson, who lived in Nevis in the 1720s and 1730s, clearly had Parke in mind when he asserted "the Weakness of some of our Governors, the wicked Lives of some others, and the insatiable Avarice of almost all of them, have brought on many of our Woes" (Robertson, *A Detection of the State and Situation of the Present Sugar Planters of Barbadoes and the Leeward Islands* [London: John Wilford, 1732], 29). The French historian Georges Butel-Dumont concurred, accusing Parke of engaging in "despotic processes" (*procédés despotiques*) and "believing that he could violate with impunity the forms and practices of the Assembly" (*violer impunement les formes et les usages de l'assemblée*) (Butel-Dumont, *Histoire et commerce des Antilles angloises* [Paris: n.p. 1758], 47). All translations are mine, unless otherwise specified.

[77] Dunn, *Sugar and Slaves*, 118.

[78] Ibid., 340.

barbarism, but were asserting their Englishness and preserving it from an unprincipled attacker. In one sense, Parke's murder was not "an isolated or accidental event," because Leeward whites had responded in a similar, though less violent, manner to other officials, including Governor Roger Osborne and the two Codringtons, who seemed to threaten their rights as Englishmen. But such instances were relatively few, and their existence implies not that Leeward settlers were perpetually in rebellion against lawful authority but that, on the contrary, they attempted to uphold their rights by the use of less confrontational tactics, moving toward violence only in circumstances in which they believed no other options existed to allow them to secure these rights.

"OPPRESSIVE AND ILLEGAL IMPRISONMENT": THE ASSEMBLY AS TYRANT?

Although Parke's murder was a unique event, the question of the rights of the Leeward Assemblies continued to trouble the political life of the islands throughout the eighteenth century. The colonists remained convinced that "the Assemblys here had all the privileges of the Commons at home," and any governor who refused to accept this interpretation was likely to come into serious conflict with his constituents.[79] But as we observed earlier in this chapter, the nature of political life in the Leewards was such that aggressive behavior on the part of even one member of the governing elite could plunge a whole Council or Assembly, and therefore an entire island, into turmoil. The problems might be particularly severe when that one man was the governor, but from the story of John Gardiner it is evident that a challenge could erupt from within the Assembly as well as from outside it.

In 1770 Gardiner, the solicitor general of St. Kitts, petitioned the Court of King's Bench and Common Pleas in London to release him from his imprisonment "by virtue of a Warrant under the Hand and Seal of the Honourable John Fahie, Esquire, the Speaker of the Assembly of this Island, and which Warrant is set forth in the Return to the Writ of Habeas Corpus."[80] Gardiner had been arrested for defending the rights of several members of the Kittitian Assembly who had walked out of a legislative

---

[79] Governor Gilbert Fleming to the Board of Trade, October 4, 1752, C.O. 152/27: Leeward Islands, Original Correspondence, 1750–4.

[80] Gardiner, *The Argument or Speech of John Gardiner, Esquire, Barrister at Law* (Basseterre, St. Kitts: Thomas Howe, 1770), viii.

session in order to express their opposition to the idea of allowing members of the Council, or upper house, of St. Kitts to vote in Assembly, or lower house, elections. This was not a trivial issue in an island where the electorate numbered in the low hundreds and "one man's vote could decide more than one election, for men voted in the several parishes where they held property." But he did not devote much of his petition to upholding the correctness of his behavior or that of the rebellious assemblymen, perhaps believing that the London court would have little interest in what might strike them as a trivial local affair.[81] Rather, he offered a more general challenge to the Assembly's right of imprisonment, arguing that, unlike Parliament, "the Assembly of this Island ... is no Court of Record" and therefore had no power to imprison Gardiner or anyone else, in the same way that "the King himself cannot imprison any Man" by his own authority, as in a Court of Star Chamber.[82]

In Gardiner's view, the St. Kitts Assembly was in no way comparable in its rights and privileges to the Parliament of Great Britain, and its "Claim of Equality with the House of Commons ... is a Claim more than most indecent; it is a Claim of Insolence and Arrogance, not warranted by Reason or the Nature of Things."[83] The Assembly claimed that its authority had been the gift of Charles I, who had granted it St. Kitts's charter of incorporation. Gardiner claimed that he had "been pretty diligent in searching the Records of this Island" for this charter but that he had not been able to locate it.[84] In his opinion, the Assembly would have to produce the original charter in order to uphold its claim to parliamentary privileges, but even should such a charter be found, it would not justify the house's actions in imprisoning him, because if "the King has granted to them a Charter of Incorporation, and that in such Charter he has given the Assembly, in express terms, an arbitrary Power to imprison whom they please, for what they please ... the King is deceived in his Grant; that the same is absolutely void, and that those who dare to execute such Powers will be adjudged Trespassers."[85]

In this last assertion, Gardiner addressed himself to the lawyer John Stanley, his "quondam Friend and very old Acquaintance," who led the

[81] T. A. Milford, *The Gardiners of Massachusetts: Provincial Ambition and the British-American Career* (Durham: University of New Hampshire Press, 2005), 92.

[82] Gardiner, *Argument*, 4. See also Mary Patterson Clarke, *Parliamentary Privilege in the American Colonies* (New Haven: Yale University Press, 1943), 98n.

[83] Gardiner, *Argument*, xi.

[84] Ibid.

[85] Ibid., 4.

prosecution. In his imprisonment of Gardiner, Stanley had claimed, citing the conventional defense of parliamentary privilege, that "without a Power of Commitment it would be impossible for the House of Assembly to do Business, as without it the solemn Debates and Business of the House would be liable to constant Interruption from the Insolence of any Ruffians who might think proper to break in upon the House."[86] According to him, the St. Kitts Assembly, "on the Day of their first Meeting, claimed a Confirmation of all their Privileges from the King's Representative the [Governor] General; one of which was the Privilege of imprisoning: And that his Excellency then granted and confirmed all of those Privileges, so claimed, to the Speaker."[87] In other words, Stanley based his defense of the Assembly's imprisonment of Gardiner on the idea that the house had acquired its privileges from its status as a parliamentary body and that the royal governor had acknowledged these privileges. In this argument, Stanley took it for granted that the St. Kitts Assembly enjoyed powers similar to those of the House of Commons and that, because the Commons had the right to imprison those who disrupted or defied it, the Assembly by analogy possessed this same right.

In response to Stanley, Gardiner formulated a two-pronged argument. He first cited his unsuccessful search for the charter referred to by Stanley as a pretext by which to make the point that, even if the king had indeed issued such a charter, he had been "deceived in his Grant," and therefore that such a document was "absolutely void, and that those who dare to execute such Powers will be adjudged Trespassers," as he considered Stanley to be.[88] Moreover, even if Stanley were to succeed in locating this elusive charter, it would not empower him to proceed against Gardiner, because it was superseded by the Act of 1727, which was "now in Force, and is ... the only Authority by which the Assembly can now legally pretend to sit, and do Business, by which they exist, and from which they can claim any Privilege."[89] Gardiner insisted that the Assembly "can claim no Powers, no Authority, no Privileges, out of, but must confine themselves to such as are expressed – are specified in, that Act. That Act

---

[86] Ibid., xi. In the following year, Stanley was appointed solicitor general of the Leewards (G. P. J. Walker, ed., "The Cayon Diary: Notes Made by John Earle of Cayon, in the Island of St. Kitts during the Second Half of the Eighteenth and the Early Years of the Nineteenth Centuries" [undated typescript, Nevis Historical and Conservation Society, Charlestown, Nevis], 5).

[87] Gardiner, *Argument*, xi.

[88] Ibid., 4.

[89] Ibid., 12.

does not give the House any Power to imprison, nor does it constitute the Assembly a Court of Record, and therefore, if they have a Power to imprison, they have it elsewhere than from that Act," in which case such a power would be null and void.[90] Explicitly, Gardiner thus argued that the St. Kitts House of Assembly had absolutely no power to legally imprison him or anyone else and that it therefore was legally obligated to release him forthwith.

It would have been logical for Gardiner to end his argument there, having presented his case for his immediate release from custody. But he did not halt his attacks on the authority of the Assembly, instead choosing to amplify his complaints by challenging not only the house's right of imprisonment but its pretensions to parliamentary status. In his view, "The Claim of Equality with the House of Commons, insisted upon by and for our Assembly, is a Claim more than most indecent; it is a Claim of Insolence and Arrogance, not warranted by Reason or the Nature of Things."[91] In Gardiner's opinion, it was outrageous that "the little, trifling, twopenny, pretended-corporate Charter Assembly of Saint Christopher's" should dare to consider itself analogous to "that illustrious Body, the House of Commons of Great Britain," to the same degree that it would be "criminal" for Gardiner or any other island resident to transfer his allegiance from the king to the governor of the Leewards, "that wretched Shadow of Royalty, His Excellency General [William] Woodley."[92] If Governor Woodley was merely the "shadow" of George III, then the Kittitian Assembly was just the shadow of the House of Commons, and a shadow could never replace the real thing in power and prestige.

To Gardiner, it was ludicrous, even grotesque, for the Assembly to consider itself in any way comparable to the House of Commons. To him, the obvious metropolitan parallel to the Assembly was not Parliament, but rather the Corporation of London, which held the responsibility for making bylaws for the city's residents. The corporation consisted of the lord mayor, the city's aldermen, and the members of London's Common Council, and had the same tripartite form as both the British Constitution and the government of St. Kitts. But according to Gardiner, the corporation remained content to legislate only on behalf of the inhabitants of the City of London and was aware that "their Bye-Laws bind not, affect

90 Ibid., 13.
91 Ibid., 8.
92 Ibid., 15.

not, the City of Westminster, the Borough of Southwark, the County of Middlesex, or any other Part of the Kingdom." The corporation's position thus stood in striking contrast to the Assembly of St. Kitts, which, he believed, was assuming parliamentary powers and privileges to which it was absolutely not entitled.[93] As in Gardiner's own case, some of those usurped powers seemed to infringe directly on the subjects' rights as free and independent Britons. For that reason, it appeared to him that his majesty's subjects in St. Kitts could never be secure in the possession of their rights as long as the Assembly compared itself to the House of Commons and refused to acknowledge its commensurate status with the Corporation of London. The corporation understood that it lacked the authority to "make a Bye Law that contradicts the Spirit of, or militates with, the Law of England," and it behoved the Assembly to accept that "the Legislature of Saint Christopher's [could not] make ... a Bye Law" to act in defiance of the common law, which granted the right of imprisonment only to courts of record.[94]

Gardiner went on to remind the Assembly that "the common Law of England is in Force within the Island, and [that] the King, his Substitutes, and all others, are as much bound by that Law here, as they are bound by the same Law at home"; after all, he demanded, "should Business, or any other lawful Occasion, oblige me to quit Great Britain and settle here, merely because I cross the Atlantic, and reside here, do I forfeit the Rights of a British Subject?"[95] Here Gardiner echoed the observation the Barbadian pamphleteer Edward Littleton had made nearly a century earlier, that the difference between Britain and its colonies was only a question of "a distance and a space" and did not imply any disparity between the innate qualities of metropolitan and colonial English subjects. Gardiner concluded his tract by assuring his audience that "we who have known the Sweets of legal British Liberty, cannot ... tamely sit by, or patiently submit to this Iron Yoke of Oppression" placed on him by the Assembly's tyranny and its usurpation of parliamentary authority.[96] For a freeborn Englishman to lose his natural rights was catastrophic under any circumstances. For such a man to be oppressed not by an autocratic ruler but by the "passionate, malicious, revengeful, ignorant, unlearned, and unlettered Men, who often compose the Majority of our

[93] Ibid., 14.
[94] Ibid.
[95] Ibid., 20.
[96] Ibid., 38.

Assemblies," however, was the ultimate indignity. "For surely it is far better, it is far nobler, to submit to the Commands of one absolute Monarch, than to the insolent despotic Orders and Directions of a Number of ignorant, malicious, unfeeling, little, contemptable Tyrants; and if we must Perish, it is more noble, far more honourable, to fall by a Lion, than submit to be gnawed to Death by Rats."[97] In Gardiner's formulation, the very fact that the Leeward colonists were entitled to the same "Sweets of Liberty" as metropolitan Britons removed any necessity for powerful local assemblies; put simply, the settlers should rest assured of Britain's commitment to liberty and the rule of law, as supported by Parliament, and had no need to turn their legislatures, whose purpose was solely to deal with matters of local interest, into bulwarks against the imagined tyranny of the mother country. Not surprisingly, when the Board of Trade considered the Kittitian case in the summer of 1771, it not only affirmed that Council members had the right to vote in Assembly elections, but accused the Assembly of having "corrupted its own Constitution by affecting a power which they have not, analogous, and coequal to that of the House of Commons"; some months later, the Board of Trade ordered Sir Ralph Payne, the new Leeward governor, to "keep the Assembly of St. Christopher more within the legal bounds of a provincial council and to hinder them from usurping authorities inconsistent with the peace and good order of the said island."[98]

Of course, by this time the assemblies of most of Britain's North American colonies were in covert or open rebellion against imperial authority. In 1765 the Leewards, particularly St. Kitts, had, in contrast to Jamaica and Barbados, made common cause with the mainland colonies in their fervent opposition to the imposition of the Stamp Act. These demonstrations appeared to have been planned some time in advance and mirrored those in North America in their use of strategies such as the burning of effigies, ceremonial processions, and the destruction of the stamps themselves. As Andrew O'Shaughnessy has found, the Kittitian demonstrations seem to have involved at least half of the white men on the island, and therefore were equivalent in their mobilization of public support to the far better-known incidents involving the Sons of Liberty in Boston and New York.[99] Under such circumstances, one might have

[97] Ibid., 25–6, 38–9.

[98] Milford, *Gardiners*, 97; Sir Probyn Inniss, *Basseterre: The Story of a West Indian Town* (Basseterre, St. Kitts: Privately printed, 1985), 20.

[99] O'Shaughnessy, "The Stamp Act Crisis in the British Caribbean," *William and Mary Quarterly* s3:51 (1994), 209.

expected the Board of Trade's refusal to validate the Assembly's claims to parliamentary privilege, and its instructions to Governor Payne to keep the assemblymen on a tight leash, to have brought the House into open revolt against metropolitan authority. Instead, the Kittitian Assembly "fell into line" upon Payne's arrival in the islands, and John Gardiner himself took his seat in the house, representing three different parishes between 1773 and 1775.[100] And, of course, none of the West Indian colonies followed those of the North American mainland into revolution against metropolitan authority.

The reasons for the West Indies' loyalty have been much debated, and many scholars have over generations agreed with John Spencer-Churchill that "the free institutions of a mere oligarchy of slave-holders failed to foster the spirit of self-reliance and united effort for the common weal which is supposed to be the essence of free institutions." Colonists such as the Kittitian Samuel Augustus Mathews might have insisted that the islands' Councils were "composed of gentlemen of the most respectable characters, men of liberal principles," and that "the Houses of Assembly at those Islands are also composed of gentlemen ... of real courage as well as independence," but the rise of antislavery sentiment toward the end of the eighteenth century, and the perceived economic and social decay of the islands in the post-Emancipation period, meant that such pronouncements about the islands' political institutions appeared laughable.[101] More recently, however, a number of scholars have taken more seriously West Indians' desire for self-government and their claims of political rights, which demanded the mother country's respect. Particular attention has been given, notably by O'Shaughnessy, Jack P. Greene, and Steven Sarson, to the islands' long tradition of self-government, to the ways in which their Assemblies cast themselves as upholding long-established rights rather than demanding new privileges, and to their insistence that "English overseas colonies were transplanted fragments of English people and their institutions, particularly in relation to land, self-legislation, and the definition of property in persons."[102] It was, of course, this

---

[100] Milford, *Gardiners*, 98.

[101] Spencer-Churchill, *The Leeward Islands* (London: Spottiswoode & Co., 1898), 24; Mathews, *The Lying Hero or an Answer to J. B. Moreton's Manners and Customs in the West Indies* (St. Eustatius: Edward Luther Low, 1793), 19–20.

[102] Michael Craton, "Property and Propriety: Land Tenure and Slave Property in the Creation of a British West Indian Plantocracy, 1612–1740," in Susan Staves and John Brewer, eds., *Early Modern Conceptions of Property* (New York, Routledge, 1996), 498.

"definition of property in persons" that was perhaps the most important
factor that forestalled the Leeward Islands and the other British colonies
in the West Indies from joining the North American colonies' rebellion
against imperial authority. On the eve of the American Revolution, the
population of the Leewards consisted of approximately 7,000 whites
and more than 100,000 blacks.[103] Less than a decade before the onset
of the revolution, an apparently deeply rooted slave conspiracy had been
uncovered on Montserrat, and in 1775 many Leeward settlers could still
remember the alarming rumors of the 1736 plot at Antigua. Throughout
the second and third quarters of the eighteenth century, the planters
had repeatedly petitioned the Crown to send more British troops to the
islands, less to protect them against French incursions than to serve as a
deterrent to potentially rebellious slaves.

Put simply, "massive slave populations made independence impossible," yet at the same time "traditions of self-government were just as
entrenched as they were in the colonies that became the United States."[104]
The fact that, when push came to shove, the Leewards chose to remain
loyal to the Crown ought not to imply that the colonists' claims to self-
rule and to an expansive conception of their rights as British subjects
were hollow. As O'Shaughnessy has pointed out, the very fact that major
riots against the Stamp Act took place in the Leewards differentiates
these islands from the other British West Indian colonies and constitutes
evidence of a long-standing commitment on the part of this colonial population to resist anything that appeared to be aggressive and unlawful
metropolitan incursions against their liberties. Moreover, "the fact that
the Leewards did not feel bound to follow the Americans into revolution a decade later [after the Stamp Act riots] further implies that the
Caribbean islands were capable of independent action."[105]

Had the political elites of the Leeward Islands displayed greater willingness to be guided in all things by the mother country, their lives would
probably have been considerably easier. In islands whose white populations were so small that it was often difficult to fill all of the seats on the
Council and in the Assembly, as well as the offices of solicitor general,

[103] Thomas Southey, *Chronological History of the West Indies* (London: Longman, 1827),
vol. 2, 419.
[104] Steven Sarson, *British America, 1500–1800: Creating Colonies, Imagining an Empire*
(London: Hodder Arnold, 2005), xviii.
[105] O'Shaughnessy, "Stamp Act," 226; Douglas J. Hamilton, *Scotland, the Caribbean, and
the Atlantic World, 1750–1820* (Manchester: Manchester University Press, 2005),
150–1.

judges, justices of the peace, constable, and so on, it would always have been a challenge to deal with the most pressing local issues: establishing control over land, slaves, and servants; coping with the difficulties created by natural disaster and foreign attack; supporting the Church of England in the face of widespread indifference; and regulating everything from tavern licensing to water conservation. To carry out all of these responsibilities was a daunting business, and it must have been at least occasionally tempting to conduct political life in a way that would minimize confrontation within each island and between the colony and the metropole. Yet in the situations described here, and in many others as well, the Leeward colonists remained unshaken in their belief that these islands, so far from Britain, so unlike it in landscape, climate, and social organization, and so challenged by problems unknown in the mother country, could be molded into recognizably English societies. Because they, like Britons at home and throughout the British Empire, "regarded liberty as the essence of Britishness," they believed not only that any curtailment of that liberty was a step along the road to tyranny, but also that it also represented a diminution of that Britishness on which their societies were centered.[106] Here again, we see the Leeward settlers at work in an act of sustained improvisation, trying to adapt metropolitan political ideals and practices to a very different world, a task that to their minds, if not always those of their governors or metropolitan officials, they largely achieved. And as the case of George Frye shows, they were equally determined to protect themselves and their communities from fellow islanders whose words and actions seemed to threaten these English, and thus British, ideals.

THE "HIGH CRIMES, AND OTHER MISDEMEANORS" OF GEORGE FRYE

George Frye, the son of a Montserratian planter and member of the island's Council, had spent much of his life in England, but returned home in 1750 when he obtained the position of captain of a regiment stationed in the Leewards and simultaneously "His Majesty [George II] was also pleased to appoint [him] to be one of the members of his council in Montserrat."[107] Soon after Frye's arrival in Montserrat,

---

[106] Greene, "Empire and Identity," 228.
[107] George Frye, *The Case of George Frye, President of the Council of the Island of Montserrat* (London: n.p., 1754), 4.

the Lords of trade and plantations were pleased to signify to Gilbert Fleming, Esq; then commander in chief [governor] of the Leeward Caribbee Islands in the absence of General Mathews, that as it appeared that his Majesty's mandates granted to him [Frye] to sit in council of that island was of a prior date to any of the mandates granted to the other members of the council there, it was his Majesty's pleasure that he [Frye] should take precedence of all the other members, though some of them had been sworn in before him.[108]

The king's granting of precedence to Frye, thus allowing him to serve as president of the Council and, in the absence of both the Leeward governor general and the lieutenant governor of Montserrat, as de facto governor of Montserrat, was an act certain to sow discord among the Montserratian elite. Island officials took issues of seniority very seriously, and as we have seen in the case of Daniel Parke, they resented any attempts on the part of the metropole to disrupt the pecking order of local politics by placing its own protégés in positions of superiority over them. Thus, Frye's sojourn in Montserrat began less than auspiciously and spiraled rapidly downward. On December 13, 1753, the Assembly published articles of impeachment against Frye. These articles of "high crimes, and other misdemeanors" offered eleven separate instances of alleged misconduct on Frye's part, charges that centered on Frye's misdeeds both as a private individual and as a government official.[109] According to the text of the articles, Frye's character was that of "a *common calumniator*, and a *common disturber of the peace*," while in his political office he "*abused the authority* he was entrusted with, by virtue of those offices, in making use of the King's processes for *sinister* and vile purposes, and to cover and encourage other violent and arbitrary proceedings, in order to deprive his Majesty's subjects of their *liberty*, and injure them in their *property*."[110]

Upon first reading, these charges appear to describe two distinct types of offenses, but no strict distinction should be drawn between Frye's private conduct and his official actions. Whether he gave offense to his fellow Montserratians as a private individual or as a member of the local administration, his actions infringed on the jealously guarded honor of local white men. As the preceding chapter described, such attacks were difficult for Leeward men to overlook when they originated in the private sphere of sociability and sexuality. When they entered the realm of politics, they were even less tolerable. A "*common calumniator*, and a

---

[108] Ibid., 4.

[109] On impeachment in colonial British America, see Peter Charles Hoffer and N. E. H. Hull, *Impeachment in America, 1635–1805* (New Haven: Yale University Press, 1984).

[110] Frye, *Case of Frye*, 26, 29, emphasis in original.

common disturber of the peace" was threatening as a member of local society. When such a person attained power over his fellow British subjects, he, like Daniel Parke, represented the ultimate danger of unrestrained tyranny. In a culture where insults often functioned as challenges to an antagonist's manliness and honor, Frye's inability or unwillingness to temper his words was guaranteed to offend the sensibilities and inflame the tempers of his auditors. Vere Langford Oliver, the early-twentieth-century chronicler of Leeward history, remarked on having read the records of Frye's case that "the offences complained of were very trivial, and all the proceedings ludicrous in the extreme," and it is difficult to deny that Frye's choice of words and actions reflected the workings of a notably unsophisticated mind.[111] Nonetheless, those who bore the brunt of Frye's insults saw these offenses as menacing rather than ridiculous.

Frye's altercation with William Dyett was described in the preceding chapter, and it is unnecessary to recount the event here. As a situation in which a seemingly trivial act of individual misbehavior triggered a violent response in rhetoric and action alike, it is representative of Frye's exploits. Several of the charges in the Assembly's articles of impeachment presented examples in which Frye employed scatological and otherwise offensive language in his interactions with others. Perhaps the least serious instance involved an incident in which Frye, "speaking of an ancient maiden lady, said, that she once drank a glass of urine, and eat some parrot's dung, to acquire a parrot and a monkey, the possessor of which would not let her have them upon any other terms."[112] This uncouth jest did not impinge directly on anyone's reputation, because it did not assign names or distinguishing features to the characters therein, but it marked Frye to many Montserratians as "a person of a lewd life and conversation" whose "most indecent and immodest manner" and use of "obscene and lewd expressions" threatened "to corrupt the morals of the people, and to bring his Majesty's government into contempt."[113] Frye's recounting of this off-color anecdote did not offer insult to any particular individual, but the fact that it was the president of the island's ruling Council who told the joke, albeit in an informal and unofficial setting, led the public to see Frye as "bringing himself, and the dignity of his office, into contempt and ridicule" and therefore as insulting the authority and reputability of Montserrat's public life, a serious problem in an

---

[111] Oliver, *Caribbeana*, vol. 2, 287.
[112] Frye, *Case of Frye*, 23.
[113] Ibid., 29.

island where the tiny size of the white population meant that the personal would always be political, and vice versa.[114] Frye's gleeful recounting of the story of this "ancient maiden lady" clearly offended many of his associates, but at least he had recounted it in a social rather than a political setting, and the anecdote did not insult particular individuals.

Far more problematic were the insults Frye issued from his seat at the head of the Council, which were aimed at locally prominent people and could in no way be decoupled from Frye's public persona. As mentioned in the preceding chapter, John Bramley, a member of the Assembly, appeared before the Court of Grand Sessions in order to serve on a grand jury, "very meanly clad with a white cap on."[115] When Frye scolded him for his slovenly appearance, Bramley defended his right to wear what he pleased, to which Frye responded by suggesting that "since he was so fond of a white cap, he would advise him to wear one on his p—k, and not keep a seraglio of negroes."[116] Frye's outburst gave offense on several levels. His criticism of Bramley implied that, as president of the Council, Frye believed that his authority extended to arbitrary infringements on his fellow islanders' freedom of action, a threat that was merely irksome in his challenge to Bramley's sartorial choices but offered a dangerous precedent for more serious incursions against individual rights. The episode of Dyett's indecent exposure and Frye's enraged response to it shows that any public taunt that referred to male genitalia, such as Frye's suggestion that Bramley place his cap on his "p—k," served as an extreme form of provocation, and Frye's charge that Bramley was sexually involved with several black women was guaranteed to enrage the latter. As has been described elsewhere, many, perhaps the majority, of white West Indian men engaged in sexual relationships with free or enslaved black women, but although interracial sex was not a secret, it was not a subject of polite conversation. Even the term "seraglio" carried defamatory overtones; it referred to the harems of Ottoman Turkish rulers and implied a highly unwelcome connection between allegedly immoral, "heathen" sexual practices and those in which Bramley supposedly engaged.[117]

---

[114] Ibid., 30.

[115] Ibid., 48. Bramley was the brother-in-law of George Wyke, whom Frye had superseded as president of the Council, and he had quarreled violently three decades earlier with Frye's father because Frye had told Leeward governor Walter Hamilton (1715–21) that Bramley was a "disaffected person" (Governor John Hart to the Board of Trade, March 16, 1724, *C.S.P. Col., 1724–1725* [London: HMSO, 1936], 63).

[116] Frye, *Case of Frye*, 48.

[117] Throughout early modern and modern European history, and particularly in the period between the sixteenth and eighteenth centuries, the Turk functioned as the ultimate

Frye's confrontation with Michael White, a prominent local planter and lawyer, was even more provocative than his dealings with Bramley. White angered Frye when the former served as counsel for Mansell Nathaniel Wilks in a lawsuit Wilks brought against Frye. By Frye's own admission, at the close of the trial he had referred to White, whom Leeward governor Thomas, himself a self-consciously dignified and honorable man, described as having "a large Estate … [and] a liberal Education, and is a Man of distinguished Honour and Probity," as "an insolent old scoundrel; Frye told him that he would beat him, but for his cowardice, and that he would sh—t upon him were it not that White might seek his revenge for it by law."[118] As in the case of his response to Bramley, Frye's words carried multiple insults. He impugned not only White's integrity but, still more gallingly in the context of a society whose principal value was personal honor, his courage, implying that White would respond to an attack with fists or feces in a cowardly, litigious manner, rather than by manly self-defense. Apparently "this nasty threat gave White too great offence ever to be forgiven" because "it furnished those who did not love him with a most provoking nick-name to call him by." According to Frye, White was "the great spring and principal mover of the impeachment," and his implacable opposition to Frye made it clear that "this shitten menace was not forgotten."[119]

White was no more inclined to forgive than he was to forget; he responded by spreading "a scandalous libel against the President and the gunner of the fort, who were pointed at under the names of Don Quixote and Sancho Panca; and having (at the same time) written those names … upon a publick tavern table."[120] Stung by the accusation of homosexuality, Frye "wrote upon the table," under the "ill-spelt" insult, the suggestion that White "learn Spanish of another aunt of his, who was housekeeper to a Jew."[121] Like the "shitten menace," this "blacken[ing] the memory of

---

"other," with the possible exception of the black African, to European Christendom, and the English popular imagination figured Turks as "cruel and tyrannical, deviant and deceiving … all that an Englishman and a Christian was not … the Other with whom there could only be holy war"; see Nabil Matar, *Turks, Moors, and Englishmen in the Age of Discovery* (New York: Columbia University Press, 1999), 13.

[118] Governor George Thomas to Board of Trade, May 30, 1764, C.O. 152/30/56; Frye, *Case of Frye*, 20. Thomas thought so highly of White that in 1764 he appointed him deputy governor of Montserrat.

[119] Frye, *Case of Frye*, 20–1. Unfortunately, the text does not inform us of the nature of this "most provoking nick-name."

[120] Ibid., 22.

[121] Ibid.

[White's] dead ancestors" by accusing them of illicit sexual behavior was an insult White could not allow to pass without response. A few days after Frye etched his challenge into the surface of the table, White "struck him over the head with his stick," but Frye "in return knocked the assailant down, and then committed him to jail; White's suspension a short time afterwards prevented his meeting with any further punishment."[122]

Equally alarming was Frye's arbitrary abuse of the powers he possessed as the president of the Montserrat Council. Many of Frye's actions encouraged observers to believe that he was bent not only on defaming his fellow islanders but also on denying those under his authority their fundamental and inalienable rights as Englishmen. One example of an attack on an individual's rights was the case of Mr. Rookesby, a passenger who had boarded Captain Thomas Woodward's shallop at St. Kitts and disembarked at Montserrat. According to Frye, "This Rookesby was a fugitive for debt, and a fellow of most infamous character."[123] Indebtedness was widespread in the Leewards and throughout the English West Indies, and to prevent debtors from running away from their creditors laws in force throughout the islands mandated that

no one shall be permitted to embark for any other part of the world without giving fourteen days notice of their intention in the secretary's office: and to make this regulation more effectual, the masters of all vessels which arrive in the islands are obliged to give security, to take no persons on board without a ticket or certificate of their having given such a regular notice.[124]

Captain Woodward had obeyed the law and had deposited his bond at the secretary's office in St. Kitts. Rather than navigate the shallop himself, Woodward employed a master to do so, and the latter allowed Rookesby to board the vessel and sail for Montserrat, leaving the unlucky Woodward in the position of having to forfeit his security to Rookesby's creditors unless Woodward could force the latter to return to St. Kitts. An anxious Woodward sent word of these developments to Frye as president of the Council of Montserrat, and the news reached the island shortly after Rookesby's arrival there.

According to his own account, Frye "was well inclined to do everything in his power towards assisting Captain Woodward." Unfortunately for Frye, however, "he had no authority to seize upon and send any

---

[122] Ibid., 26, 22.
[123] Ibid., 14.
[124] Ibid., 13.

person out of the island without his [the individual's] own consent."[125] Undeterred, Frye "devised an expedient" by which "he granted a warrant for the apprehension of Rookesby as a loose and disorderly person; this warrant was executed the same evening, and Rookesby was brought before the President, who was then at a tavern near the beach."[126] Frye immediately discharged Rookesby "for want of proof of his profligate life" and left the room. At that point, "two or three stout fellows, employed by Capt. Woodward, hurried [Rookesby] on board a vessel and carried him safe back to St. Kitts," where presumably his creditors succeeded in confronting him and Woodward was relieved of financial responsibility for his troublesome passenger.[127]

Frye's handling of the Rookesby affair "furnished matter for loud complaints against the President's tyranny and oppression."[128] Rookesby himself, as an improvident stranger, was not a particularly sympathetic figure to most Montserratians. But many islanders saw Frye's usage of him as blatantly unjust, as a sort of entrapment in which Frye employed the laws and personnel of the island's administration to seize Rookesby on specious charges, violating the principle of habeas corpus and "making use of the King's processes for sinister and vile purposes ... to deprive his Majesty's subjects of their liberty."[129] Rookesby may not have been an appealing figure to the Montserratians, but he was a British subject and as such possessed the usual rights and privileges that Frye had violated. In his own defense, Frye claimed that "he himself did nothing more ... than the granting the warrant, and discharging the fellow when brought before him; all the rest was done by Capt. Woodward without any assistance or warrant from him [Frye]." He admitted that "whether in this affair he acted legally or not must be left to others to determine," but maintained that "his intentions were praise-worthy, and the actions equitable."[130] This Machiavellian rhetoric of the end justifying the means found little public support, even among the merchants and lawyers who were likely to have

---

[125] Ibid., 14.

[126] Ibid., 15.

[127] Ibid.

[128] Ibid.

[129] Ibid., 29. William Blackstone defined personal liberty as "the power of locomotion, of changing situation, or removing one's person to whatsoever pace one's own inclination may direct, without imprisonment, or restraint, unless by due process of law" (quoted in Peter Linebaugh, *The London Hanged: Crime and Civil Society in the Eighteenth Century* [Cambridge: Cambridge University Press, 1992], 122).

[130] Frye, *Case of Frye*, 15.

disapproved of the irresponsible conduct of men such as Rookesby. To
the Assembly, Frye's use of a disingenuous and probably unlawful strategy to achieve a supposedly beneficial result was proof of the president's
duplicity and his lack of respect for the rights of English subjects, offenses
that appeared again in his treatment of Mansell Nathaniel Wilks.

Frye's difficulties with Wilks, a clerk employed by the former's brother
Edward Frye, began when Wilks hired a boat to take him to St. Kitts so
that he could carry out some business on his master's behalf. President
Frye, "having occasion to dispatch a letter to St. Kitts, sent it on board
the vessel by the fort major, who delivered it into the hands of a passenger to be forwarded; the passenger gave it to the master [of the ship],
who refused to carry it, and returned it to the President, telling him, that
his refusal was in consequence of Wilks's directions."[131] While the captain was informing Frye of this turn of events, Wilks "at that instant
coming up, confirmed what the master said, and added, that no letters
should be carried in that vessel but from such people as he and his master
approved of," a group that apparently did not include Frye.[132] Frye flew
into a rage in the face of this "flat refusal to permit what the President, as
commander in chief of the island, had a right to compel," and his anger
increased when his berating of Wilks, "instead of producing submission,
only gave rise to sawcy answers."[133] Frye appeared to resolve the conflict
by placing the letter inside a case, which he then addressed to the gunner of the fort at Basseterre, writing on the surface of the case the phrase
"Upon his Majesty's service." At that point, "the master of the shallop
durst no longer refuse to take it," lest by doing so he might involve himself in the serious misdeed of interfering in matters of government business and colonial security.[134]

Ensuring that the captain would take the letter to St. Kitts failed to
assuage Frye's anger against Wilks, whom he feared might board the shallop and set off without either the captain or the letter. Hoping to forestall
this turn of events, Frye followed Wilks to a tavern on the beach, perhaps
the same one in which he had seen Rookesby captured. Finding Wilks
within, Frye "upon his entring into the room told him, 'He saw he was
not gone yet;' to which the other making no answer, nor shewing the least

---

[131] Ibid., 16.
[132] Ibid. Wilks's master, of course, was Frye's brother Edward; unfortunately, nothing in the
text illuminates the affective nature of the relationship between the two brothers.
[133] Ibid.
[134] Ibid.

token of respect, but, on the contrary, endeavour[ed] to affront him by the insolence of his gestures."[135] Frye responded to Wilks's hostility by asking him if he knew to whom he was speaking and by informing him that it was Wilks's duty to behave in a respectful manner toward his superior. Wilks "pertly answered" that he was quite aware of his interlocutor's identity, at which point Frye demanded that Wilks leave the taproom. Wilks "peremptorily refused, and called upon the company to bear witness how he was treated, saying, the tavern was as free for him as for the President," a statement he repeated several times.[136] Frye decided that in such a volatile situation it was "incumbent upon him to maintain the dignity of his office, and consequently declared he would commit Wilks to gaol for his contempt; he accordingly sat down to a table to write a warrant for that purpose." Immediately Wilks, "with an effrontery of which there are but few examples, impudently seated himself at the same table, and drawing out a pencil began to write also, swearing, 'By G – d, he could write as well as the President.'" Again, Frye demanded that Wilks leave the room, and upon Wilks's refusal and his second appeal to the assembled taverngoers to serve as witnesses of Frye's abusive behavior toward him, Frye "turned him out with his own hands."[137]

Boiling over with rage, Frye issued a warrant for Wilks's apprehension "to answer for the insult committed upon him," and the island's constable seized Wilks and carried him before Benjamin Walker, a justice of the peace.[138] Walker, however, thwarted Frye's intent by refusing to hear the complaint "under a pretext that the warrant being to bring Wilks before the President, he, as an inferior, would not meddle with it, as it might be look'd upon as an encroachment upon the President's authority."[139] Whether Walker's response was serious or sarcastic is unclear, but in either case it indicated that Montserratians were well aware of Frye's almost pathological jealousy over questions of his authority. Frustrated, Frye drew up another warrant in which he specified that the constable was to bring Wilks before Walker. Walker signed the document but stymied the president again by requesting that Frye allow Wilks to deal with Edward Frye's business at St. Kitts before returning to face the charges. President Frye agreed, perhaps because he did not wish to be "of great prejudice" to his brother's affairs, but rather than present himself before

[135] Ibid., 16–17.
[136] Ibid., 17.
[137] Ibid.
[138] Ibid., 18.
[139] Ibid.

Frye to answer the charges, upon his return Wilks "appear[ed] upon all occasions before the President, attended by a retinue of factious people, with an air of triumph" that must have been utterly galling to Frye.[140] Frye ordered his trusty constable to seize Wilks and bring him before another justice, Michael Dyer, as Walker was intent on avoiding further involvement in this affair. After Wilks's apprehension, however, "that ingenious justice [Dyer] could not find out that there was any crime or misbehavior in offering the greatest insults to the first magistrate in the country."[141] Disgusted by Dyer's intransigence, Frye dismissed him and determined to try the case himself. He dealt with Wilks by sentencing him to spend half an hour confined in the stocks. Wilks served his punishment but immediately brought an action against Frye for this "unheard-of punishment … [inflicted] in a most ignominious and barbarous manner … without even the formality of a trial."[142] Frye's old enemy, the lawyer Michael White, served as Wilks's counsel and stirred up public outrage by referring to Frye as a "Turkish Basha," thus conjuring up visions of Oriental despotism that stood opposed to English ideals of liberty.[143] White's rhetorical strategy was successful, and the jury found in Wilks's favor, ordering that Frye pay him the sum of one hundred pounds in damages.

Frye's treatment of Rookesby and Wilks epitomized the sort of behavior his fellow islanders found unjust and even tyrannical. Throughout his tenure as president, Frye frequently overstepped what island residents regarded as the legitimate boundaries of his authority. He tried to control the lives of Montserratians to an unprecedented degree, seeking to mandate how they dressed, regulate what they said, and even restrict their access to public spaces such as taverns and force them to remain on or depart from Montserrat against their will. In some instances, Frye's offenses were verbal, while in others they involved actions, such as the arrests of Rookesby and Wilks. To the anxious Montserratian public, however, there was little difference between words and deeds, and in the most basic sense Frye's abusive rhetoric *was* also an action. Whether his weapons were words or force of arms, his behavior made it clear to all observers that he viewed himself in his role as Council president as having rights while everyone else had only duties. Frye saw himself as "having a right to compel" the ship captain to accept his letter and as possessing "a

---

140 Ibid.
141 Ibid., 19.
142 Ibid., 28.
143 Matar, *Turks, Moors, and Englishmen*, 13.

right to command all over the island," whereas it was the duty of all local residents, including Mansell Wilks, "to treat him with respect."

Frye's impeachment made it clear that governor and governed held conflicting interpretations of the "rights" of Englishmen. In his defense, Frye asserted that he had committed no deeds that merited public censure, let alone impeachment. Although the articles of impeachment "carry a terrible sound with them, and would naturally induce people to suppose that such a pompous introduction must be followed by charges of the most enormous guilt, such as selling the island to the enemy, burning houses, plundering churches, robbing the community, destroying the constitution of the country, to make himself absolute, [or] committing rapes and murders," Frye claimed that his alleged crimes amounted to nothing more than "three or four unguarded, and indecent, expressions ... speaking very freely ... telling a man who had wickedly traduced him, that he deserved to be so served ... going armed in his own defence," and a few other trifling offenses.[144] In a final attempt to justify himself to the metropolitan administration, which he hoped would overturn his conviction and allow him to regain his position of precedence in Montserrat, Frye claimed that, had he really been such a tyrant as the articles made him out to be, Wilks would not have dared to bring a suit against him, nor would a jury have found in Wilks's favor and forced Frye to pay damages to him, nor would Dyett or Rookesby have been willing to present blatant challenges to his authority. Frye asserted that the Montserratians' willingness to complain and even to take action against him proved that he was no tyrant, for a true tyrant would have so oppressed his subjects that they would have had neither the legal right nor the courage to oppose him.

For their part, most Montserratians claimed that Frye's dominion was so cruel and lawless, like that of Parke, that they were unable to restrain him with the usual political machinery. Therefore, their resistance was their only means of delivering themselves from a despotic ruler, one who "hath most grievously offended against the peace of his Majesty, his crown and dignity, the rights and liberties of the subject, the laws and statutes, and the prosperity and good government of this island."[145] When the ruler and the ruled held such divergent conceptions of their rights and duties as Englishmen, conflict was unavoidable, and when it broke out, both factions were sufficiently convinced of the seriousness of

[144] Frye, *Case of Frye*, 45, 51–2.
[145] Ibid., 31–2.

the affair that the situation was far more likely to result in violence than in compromise. Frye's display of "arbitrary power and tyranny" might have seemed fairly trivial, but in the tiny, tightly intermarried islands of the Leewards, the ability of an officeholder to "*terrify* and be *revenged* of particular persons," or simply to "deny public gestures of respect," threatened to undermine social order to its breaking point.[146]

CONCLUSION

The men who participated in the political life of the Leewards between 1670 and 1770 had a strong and well-defined sense of their identity as Englishmen, as well as of the rights and privileges that lay at the heart of English identity and that made them proud to claim the name of English subjects. This definite sense of English identity and the rights it entailed dovetailed with the islands' overriding sociocultural ethos, which emphasized individual honor as the supreme societal value and required that maintenance of one's honor in the eyes of others was of the greatest importance. This obsession with honor made Leeward society highly contentious; it encouraged individuals to see any challenge as a zero-sum game in which one could regain one's lost prestige only by diminishing that of one's opponent. The legislative and judicial records of the seventeenth- and eighteenth-century Leewards are replete with examples of interpersonal conflict, ranging from minor tavern quarrels to acts of amazing brutality, such as the killing of Daniel Parke. It was this streak of assertiveness shading into violent aggression that encouraged metropolitan Englishmen to develop a stereotype of the West Indian as someone whose contentious nature was simultaneously ludicrous and menacing.

This stereotype has continued to color modern scholars' perceptions of the character of English West Indians and the societies they created, and it has encouraged many of these historians to deride the Leewards and the other English Caribbean colonies as failed social experiments in which the norms and values of Englishness never really took hold. However, it is crucial to bear in mind that a preoccupation, even an obsession, with personal honor and a marked tendency to respond to perceived slights against one's honor with passionate and even violent words and actions

---

[146] Ibid., 30, emphasis in original; Michael J. Braddick, "Civility and Authority," in Braddick and David Armitage, eds., *The British Atlantic World, 1500–1800* (New York: Palgrave, 2002), 97. After his impeachment, Frye was suspended from the Council of Montserrat by Governor Thomas. Frye traveled to England to plead his case before the Privy Council, but he died shortly after his arrival in London, leaving the case unresolved.

not only was characteristic of the Leewards, or the British West Indian colonies more generally, but was, as Joanne Freeman has made clear, integral to the political culture of the early American republic, in which "reputation was at the heart of this personal form of politics." In both the eighteenth-century Leewards and the new American nation, "there were no organized parties ... no set teams of combat or institutionalized rules for battle." As a result, what might seem to outside observers to be trivial and even ridiculous "verbal shoving matches" could very quickly generate a climate of hostility that might have very serious, even (as in the notorious feud between Aaron Burr and the Nevis-born Alexander Hamilton) deadly, consequences. In this sense, political life in the Leewards was highly similar to that prevalent elsewhere in colonial British America and, later, in the newly independent United States. Although the members of local political elites considered themselves to be gentlemen, "men of integrity ... whose promises could be trusted; their word was their bond," *because* they were gentlemen, they were wholly committed to upholding their honor, an attribute that was "entirely other-directed, determined before the eyes of all the world."[147] Such gentlemen might prize order and self-restraint, yet the powerful imperative of protecting their honor allowed them not only to engage in but to rationalize acts of great passion, as well as verbal and even physical violence against anyone who called that honor into question.

Moreover, as this chapter has shown, it was the perceived abrogation or usurpation of their English rights that, to a considerably greater degree than questions of nationality, religious allegiance, or even sexual behavior, inflamed the passions of the political elites of the Leewards. Whether the source of the alleged tyranny was an unwelcome outsider, an overmighty local, or a governing body that appeared intent on usurping parliamentary authority, Leeward colonists were willing, even eager, to defend themselves with words and actions alike. They believed passionately that "they were occupying extensions of sovereign territory, and that this [had] allowed them to implant an English society and institutions ... the reconstitution of local government on the English model."[148] One of the most important privileges they saw as an English birthright was the right to fend off any challenge to their conception of themselves as honorable subjects of the king or queen of England, and they were

---

[147] Freeman, *Affairs of Honor: National Politics in the New Republic* (New Haven: Yale University Press, 2001), xix, xviii, xv, xvi.
[148] Craton, "Property and Propriety," 497.

unwilling to suffer without protest any challenge to this self-image. Later commentators such as V. L. Oliver decried the "ludicrous" and "trivial" nature of some of these controversies, but this judgment misses the crucial point that to Leeward colonists, imbricated as they were in local and metropolitan cultural formations that stressed masculine honor as the highest value, even such admittedly ludicrous and trivial affronts were impossible to ignore, for they presented challenges to individual and corporate identity that, if not resolved, could result only in the diminution of the affronted person's public image and self-esteem.

The story of the life and death of John Barbot played itself out in the social rather than the political sphere, but it is connected to the stories of Parke, Frye, and Gardiner, in that it depicts the dire consequences that so often attended any sort of attack on the intricately interwoven attributes of an individual's masculine honor and his rights as an English subject. At the same time, it provides an unparalleled perspective on the quotidian life of the islands, one that struck contemporary metropolitan readers initially as exotic, but at the same time as a recognizably English colonial society.

Conclusion

On Friday, January 5, 1753, John Barbot, a twenty-five-year-old attorney-at-law, was arraigned at the Court of Oyer and Terminer in Basseterre for the murder of Matthew Mills, Esquire. Barbot, the court alleged, had shot Mills at sunrise on the shore of Frigate Bay, near the salt ponds on the desolate and sparsely populated eastern end of St. Kitts.[1] The prosecution, led by John Baker, solicitor general of the Leeward Islands, made its opening statement: On November 7, 1752, on the occasion of the sale of a piece of property called Bridgwater's Estate, on the nearby island of Nevis, Barbot had quarreled with Mills about a matter relating to the terms of sale of the estate. Several witnesses claimed that they had heard Barbot several days later, on November 10, declaring to a gathering of people in Basseterre that "there was a certain gentleman in this island, whom he would either kill or be killed by in less than a fortnight."[2] Baker stated that several witnesses had seen Barbot practicing shooting a pistol later that same week and that others had seen him hastily drawing up

---

[1] *The Tryal of John Barbot, Attorney at Law, for the Murder of Mathew Mills, Esq.; to which is added, The Prisoner's Narrative of the Cause of the Difference between Mr. Mills and Himself, and the several Steps that led from thence, to the Commission of the Fact for which he suffered* (London: John Whiston and Benjamin White, 1753). The proceedings also appear in T. B. Howell, *A Complete Collection of State Trials and Proceedings for High Treason and Other Crimes and Misdemeanors, from the Earliest Period to the Year 1783* (London: Hansard, 1816), vol. 18, *17–26 George II, 1744–1753*, 1230–1323. The Mills murder is first mentioned in the legislative papers of St. Kitts in a letter of Governor Gilbert Fleming to the Lords of Trade and Plantations of December 23, 1752; see C.O. 152/27/176, Leeward Islands, Original Correspondence, 1750–4, National Archives of Great Britain, Kew, London.

[2] *Tryal*, 7.

an impromptu will at Hugh O'Donnell's tavern in Charlestown, Nevis, on November 18. On the following day, November 19, John McKenley, overseer of Spooner's Plantation near Frigate Bay, was, as he testified, awakened at daybreak by a young male slave named Coomy, whom he recognized as the property of Matthew Mills, being "the boy who always ran with the deceased." Coomy told McKenley that his "master was fighting on the bay with a gentleman come from Nevis, and that he feared his master was killed."[3] While McKenley arose and dressed, Coomy ran back to the scene of the crime; when McKenley arrived there a few minutes later, he found the slave holding his master in his arms, who "tho' still warm, had just breathed his last." When McKenley asked Coomy if he knew the identity of Mills's killer, Coomy replied that it was John Barbot, adding that, "if you will go to the sea-side I believe you will see him; for I am sure he can't be gone far." McKenley ran to the water's edge, "and there saw a canoo with four oars and a paddle, rowing from the shore towards Nevis, with somebody drest in white sitting in the stern."[4] As the canoe approached the coast of Nevis, it drew into the view of a boat coming from the nearby island of Montserrat. This vessel's master, William Johnson, testified that he "very well knew the prisoner, and saw him sitting in the canoo, drest in a white coat, and having on a laced hat." Later that day, the provost marshal of Nevis, alerted by Coomy, McKenley, Johnson, and Mr. Halburd's Peter, "a very sensible negro fellow, belonging to the canoo," who had expressed to his master that "he was afraid Mr. Barbot had done 'some mischief,'" arrested John Barbot, charged him with Mills's murder, and committed him to jail to await trial.[5]

Under Baker's direction, the prosecution proceeded to call two dozen witnesses, who testified variously that they had witnessed Barbot's quarrel with Mills at the sale of Bridgwater's Estate, had overheard Barbot announcing that he would soon kill or be killed by Mills, had seen him draw up a hasty will at O'Donnell's tavern or had been called on by him to witness the document, had rented to him a canoe and the services of two slave oarsmen, had lent him a pair of pistols, and, finally, had identified him as the sole passenger in the canoe traveling from

[3] Ibid., 8.
[4] Ibid.
[5] Ibid., 8. Nevisian slaves had made canoe trips to and from St. Kitts since at least the 1730s; a 1737 petition to the island's Assembly from "Severall the Inhabitants in Charles Towne ... Set forth the many Inconveniances of Negros trading & Going backward and forward in Canoes from this Island to St Christophers" (C.O. 186/2, Minutes of Council and Assembly of Nevis, February 12, 1737).

St.Kitts to Nevis on the morning of November 19. The final witness was Dr. Hamilton, the medical examiner of St. Kitts, who testified that he had examined Matthew Mills's corpse and found that the chest wound that had killed Mills could not have been inflicted if the deceased had been "in a posture of defence."[6] Furthermore, Mills's bullets were still in the pockets of his coat, and his pistol showed no evidence of having been discharged, circumstances which implied that his murderer had attacked him by surprise rather than engaged him in a "fair fight."

John Barbot then made his opening statement, in which he asserted that the witnesses he was about to present would, by their sworn testimony, invalidate much of the prosecution's evidence against him.[7] He called nearly twenty witnesses, the majority of whom he employed in an attempt to prove that, on November 10, the day on which Patience Dorset, one of the prosecution's witnesses, claimed she had seen and heard him at Basseterre making threats against Mills's life, he had actually been across the strait at a social gathering on Nevis. If Barbot had been able to make a convincing case that he had been at Nevis on the day in question, and therefore that Mrs. Dorset had never heard him announce his hostility to Mills, he would have been able to undercut one of the most damaging pieces of evidence against him. Unfortunately for the defendant, though, his various witnesses contradicted both him and one another. Some claimed that Barbot had indeed been at Nevis on the tenth, but others thought that he had visited on the ninth, and some witnesses admitted that they were unable to recall the precise date. The muddled nature of this testimony not only failed to disprove Mrs. Dorset's allegations, but instead did considerable damage to Barbot's credibility, making his witnesses appear as if they were either incompetent or mendacious.

Embarrassed by his failure to mount a credible defense and realizing the seriousness of his situation, Barbot attempted to save himself

---

[6] *Tryal*, 30. Leeward laws mandated that "Chirurgeons ... be commanded by the Coroner to inspect or open the dead Body" as soon as possible because "the Heat of this Climate doth sooner corrupt dead Bodies that the Northern Part of Europe, whereby they become very nauseous to Coroners, and others, when viewed by the Inquest." See "An Act for regulating the Coroner's Office; and appointing the Fees for the Coroners in this Island, and Chirurgeons, that shall be commanded to inspect dead Bodies," *Acts of Assembly, Passed in the Island of Nevis, from 1664, to 1739, inclusive* (London: John Baskett, 1740), 27.

[7] Throughout the eighteenth century, English law mandated that criminal defendants conduct their own cases, as it was popularly believed that the accused's demeanor helped to reveal the truth of his words and actions (James Epstein, "The Politics of Colonial Sensation: The Trial of Thomas Picton and the Cause of Louisa Calderon," *American Historical Review* 112 [2007], 722).

by impugning the integrity of some of the prosecution's most important witnesses. William Johnson, the mariner who had claimed that he
had seen Barbot in the canoe returning to Nevis, was, Barbot asserted,
a person of bad character, a man who had been whipped publicly for
theft at Montserrat and therefore was not a reputable witness.[8] However,
because Barbot was not able to produce any documentary evidence that
Johnson had been thus punished, his claim gained him no support and
damaged his credibility further. Barbot also tried to discount the damning testimony of John McKenley by saying that it was only hearsay and
was, moreover, "information from a slave, who, by the laws of his country [England], would have been an incompetent witness had he been
produced as such." In his summation, Barbot claimed that the evidence
against him was "very light" and that the *onus probandi*, or burden of
proof, lay on the prosecution, not on him.[9] He ended his presentation
with the statement that any person sitting in that Basseterre courtroom
was as likely as he to have killed Matthew Mills. The jury withdrew, and
within half an hour returned a verdict of guilty against Barbot.[10] William
Mathew Burt, president of the Council of St. Kitts, sentenced Barbot "to
be carried to the place from whence you came, and from thence to the
place of execution, where you are to be hanged by the neck until you
are dead, and may God have mercy on your soul."[11] Two weeks later, on
Saturday, January 20, 1753, Barbot was executed at Basseterre.

We appear to have witnessed the quick end to a simple and sordid
story, with Barbot rapidly following his victim to the grave. Yet in August
1753, the fashionable *London Magazine* printed a lengthy and detailed
account of Barbot's trial.[12] The periodical had drawn the majority of the
material from a pamphlet that had appeared in London earlier that spring,
which contained not only a verbatim transcript of the trial proceedings,

[8] *Tryal*, 31.
[9] Ibid., 36.
[10] In an act of 1723, the Assembly of St. Kitts mandated that "all Persons residing in the said
Island, seized of any Estate in Fee, or of any Freehold of the yearly Value of ten Pounds
current Money, or possessed of any Personal Estate of the Value of one hundred Pounds
current Money aforesaid, shall and may be of Jurors, to try an Issue real or personal." See
"An Act for the establishing a Court of King's-bench and Common-pleas, and for the better Advancement of Justice in the Island of St. Christopher's," *Acts of Assembly, Passed
in the Island of St. Christopher; from 1711, to 1739, inclusive* (London: John Baskett,
1739), 90.
[11] *Tryal*, 48.
[12] "Trial of John Barbot, at St. Christopher's, in the West Indies, for the Murder of Matt.
Mills, Esq.," *London Magazine*, August 1753.

but also "The Prisoner's Narrative of the Cause of the Difference between Mr Mills and Himself, and the several Steps that led from thence, to the Commission of the Fact for which he suffered." The magazine justified the attention it devoted to the Barbot affair by the fact that the story "has of late been a subject of conversation, and contains some very extraordinary circumstances." More specifically:

> We have given the more full account of the evidence upon this trial, because the proof was founded entirely upon presumption, without any one witness of the fact, which is a dangerous sort of proof, but more necessary to be admitted in the West-Indies than here at home, because negroes are not admitted as witnesses, even tho' employed in committing a crime.[13]

In the absence of the information presented by Coomy and Peter, the canoe slave, it seems likely that the jury would have been unable to convict Barbot of Matthew Mills's murder. Without Coomy's claim that Barbot was the man who had shot his master and Peter's statement that he had rowed Barbot to St. Kitts, where Barbot "had done a great deal of mischief, for, he believed, he [Barbot] had killed Mr. Mills," the evidence against Barbot, although suggestive of ill-feeling between the two men and a desire on Barbot's part for vengeance for a perceived insult, would not have been sufficient to place Barbot conclusively at the scene of the crime.[14] Because island law forbade slaves to testify against free persons, Coomy and Peter were barred from testifying on their own behalf and had to have their statements ventriloquized by the overseer John McKenley and the canoe owner, John Cribbe.

A case such as that of Barbot and Mills would likely have been of interest to the *London Magazine*'s readership even had it taken place closer to the metropole; the audience of a periodical subtitled a "Gentleman's Intelligencer" thrived on dramatic, well-documented tales of intrigue and misbehavior among the elite. The story's tropical setting, however, added to its piquancy. The fact that slaves, although not legally empowered to act as witnesses, provided the most damning evidence against Barbot signified the alien-ness of this colonial society from English legal practices. At the same time, though, the *London Magazine*'s story and Barbot's pamphlet offered readers a true slice of West Indian life, a view into the

[13] "Trial of John Barbot, at St. Christopher's in the West Indies, for the murder of Matt. Mills, Esq.," *London Magazine*, August 1753, reprinted in Vere Langford Oliver, *Caribbeana* (London: Mitchell, Hughes, and Clarke, 1919), vol. 6, 38.
[14] Oliver, *Caribbeana*, vol. 6, 36.

vie quotidienne of English West Indian plantation society at the apex of
its prosperity. Mid-eighteenth-century Londoners, eager readers of sen-
sational and frequently heavily fictionalized narratives of West Indian
decadence, might have expected the narrative of Barbot's crime and punishment to depict only a few social categories and physical locations in
the islands. Yet what comes through clearly in both the pamphlet and
the magazine article is the presence in the Leeward colonies of people
of a wide variety of occupational, racial, and social statuses: In addition
to the archetypal planter grandees such as Mills, we see legal and medical professionals (such as Barbot, Dr. Webb, and Dr. Hamilton), government officials (Solicitor General Baker), overseers (John McKenley),
working-class whites (Patience Dorset; the tavern-keeper O'Donnell; the
sailor Johnson), and even "christian-slaves" such as Peter Rowland.[15]
Equally varied as the dramatis personae are the settings of the action
in the case: the witnesses speak not only of plantations and fields, but
of taverns and communal outhouses, of beaches and public squares, of
townhouses and wharves. Although by the time of the Mills murder the
Leeward colonies were without a doubt slave societies, as opposed to
societies with slaves, accounts of the Barbot affair present a picture of
daily life in the islands that might well have struck metropolitan readers
as a reasonable colonial replication of life in England's smaller towns
and rural parishes.[16]

From the beginning of English settlement in the West Indies, metropolitan visitors and commentators were quick to fasten on the aspects of
these societies that seemed to them the most exotic, and thus the most
alien to metropolitan mores and practices. Sir Henry Colt, who sailed
through the Caribbean and stopped on Montserrat in 1631, wrote of the
island's phantasmagoric atmosphere that "I have neuer felt soe moyst an
ayre. All thinges rust, ye verye keyes in our pocketts rust, and at nights ye
clothes of our backs in touch is moyst, & stiff. We are moor drowsye and
sleepy than accustomed, & full of dreams."[17] Throughout the seventeenth

---

[15] *Tryal*, 19. For an analysis of the role of slave testimony in the Barbot affair and other
legal cases in the islands, see Natalie Zacek, "Voices and Silence: The Problem of Slave
Testimony in the Eighteenth-Century English West Indian Law Court," *Slavery and
Abolition* 24 (2003), 24–39.

[16] On the distinction between slave societies and slaveholding societies, see Philip D.
Morgan, "British Encounters with Africans and African-Americans, circa 1600–1780,"
in Morgan and Bernard Bailyn, eds., *Strangers Within the Realm: Cultural Margins of the
First British Empire* (Chapel Hill: University of North Carolina Press, 1991), 172–3.

[17] V. T. Harlow, *Colonising Expeditions to the West Indies and Guiana, 1623–1677*
(London: Hakluyt Society, 1925), 65.

and early eighteenth centuries, writers such as William Pittis and Ned Ward painted shocking pictures of the West Indies as "a sink of all filthiness," in which the tropical climate and stunted development of social and political institutions allowed white colonists to act on their basest desires. Later in the eighteenth century, as wealthy absentee planters settled in great state in London and Bath, the "creole," along with the East India Company "nabob," emerged in the popular imagination as a symbol of ill-gotten wealth and parvenu vulgarity.[18] As the century drew to a close and metropolitan commitment to abolition increased, works by, among others, James Ramsay, formerly an Anglican minister in St. Kitts, depicted West Indian society as a hell on earth, inhabited only by un-Christian tyrants and their miserable bondspeople, and representing a hideous travesty of English values. Even decades after Emancipation, historians such as James Anthony Froude criticized West Indian colonists for their failure to build recognizably English societies in the islands. Froude unflatteringly compared the cities and towns of the English islands to the splendors that to him typified the Spanish colonizing impulse. Upon visiting Havana, he was enchanted by "a city of palaces, a city of streets and plazas, of colonnades, and towers, and churches and monasteries ... a reproduction of Burgos or Valladolid, as if by some Aladdin's lamp a Castilian city had been taken up and set down again unaltered on the shore of the Caribbean Sea." By contrast, "we English have built in these islands as if we were but passing visitors, wanting only tenements to be occupied for a time ... Kingston [Jamaica] is the best of our West Indian towns, and Kingston has not one fine building in it."[19] These views of the inherent un-Englishness of the West Indian colonies have been echoed by historians from Lowell Ragatz in the 1920s to T. A. Milford in 2005.[20] However, historians have begun to reevaluate the societies of the English colonies in the West Indies, seeing them less as "disastrous social failures" than as "viable societ[ies] ... with rules and reason," and not just examples of "untrammelled individualism, self-centeredness, and lack

[18] *A True and Perfect Relation of that most Sad and Terrible Earthquake, at Port Royal in Jamaica, which Happened on Tuesday the 7th of June* (London: R. Smith, 1692); Timothy Touchstone, *Tea and Sugar, or the Nabob and the Creole* (London: J. Ridgway, 1792.

[19] Froude, *The English in the West Indies, or, The Bow of Ulysses* (London: Longmans, Green, & Co., 1888), 256.

[20] Ragatz, *The Fall of the Planter Class in the British Caribbean, 1763–1833* (New York: Century Co., 1928); Milford, *The Gardiners of Massachusetts: Provincial Ambition and the British-American Career* (Durham: University of New Hampshire Press, 2005).

of concern for the commonweal."[21] Recent work on Jamaica by, among others, Trevor Burnard, Sarah M. S. Pearsall, and B. W. Higman, and on Barbados by Larry Gragg, has encouraged scholars to rethink these long-held ideas about the presumed inability or unwillingness of seventeenth- and eighteenth-century English West Indian colonists to uphold metropolitan social, political, and cultural ideals.[22] It is to this emerging conversation that I hope this monograph will contribute.

Although the abolitionists' image of the West Indian planter as the "dull creole," the "veriest wretch on nature's face," "whose torpid pulse no social feelings move," can seem to modern sensibilities overdrawn to the point of self-parody, it is a challenge to empathize with these men and women, who made their fortunes from the labors of slaves, or even with those less economically successful West Indian whites who benefited indirectly from slavery by living in island societies in which "Every Body is ... on a level as to station," and "the poorest White person here seems to consider himself nearly on a level with the richest."[23] It is tempting to dismiss as irresponsible romanticism the georgic depiction of Leeward society by poets such as James Grainger, who lived in St. Kitts and Nevis from 1759 to 1763 and who claimed that the slaves of these "sweetly social isle[s]" were "well-fed, well-cloath'd, all emulous to gain / Their master's smile, who treated them like men."[24] Similarly, it is easy to be cynical about Samuel Augustus Mathews's and other St. Kitts planters' assertions that theirs was a "most civilized community" characterized by its commitment to English values. They offered these statements in an attempt to defend themselves and their fellow West Indian planters against the aspersions made against them by J. B. Moreton, formerly a

[21] Trevor Burnard, *Mastery, Tyranny, and Desire: Thomas Thistlewood and His Slaves in the Anglo-Jamaican World* (Chapel Hill: University of North Carolina Press, 2004), 250.

[22] See ibid.; Pearsall, "'The late flagrant instance of depravity in my Family': The Story of an Anglo-Jamaican Cuckold," *William and Mary Quarterly* 53:60 (2003): 549–82; Higman, *Plantation Jamaica, 1750–1850: Capital and Control in a Colonial Economy* (Kingston: University of the West Indies Press, 2005); and Gragg, *Englishmen Transplanted: The English Colonization of Barbados, 1627–1660* (Oxford: Oxford University Press, 2003).

[23] James Montgomery, "The West Indies," in Robert Bowyer, ed., *Poems on the Abolition of the Slave Trade* (Manchester, NH: Ayer Publishing, 1971), 29, 30; Janet Schaw, *The Journal of a Lady of Quality*, ed. Charles M. Andrews and Evangeline Walker Andrews (New Haven: Yale University Press, 1923), 85; Bryan Edwards, *The History, Civil and Commercial, of the British Colonies in the West Indies* (Philadelphia: J. Humphreys, 1806), vol. 2, 403.

[24] Grainger, *The Sugar-Cane: A Poem* (London: R. and J. Dodsley, 1766), 93, 42.

bookkeeper in Jamaica, in his *Manners and Customs of the West India Islands* (1793), and by Reverend James Ramsay's *Essay on the Treatment and Conversion of African Slaves in the British Sugar Colonies* (1784), works that capitalized on nascent antislavery sentiment in England by offering eager readers detailed descriptions of the island societies' iniquities.[25] It is even tempting to see Samuel Martin, the most self-consciously improving planter of the eighteenth-century Leewards, as insufficiently self-aware, if not deliberately mendacious, when he informed his daughter-in-law in England that his "chief pleasure" was the "Holy Rapture" of instructing his slaves in the gospel, and that he found their "charming Voices more delightfull ... than the Bath consort is to Belles & Beaux."[26]

But if such claims strike our ears as hollow, it is nonetheless important to bear in mind how important it was to Leeward colonists to consider themselves and their societies to be recognizably upholding English social ideals and practices. Moreover, although the societies that these English colonists created were, like those of Barbados, Jamaica, and the plantation colonies of the American mainland, sites of exploitation and, in all too many cases, absolute misery for the enslaved, they nonetheless should not be dismissed simply as social failures. In the century between their independence from Barbados and the outbreak of the American Revolution, Antigua and Montserrat, Nevis and St. Kitts contended with numerous challenges to the creation and maintenance of a social order that allowed these tiny islands to generate enormous wealth and to become the proverbial jewels in the crown of the first British Empire. Beset by the problems of very limited arable land, a challenging climate, and the ongoing threat of natural disaster, slave rebellion, and foreign attack, the Leeward colonies not only survived but prospered, and as they did so they at the same time succeeded in managing tensions between settlers of varied national origin and confessional allegiance. They also proved themselves able to develop social mores that accommodated a population imbalanced racially and in terms of gender and that at the same time upheld traditional English ideals relating to personal honor and the maintenance of communal order. Finally, over the course of the eighteenth century, their governing elites overcame the difficulties of a deeply problematic

[25] *An Answer to the Reverend James Ramsay's Essay, on the Treatment and Conversion of Slaves, in the British Sugar Colonies* (Basseterre: n.p., 1784), 62; Samuel Augustus Mathews, *The Lying Hero or, An Answer to J. B. Moreton's Manners and Customs in the West India Islands* (St. Eustatius: Edward Luther Low, 1793).

[26] Samuel Martin to "Daughter," June 9, 1774, Add. Mss. 41350, Martin Family Papers, vol. 5, British Library, London.

administrative structure and developed a strong sense of their political rights as "Englishmen overseas." Throughout these endeavors, they were guided by confidence in their right and ability to transform these tropical outposts into, if not "little Englands," then at least into lucrative settlements that upheld the spirit, if not always the letter, of English ways of life and thought. It was this confidence, in themselves and in their aims, that gave them a capacity to improvise, a willingness to keep what worked and to jettison what did not, which is perhaps the most notable of their achievements and constitutes their most convincing claim to inclusion in the real and imagined landscape of colonial British America.

Bibliography

I.   Manuscript Sources

United Kingdom

The British Library, London

Add. Mss. 34486
Add. Mss. 36325
Add. Mss. 41348–41350, Martin Family Papers, vols. 3–5
Egerton Mss. 2395, Thomas Povey Papers
Sloane Mss. 4049, Papers of Hans Sloane

Duke Humfrey's Library, Bodleian Library, University of Oxford

Rawlinson Mss. A.40: Thurloe's Papers, vol. 11

Rhodes House Library, University of Oxford

Society for the Propagation of the Gospel Papers, C/WIN/ANT 1

Lambeth Palace Library, London

Fulham Papers: Gibson 2
Fulham Papers, vol. 19, Leeward Islands, General Correspondence, 1681–1749

National Archives of the United Kingdom, Kew, London

C[olonial]. O[ffice]. 152/9–48: Board of Trade, Original Correspondence, Leeward Islands, 1710–70
C.O. 153/13: Board of Trade, Leeward Islands, Entry Books, 1717–21
C.O. 184/1: Board of Trade, Original Correspondence, Nevis, 1703–15
C.O. 186/1–3: Minutes of Assembly, Nevis, 1722–56
C.O. 187/1–2: Naval Office Returns, Nevis, 1720–9
C.O. 239/1: Leeward Islands: Original Correspondence, Secretary of State
C.O. 241/1–8: Minutes of Council and Assembly, St. Kitts, 1721–60

Public Record Office of Scotland, Edinburgh

GD 205/53/8: Ogilvy of Inverquharity Papers, Letter-Book of William Tullideph

Antigua, West Indies

Archives of Antigua, St. John's

Minutes, House of Assembly, Box 316

Nevis, West Indies

Nevis Historical and Conservation Society, Charlestown

"Jews of Nevis." Unattributed and undated typescript.
Walker, G. P. J., ed. "The Cayon Diary: Notes Made by John Earle of Cayon, in the Island of St. Kitts during the Second Half of the Eighteenth and the Early Years of the Nineteenth Centuries." Undated typescript.

St. Kitts, West Indies

Record Office, Basseterre

St. Christopher Deeds, Records

United States

Burke Library, Hamilton College, Clinton, NY

Beinecke Lesser Antilles Collection

Henry E. Huntington Library, San Marino, CA

Blathwayt Papers

The John Carter Brown Library, Providence, RI

Codex. Eng. 74: Thomas Hulton, "Account of Travels"

William L. Clements Library, University of Michigan, Ann Arbor

Shelburne Papers

II.   Printed Primary Sources

An Account of the Late Dreadful Earth-Quake in the Island of Mevis, St. Christophers, &c. which happen'd in the Beginning of April, of this present Year 1690. London: A. Smith, 1690.
An Account of the Late Dreadful Hurricane, which happened on the 31st August, 1772, also the Damage done on that Day in the Islands of St. Christopher and Nevis. Basseterre, St. Kitts: Thomas Howe, 1772.

Acts of Antigua. London: John Baskett, 1764.

Acts of Assembly, Passed in the Charibbee Leeward Islands, from 1690, to 1730. London: John Baskett, 1734.

Acts of Assembly, Passed in the Island of Barbadoes, from 1648, to 1718. London: John Baskett, 1732.

Acts of Assembly, Passed in the Island of Nevis, from 1664, to 1739, inclusive. London: John Baskett, 1740.

Acts of Assembly, Passed in the Island of St. Christopher; from 1711, to 1739, inclusive. London: John Baskett, 1739.

Acts of Assembly Passed in the Island of St. Christopher; from the Year 1711, to 1769. St. Christopher: Daniel Thibou, 1769.

America: or an Exact Description of the West-Indies. London: Richard Hodgkinson, 1655.

The American Gazetteer. London: A. Millar, 1746.

Anderson, John. *The History and Constitutions of the Most Ancient and Honourable Fraternity of Free and Accepted Masons.* London: J. Robinson, 1746.

An Answer to the Reverend James Ramsay's Essay, on the Treatment and Conversion of Slaves, in the British Sugar Colonies. Basseterre: n.p., 1784.

Antigua. Lucy Chester Parke, Widow, Appellant. Charles Dunbar, Esq; and John Doe his Lessee, Respondents. The Appellant's Case. London: n.p., 1740.

Baker, John. *The Diary of John Baker, Barrister of the Middle Temple, Solicitor-General of the Leeward Islands.* Philip C. Yorke, ed. London: Hutchinson & Co., Ltd., 1931.

Barclay, Patrick. *The Universal Traveller: or, A Complete Account of the Most Remarkable Voyages and Travels of the Eminent Men of our Own and Other Nations to the Present Time.* Dublin: R. Reilly, 1735.

Bellin, Jacques. *Description géographique des Isles Antilles possédées par les Anglois.* Paris: Didot, 1758.

Besse, Joseph. *The Sufferings of the People Called Quakers.* 2 vols. London: L. Hinde, 1753.

Blome, Richard. *A Description of the Island of Jamaica, with the Other Isles and Territories in America, to which the English are Related.* London: T. Milbourn, 1672.

The Present State of His Majesties Isles and Territories in America. London: T. Milbourn, 1686.

A Brief and True Remonstrance of the Illegal Proceedings of Roger Osburn (an Irish man born) Governour of Mount:Serrat one of the Caribba Islands with his Irish Complices against Samuel Waad the Younger, of Topsham in the County of Devon, Gent. And of his Barbarous and Inhuman Murthering of the said Waad in the said Island upon the First Day of May: 1654. London: n.p., 1654.

Burke, William. *An Account of the English Settlements in America.* 2 vols. London: R. and J. Dodsley, 1759.

Butel-Dumont, Georges. *Histoire et commerces des Antilles angloises.* Paris: n.p., 1758.

Caledonia; or, The Pedlar turn'd Merchant: A Tragi-Comedy, as it was Acted by His Majesty's Subjects of Scotland, in the King of Spain's Province of Darien. London: n.p., 1700.

Campbell, John. *Candid and Impartial Considerations on the Nature of the Sugar Trade.* London: R. Baldwin, 1763.

Carman, Harry, ed. *American Husbandry.* New York: Columbia University Press, 1939.

A Collection of Some Writings of the Most Noted of the People called Quakers, in their Times. Philadelphia: W. and T. Bradford, 1767.

Coppier, Guillaume. *Histoire et voyage des Indes occidentales.* Lyon: Jean Huguetan, 1645.

A Copy of the Petition of William Freeman, Esq., in behalf of himself, Mr. Mead, and others, owners of several tracts of land in the Charibbee Islands in America against Colonel Codrington, Governor of the Leeward Islands, presented in the House of Commons, with remarks thereon. London: n.p., 1702.

Dampier, William. *Voyages and Descriptions.* London: James Knapton, 1700.

Douglass, William. *A Summary, Historical and Political, of the First Planting, Progressive Improvements, and Present State of the British Settlements in North America.* 2 vols. London: R. Baldwin, 1755.

Du Tronchoy, Gautier. *Journal de la campagne des isles de l'Amérique.* Troyes: Jacques Lefebvre, 1709.

Edmundson, William. *The Journal [Abridged] of William Edmundson, Quaker Apostle to Ireland and the Americas, 1627–1712.* Caroline N. Jacob, ed. Philadelphia: Religious Society of Friends, 1968.

Edwards, Bryan. *The History, Civil and Commercial, of the British Colonies in the West Indies.* 2 vols. London: John Stockdale, 1801.

The History, Civil and Commercial, of the British Colonies in the West Indies. 2 vols. Philadelphia: J. Humphreys, 1806.

Elegy on the Mournful Banishment of James Campbel of Burnbank to the West-Indies. Edinburgh: n.p., 1721.

An English Ointment for the Scotch Mange. London: B. Bragg, 1705.

Flannigan, Mrs. Amelia. *Antigua and the Antiguans.* 2 vols. London: Saunders and Ottley, 1844.

French, George. *The History of Colonel Parke's Administration.* London: n.p., 1717.

Frye, George. *The Case of George Frye, President of the Council of the Island of Montserrat.* London: n.p., 1754.

A Full and True Account of the Besieging and Taking of Carrickfergus by the Duke of Schomberg, as also a Relation of what has lately pass'd in the Islands of Antego, Mevis, and Montserrat in the West-Indies, Where Their Majesties have been Solemnly Proclaim'd. London: Richard Baldwin, 1689.

Gardiner, John. *The Argument or Speech of John Gardiner, Esquire, Barrister at Law.* Basseterre, St. Kitts: Thomas Howe, 1770.

Gardyner, George. *A Description of the New World, or American Islands and Continent: and by what people these regions are now inhabited, and what places there are desolate and without inhabitants.* London: Robert Leyburn, 1651.

Gay, Edwin F. "Letters from a Sugar Plantation in Nevis, 1723–1732." *Journal of Economic and Business History* 1 (1928): 149–73.

Gordon, Patrick. *Geography Anatomiz'd: or, the Geographical Grammar.* London: J. and J. Knapton, 1730.

Grainger, James. *The Sugar-Cane: A Poem.* London: R. and J. Dodsley, 1766.

Gwynn, Aubrey C. "Documents Relating to the Irish in the West Indies." *Analecta Hibernica* 4 (1932): 139–286.

Hall, Clayton Colman, ed. *Narratives of Early Maryland, 1633–1684.* New York: Scribner's, 1910.

Hodges, Thomas. *Plantation Justice.* London: A. Baldwin, 1701.

Howard, John Henry. *The Laws of the British Colonies, in the West Indies and Other Parts of America, concerning Real and Personal Property and Manumission of Slaves.* 2 vols. Westport, CT: Negro Universities Press, 1970.

Howell, T. B. *A Complete Collection of State Trials and Proceedings for High Treason and Other Crimes and Misdemeanors, from the Earliest Period to the Year 1783.* London: Hansard, 1816.

Jeaffreson, John Cordy, ed. *A Young Squire of the Seventeenth Century, From the Papers (A.D. 1676–1686) of Christopher Jeaffreson.* 2 vols. London: Hurst and Blackett, 1878.

Journal of the Commissioners for Trade and Plantations. London: HMSO, 1920–38.

A Journal of the Life, Travels, Sufferings, and Labour of Love in the Work of the Ministry, of that Worthy Elder, and Faithful Servant of Jesus Christ, William Edmundson. London: J. Sowle, 1715.

Keimer, Samuel, ed. *Caribbeana.* 3 vols. Millwood, NY: Kraus Reprint Co., 1978.

Labat, Jean-Baptiste. *The Memoirs of Pere Labat, 1693–1705.* John Eaden, trans. London: Frank Cass, 1970.

Langford, Jonas. *A Brief Account of the Sufferings of the Servants of the Lord called Quakers, from their first Arrival in the island of Antegoa, under the several Governours, from the Year 1660, to 1695.* London: T. Sowle, 1706.

Laws of the Island of St. Christopher, from the Year 1711, to the Year 1791. Basseterre, St. Kitts: Edward Luther Low, 1791.

Leslie, Charles. *A New and Exact History of Jamaica.* Edinburgh: R. Fleming, 1740.

Luffman, John. *A Brief Account of the Island of Antigua.* London: T. Cadell, 1789.

Mackenzie, Roderick. *A General Survey of that Part of the Island of St. Christophers, Which formerly belonged to France.* London: J. Roberts, 1722.

Martin, Samuel. *An Essay upon Plantership.* London: A. Millar, 1765.

A Plan for Establishing and Disciplining a National Militia in Great Britain, Ireland, and in all the British Dominions of America. London: A. Millar, 1745.

A Short Treatise on the Slavery of Negroes in the British Colonies. St. John's, Antigua: Robert Mearns, 1775.

Mathews, Samuel Augustus. *The Lying Hero, or, an Answer to J. B. Moreton's Manners and Customs in the West Indies.* St. Eustatius: Edward Luther Low, 1793.

McKinnen, Daniel. *A Tour through the British West Indies.* London: J. White, 1804.

Moll, Herman. *Atlas geographus: or, a compleat system of geography, ancient and modern.* London: John Nicholson, 1717.

Montgomery, James. "The West Indies." In Robert Bowyer, ed., *Poems on the Abolition of the Slave Trade.* Manchester, NH: Ayer Publishing, 1971.

Montserrat Code of Laws from 1668, to 1788. London: R. Hindmarsh, 1790.

Morden, Robert. *Geography Rectified.* London: Robert Morden and Thomas Cockerill, 1693.

Moreton, J. B. *Manners and Customs of the West India Islands.* London: W. Richardson, 1790.

Nickalls, John L., ed. *The Journal of George Fox.* Cambridge: Cambridge University Press, 1952.

Ogilby, John. *America: being an Accurate Description of the New World.* London: Thomas Johnson, 1670.

Oldmixon, John. *The British Empire in America.* 2 vols. London: John Nicholson, 1708.

Pelleprat, Pierre. *Relation des Missions des PP. de la Compagnie de Iesus dans les Isles, et dans la terre ferme de l'Amérique meridionale.* Paris: Cramoisy, 1655.

Pilkington, Laetitia. *Memoirs of Mrs. Laetitia Pilkington, 1712–1750, Written by Herself.* London: George Routledge and Sons, 1928.

Pittis, William. *The Jamaica Lady; or, The Life of Bavia.* London: Thomas Bickerton, 1720.

Poole, Robert. *The Beneficent Bee: or, Traveller's Companion.* London: E. Duncomb, 1753.

Randall, John. *A Brief Account of the Rise, Principles, and Discipline of the People call'd Quakers, in America, and elsewhere.* Bristol: Samuel Farley, 1747.

Raynal, Abbé. *A Philosophical and Political History of the Settlements and Trade of the Europeans in the East and West Indies.* 6 vols. J. O. Justamond, trans. London: A. Strahan and T. Cadell, 1788.

Robertson, Robert. *A Detection of the State and Situation of the Present Sugar Planters of Barbadoes and the Leeward Islands.* London: John Wilford, 1732.

A Letter to the Right Reverend the Lord Bishop of London, from an Inhabitant of His Majesty's Leeward-Caribbee-Islands. London: John Wilford, 1730.

A Short Account of the Hurricane, that pass'd thro' the English Leeward Carribbee Islands, on Saturday the 30th of June 1733. London: Privately printed, 1733.

Russell, Francis. *An Essay on the Reduction of Interest.* Basseterre: Thomas Howe, 1770.

Sainsbury, W. Noel, et al., eds. *Calendar of State Papers, Colonial, America and West Indies, 1574–1739*. London: HMSO, 1860–1994.

Salmon, Thomas. *A Critical Essay Concerning Marriage*. London: C. Rivington, 1724.

Schaw, Janet. *The Journal of a Lady of Quality*. Evangeline Walker Andrews and Charles M. Andrews, eds. New Haven: Yale University Press, 1923.

Shervington, William. *Miscellanies*. St. John's, Antigua: Edward Hughes, 1763. *Occasional Poems*. St. John's, Antigua: T. Smith, 1749.

A Sermon Preached before the Free and Accepted Masons in the Town of St. John's, Antigua, on the 24th June, 1754. St. John's, Antigua: Benjamin Mecom, 1754.

Sloane, Hans. *A Voyage to the Islands Madera, Barbadoes, Nieves, S. Christophers and Jamaica*. 2 vols. London: B. M., 1707.

Smith, Wavell. *Two Letters to Mr. Wood, on the Coin and Currency of the Leeward Islands, &c*. London: J. Millan, 1740.

Smith, William. *A Natural History of Nevis, and the rest of the English Leeward Charibee Islands in America*. Cambridge: J. Bentham, 1745.

Smollett, Tobias. *The Present State of All Nations*. 8 vols. London: R. Baldwin, 1769.

Some Instances of the Oppression and Male-Administration of Col. Parke, late Governor of the Leeward Islands. London: n.p., 1713.

Southey, Thomas. *Chronological History of the West Indies*. 3 vols. London: Longman, 1827.

"Standing Up for the Liberties of my Fellow Subjects," in *The Barbadoes Packet*. London: S. Popping, 1720.

The Substance of a Letter from One of the Prisoners who were Transported from Liverpool to the West-Indies. London: n.p., n.d.

Thomas, Dalby. *An Historical Account of the Rise and Growth of the West-India Collonies*. London: John Hindmarsh, 1690.

Thompson, Edward. *Sailor's Letters: written to his Select Friends in England, during his Voyage and Travels in Europe, Asia, Africa, and America, from the Year 1754 to 1759*. 2 vols. London: T. Becket, 1766.

Touchstone, Timothy. *Tea and Sugar, or the Nabob and the Creole*. London: J. Ridgway, 1792.

A True and Perfect Relation of that most Sad and Terrible Earthquake, at Port Royal in Jamaica, which Happened on Tuesday the 7th of June. London: R. Smith, 1692.

The Tryal of John Barbot, Attorney at Law, for the Murder of Matthew Mills, Esq.; to which is added, The Prisoner's Narrative of the Cause of the Difference between Mr. Mills and Himself, and the several Steps that led from thence, to the Commission of the Fact for which he suffered London: John Whiston and Benjamin White, 1753.

"Tryal of John Barbot, at St. Christopher's, in the West Indies, for the Murder of Matt. Mills, Esq." *London Magazine* (August 1753).

Uring, Nathaniel. *A Relation of the late Intended Settlement of the Islands of St. Lucia and St. Vincent, in America*. London: J. Peele, 1725.

The Virginia Gazette

Vokins, Joan. *God's Mighty Power Magnified*. London: Thomas Northcott, 1691.

Ward, Edward. *A Trip to Jamaica: With a True Character of the People and the Island*. London: J. How, 1700.

Whistler, Henry. "An Account of Barbados in 1654." In N. C. Connell, "An Extract from Henry Whistler's Journal of West Indian Expedition under the Date 1654." *Journal of the Barbados Museum and Historical Society* (1938).

W. S. A. B. *The Antigonian and Bostonian Beauties*. Boston: D. Fowle, 1790.

Young, Sir William. *A Tour through the Several Islands of Barbados, St. Vincent, Antigua, Tobago, and Grenada in the Years 1791 and 1792*. London: John Stockdale, 1801.

III. Secondary Works

Abbott, Mary. *Family Ties: English Families, 1545–1920*. London: Routledge, 1993.

"AHR Forum: The New British History in Atlantic Perspective." *American Historical Review* 104 (1999): 426–500.

Akenson, Donald Harman. *If the Irish Ran the World: Montserrat, 1630–1730*. Montreal: McGill-Queen's University Press, 1997.

Amussen, Susan Dwyer. *Caribbean Exchanges: Slavery and the Transformation of English Society, 1640–1700*. Chapel Hill: University of North Carolina Press, 2007.

An Ordered Society: Gender and Class in Early Modern England. Oxford: Basil Blackwell, 1988.

Arbell, Mordechai. *The Jewish Nation of the Caribbean: The Spanish–Portuguese Jewish Settlements in the Caribbean and the Guianas*. Jerusalem: Gefen Publishing House, 2002.

Aspinall, Algernon E. *West Indian Tales of Old*. New York: Negro Universities Press, 1969.

Atherton, Gertrude. *The Conqueror*. New York: Macmillan, 1902.

Augier, F. R., and S. C. Gordon. *Sources of West Indian History*. London: Longman, 1962.

Bagwell, Richard. *Ireland under the Stuarts and during the Interregnum*. 2 vols. London: Longmans, Green, 1909.

Bailyn, Bernard. "Politics and Social Structure in Virginia." In James M. Smith, ed., *Seventeenth-Century America*. Chapel Hill: University of North Carolina Press, 1959.

Barash, Carol. "The Character of Difference: The Creole Woman as Mediator in Narratives about Jamaica." *Eighteenth-Century Studies* 23 (1990): 406–24.

Barnard, T. C. *Making the Grand Figure: Lives and Possessions in Ireland, 1641–1770*. New Haven: Yale University Press, 2004.

Beckles, Hilary M. A 'riotous and unruly lot': Irish Indentured Servants and Freemen in the English West Indies, 1644–1713." *William and Mary Quarterly* s3:47 (1990): 503–22.

White Servitude and Black Slavery in Barbados, 1627–1715. Knoxville: University of Tennessee Press, 1989.

"White Women and Slavery in the Caribbean." *History Workshop Journal* 36 (1993): 66–82.

Berleant-Schiller, Riva. "Free Labor and the Economy in Seventeenth-Century Montserrat." *William and Mary Quarterly* s3:46 (1989): 539–64.

Bethencourt, Cardozo de. "Notes on Spanish and Portuguese Jews." *Publications of the American Jewish Historical Society* 29 (1925): 7–38.

Blake, Martin J. *Blake Family Records, 1300 to 1600*. London: Elliot Stock, 1902.

Blake Family Records, 1600 to 1700. London: Elliot Stock, 1905.

Bonomi, Patricia U. *The Lord Cornbury Scandal: The Politics of Reputation in British America*. Chapel Hill: University of North Carolina Press, 1998.

Bosher, J. F. "Huguenot Merchants and the Protestant International in the Seventeenth Century." *William and Mary Quarterly* s3:52 (1995): 77–102.

Boucher, Philip P. *France and the American Tropics to 1700: Tropics of Discontent?* Baltimore: Johns Hopkins University Press, 2008.

Bourne, Ruth. *Queen Anne's Navy in the West Indies*. New Haven: Yale University Press, 1939.

Bowers, Claude G. "Hamilton: A Portrait." In Jacob Ernest Cooke, ed., *Alexander Hamilton: A Profile*. New York: Hill and Wang, 1967.

Braddick, Michael J. "Civility and Authority." In Michael J. Braddick and David Armitage, eds., *The British Atlantic World, 1500–1800*. New York: Palgrave Macmillan, 2002.

Brathwaite, Edward Kamau. "Creative Literature of the British West Indies During the Period of Slavery." *Savacou* 1 (1970): 46–73.

Brown, Kathleen M. *Good Wives, Nasty Wenches, and Anxious Patriarchs: Gender, Race, and Power in Colonial Virginia*. Chapel Hill: University of North Carolina Press, 1996.

Brown, Vincent. "Spiritual Terror and Sacred Authority in Jamaican Slave Society." *Slavery and Abolition* 24 (2003): 24–53.

Buisseret, David. "The Elusive Deodand: A Study of the Fortified Refuges of the Lesser Antilles." *Journal of Caribbean History* 6 (1976): 43–80.

Burnard, Trevor. "Ethnicity in Colonial American Historiography: A New Organising Principle." *Australasian Journal of American Studies* 10 (1992): 1–14.

"A Failed Settler Society: Marriage and Demographic Failure in Early Jamaica." *Journal of Social History* 28 (1994): 63–82.

Mastery, Tyranny, and Desire: Thomas Thistlewood and His Slaves in the Anglo-Jamaican World. Chapel Hill: University of North Carolina Press, 2004.

"'A Matron in Rank, a Prostitute in Manners': The Manning Divorce of 1741 and Class, Race, Gender, and the Law in Eighteenth-Century Jamaica." In Verene A. Shepherd, ed., *Working Slavery, Pricing Freedom: Perspectives from the Caribbean, Africa, and the African Diaspora*. New York: Palgrave, 2002.

"Slave Naming Patterns: Onomastics and the Taxonomy of Race in Eighteenth-Century Jamaica." *Journal of Interdisciplinary History* 31 (2001): 225–46.

"Theater of Terror: Domestic Violence in Thomas Thistlewood's Jamaica." In Christine Daniels and Michael V. Kennedy, eds., *Over the Threshold: Domestic Violence in Early America*. New York: Routledge, 1999.

"Thomas Thistlewood Becomes a Creole." In Bruce Clayton and John A. Salmond, eds., *Varieties of Southern History*. Westport, CN: Greenwood Press, 1996.

Calder, Angus. *Revolutionary Empire*. New York: Dutton, 1981.

Chernow, Ron. *Alexander Hamilton*. New York: Penguin, 2004.

Clarke, Mary Patterson. *Parliamentary Privilege in the American Colonies*. New Haven: Yale University Press, 1943.

Clymer, Lorna. "Cromwell's Head and Milton's Hair: Corpse Theory in Spectacular Bodies of the Interregnum." *The Eighteenth Century* 40 (1999): 91–112.

Colley, Linda. *Britons: Forging the Nation, 1707–1837*. New Haven: Yale University Press, 1992.

Conway, Stephen. "From Fellow-Nationals to Foreigners: British Perceptions of the Americans, circa 1739–1763." *William and Mary Quarterly* s3:59 (2002): 65–100.

Cooke, Jacob Ernest. *Alexander Hamilton*. New York: Scribner's, 1982.

Cooper, Donald B. *The Establishment of the Anglican Church in the Leeward Islands*. Stillwater: University of Oklahoma Press, 1966.

Corfield, Penelope J. "Dress for Deference and Dissent: Hats and the Decline of Hat Honour." *Costume* 23 (1989): 64–79.

Craton, Michael. "Property and Propriety: Land Tenure and Slave Property in the Creation of a British West Indian Plantocracy, 1612–1740." In Susan Staves and John Brewer, eds., *Early Modern Concepts of Property*. New York: Routledge, 1996.

Testing the Chains: Resistance to Slavery in the British West Indies. Ithaca, NY: Cornell University Press, 1982.

Cullen, Louis M. "Galway Merchants in the Outside World, 1650–1800." In Diarmuid O'Cearbhaill, ed., *Galway Town and Gown*. Dublin: Gill and Macmillan, 1984.

"The Irish Diaspora of the Seventeenth and Eighteenth Centuries." In Nicholas Canny, ed., *Europeans on the Move: Studies on European Migration, 1500–1800*. Oxford: Clarendon Press, 1994.

Cundall, Frank, et al. "Documents Relating to the History of the Jews in Jamaica and Barbados in the Time of William III." *Publications of the American Jewish Historical Society* 23 (1915): 25–9.

Davies, K. G. *The Royal African Company*. New York: Longmans, Green, 1957.

Davis, David Brion. *Slavery and Human Progress*. New York: Oxford University Press, 1984.

Dayfoot, Arthur Charles. *The Shaping of the West Indian Church, 1492–1962*. Gainesville: University of Florida Press, 1999.

Demets, Bishop Antoine. *The Catholic Church in Montserrat, West Indies*. Plymouth, Montserrat: Privately printed, 1980.

Devine, T. M. *Scotland's Empire and the Shaping of the Americas, 1600–1815*. Washington, DC: Smithsonian Books, 2003.

Dobbin, Jay D. *The Jombee Dance of Montserrat: A Study of Trance Ritual in the West Indies*. Columbus: Ohio State University Press, 1986.

Dodsworth, Francis. "*Virtus* on Whitehall: The Politics of Palladianism in William Kent's Treasury Building." *Journal of Historical Sociology* 18 (2005): 282–317.

Dunn, Richard S. "The Barbados Census of 1680." *William and Mary Quarterly* s3:26 (1969): 3–30.

Sugar and Slaves: The Rise of the Planter Class in the English West Indies, 1624–1713. Chapel Hill: University of North Carolina Press, 1973.

Durham, Harriet Frorer. *Caribbean Quakers.* Hollywood, FL: Dukane Press, 1972.

Dyde, Brian. *Out of the Crowded Vagueness: A History of the Islands of St. Kitts, Nevis & Anguilla.* Oxford: Macmillan, 2005.

Eltis, David, Frank Lewis, and David Richardson. "Slave Prices, the African Slave Trade, and Productivity in Eighteenth Century South Carolina: A Reassessment." *Journal of Economic History* 66 (2006): 1066–71.

Emery, Noemie. *Alexander Hamilton: An Intimate Portrait.* New York: Putnam, 1982.

English, T. Savage. *Ireland's Only Colony: Records of Montserrat, 1632 to the End of the Nineteenth Century.* London: West India Committee Library, 1930.

Epstein, James. "The Politics of Colonial Sensation: The Trial of Thomas Picton and the Cause of Louisa Calderon." *American Historical Review* 112 (2007): 712–41.

Faber, Eli. *Jews, Slaves, and the Slave Trade.* New York: New York University Press, 1998.

A Time for Planting: The First Migration, 1654–1820. Baltimore: Johns Hopkins University Press, 1992.

Felsenstein, Frank. *Anti-Semitic Stereotypes: A Paradigm of Otherness in English Culture, 1660–1830.* Baltimore: Johns Hopkins University Press, 1995.

Fergus, Howard. "Montserrat 'Colony of Ireland': The Myth and the Reality." *Studies* (1981): 325–40.

Montserrat: History of a Caribbean Colony. London: Macmillan, 1994.

Fischer, Kirsten. *Suspect Relations: Sex, Race, and Resistance in Colonial North Carolina.* Ithaca: Cornell University Press, 2002.

Forbes, Susan. "Quaker Tribalism." In Michael Zuckerman, ed., *Friends and Neighbors: Group Life in America's First Plural Society.* Philadelphia: Temple University Press, 1982.

Forde-Jones, Cecily. "Mapping Racial Boundaries: Gender, Race, and Poor Relief in Barbadian Plantation Society." *Journal of Women's History* 10 (1998): 9–31.

Fothergill, Gerald. *A List of Emigrant Ministers to America, 1690–1811.* Baltimore: Genealogical Publishing Company, 1985.

Foucault, Michel. *The History of Sexuality: An Introduction.* Robert Hurley, trans. New York: Pantheon, 1978.

Freeman, Joanne B. *Affairs of Honor: National Politics in the New Republic.* New Haven: Yale University Press, 2001.

Friedman, Lee M. "Wills of Early Jewish Settlers in New York." *Publications of the American Jewish Historical Society* 23 (1915): 147–61.

Frohnsdorff, Gregory. "'Before the Public': Some Early Libraries of Antigua." *Libraries & Culture* 38 (2003): 1–23.

Froude, James Anthony. *The English in the West Indies, or, The Bow of Ulysses.* London: Longmans, Green, & Co., 1888.

Galenson, David. "Servants Bound for Antigua, 1752–56." *Genealogists' Magazine* 19 (1978): 277–9.

White Servitude in Colonial America. Cambridge: Cambridge University Press, 1981.

Gaspar, David Barry "Ameliorating Slavery: The Leeward Islands Slave Act of 1798," In Robert L. Paquette and Stanley R. Engerman, eds., *The Lesser Antilles in the Age of European Expansion*. Gainesville: University Press of Florida, 1996, pp. 241–258.

Bondmen and Rebels: A Study of Master–Slave Relations in Antigua. Baltimore: Johns Hopkins University Press, 1985.

"Runaways in Seventeenth-Century Antigua." *Boletin de Estudios Latinamericanos y del Caribe* 26 (1979): 3–13.

"'To Bring Their Offending Slaves to Justice': Compensation and Slave Resistance in Antigua, 1669–1763." *Caribbean Quarterly* 30 (1984): 45–59.

Goveia, Elsa V. *Slave Society in the British Leeward Islands at the End of the Eighteenth Century*. New Haven: Yale University Press, 1965.

A Study on the Historiography of the British West Indies. Washington, DC: Howard University Press, 1980.

Gragg, Larry D. *Englishmen Transplanted: The English Colonization of Barbados, 1627–1660*. Oxford: Oxford University Press, 2003.

"A Puritan in the West Indies: The Career of Samuel Winthrop." *William and Mary Quarterly* s3:50 (1993): 768–86.

Graham, Michael, S.J. "Popish Plots in Early Maryland." *Catholic Historical Review* 79 (1993): 208–15.

Green, Cecilia A. "Hierarchies of Whiteness in the Geographies of Empire: Thomas Thistlewood and the Barretts of Jamaica." *New West Indian Guide* 80 (2006): 5–43.

Greene, Jack P. "Changing Identity in Colonial British America: Barbados as a Case Study." In Nicholas Canny and Anthony Pagden, eds., *Colonial Identity in the Atlantic World*. Princeton, NJ: Princeton University Press, 1987.

"Empire and Identity." In P. J. Marshall, ed., *The Oxford History of the British Empire*, vol. 2: *The Eighteenth Century*. Oxford: Oxford University Press, 1998.

Grenfell, Joyce. *Nevis, Queen of the Caribees*. London: Macmillan, 1994.

Guttridge, G. H. *The Colonial Policy of William III in America and the West Indies*. Cambridge: Cambridge University Press, 1922.

Hamilton, Allan McLane. *The Intimate Life of Alexander Hamilton*. New York: Scribner's, 1911.

Hamilton, Douglas J. *Scotland, the Caribbean, and the Atlantic World, 1750–1820*. Manchester: Manchester University Press, 2005.

Hancock, David. *Citizens of the World: London Merchants and the Integration of the British Atlantic Community, 1735–1785*. Cambridge: Cambridge University Press, 1995.

"Commerce and Conversation in the Eighteenth-Century Atlantic: The Invention of Madeira Wine." *Journal of Interdisciplinary History* 29 (1998): 197–220.

Harlow, V. T. *Colonising Expeditions to the West Indies and Guiana, 1623–1677*. London: Hakluyt Society, 1925.

Hemphill, C. Dallett. *Bowing to Necessities: A History of Manners in America, 1620–1860.* New York: Oxford University Press, 1999.

Hershkowitz, Leo. "Original Inventories of Early New York Jews." *American Jewish History* 90 (2002): 239–323.

Wills of Early New York Jews, 1704–1799. New York: American Jewish Historical Society, 1967.

Higham, C. S. S. *The Development of the Leeward Islands under the Restoration, 1660–1688.* Cambridge: Cambridge University Press, 1921.

"The Early Days of the Church in the West Indies." *Church Quarterly Review* 92 (1921): 117–20.

"The General Assembly of the Leeward Islands." *English Historical Review* 41:162 (1926): 190–209.

"The General Assembly of the Leeward Islands," Part II, *English Historical Review* 41:163(1926): 366–388.

"The Negro Policy of Christopher Codrington." *Journal of Negro History* 10 (1925): 150–3.

Higman, B. W. *Plantation Jamaica, 1750–1850: Capital and Control in a Colonial Economy.* Kingston: University of the West Indies Press, 2005.

Hill, Christopher. *The World Turned Upside Down: Radical Ideas During the English Revolution.* New York: Viking Press, 1972.

Hoetink, Harmannus. *The Two Variants in Caribbean Race Relations.* Eva M. Hooykaas, trans. Oxford: Oxford University Press, 1967.

Hoffer, Peter Charles, and N. E. H. Hull. *Impeachment in America, 1623–1805.* New Haven: Yale University Press, 1984.

Hubbard, Vincent K. *Swords, Ships, and Sugar: A History of Nevis to 1900.* Placentia, CA: Premiere Editions, 1991.

Hulme, Peter. *Colonial Encounters: Europe and the Native Caribbean, 1492–1797.* London: Methuen, 1986.

Hulme, Peter, and Neil L. Whitehead, eds. *Wild Majesty: Encounters with Caribs from Columbus to the Present Day.* Oxford: Clarendon Press, 1992.

Hurwitz, Samuel J., and Edith Hurwitz. "The New World Sets an Example for the Old: The Jews of Jamaica and Political Rights, 1661–1831." *American Jewish Historical Quarterly* 55 (1965): 37–56.

Inniss, Sir Probyn. *Basseterre: The Story of a West Indian Town.* Basseterre, St. Kitts: Privately printed, 1985.

James, Mervyn. "English Politics and the Concept of Honour, 1485–1642." *Past and Present,* s3 (1978): 1–92.

Jefferys, Edward Miller. *Jefferys of Worcestershire, Nevis, Philadelphia.* Philadelphia: Privately printed, 1939.

The Jewish Community in Early New York, 1654–1800. New York: Fraunces Tavern Museum, 1980.

Johnston, J. R. V. "The Stapleton Sugar Plantations in the Leeward Islands." *Bulletin of the John Rylands Library* 48 (1965): 175–206.

Kaplan, Benjamin J. "Fictions of Privacy: House Chapels and the Spatial Accommodation of Religious Dissent in Early Modern Europe." *American Historical Review* 107 (2002): 1031–64.

Karras, Alan L. *Sojourners in the Sun: Scottish Migrants in Jamaica and the Chesapeake, 1740–1790*. Ithaca, NY: Cornell University Press, 1992.

"The World of Alexander Johnston: The Creolization of Ambition, 1762–1787." *Historical Journal* 30 (1987): 53–76.

Kelsick, Cecil A. "The Constitutional History of the Leewards." *Caribbean Quarterly* 6 (1960): 177–209.

Langford Paul. *A Polite and Commercial People: England, 1727–1783*. Oxford: Oxford University Press, 1989.

Laws, William. *Distinction, Death, and Disgrace: Governorship of the Leeward Islands in the Early Eighteenth Century*. Kingston: Jamaican Historical Society, 1976.

Layman, A. *Antigua: The Story of the Cathedral and Parish Church of St. John, 1678–1932*. London: Privately printed, 1933.

Lazarus-Black, Mindie. *Legitimate Acts and Illegitimate Encounters: Law and Society in Antigua and Barbuda*. Washington, DC: Smithsonian Institution Press, 1994.

"The Leeward Islands: Their Past and Present Condition." *Proceedings of the Royal Colonial Institute* 12 (1881).

Lemon, James. *The Best Poor Man's Country: A Geographical Study of Early Southeastern Pennsylvania*. Baltimore: Johns Hopkins University Press, 1972.

Levy, Babette M. *Early Puritanism in the Southern and Island Colonies*. Worcester, MA: American Antiquarian Society, 1960.

Lewis, Gordon K. *Main Currents in Caribbean Thought: The Historical Evolution of Caribbean Society in Its Ideological Aspects*. Baltimore: Johns Hopkins University Press, 1983.

Linebaugh, Peter. *The London Hanged: Crime and Civil Society in the Eighteenth Century*. Cambridge: Cambridge University Press, 1991.

Lockridge, Kenneth A. *On the Sources of Patriarchal Rage: The Commonplace Books of William Byrd and Thomas Jefferson and the Gendering of Power in the Eighteenth Century*. New York: New York University Press, 1992.

Loker, Zvi. *Jews in the Caribbean: Evidence on the History of the Jews in the Caribbean Zone in Colonial Times*. Jerusalem: Institute for Research on the Sephardi and Oriental Jewish Heritage, 1991.

Lorimer, Joyce. *English and Irish Settlement on the River Amazon, 1550–1646*. London: Hakluyt Society, 1989.

Lowenthal, David. "The Wayward Leewards." In Karen Fog Olwig, ed., *Small Islands, Large Questions: Society, Culture, and Resistance in the Post-Emancipation Caribbean*. London: Frank Cass, 1995.

West Indian Societies. New York: Oxford University Press, 1972.

Mackie, Erin, ed., *The Commerce of Everyday Life: Selections from "The Tatler" and "The Spectator."* New York: Bedford Books / St. Martin's Press, 1998.

Mackie, Erin Skye. "Cultural Cross-Dressing: The Colorful Case of the Caribbean Creole." In Jessica Munns and Penny Richards, eds., *The Clothes That Wear Us: Essays on Dressing and Transgressing in the Eighteenth Century*. Newark: University of Delaware Press, 1999.

Manchester, Kathleen D. *Historic Heritage of St. Kitts, Nevis, Anguilla.* Privately printed, 1971.

Mancke, Elizabeth. "Another British America: A Canadian Model for the Early Modern British Empire." *Journal of Imperial and Commonwealth History* 25 (1997): 1–36.

Marcus, Jacob R. "The American Colonial Jew: A Study in Acculturation." The B. G. Rudolph Lecture in Judaic Studies, Syracuse University, 1968.

The Colonial American Jew. 2 vols. Detroit: Wayne State University Press, 1970.

Mason, Keith. "The World an Absentee Planter and His Slaves Made: Sir William Stapleton and His Nevis Sugar Estate, 1722–1740." *Bulletin of the John Rylands Library* 75 (1993): 103–31.

Matar, Nabil. *Turks, Moors, and Englishmen in the Age of Discovery.* New York: Columbia University Press, 1999.

McConville, Brendan. *The King's Three Faces: The Rise and Fall of Royal America, 1688–1776.* Chapel Hill: University of North Carolina Press, 2006.

McDonald, Forrest. *Alexander Hamilton: A Biography.* New York: Norton, 1979.

McNamara, Martha J. *From Tavern to Courthouse: Architecture and Ritual in American Law, 1658–1860.* Baltimore: Johns Hopkins University Press, 2004.

Mendes, George I. "The Historical Notes of the Early Years of the Island of Montserrat." *Leeward Islands Review and Caribbean Digest* 1 (1937): 9–17.

Mereness, Newton D., ed. *Travels in the American Colonies.* New York: Antiquarian Press, 1961.

Merrill, Gordon C. *The Historical Geography of St. Kitts and Nevis, the West Indies.* Mexico City: Instituto Panamericano de Geografía y Historia, 1958.

Messenger, John. "The 'Black Irish' of Montserrat." *Eire-Ireland* 2 (1967): 24–40.

"The Influence of the Irish in Montserrat." *Caribbean Quarterly* 13 (1967): 3–26.

"Montserrat: The Most Distinctively Irish Settlement in the New World." *Ethnicity* 2 (1975): 281–303.

Milford, T. A. *The Gardiners of Massachusetts: Provincial Ambition and the British-American Career.* Durham: University of New Hampshire Press, 2005.

Miller, Helen Hill. *Colonel Parke of Virginia: "The Greatest Hector in the Town."* Chapel Hill, NC: Algonquin Books, 1989.

Miller, John. "'A Suffering People: English Quakers and Their Neighbours, c. 1650–c. 1700." *Past and Present* 188 (2005): 71–103.

Miller, John Chester. *Alexander Hamilton and the Growth of the New Nation.* New York: Harper and Row, 1964.

Miller, Kerby A. *Emigrants and Exiles: Ireland and the Irish Exodus to North America.* New York: Oxford University Press, 1985.

Mitchell, Broadus. *Alexander Hamilton: Youth to Maturity, 1755–1788.* New York: Macmillan, 1957.

Morgan, Edmund S. *American Slavery, American Freedom: The Ordeal of Colonial Virginia*. New York: Norton, 1975.

Morgan, Jennifer L. *Laboring Women: Reproduction and Gender in New World Slavery*. Philadelphia: University of Pennsylvania Press, 2004.

Morgan, Kenneth. *The Bright-Meyler Papers: A Bristol West-India Connection, 1732–1837*. New York: Oxford University Press, 2008.

Morgan, Philip D. "British Encounters with Africans and African-Americans, circa 1600–1780." In Philip D. Morgan and Bernard Bailyn, eds., *Strangers Within the Realm: Cultural Margins of the First British Empire*. Chapel Hill: University of North Carolina Press, 1991.

Morris, DuBois Schanck, Jr. "Aspects of Toleration and Tribulation in the West Indies." In Peter Steven Gannon, ed., *Huguenot Refugees in the Settling of Colonial America*. New York: Huguenot Society of America, 1985.

Morris, Mr. "The Colony of the Leeward Islands." *Proceedings of the Royal Colonial Institute* 22 (1890): 225–63.

Morton, H. V. *A Traveller in Rome*. London: Methuen, 1957.

Mulcahy, Matthew. *Hurricanes and Society in the British Greater Caribbean, 1624–1783*. Baltimore: Johns Hopkins University Press, 2006.

Naipaul, V. S. *The Loss of El Dorado*. London: Andre Deutsch, 1969.

Nash, R. C. "Huguenot Merchants and the Development of South Carolina's Slave-Plantation and Atlantic Trading Economy, 1680–1775." In Bertrand van Ruymbeke and Randy J. Sparks, eds., *Memory and Identity: The Huguenots in France and the Atlantic Diaspora*. Columbia: University of South Carolina Press, 2004.

"Irish Atlantic Trade in the Seventeenth and Eighteenth Century." *William and Mary Quarterly* s3:42 (1985): 329–56.

Norton, Mary Beth. "Gender and Defamation in Seventeenth-Century Maryland." *William and Mary Quarterly* s3:44 (1987): 3–29.

Ohlmeyer, Jane H. "A Laboratory for Empire? Early Modern Ireland and English Imperialism." In Kevin Kenny, ed., *Ireland and the British Empire*. Oxford: Oxford University Press, 2004.

Oliver, Vere Langford. *Caribbeana: Being Miscellaneous Papers Relating to the History, Genealogy, Topography, and Antiquities of the British West Indies*, vols. London: Mitchell, Hughes and Clarke, 1909–19.

The History of the Island of Antigua. 3 vols. London: Mitchell and Hughes, 1894–9.

The Monumental Inscriptions of the British West Indies. Dorchester: Friary Press, 1927.

Olwig, Karen Fog. *Global Culture, Island Identity: Continuity and Change in the Afro-Caribbean Community of Nevis*. Chur, Switzerland: Harwood Academic Publishers, 1993.

O'Shaughnessy, Andrew Jackson. *An Empire Divided: The American Revolution and the British Caribbean*. Philadelphia: University of Pennsylvania Press, 2000.

"The Stamp Act Crisis in the British Caribbean." *William and Mary Quarterly* s3:51 (1994): 203–26.

Pactor, Howard S. *Colonial British Caribbean Newspapers: A Bibliography and Directory.* New York: Greenwood Press, 1990.

Pares, Richard. *Merchants and Planters.* Cambridge: Cambridge University Press, 1960.

War and Trade in the West Indies, 1739–1763. London: Frank Cass, 1963.

A West-India Fortune. London: Longmans, Green, 1950.

Pascoe, C. F. *Two Hundred Years of the S.P.G.: An Historical Account of the Society for the Propagation of the Gospel in Foreign Parts, 1701–1900.* 2 vols. London: Society for the Propagation of the Gospel, 1901.

Paton, Diana. *No Bond but the Law: Punishment, Race, and Gender in Jamaican State Formation, 1780–1870.* Durham, NC: Duke University Press, 2004.

Pearsall, Sarah M. S. "'The late flagrant instance of depravity in my Family': The Story of an Anglo-Jamaican Cuckold." *William and Mary Quarterly* 53:60 (2003): 549–82.

Pitman, Frank Wesley. *The Development of the British West Indies.* New Haven: Yale University Press, 1917.

"The West Indian Absentee Planter as a Colonial Type." *Proceedings of the Pacific Coast Branch of the American Historical Association* (1927): 113–27.

Pluchon, Pierre. *Negres et juifs: Le racisme au siècle des Lumières.* Paris: Tallandier, 1984.

Pope, Peter E. *Fish into Wine: The Newfoundland Plantation in the Seventeenth Century.* Chapel Hill: University of North Carolina Press, 2004.

Price, Jacob M. *Perry of London: A Family and a Firm on the Seaborne Frontier.* Cambridge, MA: Harvard University Press, 1992.

Pulsipher, Lydia M. "Galways Plantation, Montserrat." In Herman J. Viola and Carolyn Margolis, eds., *Seeds of Change: A Quincentennial Commemmoration.* Washington, DC: Smithsonian Institution Press, 1991.

Seventeenth-Century Montserrat: An Environmental Impact Statement. Norwich: Geo Books, 1986.

Pulsipher, Lydia M., and Conrad M. Goodwin. "'Getting the Essence of It': Galways Plantation, Montserrat, West Indies." In Paul Farnsworth, ed., *Island Lives: Historical Archaeologies of the Caribbean.* Tuscaloosa: University of Alabama Press, 2001.

"A Sugar Boiling-House at Galways: An Irish Sugar Plantation in Montserrat, West Indies." *Post-Medieval Archaeology* 16 (1982): 21–7.

Rabin, Dana. "The Jew Bill of 1753: Masculinity, Virility, and the Nation." *Eighteenth-Century Studies* 39 (2006): 157–71.

Ragatz, Lowell J. *The Fall of the Planter Class in the British Caribbean, 1763–1833.* New York: Century Co., 1928

Ramagosa, Carol Walter. "Eliza Lucas Pinckney's Family in Antigua, 1668–1747." *South Carolina Historical Magazine* 99 (1998): 238–58.

Richardson, Bonham C. *Igniting the Caribbean's Past: Fire in British West Indian History.* Chapel Hill: University of North Carolina Press, 2004.

Robson, G. R. "An Earthquake Catalogue for the Eastern Caribbean." *Bulletin of the Seismological Society of America* 54 (1964): 785–832.

Rocher, Rosane, and Michael E. Scorgie. "A Family Empire: The Alexander Hamilton Cousins, 1750–1830." *Journal of Imperial and Commonwealth History* 23 (1995): 189–210.

Root, Winfred T. "The Lords of Trade and Plantations, 1675–1696." *American Historical Review* 23 (1917): 20–41.

Rouse, Parke, Jr. *James Blair of Virginia*. Chapel Hill: University of North Carolina Press, 1971.

Royster, Charles. *The Fabulous History of the Dismal Swamp Company: A Story of George Washington's Times*. New York: Knopf, 1999.

Rozbicki, Michal J. *The Complete Colonial Gentleman: Cultural Legitimacy in Plantation America*. Charlottesville: University of Virginia Press, 1998.

"The Curse of Provincialism: Negative Perceptions of Colonial American Plantation Gentry." *Journal of Southern History* 63 (1997): 727–52.

Rutman, Darrett B., and Anita H. Rutman. *A Place in Time: Middlesex County, Virginia, 1650–1740*. New York: Norton, 1984.

Sarson, Steven M. *British America, 1500–1800: Creating Colonies, Imagining an Empire*. London: Hodder Arnold, 2005.

Schachner, Nathan. *Alexander Hamilton*. New York: Appleton-Century, 1946.

Secor, Robert. "Ethnic Humor in Early American Jest Books." In Frank Shuffelton, ed., *A Mixed Race: Ethnicity in Early America*. New York: Oxford University Press, 1993.

Shapin, Steven M. *A Social History of Truth: Civility and Science in Seventeenth-Century England*. Chicago: University of Chicago Press, 1994.

Sheridan, Richard B. *Doctors and Slaves: A Medical and Demographic History of Slavery in the British West Indies, 1680–1834*. Cambridge: Cambridge University Press, 1985.

"An Era of West Indian Prosperity, 1750–1775." In Richard B. Sheridan, ed., *The Development of the Plantations to 1750*. Bridgetown, Barbados: Caribbean Universities Press, 1970.

"Letters from a Sugar Plantation in Antigua, 1734–1758." *Agricultural History* 31 (1957): 3–23.

"Planters and Merchants: The Oliver Family of Antigua and London." *Business History* 13 (1971): 104–13.

"The Rise of a Colonial Gentry: A Case Study of Antigua, 1730–1775." *Economic History Review* s2:13 (1961): 342–57.

"Samuel Martin: Innovating Sugar Planter of Antigua, 1750–1776." *Agricultural History* 34 (1960): 126–39.

Sugar and Slavery: An Economic History of the British West Indies, 1623–1775. Baltimore: Johns Hopkins University Press, 1974.

"The Wealth of Jamaica in the Eighteenth Century." *Economic History Review* 18 (1965): 285–303.

Shields, David S. *Civil Tongues and Polite Letters in British America*. Chapel Hill: University of North Carolina Press, 1997.

Shilstone, E. M. *Monumental Inscriptions in the Jewish Synagogue at Bridgetown, Barbados, with Historical Notes from 1650*. Barbados: Macmillan, 1988.

Smith, S. D. *Slavery, Family and Gentry Capitalism in the British Atlantic: The World of the Lascelles, 1648–1834*. Cambridge: Cambridge University Press, 2006.

Snyder, Holly. "Rules, Rights and Redemption: The Negotiation of Jewish Status in British Atlantic Port Towns, 1740–1831." *Jewish History* 20 (2006): 147–70.

Spencer-Churchill, J. *The Leeward Islands*. London: Spottiswoode & Co., 1898.

Spurdle, F. G. *Early West Indian Government*. Christchurch, New Zealand: Whitcomb and Tombs, 1963.

Statt, Daniel. *Foreigners and Englishmen: The Controversy over Immigration and Population, 1660–1760*. Newark: University of Delaware Press, 1995.

Stern, Malcolm H. *First American Jewish Families: 600 Genealogies, 1654–1977*. Cincinnati: American Jewish Archives, 1978.

"A Successful Caribbean Restoration: The Nevis Story." *American Jewish Historical Quarterly* 61 (1971): 22–5, 327.

Stewart, Maaja A. "Inexhaustible Generosity: The Fictions of Eighteenth-Century British Imperialism in Richard Cumberland's *The West Indian*." *The Eighteenth Century* 37 (1996): 42–55.

Stone, Lawrence. *The Crisis of the Aristocracy, 1558–1641*. New York: Oxford University Press, 1967.

The Family, Sex, and Marriage in England, 1500–1800, abridged ed. New York: Harper and Row, 1979.

Sypher, Wylie. "The West Indian as a 'Character' in the Eighteenth Century." *North Carolina Studies in Philology* 36 (1939): 503–20.

Taylor, Alan. "'The Hungry Year': 1789 on the Northern Border of Revolutionary America." In Alessa Johns, ed., *Dreadful Visitations: Confronting Natural Catastrophe in the Age of Enlightenment*. New York: Routledge, 1999.

Terrell, Michelle M. *The Jewish Community of Early Colonial Nevis: A Historical and Archaeological Study*. Gainesville: University Press of Florida, 2005.

Thompson, Lynda M. *The 'Scandalous Memoirists': Constantia Phillips, Laetitia Pilkington, and the Shame of 'Publick Fame.'* Manchester: Manchester University Press, 2000.

Thoms, D. W. "The Mills Family: London Sugar Merchants of the Eighteenth Century." *Business History* 11 (1969): 3–10.

Truxes, Thomas. *Irish–American Trade, 1660–1783*. Cambridge: Cambridge University Press, 1988.

Tyson, George F., Jr., and Carolyn Tyson. *An Inventory of the Historical Landmarks of St. Kitts–Nevis*, rev. ed. St. Thomas, Virgin Islands: Island Resources Foundation, 1974.

Upton, Dell. *Holy Things and Profane: Anglican Parish Churches in Colonial Virginia*. New Haven: Yale University Press, 1986.

Vaughan, Megan. *Creating the Creole Island: Slavery in Eighteenth-Century Mauritius*. Durham, NC: Duke University Press, 2005.

Warshow, Robert. *Alexander Hamilton: First American Business Man*. Garden City, NY: Garden City Publishing Company, 1931.

Watson, Michael. "The British West Indian Legislatures in the Seventeenth and Eighteenth Centuries: An Historiographical Introduction." In Philip Lawson, ed., *Parliament and the Atlantic Empire*. Edinburgh: Edinburgh University Press, 1995.

Watts, David. *The West Indies: Patterns of Development, Culture and Environmental Change since 1492*. Cambridge: Cambridge University Press, 1987.

Webb, Stephen Saunders. *Lord Churchill's Coup: The Anglo-American Empire and the Glorious Revolution Reconsidered*. New York: Knopf, 1995.

Wells, Robert V. *The Population of the British Colonies in America before 1776: A Survey of Census Data*. Princeton, NJ: Princeton University Press, 1975.

Wheeler, Marion M. *Montserrat, West Indies: A Chronological History*. Plymouth, Montserrat: Montserrat National Trust, 1988.

Williams, Eric. *From Columbus to Castro: The History of the Caribbean*. New York: Vintage Books, 1984.

Wilson, Kathleen. *The Island Race: Englishness, Empire, and Gender in the Eighteenth Century*. New York: Routledge, 2003.

Wilson, Samuel M. "Caribbean Diaspora." *Natural History* 102 (1993): 54–60.

Wolf, Lucien. "The Family of Gideon Abudiente." In Lucien Wolf, ed., *Essays on Jewish History*. London: Jewish Historical Society of England, 1934.

Wood, Peter. *Black Majority: Negroes in South Carolina from 1670 through the Stono Rebellion*. New York: Norton, 1974.

Wright, Neil, and Ann Wright. "Hamilton's Sugar Mill, Nevis, Leeward Islands, Eastern Caribbean." *Industrial Archaeology Review* 13 (1991): 114–41.

Zacek, Natalie A. "Sexual Transgression and Social Control in the English Leeward Islands, 1670–1763." In Merril D. Smith, ed., *Sex and Sexuality in Colonial America, 1492–1800*. New York: New York University Press, 1998.

"Voices and Silence: The Problem of Slave Testimony in the Eighteenth-Century English West Indian Law Court." *Slavery and Abolition* 24 (2003): 24–39.

Zahedieh, Nuala. "The Capture of the *Blue Dove*, 1664: Policy, Profits, and Protection in Early English Jamaica." In Roderick A. MacDonald, ed., *West Indies Accounts*. Barbados: University of the West Indies Press, 1996.

IV.   Dissertations, Theses, and Unpublished Papers

Quintanilla, Mark S. "The 'Monmouth Men' in the West Indies." Ph.D. dissertation, Arizona State University, 1993.

Rouse-Jones, Margaret Deanne. "St. Kitts, 1713–1763: A Study of the Development of a Plantation Colony." Ph.D. dissertation, Johns Hopkins University, 1977.

Snyder, Holly. "'Usury, to the English Mind': The Image of the Jewish Merchant in the British Atlantic World." Paper presented to the Ninth Annual Conference of the Omohundro Institute of Early American History and Culture, New Orleans, June 2003.

Wilkie, Everett. "The Image of the Scot as Colonizer." Paper presented to "The Scots in the Atlantic World," John Carter Brown Library, Providence, RI, June 1994.

V. Internet Resources

http://www.tc.umn.edu/~terreo11/Synagogue.html: The Official Homepage of
the Nevis Synagogue Archaeology Project.
http://www.librarycompany.org/Economics/2002Conference/papers.htm:
Matthew Mulcahy, "Weathering the Storms: Hurricanes and Plantation
Agriculture in the British Greater Caribbean," Program in Early American
Economy and Society, Library Company of Philadelphia.
http://www.candoo.com/genresources/antiguafilms.htm: Antigua Film Project.

Index

Printed in Great Britain
by Amazon

29339933R00175